Judaism without Jews

Judaism without Jews

Philosemitism and Christian Polemic in Early Modern England

Eliane Glaser

© Eliane Glaser 2007

All rights reserved. No reproduction, copy or transmission of this publication may be made without written permission.

No paragraph of this publication may be reproduced, copied or transmitted save with written permission or in accordance with the provisions of the Copyright, Designs and Patents Act 1988, or under the terms of any licence permitting limited copying issued by the Copyright Licensing Agency, 90 Tottenham Court Road, London W1T 4LP.

Any person who does any unauthorised act in relation to this publication may be liable to criminal prosecution and civil claims for damages.

The author has asserted her right to be identified as the author of this work in accordance with the Copyright, Designs and Patents Act 1988.

First published 2007 by
PALGRAVE MACMILLAN
Houndmills, Basingstoke, Hampshire RG21 6XS and
175 Fifth Avenue, New York, N.Y. 10010
Companies and representatives throughout the world

PALGRAVE MACMILLAN is the global academic imprint of the Palgrave Macmillan division of St. Martin's Press, LLC and of Palgrave Macmillan Ltd. Macmillan® is a registered trademark in the United States, United Kingdom and other countries. Palgrave is a registered trademark in the European Union and other countries.

ISBN-13: 978–0–230–50774–6   hardback
ISBN-10: 0–230–50774–3   hardback

This book is printed on paper suitable for recycling and made from fully managed and sustained forest sources.

A catalogue record for this book is available from the British Library.

Library of Congress Cataloging-in-Publication Data

Glaser, Eliane, 1973–
  Judaism without Jews : philosemitism and Christian polemic in early modern England / Eliane Glaser.
    p. cm.
    ISBN-13: 978-0-230-50774-6 (cloth)
    ISBN-10: 0-230-50774-3 (cloth)
     1. Jews—England—History—17th century. 2. Philosemitism—Great Britain. 3. Christianity and other religions—Judaism. 4. Judaism—Relations—Christianity. 5. England—Ethnic relations. I. Title.

DS135.E5.G57 2007
942'.004924—dc22   2006051576

10 9 8 7 6 5 4 3 2 1
16 15 14 13 12 11 10 09 08 07

Printed and bound in Great Britain by
Antony Rowe Ltd, Chippenham and Eastbourne

Contents

Acknowledgments	vi
Introduction	1
1. Anglo-Jewish History and Early Modern England	7
2. Puritans and Judaism: From Scholarship to Sedition	30
3. Anglicans and Judaism: From Ceremony to Legalism	64
4. Religious Toleration: Jews and Jewish Precedents in the Christian Church and State	92
5. Contesting Readmission: Common Law and the English Constitution	113
Conclusion	130
Notes	133
Bibliography	189
Index	214

Acknowledgments

Judaism without Jews is a greatly revised version of a Ph.D. thesis completed at Birkbeck College, London in 2000. My research between 1996 and 2000 was funded by a studentship from the Arts and Humanities Research Board and a grant from the ATP Trust. I am grateful to Alan Stewart for being such a dedicated Ph.D. supervisor, to Ceri Sullivan for her periodic injections of energy and to Warren Boutcher and James Shapiro, my Ph.D. examiners, whose insightful comments prompted me to turn the thesis into a book. I would like to thank Lisa Jardine and Quentin Skinner for their encouragement, and Andrew Hadfield and Matthew Dimmock for inviting me to present some recent work at a conference at Sussex University entitled 'Religions of the Book', which helped me to refine my ideas further. Ariane Koek, Charlie Taylor, Alice Feinstein and other colleagues at the BBC enabled me to take time off work in order to write. I am particularly grateful to Palgrave Macmillan's two anonymous readers for their astute reports, which helped me to improve the book. Part of Chapter 5 first appeared in *Reformation* as '"Reasons ... theological, political, and mixt of both": A Reconsideration of the "Readmission" of the Jews to England'; I would like to thank Ashgate for permission to reprint that material here. A great many scholars provided inspiration and intellectual companionship during my Ph.D., especially Andy Gordon, Sue Wiseman, Paul Sheehan, Piyel Haldar, Patricia Brewerton, Markman Ellis and Richard Hamblyn. Paul Laity read the manuscript in its final stages, and Tom Morris and Emma Satyamurti helped me put the finishing touches to the book. Finally, I would like to thank Will Fisher and Paul Myerscough for reading my work and for being constant guides; and David Schneider for making me feel at home in the world of Jews without Judaism.

Introduction

In the long history of Anglo-Jewry, one moment stands out: Oliver Cromwell's decision, in 1656, to readmit the Jews to England, more than 350 years after they had been expelled by Edward I. The story of England's transformation from medieval antisemitism to Renaissance philosemitism is well known: in 1655, Menasseh ben Israel, the leading rabbi and physician, travelled from his native Amsterdam to England on a mission to persuade Cromwell to let the Jews back in. Cromwell listened to Menasseh's proposal, and, later that year, brought together a group of merchants, lawyers and theologians to assess the pros and cons of readmitting the Jews; a gathering which became known as the Whitehall Conference. Although the Conference failed to reach a decision, the story goes, Cromwell subsequently granted the Jews already resident in London informal permission to establish a community. Thereafter the Jewish presence in England was gradually consolidated, and 1701 saw the inauguration of the large synagogue at Bevis Marks in the City of London.

The anniversary of the readmission of the Jews to England has long been celebrated by the Anglo-Jewish community. Throughout 2006, there was a calendar of events to celebrate the 350th anniversary, including a festival in London's Trafalgar Square; a commemorative service at Bevis Marks, attended by Prime Minister Tony Blair; as well as concerts, lectures and official banquets. In 1956, celebrations for the 'Tercentenary of the Resettlement of the Jews in Great Britain' began in January with an exhibition of Anglo-Jewish art and history at the Victoria and Albert Museum; in March, the London Philharmonic Orchestra performed a concert at the Royal Festival Hall; in May, a tercentenary banquet was held at the Guildhall, attended by Prime Minister Anthony Eden; and the festivities concluded in June with a garden party at Lambeth Palace.[1] During a speech at the Tercentenary banquet, Lord Samuel, the first high commissioner in Palestine, summarised the story of readmission thus:

> When the Puritan movement took hold in the sixteenth and seventeenth centuries, an intense interest in the Bible spread among the English people ... the people of the Old Testament, their dispersal, the prophecies of their return, were subjects of continual discussion ...

when a delegation of the Jews of Amsterdam came over to ask for leave to establish a community here . . . [Cromwell] and his Council gave them a favourable hearing. Permission was granted, and in the year 1656 the first pioneers came over, and settled in London.[2]

In a commemorative volume produced for the 250th anniversary in 1906, the Anglo-Jewish historian Lucien Wolf described the Whitehall Conference as 'epoch-making not only in Jewish, but also in English, history', and in a speech reproduced in the volume, the MP James Bryce claimed that 'nowhere in the modern world have the Jews found so tranquil and peaceful a home as here in this England of ours. We Englishmen are very proud of that'.[3]

Earlier accounts of the events of 1656 produced a rather less positive impression, however. After the Whitehall Conference had ended, Menasseh ben Israel expressed his disappointment at its inconclusive outcome:

> Mens judgements and sentences were different. Insomuch, that as yet, we have had no finall determination from his Serene Highnesse. Wherefore those few *Jewes* that were here, despairing of our expected successe, departed hence. And others who desired to come hither, have quitted their hopes, and betaken themselves some to *Italy*, some to *Geneva*, where that Commonwealth hath at this time most freely granted them many and great priviledges.[4]

The Baptist preacher Henry Jessey, who wrote an account of the Whitehall Conference, described how the failure of Menasseh's efforts brought expectations of a Jewish readmission to a decisive halt:

> Many Jewish Merchants had come from beyond the seas to *London*, and hoped they might have enjoyed as much privilege here, in respect of Trading, and of their Worshipping . . . here, in Synagogues, publickly, as they enjoy in *Holland* . . . But after the conference and Debate at *White-Hall* was ended, they heard by some, that the greater part of the Ministers were against this: therefore they removed hence again to beyond the Seas, with much grief of heart, that they were thus disappointed of their hopes . . . and this Jewish Project was never afterwards revived.[5]

In 1738, the historian and antiquary D'Blossiers Tovey (1692–1745) published *Anglia Judaica*, the first history of the Jews in England.[6] Tovey concluded his narrative of Menasseh's quest with the following words: 'I shall therefore say no more of him, than that He was born in Portugal in 1604, and died in the Year 1657, about which Time he left England, having obtain'd nothing more from Oliver, and his Council, than the bare Consideration of his Petition'.[7]

At first glance, it seems extraordinary that the same events could have produced such contrasting interpretations. In 1894, Lucien Wolf noted that 'historical critics have differed as to the exact legal value of the work performed by the Whitehall Conference', and described with regret 'the controversy which has raged around this question'.[8] As the first chapter of this book will illustrate, the events of the mid-seventeenth century were, in reality, ambiguous; and historians interpreted them in very different ways in the centuries that followed. Something happened, however, during Wolf's lifetime, to solidify the more sanguine version of the events of 1656; indeed, the first celebration of Cromwell's readmission of the Jews was held in 1894. By the end of the century, the controversy that Wolf lamented had all but disappeared.

The first chapter of this book explores the development of Anglo-Jewish history in Victorian England, and the reasons why readmission came to be celebrated as the birth of the modern Jewish community. It places the creation of that historical tradition in the context of the concerns of both the Jewish community and of the wider British culture; at a time of changing attitudes towards Cromwell, religious tolerance and immigration. The late nineteenth century witnessed a resurgence of interest, furthermore, in the European Renaissance; Jacob Burnhardt's influential study, *The Civilization of the Renaissance in Italy*, first published in 1860, identified the boundary between the medieval and the Renaissance periods as the transition to the modern age and the birth of the individual, and this was consolidated, in turn, by a new appreciation of the innovatory genius of Shakespeare. In this atmosphere, it was relatively easy to regard 1656 as a watershed in Anglo-Jewish history. But with the eulogising interpretation of that moment came a particular understanding of Christian attitudes not only to Jews, but also to the Jewish religion, in the period prior to the mid-seventeenth century. The interest which Christians undoubtedly displayed towards Judaism in post-Reformation England came to be seen in the light of the events of 1656, and inextricably linked to the story of readmission; and Anglo-Jewish history took on a teleological aspect which continues to exert its influence today. The remainder of this book seeks to place Christian interest in Judaism back into the context of the religious and political concerns of the late sixteenth and early to mid-seventeenth centuries.

Accordingly, Chapters 2–5 explore the thesis that the 100 years prior to 1656 saw a remarkable increase in Christian enthusiasm for Jewish ideas, not necessarily for the purposes of laying the ground for the Jews' toleration and readmission, but rather because the factional divisions and doctrinal debates that resulted from the Reformation, and the political instability which came to dominate the mid-seventeenth century, produced an oppositional landscape in which references to Judaism proved to be an invaluable polemical resource. Through an analysis of a series of religious and political debates, these chapters illustrate the particular ways in which Judaism was employed in the articulation of an evolving, but contested, church and state. Chapter 2 reformulates the association – established in the midst of the nineteenth-century Puritan revival – between early modern Puritans and Jews, arguing that Puritans from the sixteenth century onwards were indeed interested in Hebrew and the Old Testament, and even in observing Jewish festivals such as the Sabbath and Passover; but that they did so for specific, pragmatic reasons.

Furthermore, it was not only Puritans who identified with Jews in the early modern period. Chapter 3 explores the little-known alliance between Anglicans and Judaism; a phenomenon which is all but ignored in Anglo-Jewish history in favour of the emphasis on Puritan philosemitism. As this chapter illustrates, however, the Conformists' love of religious ritual and beauty, particularly during the Laudian church reforms of the 1630s, sometimes led them to adopt Jewish ideas. Christian enthusiasm for Judaism was differentiated, it seems, according to the issue at hand. Comparing the manner in which Judaism was invoked across these decades and debates reveals a striking variation in the affiliation of those Christians who made use of these ideas, and even inconsistencies within the same group over time. This book attempts to throw light, therefore, both on the way in which early modern Christians recruited Judaism, and on the shifting and contentious atmosphere of early modern Christian culture itself.

Jewish ideas became especially useful in debates about religious toleration, when commentators invoked the precedent of the Sanhedrin, the ancient Jewish court, in order to articulate a church–state model which could accommodate religious difference. Historical accounts of religious toleration have tended to regard the emergence of the principle of freedom of conscience in the seventeenth century as a necessary precondition for the practical toleration of both dissident Christians and Jews; but, as Chapter 4 reveals, participants in debates about toleration rarely made the connection between the Jewish ideas they were putting to use and the existence of Jewish people. Chapter 5 addresses what is regarded as the culmination of Christian philosemitism: the proposals to readmit the Jews to England in the mid-1650s. Even though these proposals failed to deliver, they prompted a great deal of debate. This chapter reveals that, even here, there was another dimension to those debates; one that had to do with conflicting legal traditions, constitutional politics and English nationhood.

This book is indebted to the work of a number of scholars within the disciplines of Anglo-Jewish history, early modern history and English literature. The influential Anglo-Jewish historian Cecil Roth published his *History of the Jews in England* in 1941.[9] With an earlier generation of Jewish historians in mind, including Lucien Wolf, Roth attempted in his *History* to 'eschew the parochial and personal aspect which has hitherto monopolized attention and to write the history of the Jews in England rather than the *memorabilia* of the community of London, which have engaged the attention of previous writers'.[10] Although Roth attempted to be sceptical rather than celebratory, his work, nonetheless, contributed to an ongoing positivist Jewish historical tradition. In 1994, the pre-eminent historian of Anglo-Jewry David Katz inverted Roth's title in *The Jews in the History of England, 1485–1850*. Katz's starting point was an awareness – echoing, in a sense, that of Roth – that Jewish history tends to be confined to its own ghetto: 'Like anthropologists writing on a wide variety of cultures, historians of Jewish England meet with historians of Jewish France and Jewish Germany, and look for common features rather than trying to integrate Jewish history into the surrounding culture'.[11] At the same time, Katz noted that Jewish subject matter tends to be marginalised in the work of British historians, who often all but ignore the important place of Judaism in 'mainstream' history.[12] Monographs such as *The Jews in the History of England, Philo-Semitism and the Readmission of the Jews to England* (1982) and *Sabbath and Sectarianism in Seventeenth Century England* (1988) are invaluable in their thoroughness and scope, and this book is indebted to his research.[13] However, Katz's own principle – that Jewish history should be placed in the context of British history – could be pushed farther; if his work succeeds in documenting the extent to which early modern English Christians were interested in Jews and Judaism, this study uses textual analysis to distinguish between different forms of interest in the context of historically specific debates. Moreover, despite its admirable historiographical self-awareness, Katz's work tends to reinforce traditional assumptions about the founding of modern Anglo-Jewry.[14]

Another essential contribution to the field, this time from the discipline of English Literature, appeared in 1996: James Shapiro's *Shakespeare and the Jews*. Shapiro's virtuosic study explores literary and non-literary portrayals of Jews and Jewishness in the context of the early modern formation of English national identity. *Shakespeare and the Jews* is a wide-ranging, nuanced and critically aware book which places Anglo-Jewish history in the field of cultural representation. Shapiro writes in his conclusion: 'Only gradually are historians acknowledging the extent to which English Reformation thought was preoccupied with Jewish questions, and how, as a result, emerging political, social, and religious institutions were influenced by Jewish models'; this book takes Shapiro's cue as one of its starting points.[15] It builds, too, on the insights of historians of modern Anglo-Jewry, especially David Cesarani and Tony Kushner. Kushner has observed that 'in the search to "reclaim the past", *critical* historical analysis can be forgotten. The search for roots and the "celebration" of continuous presence can take precedence over the need to locate contexts and to provide relevance'.[16] This book applies that observation to Christian philosemitism in the early modern period.[17]

1
Anglo-Jewish History and Early Modern England

In 1906, during a speech to celebrate the 250th anniversary of readmission, Lucien Wolf praised the two men he regarded as the pioneers of philosemitism in England:

> Cromwell, the great-hearted Protector, and Menasseh ben Israel, the devoted Jew . . . it was their spirit of toleration and justice which invested [the Whitehall Conference] with all it had of dignity and usefulness . . . they are the figures of a Christian and a Jew, standing together in the dawn of English liberty, twin champions of a wronged people, and heralds of a free state. It is a picture on which we do well to dwell . . . which in its stability and fruitfulness serves as a beacon of toleration and liberty to the dark places that still linger on the face of God's earth.[1]

The encounter between Menasseh and Cromwell symbolised, for Wolf, the beginning of a new era: the 'dawn of English liberty' and the 'herald[ing]' of a 'free state'. For him, as for other Anglo-Jewish historians, the English Renaissance was highly significant, as it produced not only a cultural rebirth but also the Renaissance of the Jewish people. During that period, England had become a unique and unprecedented haven for the Jews, the 'wronged people'. Wolf's reference to 'the dark places that still linger on the face of God's earth' was, furthermore, a reminder that he was also talking about his own age. The description of England as a 'free state' and a place of 'liberty' fitted a notion of English identity that had developed during the Victorian era. The 'dark places' were the areas of Continental Europe and Russia which had hosted violent pogroms against the Jews in the late nineteenth century: the Jews were being 'wronged' again.[2] Britain could consider itself an exception to this dominant European prejudice, but only up to a point; and there is a note of persuasion in Wolf's speech. Because by the turn of the century, the waves of Jewish immigration from eastern Europe were prompting a backlash of antisemitism and xenophobia, and in the same year as Wolf gave his speech, Parliament passed the Aliens Act, designed to set up a new system of immigration control. This chapter describes how a combination of pride and anxiety led Anglo-Jewish historians of the late nineteenth and early twentieth centuries to focus their attention on the early modern period, and to formulate a particular understanding of Christian references to Judaism in that period which was to hold sway long after their time. In order to unpack this interpretation, the chapter begins by outlining the events which have so concerned Anglo-Jewish historians, before turning its attention to the development and character of the resulting historical tradition.[3]

Jews in early modern England

In contrast to the dominant strain of Jewish history – a lachrymose narrative of antisemitism and adversity – the history of the Jews in England stands out as a philosemitic exception.[4] This reputation is based, however, only on the post-Reformation era; medieval England's treatment of Jews was rather less edifying. A Jewish presence in England was probably first established with the arrival of William the Conqueror, and at its height, medieval Jewry was a thriving community of about 5,000 people. The community's primary occupation was money-lending, which was regarded as a sin by the church, but tolerated, in practice, as a fact of commercial life. Although the community thereby accumulated great wealth, it lost its wealth over time as successive kings imposed a series of punitive taxes. In 1275, usury was declared illegal, and the community found itself depleted both numerically and financially. When Edward I returned from Gascony in 1290, deep in debt, he resorted to asking his Parliament for money. The representatives of the shires and boroughs demanded, in return for granting a special tax, the expulsion of the Jews. The thirteenth-century expulsion is discussed in more detail in Chapter 5.

In 1290, therefore, England became the first country to expel its Jewish population. As medievalist historians Kenneth Stow and Robert Stacey have argued, however, the factors prompting this apparently egregious and decisive event were complex: a combination of Judeophobia, politics and economics.[5] Despite the events of 1290, moreover, the Jewish presence in England never entirely disappeared. After Jews were expelled from the Iberian peninsula in 1492, many migrated to northern Europe. There were Spanish and Portuguese Jews in England during the reign of Henry VIII, and in the Elizabethan era, they became more prominent; one of the most notorious was Roderigo Lopez, the Queen's physician, who was executed in 1594 for conspiring to poison her.[6] During the late sixteenth century, there were up to 200 Jews living in England, mainly in London; although there was also a small community of Jewish traders in Bristol. In 1609, their numbers were reduced by the expulsion of Portuguese merchants residing in London, but in 1630, England signed a treaty with Spain which meant that Spanish and Portuguese subjects, some of whom were Jews, were exempt from the laws against recusants. A secret Jewish community was gradually established by merchants such as Antonio Fernandez Carvajal.[7] These were not only *conversos* – Jews who had converted to Christianity – but also crypto-Jews who worshipped in private.[8] Not only did this community exist, but it was also known about: the Royalist writer and spy, James Howell, wrote from London to a friend in Amsterdam in 1653: 'Touching Judaism, some corners of our city smell as rank of it as doth your's there'.[9] A convert named Paul Isaiah wrote in 1655 that 'though perhaps there may not be now in England, any great numbers of professed Jews (some to my own knowledge there are, who have their synagogues, and there exercise Judaism) yet, they who live here, as often as they are bound to use their office of prayer (which is twice a day) so often are they bound to blaspheme Christ'.[10]

While the number of Jews in England was growing, contact between Christians and Jews both in England and on the Continent increased. A number of English Christians became interested in millenarian ideas involving the discovery of dispersed members of the 12 tribes of Israel and their conversion to Christianity, considered by some to prefigure Christ's Second Coming.[11] In 1644, a Marrano Jew named Aaron ha-Levi, also known as Antonio de Montezinos, returned from Quito Province in what is now Ecuador to his home in Amsterdam. A year later, he told Menasseh ben Israel that he had met Israelites descended from the tribe of Reuben living there in secret. Menasseh included Montezinos's account in a book entitled *The Hope of Israel*, which he published in Latin and Spanish in 1650. Later that year, *The Hope of Israel* was translated into English by Moses Wall, a friend of John Milton, and published with a dedication to Parliament.[12] Menasseh also sent a French version of Montezinos's testimony to the millenarian preacher John Dury, which was translated into English and published as part of Thomas Thorowgood's *Iewes in America* in 1650.[13] John Dury, along with his friend and patron Samuel Hartlib, was hoping to found a new Jerusalem in England, where doctrinal differences between Protestants would be eliminated, and where a college of Jewish studies would be founded in order to encourage the conversion of Jews to Christianity.

Menasseh ben Israel did not confine his efforts to the readmission of the Jews to England, however. During this period, the migration of Marrano and Sephardi exiles from Brazil, Spain and Venice to the Dutch republic was at its height, and the Jewish community in Amsterdam was actively pursuing schemes to accommodate these people elsewhere.[14] In 1649, two English citizens resident in Amsterdam, Johanna Cartenright and her son Ebenezer, published a petition to Lord Fairfax and the Council of War: it requested that Jews 'be received and permitted to trade and dwell amongst you in this Land, as now they do in the Nether-lands'; this petition was, however, ignored.[15] In 1651, Menasseh himself petitioned the English government to readmit the Jews, and a committee was set up in November 1651 to discuss the matter. In 1654, Menasseh became ill, and sent his son Samuel to England to follow up the petition, along with Manuel Martinez Dormido, alias David Abrabanel, a Spanish Jew who was living in Amsterdam. They arrived in London in October, and sent two further petitions to Cromwell. The first petition included a request by Dormido to the English government to help him recover his property, and the second asked the government to reconsider readmitting the Jews. Both petitions were rejected by the Council, but in February 1655, Cromwell responded to Dormido's financial request, sending a letter to the king of Portugal asking for help on his behalf. It is likely that Dormido, along with a number of Jews in England at that time – including Antonio Carvajal – was acting as an intelligencer for Cromwell's government. Furthermore, in October 1655, England went to war with Spain to compete over South American trade, and it was thought that the Jews might have useful mercantile connections in South America.[16] With the outbreak of war, the English authorities announced that they would confiscate the goods and property of any Spaniards living in England. In March 1656, a wealthy crypto-Jew living in London named Antonio Rodrigues Robles was charged with being a spy. Robles sent Cromwell a petition in which he attempted to keep hold of his property by identifying himself as a Portuguese Jew. The authorities decided that since Robles had been attending Mass, and was not circumcised, this 'induceth vs to conceave he is noe Jew or one that walkes under loose principles, and very different from others of that profession', concluding that they 'upon examinacon doe not finde any convicting evidence to cleare vp either the Nation or Religion of the peticoner', and Robles was allowed to keep his property.[17]

Towards the end of 1655, Menasseh arrived in London and presented Cromwell with a *Humble Address*, entreating the Protector once again to readmit the Jews to England, on the basis, firstly, that since the millennium was approaching, the Jews must be gathered together, and, secondly, that the Jews could be of material benefit to the English Commonwealth.[18] Menasseh also asked for the establishment of a public synagogue and cemetery, as well as religious toleration, the freedom to trade and the right to try cases according to Mosaic Law. The Council of State appointed a sub-committee to investigate these requests, which came up with a list of seven conditions which would have to be met before Menasseh's proposals could be countenanced. In November, a delegation of theologians, merchants and lawyers was selected to determine whether these seven safeguards would be sufficient to allow the Jews to be readmitted; these delegates comprised the Whitehall Conference, which opened in December 1655. The delegates found, however, that they were unable to arrive at a consensus, and the Conference was dissolved.[19] According to a later account, written by Nathaniel Crouch, Cromwell made a speech which attempted to persuade the delegates to arrive at a more settled verdict: 'He had hoped by these Preachers to have had some clearing of the Case, as to matter of Conscience; but seeing these agreed not, but were of different Opinions, it was left more doubtful to him and the Council than before'.[20] It is difficult to determine what Cromwell's own view of the prospect of readmission actually was. In Crouch's account, Cromwell emphasised that his only interest lay in the fulfilment of biblical prophecy, as 'he had no ingagement to the Jews but what the Scriptures held forth'.[21]

In March 1656, Menasseh attempted yet again to persuade the English government to readmit the Jews, along with six members of England's existing Jewish community. They produced a document entitled 'The Humble Petition of The Hebrews at Present Residing in the citty of London', and sent it to Cromwell. The petition requested 'such Protection may be graunted vs in Writing as that wee may therewth meete at owr said priuate deuosions in owr Particular houses without feere of Molestation either to owr persons famillys or estates'. It also requested permission to establish a Jewish cemetery outside the city limits. Cromwell referred the petition to his Council of State, but it was ignored.[22] Menasseh attempted one last time to persuade Cromwell, by publishing a defence of the Jewish race, the *Vindiciae Judaeorum*. But after this too fell on deaf ears, Menasseh was forced to admit defeat.

He appealed to Cromwell for financial help, but with limited success. In September 1657, his son Samuel died, and Menasseh attempted to take his body back to the Dutch Republic bury him there. He did not complete the journey, however; and died in Middleburg. His widow remained in London, and her subsequent requests to Cromwell for help were also unheeded.

Although Menasseh went away empty-handed, a Jewish community was gradually established in the second half of the seventeenth century; but it was a slow and difficult process. In December 1656, a floor of a building in Creechurch Lane, in the City of London, was leased to Antonio Carvajal, and a small Jewish congregation started to worship there. Steadily, the congregation became more established: Samuel Pepys records in his diary a visit to the synagogue in 1659, and John Greenhalgh describes the synagogue in a letter dated 1662.[23] In February 1657, a small plot of land was acquired by the community and subsequently used as a cemetery.[24] In 1701, the large synagogue in Bevis Marks in the City opened; but according to the records there, only four people were buried in the cemetery between 1657 and 1660. In this period, Jews were customarily buried with Roman Catholics, and of the Jews known to have been resident in England before 1659, about two thirds were buried in Christian cemeteries.[25]

Estimates vary as to the number of Jews who arrived in England after the Whitehall Conference. Taking an average of the figures, between 1656 and 1701 the Jewish population increased from between 100 and 200 to between 500 and 800.[26] To put this increase into context, other foreigners arrived in England in much greater numbers during the same period. In 1681, the king announced to the Huguenots of France that they were welcome to come and settle in England; between 50,000 and 100,000 arrived. By 1709, an estimated 13,000 persecuted Protestants from the German Palatinate had arrived in England, and Parliament passed its first naturalisation law for their benefit. Furthermore, Jewish populations elsewhere in Europe increased substantially in this period; Berlin Jewry, for example, increased from a few dozen in 1671 to nearly 1,000 by 1700.[27]

Although the status of the Jews in England remained unstable in the second half of the seventeenth century, with a great deal of Judeophobic harassment and conversion to Christianity, there is little doubt that the community became better established under Charles II. The synagogue in the building in Creechurch Lane was expanded, and in 1663 the community appointed a governing committee; in 1664, they recruited, temporarily, a rabbi from Amsterdam. Soon after Charles II's accession, the lord mayor and corporation of the City of London petitioned the king to enforce the expulsion order of 1290, but he refused. When the Conventicle Act of 1664 came into force, banning any religious services which did not conform to the Church of England, the Earl of Berkshire and Paul Rycaut, an associate of English merchants in the Levant who resented Jewish competition, attempted to use the Act to blackmail Jews. Dormido and two other members of the community petitioned the king for protection, and the privy council responded in their favour, declaring that the Jews might 'promise themselves ye effects of ye same favour as formerly they have had so long as they demeane themselves peaceably and quietly with due obedience to his Maties Laws & without scandal to his Government'.[28] This was the first official statement in favour of the toleration of Jews in England. Another attempt to expel the Jews failed in 1674, and in 1685, after two brothers, Thomas and Carleton Beaumont, had 37 Jewish merchants arrested for not attending church, the king reassured the community again.[29] There were several other attempts by English merchants and their supporters to disturb and expel the Jewish population, but they were resisted by both Charles II and James II.

Early interpretations of 1656

The establishment of a Jewish community in the second half of the seventeenth century was, therefore, an ambiguous and fitful process; and as a result, during the following century and a half, the question of who had readmitted the Jews to England, and indeed of whether they had been readmitted at all, was subject to considerable debate. Furthermore, those who made claims either way were motivated by partisan attitudes towards Cromwell and Charles II. Shortly after Charles's accession, a merchant named Thomas Violet sent a petition of his own to the king asking him to expel the Jews. In his petition Violet described the Whitehall Conference and its aftermath, writing that

> Upon several days hearing, *Cromwell* and his Councel did give a Toleration and Dispensation to a great number of Iewes to come and live here in *London*, and to this day they do keep publick Worship in the City of *London*, to the great dishonour of Christianity, and publick scandal of the true Protestant Religion, and to the great damage of the Kingdome, especially our merchants, whose trade they engross, and eat the children's bread.[30]

Violet continues, sarcastically: 'May it please your Sacred Majestie, to behold *Cromwells* blessed Reformation, he stops the mouths of all Orthodox Ministers, both in publick and private, not permitting them to teach School to put bread in their heads, and at the same time invites into this Nation the Iewes, who killed the Lord Iesus'.[31] In Violet's description, the readmission of the Jews becomes a nightmarish spectre:

> Oliver Cromwell's design to bring in the Iewes amongst us, was to make them Farmers of the Customs, and Excise, and to have naturalised them, by that means to have drawn into this Nation the principal Iewes in the World, with their Estate and Credit, which if death had not suppressed the Tyrant, he would have made these Iewes very instrumental to carry on his designs by furnishing Cromwel with vast sums of treasure; Anthony Fardinando the great Iew, told me the Iewes were to advance one Million of Money, to have libertie to bring in two thousand Iewish Merchants, and their Families, to be naturalized, had that design gone on, which was prevented by the death of the Tyrant Oliver, All the English Merchants of this Nation would have been supplanted of their birth-right, and oppressed by the griping extortion of the Iewes.[32]

This fanciful projection, with its wildly exaggerated detail, resembles another commonly repeated rumour: that the Jews were plotting to take over St Paul's Cathedral and use it as a synagogue.[33] Furthermore, although Thomas Violet complains about Cromwell's generosity to the Jews, he maintains nevertheless that formal readmission has not yet taken place:

> The Iewes being banished by Act of Parliament, as appears by the Records of the Tower, cannot be restored but by Act of Parliament ... so that the Iewes being banished by common consent in Parliament, and their Estates and Lands sold by the King, as appears by many Records in the Tower they were, and this Act never repealed. It is Felony for any Iew to be found in England, by the Law, neither can any man give them Protection, but by common Consent in Parliament.[34]

Violet expresses the hope that Charles II and his Parliament will 'shew their detestation of so wicked a design, as of suffering the Iewes to make their abiding amongst us, if this toleration should continue, and be admitted among us, it would check and hinder the growth of the Gospel of Christ'.[35] Violet's account suggested, therefore, that Cromwell had unlawfully tolerated the Jews; but his accusations also served as flattery to the new king. Violet was not the only commentator to refer to readmission as a potential possibility rather than an accomplished fact: in a book published in 1692, the bishop of Lincoln, Thomas Barlow, was still debating 'the Damage or Benefit, the Conveniences of Inconveniences which may accrue to the State by [the Jews'] Admission or Rejection'.[36] He did not seem to think the Jews had been readmitted as yet:

> If indeed the admission, and tolleration of them were disadvantageous to the Gospel, and really tended to the abolition or diminution of the true Faith, or the subversion and hinderance of Christianity, it were certainly neither pious in the supreme Magistrate, nor prudent to admit them; but he ought (in this case) rather to expell them if they were here, then readmit them, now they are away . . . in short, (if after all things considered) the Wisdom of the State shall judge it convenient and beneficial for the Publick to readmit the Jews, (and we are bound in Charity to think that unless they judge so they will not admit them) then they are in Duty bound to do it, notwithstanding any Displeasure (or pretended Scandal) which their Subjects will or can conceive against them for so doing.[37]

Some commentators believed that it was Charles II rather than Cromwell who had readmitted the Jews, on account of his government's explicit statements in their favour.[38] D'Blossiers Tovey wrote in his 1738 chronicle *Anglia Judaica* that 'King *Charles* the *second* must justly be consider'd as their *Introducer* . . . about the Year sixty four, or five, great Numbers of them came into England, and have continu'd to this present Time'.[39] In 1753, 15 years after the publication of *Anglia Judaica*, the Jewish Naturalisation Act passed through Parliament. Known as the 'Jew Bill', this Act, designed to enable the naturalisation of foreign-born Jews, prompted such an outcry that it was repealed a few months later. The public reaction to the Jew Bill was illustrated in satirical prints by William Hogarth, and it became the subject, too, of a large pamphlet debate. Some contributors to the Jew Bill controversy believed the Jews had been readmitted by Cromwell a century earlier: an anonymous pamphleteer, writing as a Jew in favour of the Bill, describes how 'from 1291, we had no Re-admission into *England* till 1655, being the Space of 364 Years. The Wisdom of *Cromwell* then brought us into this Country again by a Treaty with *Manasseh Ben-Israel*, wherein the *Jewish* Nation were restored to the Exercise of their Worship in *England*'.[40] To others, it appeared that the readmission of the Jews was being mooted as if it had not already happened: an anonymous pamphlet entitled *An Historical Treatise concerning Jews and Judaism, in England* contained 'a Confutation of the Arguments made use of for their Re-admission'.[41] The *Historical Treatise* offered a catalogue of reasons why the Jews should not be allowed to return; it described itself as

> A circumstantial Narrative of the Punishments that People have from time to time undergone in this Kingdom, since the Reign of Edward I. With an Account of their particular Crimes and Impieties which occasion'd them. Collected from our Historians and ancient established Laws; by which it appears, that a Jew has no Right to appear in England, without a Yellow Badge fixed on the upper Garment . . . that Synagogues are to be suppressed, and that no Rabbi, on Pain of Death, is to pervert any one to Judaism, and that a Return of the Jews after their Expulsion, renders them incapable of receiving any Benefit from our Laws.[42]

Also writing against the Bill, the London clergyman William Romaine described how Edward I expelled the Jews from England, after which time, Romaine writes, 'we read nothing of them till the Time of *Cromwell*, and even he was not hardy enough to give them a Licence to return: He only connived at it, as did King *Charles* II and King *James*, and since the Revolution they have continued on the same Footing: For they could never be made natural-born Subjects, while the Act of Parliament, by which they were outlawed, was in full Force against them'.[43] There is a reason why the verdict on 1656 varied so widely in 1753: the Jew Bill controversy was inflected by the Parliamentary politics of the time, with – broadly speaking – Whigs in favour of the Bill, and Tories against. The anonymous pamphleteer, a Whig, was a supporter of Cromwell and religious liberty, while William Romaine, a Tory, was vehemently against both Cromwell and the Jews.[44]

The controversy over the circumstances of the Jews' readmission continued well into the nineteenth century. In a study published in 1830, entitled *A History of the Establishment and Residence of The Jews in England; with an enquiry into their Civil Disabilities*, the barrister Elijah Blunt concluded a description of the Whitehall Conference and its aftermath with the following words:

> As the circumstances above related are all that is known of the proceedings that took place under the Commonwealth, there seems no sure foundation for the assertion which is frequently made, that

Cromwell first permitted the re-establishment of the Jews in England. After the Restoration, however, they seem to have begun, by degrees, to take up their residence in this country; and in the latter end of the year 1660, an order of the Lords of the Council was presented to the House of Commons, recommending to the house to take into their consideration, measures for the protection of the Jews.[45]

By contrast, William Godwin attempted to prove, in a footnote to his *History of the Commonwealth* (1824–8), that it was Cromwell and not, as Blunt and D'Blossiers Tovey had asserted, Charles II who readmitted the Jews.[46] By the end of the nineteenth century, Godwin's view had decisively prevailed, prompting the question, first, of how the controversy had disappeared; and second, of what motivated those who decided not only that Cromwell had readmitted the Jews, but also that he was right to do so.

1656 in the Victorian age

The nineteenth century witnessed a transformation in the Anglo-Jewish community's view of its origins, and in the location of those origins in the seventeenth century, and this transformation was mirrored by the English nation at large – in part, as a result of Victorian philosemitism. From the early nineteenth century onwards, there was a dramatic increase in the number of books written about Jewish history – from the destruction of the Temple in Jerusalem to the present day – and these books were mostly by Christians.[47] One author, James Huie, explained in the preface to his *History of the Jews, From the Taking of Jerusalem by Titus to the Present Time* (1840) that 'the very peculiar interest at present taken in the condition of the Jews, and the recent movement in their favour' had prompted him to write the book. Huie was presumably referring to the events of the previous decade: in 1837, Moses Montefiore, the Jewish philanthropist and president of the Board of Deputies, was elected to a fellowship at the Royal Society, and knighted in the same year.[48] At the same time, David Salomons, who would later become London's first Jewish Lord Mayor, was campaigning to take up a seat on the Corporation. During the 1830s, 'Parliamentary Emancipation', the notion that incumbent MPs would not have to swear an Anglican oath in order to sit in Parliament, was publicly mooted for the first time. The reaction to what became known as the Damascus Affair in 1840 enhanced a sense of British philosemitism further; in February 1840, a

Sardinian Capuchin monk, Father Thomas, disappeared along with his Arab servant, and they were rumoured to have been murdered by Jews who drained their blood to make Matzahs, or unleavened bread, for Passover: the traditional blood libel. Several leaders of the Jewish community in Damascus were interrogated and tortured; three died. In Britain, non-Jewish politicians, journalists and clergymen publicly dismissed these rumours, and a group of British merchants and bankers met at Mansion House, the headquarters of the Lord Mayor and Corporation of London, in support of the Jews.[49] In 1858, after 11 years of public debate, Baron de Rothschild took up a seat in the House of Commons, becoming the first Jew to be made an MP without swearing an Anglican oath. Rothschild never actually made a speech in Parliament; but this moment became known as the Emancipation.

For nineteenth-century Christian philosemites, defending the Jews was not incompatible with their conversion to Christianity. James Huie writes in his preface: 'If the account now given of what has been hitherto done shall, by the divine blessing, in any degree promote the cause of Israel's conversion, the time and labour which the author expended upon collecting the materials will not have been thrown away'.[50] The dedication to another book by Jack Myers, entitled *The Story of the Jewish People*, illustrates the benefit which Myers hopes his work will provide to both Jewish and Christian readers alike:

> Being Jews, they may feel greater pride of race and faith when they learn something of their ancestors who lived noble lives and died heroic deaths in days of old. Or, being non-Jews, they may perhaps see in clearer and more accurate perspective the real meaning of Jewish history – the history of Judaism and those who have upheld its banner in the fierce blast of prejudice, ill-will, and persecution through the ages.[51]

For Myers, the 'real meaning of Jewish history' was a sympathetic form of missionary Protestantism. Myers was not alone in this attitude; another writer, James Hosmer asks in his preface, 'Among its tragedies is there any quite so dark as the story of the Jews? Where else are problems presented which so defy satisfactory solution? . . . Where else is there anguish so deep and long-continued?'[52] Nineteenth-century histories of the Jews were characterised by a philosemitic desire to put an end to the persecution of the Jews – by rescuing them from Judaism.[53]

Moreover, from the 1870s onwards, British Jews began to face a new type of antisemitism, based on race rather than religion, which implied that they could never become fully English because they were fundamentally alien.[54] The Jews began to experience pressure to conform to certain ideals of citizenship and respectability – in other words, to assimilate. This development was prompted, in large part, by the mass immigration of Eastern European Jews to England which began at this time.[55] Tens of thousands of Jews fleeing persecution in Russia and Poland arrived; the resulting anti-immigration sentiment was to culminate, ultimately, in the Aliens Act of 1905. In this context, the English Jewish community became anxious that the relatively comfortable *status quo* they had established within English society would be threatened. They regarded the new immigrants, moreover, as a rather different kind of Jew, with radical politics and working-class Eastern European culture. During the 1890s, the British Jewish community set up organisations such as the Russo-Polish Committee and the Jewish Lads' Brigade in an attempt to anglicise the immigrants and turn them into patriotic, respectable Jews.

The English Jewish community also turned its attention to the establishment of a foundational historical tradition. The scholar and Jewish community leader, James Picciotto, who claimed to be the first Jewish historian of English Jewry, published his *Sketches of Anglo-Jewish History* in 1875, and Lucien Wolf's work began to appear shortly afterwards.[56] Jewish scholars, many of them writing outside the academy, were keen to emphasise the well-established status of Jews in England, and accordingly, began to tell a positive story about Jews in the nation's past. They were not the first to undertake Anglo-Jewish history: Sidney Lee, the Shakespeare scholar and the first editor of the Dictionary of National Biography, had written about the Jews of the Elizabethan period in the mid-nineteenth century;[57] but during the 1880s, the history of the Jews in England was consolidated and institutionalised.[58] In 1887, an exhibition of Anglo-Jewish history was held at the Royal Albert Hall, and in 1893 the Jewish Historical Society of England was founded by Lucien Wolf and the Jewish scholar Israel Abrahams, who declared that 'the new era for scientific Jewish historical research' had begun.[59]

The Jewish community was not alone in writing history with apologetical motivations; historical scholarship in general was becoming a patriotic project. In an essay entitled 'The Science of Jewish History', Abrahams described the circumstances under which the new European organisations for the study of Jewish history had been created:

> They arose out of the wave of nationalism which passed over Europe and America in the middle of the nineteenth century. In every country local patriotism led to pride in the local past, and the new spirit of

history can be traced, not so much to the idea of a general evolution in human affairs, which was one of the pet theories of the nineteenth century, as to the national idea, to which equally the nineteenth century gave birth in every State of Europe.[60]

The birth of Anglo-Jewish history coincided, moreover, with the formalisation of history as a discipline in British universities, and the founding of organisations such as the British Academy and the English Association.[61] Anglo-Jewish history went hand in hand with this dominant historical enterprise, but it also had particular motivations of its own.

From its inception, Anglo-Jewish history was divided into three periods: the medieval period, the 'Middle Period' and the modern period. The medieval period, which extends up to the expulsion of the Jews by Edward I in 1290, was thought of as the first, negative phase of Jewish life in England: a time of Judeophobia and persecution. The period between 1290 and 1655 was classified by Wolf as the 'Middle Period' of Anglo-Jewish history,[62] and it was the study of this 'Middle Period' that was pioneered by Sidney Lee, who wrote about the secret Jews and *conversos* of Elizabethan England. The 'Middle Period' was thought to have come to an end in 1656, and in this narrative of steady progress, that date stood out as a significant turning point; accordingly, from the birth of the Jewish Historical Society onwards, scholars concentrated, almost exclusively, on the 'Middle Period' of Jewish history and the readmission. This emphasis on a definitively positive chapter in Jewish history served an important purpose at a time of communal insecurity: to express gratitude to the English nation for welcoming the Jews and to emphasise that Jewish immigration had a successful precedent.[63] The first 'Resettlement Day' was held in 1894, and the anniversaries of readmission became increasingly elaborate, culminating in the large-scale celebrations of the 250th anniversary in 1906, just months after the Aliens Act was passed. It was as if the troubling formulation of an ethnic category of 'Jew' in the 1870s resulted, through a process of compensatory projection, in the positing of a sanctioned transformation from *conversos* and crypto-Jews to 'real' Jews in 1656.

The Jewish community was in need of a firm historical foundation, therefore, and Victorian philosemites were keen to lend a sympathetic hand; but why did this project come to be associated so exclusively with Cromwell? The explanation lies in the fact that the Whig support for Cromwell that was already in evidence during the Jew Bill controversy of 1753 evolved during the nineteenth century into full-blown hagiography. This was a dramatic transformation; before the nineteenth century, Cromwell had been dismissed, mostly, as a villainous and radical insurrectionist; but as the century went on, he came to be regarded as a heroic, noble revolutionary: in the words of Raphael Samuel, he was transformed from 'a usurper, a soldier or a statesman' into 'a soul-striver'.[64] Godwin's *History of the Commonwealth* contributed to this new portrait of Cromwell as a tolerant liberal, and Thomas Carlyle's *Letters and Speeches of Oliver Cromwell*, published in 1845, went even further: Carlyle's portrayal had the effect of granting Cromwell a new status as a misunderstood and underestimated hero. In turn, the readmission story was recruited by the wider English establishment into its elevation of Cromwell's reputation.[65] Godwin describes Cromwell resolving to readmit the Jews in definitive terms:

> After the lapse of three hundred and sixty-five years, Cromwell determined to signalise himself by putting an end to this proscription. It was an enterprise worthy of his character. His comprehensive mind enabled him to take in all its recommendations and all its advantages. The liberality of his disposition, and his avowed attachment to the cause of toleration, rendered it an adventure becoming him to achieve. As a man, he held that no human being should be proscribed among his fellow-men for the accident of his birth.[66]

Despite the lack of evidence, a firm belief in Cromwell's benign sympathy towards the Jews took hold.[67] A few years after the founding of the Jewish Historical Society of England in 1893 and the first anniversary of readmission in 1894, the status of Cromwell reached its peak. In 1899, a statue to commemorate the tercentenary of Cromwell's birth was erected by the Liberal government, and there were celebrations held around the country.[68]

The dramatic improvement in Cromwell's reputation was made possible, in turn, by an elevation of the status of Puritanism. Prior to the nineteenth century, broadly speaking, Nonconformists had felt marginalised and compromised by their regicide past, and Puritanism was sidelined in histories of the Civil War in favour of the order restored by Charles II and the generosity of the 1688 Act of Toleration.[69] During the nineteenth century, however, both the Nonconformist tradition and its roots in the Civil War period were consolidated. A significant influence on the transformation of Puritanism's reputation was, again, Godwin's *History of the Commonwealth*, which helped to vindicate Britain's dissenting tradition. Godwin wrote an account of the Interregnum which presented it in more positive terms than before; in 1845, Thomas Carlyle declared in his *Letters and Speeches of Oliver Cromwell* that 'Puritanism was the last of all our Heroisms'; and S.R. Gardiner's volumes of Puritan history started to appear in 1876.[70] Nonconformists were not only granted a greater degree of toleration but also became more politically powerful, and by the 1880s, the events of the mid-seventeenth century were referred to in flattering terms as 'The Puritan Revolution'.[71]

The rise of Puritanism in the nineteenth century occurred, furthermore, at a time of intense sectarian divisions; and debates about religious toleration and the relationship between church and state proliferated. Although Puritanism was a single denomination, it had aquired, through its prominent lobbying for religious liberty, an image of a more generic inclusiveness; and Puritan writers identified their forebears as the tolerationist 'pioneers' of the 1640s and 50s.[72] This reading of the seventeenth century through the lens of the nineteenth did entail, however, a certain amount of wishful thinking. The inclusive aspect of Nonconformity, for example, was more of a reality in the nineteenth century than in the seventeenth, and Victorian commentators often elided their own liberalism with seventeenth-century religious liberty:[73] Godwin was not alone in associating religious freedom with freedom of thought and ascribing this virtue to seventeenth-century Independents.[74]

The sceptical legal historian H.S.Q. Henriques, writing in the first years of the twentieth century, recognised early on the idealistic nature of nineteenth-century representations of seventeenth-century Puritanism and of Cromwell's treatment, not only of dissident Christians, but also of Jews:

> During our own and our fathers' times a great change has taken place in the opinions men have formed of Cromwell's character and his place in the history of his country. It was at one time the fashion to write him down a self-seeking hypocrite; but thanks to the powerful advocacy of Thomas Carlyle and other writers contemporary with and subsequent to Carlyle, he has become a great statesman, nay, a hero . . . and so in the course of the apotheosis of the great Oliver, his virtue as an upholder of Religious Toleration has been much dilated upon; and his conduct towards the Jews has been selected as one instance of it. But it should not be forgotten that by the men of his own time Toleration, in those who held the reins of government, was regarded as a vice rather than a virtue; and accordingly it was not

his supporters, but his political opponents, such as Walker, Evelyn, and Burnet, who laid most stress on the favours he was alleged to have shown to the Jews.[75]

Undaunted, Anglo-Jewish historians in the late nineteenth century chose Cromwell as their protector, in tandem with their British hosts, and the comparatively definitive gestures of toleration made by Charles II and James II towards the Jews were downplayed and explained as the result of pragmatic, rather than benign, motives.[76] By 1905, the year before the 250th anniversary, H.S.Q. Henriques was one of the only writers still admitting any doubt on the issue.[77] Henriques's expertise was that of a legal historian, and he took a systematic, analytical approach to the evidence for readmission presented by Wolf and others:

> The theory itself rests upon no sufficient evidence, and the statements which are put forward as corroborating it are either wholly irrelevant or absolutely inconsistent with it; the excuse for dealing with it at such length must be that for a number of years a learned society claiming an important place in the Jewish community has held a public dinner in the early days of February to celebrate what it has been pleased to call 'Resettlement Day'. The dinner was announced in 1900, but not held, owing to the death of Queen Victoria; it has not since been revived, possibly because the organisers have discovered the futility of attempting to create an anniversary for which there is no historical justification.[78]

Henriques was evidently unaware that the anniversary would be revived the following year; despite his own scepticism, the weight of historical justification and public celebration was, by this time, overwhelming.[79]

An informal readmission

Anglo-Jewish historians had a clear motivation for determining readmission as a decisive event but they still faced the problem of making the facts support their case. Cromwell's Whitehall Conference had come to nothing, and there was no evidence that he had readmitted the Jews by any other route. The only way of arguing that readmission did happen under Cromwell was to shift the focus of attention away from Menasseh's efforts, and towards the subsequent actions of the Jewish community already resident, undercover, in England. Accordingly, a tradition was established according to which the readmission of the Jews to England was thought to have occurred not as the result of a formal act, but rather informally, with Cromwell assuring the Jews of London that he would tolerate their presence, and the Jews taking steps to establish an open community. Informal readmission was even considered advantageous, the idea being that countries which formally tolerated Jews through the passing of laws could then revoke them at a later date.[80] This belief in the virtue of informal readmission had its origin, indeed, in the patriotic notion that the English style of toleration was uniquely *ad hoc* and unofficial. In a presidential address to the Jewish Historical Society of England in October 1955, Cecil Roth described readmission as 'so gradual a process – and in this so typically English – that it is difficult to say when it began, and when the Middle Period with which I am dealing here in reality ended . . . the Resettlement was based not on doctrine, but on fact; it resulted not from a dramatic action, but from experiment, thereby becoming as it seems to me all the more English in its nature'.[81]

Central to the informal readmission thesis was the belief that Cromwell granted the requests of the March 1656 petition verbally.[82] Wolf wrote in 1888 that 'the precise terms of this grant, which was doubtless oral, have not been preserved', but 'we may assume that it was a kind of informal *fays ce que voudras*, the Protector relying on the tried discretion of the Jews'.[83] Later on, Roth admitted there was no written evidence that the petition was answered favourably, but claimed that the London Jews' requests for permission to establish a synagogue and cemetery were agreed to, nonetheless.[84] A recurrent trope in accounts of readmission is that of a document which has been lost or destroyed, and according to a conspiracy theory developed by Roth in 1961, two crucial pages were cut out of the minute book of the Council of State; pages which would have contained a favourable reply to the petition. Roth writes that a 'Miss Daphne Gifford, of the Public Record Office, re-examining the Order Book of the Council of State for 25 June 1656 . . . observed . . . a curious fact, which no previous enquirer had noticed or thought fit to place on record – *that the pages containing the minutes for that day's proceedings are missing*. Here obviously we have the key to the mystery which we are attempting to solve'. Roth continues, '*It is now possible to state categorically that the decision authorising Jewish public worship in England, after a lapse of 366 years, was reached on Wednesday, 25 June 1656*'. Roth never referred to this 'discovery' again, but Cromwell's verbal assurance has lived on in subsequent accounts.[85]

It followed that if Cromwell had verbally granted the terms of the petition, then a synagogue and cemetery were established soon after.

Accordingly, a great deal of historical research was invested in the search for evidence of these two institutions.[86] In 1924, Wilfred Samuel, the scholar and founder of the Jewish Museum in London, claimed in a book entitled *The First London Synagogue of the Resettlement* that the establishment of the synagogue in Creechurch Lane and the leasing of land for a cemetery 'were in fact the outcome of the Petition to Oliver Cromwell of March 1656, consideration of which had been stayed until the summer of that year'.[87] Moreover, evidence that they were founded was not enough; there was also considerable investment in demonstrating that these institutions were known about and – at least informally – sanctioned by the English authorities. In his essay on the establishment of 'The First London Synagogue', Samuel emphasised that 'these proceedings – albeit discreetly conducted – were authorised and *publici juris*'.[88] This combination of discretion and visibility is a recurrent feature of accounts of 1656.

Similarly detailed, almost forensic, evidence was called upon to prove public awareness of the cemetery. Samuel placed great emphasis on his discovery that the bells of the church of St Katherine Creechurch rang for the burial of prominent London Jews, writing that 'I must confess to a feeling of amazement when I unearthed these facts, and I think my Jewish readers will share my surprise and gratification at the kindly and tolerant attitude of the Church towards the newly formed Jewish congregation'.[89] Samuel also paid a lot of attention to a Parish Account Book entry of February or March 1656–7 which refers to an amount 'paid for warning the workmen before the Court of Aldermen that were Imployed in building the Jewes Synagogue'.[90] It was not in Samuel's interests to observe the paradox inherent in unearthing hidden yet widespread official acknowledgement.

The attempt to fix readmission as a definite event resulted in a number of historiographical problems. One such problem concerned the date on which the modern era of Anglo-Jewry began. From 1894 onwards, 4 February was established as a convention, because it was at one time thought that this was the date on which Cromwell gave his verbal assurance to the community that the terms of their petition would be granted, but it was 1658, not 1656, which was being celebrated.[91] In 1924, Samuel pointed out that this was simply the date on which Cromwell dissolved his Parliament.[92] By 1906, when the 250th anniversary was celebrated, the official year of readmission had shifted back to 1656, while the traditional month of celebration, February, remained in place. By 1956, the 4 February tradition had been abandoned, and readmission was celebrated over the course of several months.

Another problem concerned the extent to which the events of 1656 constituted the beginning of a new era. Alongside the desire to present 1656 as a decisive turning-point, there existed a contradictory desire to present the 'Middle Period' as one in which Jews were never entirely absent from England. According to this competing narrative, Jews maintained a continuous presence in England through the ages. This contradictory phenomenon is illustrated by two statements written by Wolf in 1887: 'Fully five years before Menasseh ben Israel came to England there was a small Jewish congregation in London, and a Jewish marriage was solemnised in its midst. The members were secret Jews, but they do not seem to have incurred any danger by the fact of their race and religion being known' and later, 'in 1656 Cromwell put an end to the long period of Jewish outlawry by permitting the formation of a Jewish congregation in Aldgate, and the acquisition of a burial ground in Mile End'.[93] In a lecture delivered at the Anglo-Jewish Historical Exhibition, Wolf emphasised the importance of establishing that there were Jews living in England between their 'expulsion' in 1290 and their 'readmission' in 1656 because it 'fills up important blanks, and completes the thread which connects the years 1290 and 1656'.[94] The assertion of continuity before and after 1656 allowed historians to portray the Anglo-Jewish community as always having had an abiding presence in the country, despite the eruptions of Judeophobia. However, this version of events sits uncomfortably with the notion that 1656 brought about a rupture with the past.

The situation was complicated, moreover, by the fact that, at a certain point in the story, Menasseh ben Israel's activities and those of the London Jewish community came together. There were benefits to be gained from both interpretations. For historians who argued that readmission was a result of Menasseh's arrival and his efforts to resettle Dutch Jews in England, the event became a foreign import, an influx of foreign Jewry: in other words, a true readmission. For historians who argued, on the other hand, that after Menasseh's mission failed, the real impetus for readmission came from London's Jewish community, the moment of readmission could be integrated, more seamlessly, into the assertion of a continuous Jewish presence in England. According to the latter scenario, however, the origins of the Jewish community in England were therefore to be found in the community which was present during the reign of Henry VIII and Elizabeth I, thus compromising the notion that the readmission was a readmission at all. This tension between continuity and change produces a curious effect: in accounts written by historians invested in readmission as a decisive event, that community seems, at the moment of Menasseh's arrival, to be mysteriously absent; indeed, the Jewish community in London prior to 1656 appears and disappears according to the fluctuations of opposing historiographical imperatives.[95]

From Jews to Judaism

Although modern historians of Anglo-Jewry are aware of the apologetical nature of accounts written by an earlier generation, the traditional – and problematic – narrative of readmission remains prevalent, and 1656 is still portrayed as more than a sum of its parts.[96] As far as non-specialist accounts are concerned, the claim that Cromwell welcomed the Jews back into England is still made without nuance or qualification.[97] Readmission continues to be the central founding event of Anglo-Jewish history,[98] and it is rare, indeed, to find any accounts which question the facts or the interpretation of readmission at all.[99] Anglo-Jewish history remains teleological in character,[100] and the same narratives are repeated time and again: namely, that the English attitude towards Jews in the Roman Catholic medieval period was one of intense antisemitism; that with the Reformation and the rise of Protestantism, and especially Puritanism, Christian attitudes were gradually transformed from antisemitism to philosemitism; that interest in Hebrew, the Talmud and Kaballah spread, and Christian contact with Jews resident in England and on the Continent increased; and that the mid-seventeenth century saw the rise of religious toleration, which eventually culminated in the Jews' informal readmission.[101]

It is certainly the case that Christians were greatly preoccupied with Judaism in the sixteenth and seventeenth centuries. Pamphlets, tracts, sermons and literary works of the period contain detailed references to the Jewish religion, Jewish history, the Hebrew language and Jewish mysticism.[102] Major protagonists in the formation of the early modern church and state, including John Foxe and Richard Hooker, as well as a multitude of scholars and writers, such as Hugh Broughton and John Selden, repeatedly referred to Judaism and the ancient Jewish constitution.[103] During the Interregnum, as the church fractured into varied and extreme religious persuasions, this interest in Judaism increased and intensified, but it was always highly ambivalent in character: the anxiety of influence resulting from Christianity's Jewish origins permeated theological discourse, and early modern Christians moved between two versions of Judaism – one typological, the other heretical – with almost incomprehensible agility.

In the work of Anglo-Jewish historians, this enthusiasm for Jewish ideas has been and continues to be represented as the precursor of sympathy for Jewish people. And yet the trajectory from Judeophobia to philosemitism did not always run in the same direction, and English attitudes towards Jews tended to fluctuate throughout the early modern period. For example, in 1623, William Sclater (1575–1626), rector of Pitminster, mused, 'how would my soule wish rather to be a Iew, that dissolute nature might be restrayned in mee by lawes, and my Conscience inioy the sweete comforts found in obedience'.[104] By contrast, for the Puritan controversialist William Prynne (1600–1669) in 1656, Jewishness signified whatever it was that Christians did not like: 'Better we cannot express more cut-throat dealing then thus, *None but a Jew would have done so*; lower we cannot prize any one of most abject condition, then by comparing him to a *Jew*'.[105] Prynne not only saw Jews in a negative light, but also declared this view to be a generalised cliché, at the very moment when support for the Jews might be assumed to have reached its peak.

In both these cases, Sclater and Prynne alike are not declaring straightforwardly what they think of Jews; rather, they are comparing themselves or others with them. This formulation is axiomatic; Christians rarely referred to Jews in a neutral, disinterested fashion. More commonly, they either used Judaism as a way of insulting other Christians, or they identified with Jews themselves. Indeed, a common habit among early modern Christians was not only the adoption of Jewish ideas, but also the adoption of Jewish practices. Scholars have struggled to account for why Christians practised Jewish customs, often regarding such behaviour as eccentric. 'Judaizing' was a complex and ambiguous process, however; because in the process of becoming 'Jewish', Judaism lost its essential quality: a paradox which was subject to considerable debate.[106] In fact, Jewishness was frequently imagined less as a characteristic of the Jewish people, and rather as one which could be attached to Christians. The *Oxford English Dictionary* cites John Milton as being the first to define Judaism (in 1641) not as a religion but as 'the act of Judaizing; adoption of Jewish practices on the part of Christians; a practice or style of thought like that of the Jews', but this meaning can be found considerably earlier.[107] From at least the second half of the sixteenth century, the label 'Jewish' could indicate not only a preference for Jewish ideas, but also the threat of becoming Jewish through that very preference.[108] To the extent that Judaism was thus regarded as a mobile characteristic which could be adopted by Christians, it was not necessarily an integral, non-Christian category. This is not to say that Christians lacked a strong sense that Jews were different, or abhorrent.

But, as the remainder of this book will argue, Jewishness did not necessarily signify a connection to the Jewish people.[109]

Judaism was a mobile characteristic, indeed, not only in terms of identity, but also in terms of discourse. When William Sclater wrote 'how would my soule wish rather to be a Iew', he was not simply expressing his love for Judaism. Read in context, his words are a contribution to the controversy over the payment of church tithes in the early seventeenth century, in which the employment or rejection of Jewish precedents was a major crux of the debate. Advocating the application of Jewish precedents, Sclater was presenting the Jews as exemplars of discipline and virtue. Thus what appears to be evidence of philosemitism is, here and – as the following chapters will illustrate – elsewhere, evidence of the instrumentality of Jewishness for Christians engaging in particular debates. Reading Sclater's and other Christians' words in context does not negate the interest in Judaism which undoubtedly existed in this period, but it does show how the nature of that interest was inflected differently depending on the controversy at hand. Attempts to understand early modern Christian Judaizing have been dominated by the events of 1656; but if early modern interest in Judaism was not about laying the foundations of an Anglo-Jewish community, what was it about? The remainder of this book seeks to answer that question.

2
Puritans and Judaism: From Scholarship to Sedition

'This Controversiall age'[1]

In 1621, Bishop Richard Montagu broke off from his reply to a tract written by the lawyer and scholar John Selden to make a more general complaint:

> Now consider the times as they goe with us at this day, wherein . . . reproofe and refutation is of principall imployment. Controversies upon all hands, are so multiplied . . . in the Church: so extended, inlarged, maintained upon all sides, with opposition: driven unto such strait issues, and nice differences with strength of wit: learning aduanced by industry unto such a pitch; that unlesse we will with shame enough sit still, and let the Aduersary carry all before him . . . needs we must . . . carry Libraries about us in our braines.[2]

Bishop Montagu was not alone in his frustration; in 1644, the Nonconformist minister Thomas Goodwin referred disparagingly to the 'controversies afoot in these times of contradiction',[3] and two years later the Scottish Presbyterian George Gillespie admitted: 'I have often and heartily wished that I might not be distracted by nor ingaged into polemick Writings, of which the World is too full already . . . and I did accordingly resolve that in this Controversiall age I should be slow to write, swift to read and learne'.[4] When viewed through the lens of nineteenth-century historiography, the early modern period seemed to be a time of tolerance, innovation and grand ideas; but contemporaries' perceptions were rather different. Contrary to dominant impressions of the Renaissance as a time of predominantly literary production, it was tracts, pamphlets and printed sermons which made up the bulk of texts printed at this time, and these texts were riddled with controversy.⁵

The evolving church, state and legal system were developed, during the sixteenth and seventeenth centuries, through the vehicle of debate, and conflicts between religious or political positions were played out over what sometimes appear to be nugatory points of religious doctrine, parliamentary precedent or aspect of law. As Joad Raymond has shown, furthermore, printed controversies conformed to certain rules: if a tract or a pamphlet was written by one faction, it had to be answered by the opposition, otherwise it could be considered irrefutable; this genre became known as animadversion.⁶ Not only had the general gist to be answered but also each point had to be considered in turn; and, with other commentators becoming involved, the controversies were prone to escalate, resulting in complex families of interrelated texts. Great masses of evidence were cited to support each side of the case, drawn from the Bible, the church fathers or historical texts. In a reply to the Congregationalist minister John Goodwin, William Prynne boasts about the large number of sources he has located: 'Both Scripture, Fathers, Councels, Acts of Parliament, the suffrages of all forraigne Reformed Churches, Writers, and our owne learnedest Bishops, Authors in all times . . . direct Acts, Resolutions of Parliament, Patents, unanswerable Law-authorities, and Reasons'. Prynne continues, throwing down the gauntlet: 'When you can produce as many good authorities, Reasons from Scripture, Antiquity, Acts of Parliament, Writers of all sorts . . . as I have done . . . I shall then excuse you from arrogancy and schisme, but till this be done, (as I presume it will never be) the guilt . . . wil stick fast upon you'.⁷ Prynne's daunting challenge illustrates the expectations facing participants in these debates.⁸

The polemical literature of the early modern period produces the impression, therefore, of a religious landscape split into a multitude of factions; the three most important being residual Roman Catholics, Conformist Protestants – or Anglicans – and Puritans. Although an outlawed minority, Roman Catholics continued to publish texts sympathetic to their cause, but the majority of the debates were between Conformist Protestants, who presented themselves as being part of the religious establishment, and Puritans, who claimed that the English church was in need of further reformation, and who opposed what they regarded as the hierarchical, ungodly nature of the church's administration. Within these three camps there were smaller factions and denominations, and over time, religious allegiances shifted, resulting in a highly differentiated and oppositional religious scene. The polemical texts of the period also contained deep political divisions, and arguments about monarchy, parliament and law were commonplace; the Civil War and the Interregnum brought these into sharp focus. In an age when no clear distinction between religion and politics was yet in place, controversies about the relationship between church and state were abundant and complex.[9]

The extent to which this partisan discourse actually reflected the existence of 'real', clearly demarcated religio-political groups has long been subject to debate.[10] To a large extent, as the following chapters will argue, early modern commentators opposed one another so vociferously precisely because the boundaries between different factions were shifting and uncertain. Controversy was a way of defining not only the nature of the opposition, but also one's own allegiance and identity, and terms of abuse were also terms of definition; William Prynne protests in a 1637 dedication to Charles I that 'those who are now slaundered under the name of Puritans, are your best and loyallest Subjects, because most hated and slaundered by Iesuites, Priests and Traytors, who would Father all villanies and treasons on them; And hate them most of any people'. On the other side, Bishop Richard Montagu complains about being slandered as a Conformist: 'One mans opinion is not (God forbid it should be) the generall resolution of the Church: howbeit wee are much wronged and preiudiced this way, by our adversaries, that impute unto us euery Dreamers idle speculations, as the generally maintayned doctrine of the Church of *England*'.[11] Puritans accused Conformists of being covert Roman Catholics, and Roman Catholics slandered not just Puritans but all Protestants as schismatics, thus eliding internal Protestant divisions.[12]

Early modern Christians were distinctly uncomfortable with the disunity which this controversy indicated. At a time when Christians believed wholeheartedly in the existence of religious truth, the proliferation of religious debate was regarded as deeply threatening; not least because far from resolving conflicts about Christian belief and practice, these controversies served to widen the gap between denominational positions. Furthermore, controversy was regarded as nothing less than a threat to the very stability of the country. John Goodwin attacks William Prynne not only because he disagrees with him, but also on the grounds that Prynne's intemperate polemic is in danger of damaging public order: 'if Master *Prin* had such a sense of the publike divisions, he would not have gone to make the breach wider by setting forth *Quaeries* stuft with such invectives'.[13] In the revised 1607 edition of his *Catholic Doctrine of the Church of England,* Thomas Rogers, chaplain to Archbishop Bancroft, describes Puritans as 'iudaizers who spread heretical doctrine', and Sunday sabbatarianism as one such heresy which 'disturbeth the peace both of the Common-weale, and Church; and tendeth unto Schism in the one, and Sedition in the other'.[14] Nevertheless, these writers were unwittingly committed to a counterproductive strategy of dogmatic refutation, since to arrive at a consensus would be to dilute the correct interpretation of God's Word, and to open up the possibility of political confusion. Within this Christian culture of debate, as Rogers's words illustrate, Judaism provided a rich and versatile tool with which commentators could attack their opponent; and a variety of Christian factions formed triangular structures of argument between themselves, the opposing faction and Jews. At times, Christians aligned themselves with 'positive' aspects of Jewishness such as chosenness and biblical truth; at others they associated their opponents with 'negative' aspects of Jewishness such as legalism and post-biblical heresy.[15] Representations of Jews and Judaism oscillated, therefore, between virtuous Old Testament Israelite and post-Pauline anachronism, rendering Jews a uniquely flexible instrument in polemical discourse.

'I am a Puritan', says a character in Robert Davenport's play *A New Trick to Cheat the Devil* (1639)

One that will eat no pork,
Doth use to shut his shop on Saturdays,
And open them on Sundays; a Familist
And one of the arch limbs of Belzebub
A Jewish Christian and a Christian Jew.[16]

Ben Jonson's Puritan character Zeal-of-the-land Busy in *Bartholomew Fayre* (1631) is also aware of the fact that, as a Puritan, he is associated with the Jewish faith. Busy reacts defensively to his continuously being labelled 'Rabbi' by announcing his intention to eat Pork: 'I will eat exceedingly, and prophesy; there may be good use made of it, too, now I think on't: by the publike eating of swine's flesh, to profess our hate and loathing of Iudaisme, whereof the brethren stand taxed. I will therefore eat, yea, I will eat exceedingly'. His companion, the Proctor Littlewit, answers, 'Good, I'faith, I will eat heartily too, because I will be no Jew, I could never away with that stiff-necked generation'.[17] As these plays suggest, and as Anglo-Jewish historians have long argued, the association between Puritanism and Judaism was firmly in place as the seventeenth century got underway. This chapter will provide further illustration of this association, but it will also demonstrate that while Protestants, and in particular Puritans, did identify themselves with

Jews, and while Roman Catholics and Conformists made use of this identification in order to demonise their Reformed opponents, the Puritan preference for Judaism was not unmotivated. Through an analysis of a series of debates in the late sixteenth and early seventeenth centuries, this chapter demonstrates the pragmatic dimensions of Puritan philosemitism.

I

Puritan Hebraism

Throughout the Long Reformation, Puritans attempted to strip away what they regarded as corrupt layers of episcopal authority and Popish ceremonialism, and reclaim the original, apostolic Christian faith. They justified their position by invoking the Bible, in particular the Old Testament, and they believed that scripture should be read in the original Hebrew. Puritans advocated the use of Hebrew in biblical translation and scriptural exegesis, and they identified with the biblical Chosen People. In addition, many Puritans became scholars of post-biblical Jewish literature such as the Talmud; and, most heterodox of all, some even began to adopt Jewish practices and customs such as the Sabbath and Passover. Conformists responded by labelling Puritans 'Judaizers' as a means of both religious and political suppression.

The rise of Hebrew in sixteenth-century England is an extraordinary phenomenon.[18] Over the course of the century, English universities adopted a new humanist curriculum which insisted on a return to the ancient languages, and Hebrew was included alongside Latin and Greek. During Henry VIII's reforms of the university curriculum, permanent teaching positions were created for the three ancient languages. Continental refugees such as John Drusius, Immanuel Tremellius and Anthony Chevallier assisted the development of Hebrew studies at the Universities, and college lectureships in Hebrew soon followed. While Hebrew was already institutionally in place in the Christian education system, it was adopted with particular alacrity by Puritans. At Cambridge, Hebrew studies was pioneered by Puritans such as Sir Walter Mildmay, Elizabeth's Chancellor, Laurence Chaderton, the Hebraist and master of Emmanuel College and William Whitaker, Regius Professor of Divinity and Master of St John's College. At Oxford, it was instituted by Thomas Sampson and Laurence Humphrey, Heads of Houses at Christ Church and Magdalen Colleges, respectively.[19] Hebrew grammar was translated by the Puritan scholar John Udall, who had acquired knowledge of Hebrew from Edward

Lively at Cambridge, and printed in English in 1593.[20] Significantly, Udall was suspected of involvement in producing the Nonconformist Marprelate tracts, which criticised the bishops and the Church of England, and imprisoned for his Nonconformist sympathies. The inclusion of Hebrew alongside the Classical languages in the Humanist curriculum led Nonconformists to be characterised as arcane scholars, and this scholarship was not regarded as 'pure': Conformists and Roman Catholics accused them of a kind of heterodox Hebraic humanism.[21]

During the Long Reformation, biblical translation was frequently the subject of intense debate.[22] Protestants were fostering a greater emphasis on the biblical underpinnings of religion, and since scripture was habitually invoked in ecclesiastical controversy, the accuracy of the current version was continually contested; in turn, translators were evidently alarmed that the Word could become compromised through its entanglement in ecclesiastical controversy. Underlying these discussions about scriptural truth lay the fear that finding a perfect biblical translation was an impossible task. In response, Puritans tended to argue that the text of scripture should be translated according to the Hebrew original, while, broadly speaking, Roman Catholics and Conformists favoured the Latin Vulgate. Puritan reliance on the Hebrew language and Jewish precedents was driven, therefore, by a doctrine of uncompromising scripturalism. During debates over whether the church or the Bible was the ultimate religious authority, Puritans stressed the sufficiency of scripture to determine questions of doctrine and church government, while Conformists often classified such questions as *adiaphora*, or as 'things indifferent' and therefore within the power of the church officials to determine.

As scripture was so important, there needed to be a learned ministry to interpret it correctly in the original languages. A popular topic of consternation in Puritan polemic, therefore, was the incompetent scholarship of clergymen. The Puritan minister Edward Dering doubted in 1577 'that there was ever Nation which had so ignoraunt Ministers'.[23] The ignorant clergy features prominently in the Puritan manifesto, *A Second Admonition to the Parliament* (1572). Its authors divided the minister's role into two functions: that of pastor, with its disciplinary function, and that of teacher, with its exegetical function.[24] It was the latter which was accorded the vital role of finding scriptural answers to ecclesiastical questions, and which was associated with proficiency in Hebrew. The Puritan leader Thomas Cartwright (1535–1603) cites the evidence of 'Hebrew Doctours' to emphasise the importance of biblical interpretation, quoting in Hebrew, and continues, 'the Scripture stayeth yt selfe upon, or presumeth an understanding reader: withowt the whiche yt shall seme very unsufficient / that ys most perfect'.[25] As a result of Puritan attacks on members of the ecclesiastical hierarchy on the basis of their ignorance of Hebrew, Conformists were liable to associate Puritan expertise in the language with nonconformity. The Jesuit scholar Gregory Martin claims, for example, that Puritans called attention to their superior knowledge of Hebrew and Greek in order to appear scholarly in the eyes of the populace: the Puritans 'may alwaies have this evasion, It is not so in the Hebrue, it is otherwise in the Greeke, and so seeme ioly fellowes and great clerkes unto the ignorant people'.[26]

One of the most well-known Hebrew scholars of the period was Hugh Broughton (1549–1612). Broughton studied Hebrew at Cambridge under the Huguenot refugee Anthony Chevallier, and Walter Mildmay acted as his patron. He met and debated with various rabbis at Frankfurt, Worms and Middleburg,[27] and published more than 40 tracts on biblical translation and exegesis, biblical genealogy and the Hebrew language, many of which made extensive use of rabbinic sources. Hugh Broughton was so much in favour of Hebrew that he expresses, at one point, the desire 'to speake in England the tongue of Eber'.[28] Broughton was a Protestant millenarian who believed passionately in the conversion of the Jews: in 1609, he petitioned James I for a sum of money to translate the New Testament into Hebrew for this purpose. Broughton is notable not only for associating the Hebrew language with contemporary Jews, having improved his Hebrew language skills in the course of encounters with them, but also for applying their methods of biblical exegesis.

Broughton is often represented, in contemporary as well as modern accounts, as a maverick and abstruse eccentric. In Ben Jonson's *The Alchemist* (1610), the character Face describes Dol Common as:

> a most rare schollar:
> And is gone mad, with studying *Broughtons* workes.
> If you name but a word, touching the *Hebrew*,
> She falls into her fit, and will discourse
> So learnedly of Genealogies,
> As you would runne mad, too, to heare her, Sir.[29]

For Broughton himself, however, biblical translation was not simply a matter of disinterested erudition. He believed his scholarship to be motivated by public interest, dedicating his 1596 commentary on the book of Daniel to the Privy Council with the declaration: 'I think my commentations upon him somewhat profitable to the good of our state'.³⁰ In his 1597 *Epistle to the Nobilitie of England*, an appeal for a new translation of the Bible, Broughton claims disapprovingly that Roman Catholics have obscured the truth of Scripture,³¹ and continues, 'the booke which we call the Bible is the Hebrewe for the olde, the Greeke for the newe . . . translations are but so farre as they are true and exact from the originall . . . by the originall their cleareness and authoritie must aye be strengthened by the Ebrew'.³² Broughton even laments that the New Testament was not written in Hebrew, claiming that if it were, it would be valued more highly.³³ Broughton's concern is not simply to point out that the truth of the Bible has been obscured through incorrect translation, but to lay the blame for this at the door of the Roman Catholics. He fears, furthermore, that if these faults are not corrected, this will add fuel to the fire of unreformed attacks on the Reformed church. Commenting on an error which he believes to exist in the Geneva version, Broughton continues, 'you see the text, and the note: whiche if wee all would graunt currant, then would the papistes earnestly triumph, that we Protestauntes confesse the text to bee corrupted: That will I neuer doe, while breadth standeth in my brest'.³⁴

Broughton blames not only the Roman Catholics, but also the English church for incompetence in Hebrew. He complains that 'the church never had yet seaven that spent their life in vowelled Ebrew and Greke exact antiquity, for the Bibles use'.³⁵ Broughton's Hebraism is motivated, indeed, by his opposition to an episcopacy which, he believes, privileges power over scholarship. He traces the development of this predicament from the very beginnings of Christianity:

> as the Iewes rejected Governours, because they would judge in their owne lawes: so in tyme Scholers would among us: pretending that Politicians in heathen studies were not fitt. But Christianity having no new matter, but the incarnation of the Angel of our Covenant, the Eternall king of glorie, and his Resurrection: having, I say, no new matter but that, wherein the world would staggar, suffereth not Scholars to beare such sway: but requireth others, *Politicia[n]s* always to be *Bishops* in their *Paroches*, to censure the Messengers of the Church; who should read learnedly the Bible: (which few can doe, and which labor spendeth all a mans youth) And all the sage should speak upon request: and the rest judge. In such assemblies, one day might open all the Bible: while plaine matters be only touched, and only difficulties be handled. But men love darkenes: and will haue other *Elohim* [gods] then God willeth.³⁶

In other words, just as the Jews opposed external interference in their affairs, preferring to govern themselves according to Jewish law as administered by the Sanhedrin, the Jewish court, contemporary Christians should reject episcopal rule, based as it is on 'politique' rather than biblical principles. However, since authentic Christianity is barely distinguishable from biblical Judaism, a radical idea ('wherein the world would staggar'), Christians have looked to the bishops to impose order rather than studying scripture directly. Broughton wishes that 'assemblies', Presbyterian councils, be established so that Christians can govern themselves with the guidance of the Bible. Not surprisingly, Broughton was identified as a subversive Nonconformist: his lectures in St Paul's churchyard attracted suspicion, and he engaged in disputes with the staunchly anti-Puritan Archbishop Whitgift (1530–1604) and Thomas Bilson (1547–1616), Bishop of Winchester. In fear of prosecution by the High Commission, he left on the first of many continental excursions at the end of the 1580s. Broughton accused Whitgift of hindering his proposed retranslation of the Geneva Bible, and held the 1568 Bishops Bible in such contempt that in 1597 he was pressing for a new translation.[37] Prefacing a tract called *An Explication of the article* to Queen Elizabeth in 1599, Broughton complains that a certain prelate (Whitgift) has been attempting to suppress his work: he reports that this prelate 'wrote unto the stationers to hinder a commentary of myne upon Daniel', and he states that Whitgift 'gaue out word that I should be stayed from preaching'.[38] Broughton's Hebrew scholarship is inextricably linked to his Nonconformist agenda.

If Hugh Broughton's knowledge of Hebrew was informed by his Puritan sympathies, a rather more overtly partisan figure from the period, John Field (d. 1588), was also interested in Hebrew, although this is not a feature of his posthumous reputation. John Field (d. 1588) was one of the most active organisers of the Puritan movement in the Elizabethan period; Field and his collaborator Thomas Wilcox were imprisoned in Newgate in July 1572 for producing the subversive tract, *An Admonition, to the Parliament*, and Whitgift denounced them as heretical. Patrick Collinson's influential portrayal of Field emphasises his role as a 'revolutionary'.[39] For Field, Hebrew was a useful subject with which to criticise the English church for being insufficiently reformed. Field blames the continuing influence of the Roman Catholic Church for the current lack of Hebrew proficiency in England. He complains that

> all men of learning and iudgement knowe that the time wherin [the Roman Catholics'] errors were most palpable & rife, all kind of good

learning was worne out, the knowledge of tongues decreased . . . for to themselues Hebrewe letters though (as they say) they be as big as Okes, yet they were Pitchforkes and staples, and as for Greeke, they were so farre from understanding of it, that not one amongest a thousande coulde read it.[40]

The metaphor 'Pitchforkes and staples' is a reference to the shape of the Hebrew letters *shin* and *chet*. Field argues that 'the credite of the ancient bookes is to bee examined from the Hebrue volumes, and the newe from the Greeke . . . we ought evermore to repaire to the founteines . . . it is a necessary labour to learne to understand it, in its owne language'.[41] Although John Field does not appear to have any proficiency in the language himself, he appeals to the connotations of Hebrew in the service of his Puritan agenda. Broughton and Field, figures who have very different reputations, both advocate the study of Hebrew because they regard it as the fountainhead of the Bible, and therefore the most reliable linguistic tool for scriptural exegesis;[42] and both advocate Hebrew as part of a polemical attack on episcopacy. In the course of their arguments, the study of Hebrew ceases to be simply a philological enterprise and becomes an instrument of religio-political controversy.

The Chosen People

Puritans favoured the Old Testament because they considered it the most authentic part of scripture, and also because they often identified with the Chosen People. The Old Testament embodied, for them, the original and direct access to God enjoyed by the Israelites, a relationship which Puritans were keen to emulate. It also provided narratives which fitted the Reformed world view: the exodus from Egypt prefigured deliverance from the Roman Catholic past, and the Prophets foretold the apocalypse implicit in millenarian notions of Protestant history and destiny. The authors of the *Admonition* complain that all this means little to the Conformists: 'When the old Testament is read, or the lessons, they make no reverence, but when the gospel commeth, then they al stand up. For why, they thinke that to be of greatest authoritie'.[43] As Patrick Collinson and others have observed, identifications between English Christians and biblical Israel were already in place well before the Reformation, but they were modified according to the Elizabethan Puritan agenda.[44] It is the details of this modification, however, and the ways in which they were refined in relation to Judaism, which are significant here. Puritan commentators drew parallels between God's relationship with the Jews and his relationship to the English church as a whole: the English church, like the biblical Israelites, was insufficiently reformed and therefore threatened with God's anger. But, more daringly, they also suggested that it was only the Puritan minority within an idolatrous English church which was now God's Chosen, and the threat of God's punishment served as a warning to the less committed. At stake, in other words, was whether the Chosen People metaphor applied to the English church, or only the Puritans within it.

Parallels with Old Testament Israelites were, therefore, a flexible political, as well as doctrinal, resource. The authors of *An Admonition, to the Parliament*, Anthony Gilby, John Field and Thomas Wilcox, also produced and translated commentaries, paraphrases and sermons on Old Testament books. In the prefaces and introductions to these texts, they cast the drama of the continuing English Reformation in biblical language, making abundant use of terms such as 'Gentiles' and 'uncircumcised Philistins'. The imperfect church was Babylon or Egypt, and the perfect church Jerusalem.[45] Edward Dering writes of 'the holye Ghoste, whose government hath made thee free from the bondage of Egypt, from the spyrituall Babylon, from Pope, and Papacie, which shame hath shaddowed, and shall at the last close it up for ever.'[46] Although these labels ostensibly referred to Roman Catholics, they could also be interpreted as an implicit attack on the Popishness still remaining in the Anglican Church. In the dedication to his commentary on the prophet Micah, Anthony Gilby declares that prelacy is the sixteenth-century equivalent of Old Testament idolatry. Gilby describes how 'oure governours' have 'banished the outwarde shewe' of idolatry, and 'have seemed to chaunge [its] kinde', but that it remains in essence.[47] The book of Micah predicts the destruction of Jerusalem, the regeneration of the Israelites and the advent of a Messiah, and therefore lends itself well to Protestant apocalyptic polemic. For Gilby, Micah 'uttereth the flattery of theyr chaplaines (as we do cal them) the false prophetes . . . let us therefore remember the olde worlde before us plagued for synne, drowned for theyr wickednesse, and feare of the fire of Godde's wrath, threatened by the prophetes, to be kindeled in these laste times, to the everlasting destruccion of all evill doers'.[48] The Puritan minister Christopher Fetherstone draws an explicit parallel between the construction of the Israelites' temple and the completion of the English Reformation. In the dedication to his commentary on the prophet Haggai, Fetherstone writes: 'when I call to minde . . . the building of the Lordes Temple by the Iewes of elder dayes, and there-withall take a vew of the truth of that material temple, of the Church I meane, generally, and more particularly here in England, this angle [outlying corner] of the world: me thinks I may full wel compare these two buildings together'. By the side of this passage in the British Library copy, a marginal manuscript note reads, 'the state of Englande and the Jewes compared'.[49]

Those who were interested in biblical Jewry were plagued by concerns, however, about whether the Old Testament contained universal precepts which applied to Christians as well as Jews, or whether they applied only to Jews. Conformists often protested that whereas they used the Old Testament legitimately, Nonconformists used it Jewishly. This is a popular topic in anti-Puritan rhetoric, and Conformists regularly accused Puritans of Jewish legalism, of taking Jewish laws which had been abrogated by the coming of Christ literally. Whitgift, for example, claims that certain prescriptions in Deuteronomy to keep God's commandments apply only to the Jews under the Law, concluding: 'thus you see how farre I am from . . . thinking that the olde testament doth not apperteine unto us: and yet I am not so Jewishe, to thinke that we are bound either to the ceremoniall or iudiciall law.[50] Later, Whitgift accuses Cartwright of adopting from the Old Testament not only the universal moral law but also the Jewish ceremonial law, abrogated, or declared redundant, by Christ:

> Where you say, that we have the same lawes to direct us in the service of God, that they had, if you meane the same morall lawes you say truly, but nothing to the purpose: if you meane the same ceremoniall lawes (which properly are sayd to be lawes directing them in the service of God) then doe you *Iudaizare, play the Iewe*.

A printed marginal note by this passage reads, 'The assertion of T.C. tendeth to Judaisme'.[51] It is hardly surprising that Whitgift is so explicit in his labelling of Cartwright as a Judaizer. In his reply to Whitgift's answer to the *Admonition*, Cartwright had gone so far as to declare that

> if the Jewes had precepts of every the least action / whych told them precisely how they should walke: how is not their case in that poynt better then oures / whych because we have in many things but generall rules / are to seeke oftentimes / what is the will of God whych we should follow.[52]

Whitgift clearly considers this issue to be of grave importance, given the high risks attached to emulating the Jews: 'I muste crave pardon of the

Reader, for making suche excursions out of the way, for I am compelled to followe you, whiche interlace your booke with suche by-matters, and those so suspicious and daungerous, that I can not safely passe them over with silence'.[53] He is acknowledging, here, the demands of printed controversy, which compel him to address, as Cartwright had done, the issue of Jewish legalism. As a Conformist, Whitgift is loath to address 'Jewish questions' at all. Cartwright responds to Whitgift's suspicions with care, writing 'it remaineth to see / whether in the matter off the iudiciall lawe / that which I have set downe be straunge / and dangerous (as the A[nswerer] surmiseth) or no'.[54] Cartwright's equivocation here is provocative, and this exchange illustrates the subtle way in which Judaism is recruited into a pivotal controversy between Puritans and Anglicans in the late sixteenth century.

The Continent and 'Jewish' influence

John Field, Hugh Broughton and William Fulke were invested in applying Jewish knowledge to the true reformation of the English church. Although their concerns appear domestic, their 'Judaizing' was heavily inspired by continental writers. Puritans such as John Field, Thomas Wilcox and Philip Sidney produced and translated commentaries on French tracts and sermons by Jean Calvin, Theodore Beza, Philippe de Mornay and the Swiss Protestant minister Pierre Viret, among others. These texts provided a rich source of parallels between Reformers and Old Testament Israelites, and also a variety of Talmudic and Jewish historical references.[55] English Puritans appropriated these sources in their search for Jewish material, and they foregrounded, in the prefaces and dedications to their translations, their alliances with Reformers abroad. These continental texts bolstered the nonconformity of English Puritans because they contributed to their reputation as Judaizers, and also because appeals to reformed churches abroad implied criticism of the English church.

English Nonconformists had always enjoyed strong links with the Continent.[56] In their translations and commentaries, English Puritans described the plight of Reformers in a variety of locations ranging from Roman Catholic Paris to Protestant Geneva. Numerous printed accounts of the St. Bartholomew's Day massacre of 1572 were produced, mostly by French Calvinist refugees in Geneva and other Protestant publishing centres around Europe.[57] The printer Henry Bynneman published numerous accounts of the massacre in London.[58] Large numbers of French Protestant refugees subsequently arrived in England, where they proceeded to publicise events across the Channel. The Puritan John Stubbs'

Discoverie of a gaping gulf whereinto England is like to be swallowed by another French marriage (1579), arguing against Elizabeth's proposed marriage to The Duc d'Anjou, was heavily influenced by Huguenot propaganda.⁵⁹

In contrast to Paris, Geneva had represented an ideal to English Puritans ever since the Marian exiles had settled there in the 1550s, under the leadership of the English reformer John Knox. During the 1520s, Geneva had become a reformed city-state; a kind of Protestant Rome. Calvin was religious leader from the 1540s, succeeded by Beza. In 1559, the Geneva Academy was created, with Beza as its first rector, and it became an important training centre for Protestant leaders from other countries. Its humanist curriculum included Hebrew as well as Latin and Greek. Many English Puritans studied there, and Thomas Cartwright was one of its lecturers. English Puritans continued to visit Geneva throughout Elizabeth's reign; taking courses at the Academy, and building contacts with other ardent Reformers.⁶⁰

English Puritans imported references to Judaism as they imported and translated continental Protestant propaganda. Philippe de Mornay's *Trewnesse of the Christian Religion* (1587), translated by the Puritan Arthur Golding, is full of detailed marginal references to Midrashic and Talmudic commentaries.⁶¹ In the preface, Mornay announces his intention to refer to a wide variety of Jewish sources in order to provide external proofs that Christianity is the true religion:

> I will alledge their ancient doctors, dispersed as well in their Cabales as in their Talmud, which are their bookes of greatest authoritie and most credit. And diverse times I will interlace the Commentaries of their late writers, which generally have bene most contrarie to the Christen doctrine, whom (notwithstanding) the truth hath compelled severally to agree, in expounding the Texts whereon the same is cheifly grounded.⁶²

Geneva was, therefore, a source of Hebrew learning for English Puritans, and this learning was put into practice: translations of tracts by Genevan Protestants such as Calvin and Beza were used as pretexts for comparisons drawn between Old Testament Israelites and contemporary Reformers. In the preface to his 1581 translation of Beza's psalm paraphrases, Anthony Gilby confesses that 'the which terrible words and threatenings against Gods chosen people, when I read them, they cause me to tremble and feare for our state heere in England . . . for besides that our religion is not yet brought to ful perfection in these 22 yeares . . . the horrible sinnes of former times are not yet purged with true teares of repentance'.[63] Gilby's act of translation is no dry academic exercise.

Indeed, the publishing connections which linked English Puritans with reformed writers on the Continent were extensive. The French Protestant Philippe de Mornay, the Puritan activist John Field, the poet Philip Sidney and continental reformers such as Beza, Calvin and Franciscus Junius were associated with one another in print, indicating that psalm paraphrases and sermon translations served an English Puritan agenda, and one which was influenced, moreover, by the Hebrew language and Jewish scholarship. John Field's *Christian Meditations* (1587) and his *A Treatise of the Church* (1579) were translations of Philippe de Mornay, the chief advisor to the Huguenot Henri of Navarre, and Field also translated thirteen of Calvin's sermons in 1579 and a translation of a tract by Beza entitled *The Iudgement of a Most Reverend and Learned Man from Beyond the Seas* in 1580.[64] Philip Sidney is said to have begun the translation of Mornay's *Trewnesse of the Christian Religion* (1587) before passing the task to Arthur Golding, the Puritan clergyman and translator.[65] Sidney's sister, the Countess of Pembroke, translated Philippe de Mornay's *Discours de la vie et de la mort* in 1590.[66] Franciscus Junius was a Calvinist minister and German philologist at Antwerp who served as an army chaplain to William of Orange, and held a chair in theology at the University of Leiden. In 1580, he dedicated his *Grammatica Hebraeae Linguae* to Philip Sidney with the following words:

> The reason, obviously, why I like to offer it to your country, is that I conclude from long conversations which I used to have with some of your fellow countrymen that they particularly were friends of art and friends of Hebrew; that their souls breathed only Hebraic flowers, so to speak; that their voices intoned only Hebrew; that their minds investigated only Hebrew problems and were intent only upon their solution: finally, to be brief, that their houses seemed to be all decorated with Hebrew letters and their table-talk never without them.[67]

This extraordinary passage illustrates the Nonconformist enthusiasm for Hebrew in England, as well as the role of literary figures such as Philip Sidney in transmitting Hebraic scholarship from the Continent to England in order to feed this enthusiasm.

Franciscus Junius and another Hebraist, Immanuel Tremellius, produced a new Latin translation of the Old Testament in 1580, designed as a Protestant alternative to the Vulgate, which carried Papist connotations.[68] In *An Apologie for Poetrie*, Sidney describes Junius and Tremellius as helping to propagate the idea of the Old Testament as a source of poesy:

> The chief [poets], both in antiquity & excellencie, were they that did imitate the inconceivable excellencies of GOD. Such were, *David* in his Psalmes, *Solomon* in his song of Songs, in his Ecclesiastes, and Proverbs: *Moses* and *Debora* in theyr Hymnes; and the writer of *Iob*; which beside other, the learned *Emanuell Tremelius*, & *Franciscus Iunius*, doe entitle the poeticall part of the Scripture.[69]

The notion that the psalms were a source of both spiritual wisdom and poetic eloquence, and that David was a *vates* or prophet figure, to be imitated by the Renaissance psalm versifier or translator, was motivated with strong sectarian motives. Elizabethan translators interpreted the psalms as containing latent criticisms of both ecclesiastical and temporal authorities.[70] Sidney's own psalm paraphrases, written in the 1580s and completed by his sister, drew heavily on the Protestant Geneva version of the Bible, produced in 1559, and the 1535 Coverdale Bible.[71] Many of the psalm translations and paraphrases which appeared during Elizabeth's reign were produced by Puritans such as John Stubbs (1582), Anthony Gilby (1580) and Thomas Wilcox (1586), and published by Puritan presses such as that of Thomas Vautrollier, who also published accounts of Protestant oppression in France.[72] The English Puritanism of John Field or Anthony Gilby should be understood, then, in the context of carefully constructed relations with continental Reformers. Psalm translations and paraphrases, along with Hebrew and Talmudic sources, were imported from the Continent and annexed to a domestic Nonconformist agenda.

II

Post-biblical Judaism: Christ's descent into Hell

Puritan interest in Hebrew did not stop at versions of the Bible: it extended into the study of post-biblical Jewish literature, a genre which was not so easily absorbed into the Christian corpus.[73] In fact, Conformists were vehemently against the Puritan study of rabbinic or Talmudic literature, since the later the Jewish source in question, the less trustworthy it was; Jews became increasingly reprehensible and heretical the longer they chose to ignore the teachings of Christ. The

Roman Catholic biblical translator Gregory Martin challenges the Puritan minister William Fulke sarcastically: 'are not your scholars (thinke you) much bound unto you, for giving them in steede of Gods blessed worde and his holy Scriptures, such translations, heretical, Iudaical, profane, false, negligent, phantastical, new, naught, monstrous?'[74] And yet despite these attacks from Conformists and Roman Catholics, Puritans continued to employ post-biblical literature; and moreover, not only in their interpretation of the Old Testament, but also, rather surprisingly, in their interpretation of the New Testament. An exploration of an individual example of this practice reveals the highly politicised nature of what appears, on first viewing, to be simply a point of arcane doctrinal disagreement: the interpretation of Christ's harrowing of Hell.

The nature of Christ's descent into Hell in the Gospels of Matthew and Luke became a highly contentious issue during Elizabeth's reign, and appeared frequently in the pamphlet literature of the period. Explanations of the descent varied – some theologians regarded it as enabling Christ's victory over the powers of evil, while others connected it to the Dereliction on the Cross, the full bearing by Christ of the sins of mankind. Yet another interpretation regarded it as Christ's visit to *Limbus Patrum*, or the place where pre-Christian people waited for the creation of Heaven, in payment for the sins of Adam.[75] Conformists such as John Whitgift and Thomas Bilson thought that Christ did indeed descend to Hell. Puritans including Hugh Broughton and William Fulke, on the other hand, argued that he descended only to the grave, and that his sufferings were not the physical experience of Hellfire but the metaphorical sufferings of his soul, for the sins of mankind.[76]

Debates which contested the meaning of the episode involved frequent recourse to the Hebrew language, because it was believed that resolution could be achieved by determining the etymology of certain key words. Broughton and Fulke appealed to the Hebrew word *sheol*, cited in rabbinic commentaries, which they took to mean 'grave'. However, they had to deal with the fact that a word which appears in the New Testament, *gehenna*, is derived from the Hebrew word *ge-hinnon* which the Jews took to mean Hell rather than the grave, and also that Rashi, the leading commentator on the Bible and the Talmud, had written in a commentary on Genesis that according to the midrashic commentary on the Bible, the word *sheol* means *gehenna*.[77] Undaunted, writers like Broughton and Fulke emphasised repeatedly that those who did not take *sheol* to mean 'grave' were simply displaying their incompetence in Hebrew. Indeed, Broughton aimed to prove that 'the New Testament speaketh most agreably to the Rabbines speech'.[78] The irony, of course, as Broughton himself points out, was that the Jews had no stake in the question of Christ's journey after death, since they did not believe in the incarnation.[79]

Prompted by his opponents' recourse to arguments drawn from rabbinical authorities, Bilson accuses those who argue that Christ did not descend to Hell of Jewish bias, which was associated, for him, with heretical appeals to the heathen Classics:

> Neither Jewish *Rabbines* with their grammaticall observations, nor Greeke *poets* with their fantasticall imaginations may be suffered to contradict it. Howe easie it is to wrangle with the words, NEPHESH, SHEOL, and HADES a meane scholar maie soon perceive; but I hold it no sound course to fetch the explication of the mysteries of christian religion, either from such impudent impugners of it, as were the *Rabbines*, or from such ignorant deluders of it, as were the prophane *poets* . . . and therefore they may spare their paines, that promise us so manie thousand deponentes both Jewish and heathen, that *Sheol* and *Hades* do not signifie hell.[80]

Henry Jacob accuses Bilson in turn of culpable and hostile ignorance towards Hebrew: 'it seemeth, your not considering (or not caring for) the use and maner of the Hebrue toung causeth your mistaking as in these places'.[81] Broughton is less tentative than Jacob in his use of postbiblical Jewish sources. He complains in his answer to Whitgift:

> all Ebrewes Doctor Bilson reiecteth for their grammer sence of *Sheol*. None ever rejected all Latins for Latine, or French for the French: yet D. Bilson dareth reject all Hebrewes for Hebrew. By the same doctrine he might teach never to hope for sound knowledge in any parte of the lawe: no not for one letter: whether it hath the forme that God wrought in the two tables or a later invented . . . for all this no D. without Rabbins helpe can tell what wordes make the Bible . . . so D. Bilson missed much for Rabbins, to the ruine of Religion, and to augment Sathans blindnes.[82]

Broughton correctly detects Bilson's and Whitgift's antipathy towards Jewish sources.

The controversy over Christ's descent into Hell had far-reaching implications; at stake was not only doctrine, but also church discipline. In fact, like so many ecclesiastical controversies of the period, its political ramifications were thematically irrelevant to its content. In other words, simply arguing for or against the proposition that Christ descended to Hell was indicative of the commentator's factional alignment. Christ's descent is the subject of Article III of Elizabeth's Thirty-Nine Articles, issued by Convocation in 1563, and it also appears in the Apostles' Creed, a statement of faith compiled in the primitive church and prescribed by the Book of Common Prayer. Denying any of the articles was interpreted as subversive and schismatic behaviour. Conformists promoted associations between the denial that Christ descended to Hell, and nonconformity: Bishop Bilson accuses his Puritan opponents of 'coin[ing] new articles of the Creed'.[83] In his preface to *The Survey of Christs Sufferings*, Bilson warns James I of 'some mens too much forwardnesse to innovate as well the doctrine as the discipline of the Church of England (they thinking those devices always best, which are newest)'.[84] The anonymous author of a reply to Broughton's work on Christ's descent into hell calls him 'a fugitive abroad, a schismatike at home, a tormentor of soules with mystical riddles'.[85] Henry Jacob and his Puritan allies responded that Articles of Faith, which are not underpinned by scripture, are heretical.[86] In fact, Broughton provocatively interprets Bilson's tract not as a theological contribution to the debate in question, but rather as a partisan defence of episcopacy, claiming that in writing his two tracts Bilson 'tooke in hand to defend Ar[chbishop] Whitgift: that our Lord his soule went hence to Hel: and not hence to heaven', and adding Bishop Bancroft to his list of offending prelates.[87] He complains, furthermore, that these prelates have 'imprisoned many, persecuted more, and urged some to death upon consequentes for denying that our Lord went hence to Hell',[88] and is quite explicit in his anti-episcopal sentiments, declaring: 'it is a pitifull thing that Bishops should be found infinitly fuller of error for the grounds of faith, and learned studies, then any other in all the Kingdome ... it is a most high iniurie against God and the Kinge, that the Church is led amisse by Bishops errors'.[89]

In this debate, as in the one about the use of Hebrew in biblical translation, Broughton is labelled by his opponents not only as a schismatic, but also as a Judaizer. The anonymous author of *Master Broughtons Letters* pours scorn on Broughton's '*Rabbinicall oracles*', and sarcastically qualifies Broughton's claims that Whitgift is unlearned: 'your meaning is he hath not spent his yeeres in the *Hebrew Rabbins*'.[90] Broughton's opponent criticises his 'Rabbinical rubbish ... by your continuall reading those fabulous masters, bringing into light nothing but fantasticall and partie coloured pild [pillaged] conceits half mad, halfe foolish; and by sucking of their traditions, as of their milke, you have taken in their conditions'.[91] The imagery here implies an unhealthy reliance on Jewish sources: a sense that Broughton's borrowings have corrupted him. The suckling metaphor also suggests that by consulting Jewish authorities, Broughton is in danger of turning Jewish in a physical sense, too. The use of Hebrew in this ecclesiastical controversy is an example of the sheer enthusiasm, on the part of sixteenth-century Puritans, for Jewish sources, but also the ways in which the use of those sources becomes a marker of factional allegiance.

John Selden and the tithes controversy

The employment of Judaism in ecclesiastical controversy continued to be acknowledged as a Puritan strategy, by commentators from a variety of denominations, well into the seventeenth century. If Hugh Broughton was the foremost Hebraist of the sixteenth century, John Selden (1584–1654) took on that role in the seventeenth. A Common lawyer, legal historian, philologer and antiquary, Selden became extremely knowledgeable not only about the Hebrew language but also about Jewish history and Jewish exegetical writings such as the Talmud.[92] Selden had acquired his Jewish knowledge from continental Hebraists such as Johannes Reuchlin and Theodore Beza, and studied Talmud with several of his contemporaries, including William Welwood, professor of mathematics and law at St. Andrews University, and Petrus Cunæus, the author of *De Republica Hebraeorum* (1617).[93] The Continent was a source of both Jewish scholarship and of Common law, and the association between continental jurisprudence and Judaism was already in place via the works of philologist, historian and legal scholar Joseph Justus Scaliger and the Dutch jurist and scholar Hugo Grotius, who also provided Selden with information about Hellenic and post-biblical Jewish history and Talmudic literature.[94] The Common Law method known as the *mos gallicum* or 'French way' involved the application of historical and philological analysis to a wide range of literary and religious texts in order to solve legal problems.[95] Common Law emphasised the accumulated weight of empirical precedent over the application of universal, abstract principles. Selden applied this Common Law methodology to classical literature and to English history, and also to Jewish historical and exegetical texts.[96] As the following pages will reveal, the controversy over the payment of tithes in the early seventeenth century associated Common Law and nonconformity with Jewish scholarship.

Selden produced numerous lengthy tracts on Jewish history and law, including a book about marriage and divorce among the ancient Jews, *Uxor Hebraica* (1646), on the succession to property and goods in ancient Jewish law, on religious hierarchies among the Jews (*De Successione in Pontificatum Ebraeorum*, 1638), on the question of the abrogation of Jewish law (*De Jure Naturali et Gentium juxta Disciplinam Ebraeorum*, 1640) and on the Sanhedrin, or Jewish court (*De Synedriis*, 1653).[97] In 1618, Selden published a treatise on the history of tithe-paying through the ages. He presented his tract as a work of disinterested scholarship, denying in the preface that it is 'any thing else but it self, that is, a meer Narration, and the *Historie of Tithes*';[98] Selden professes simply to be tracing past evidence of tithe payment, especially among the Jews. Selden's self-presentation as an even-handed historian has been successfully transformed, in the nineteenth and twentieth centuries, into a hagiographical portrait of Selden as an early pioneer of neutral historical empiricism. The historian and translator Jonathan Ziskind claims, for example, that 'Selden does not use his scholarly works on Jewish subjects to engage in polemic. He simply lets the ancient textual evidence speak for itself'.[99] Selden's contemporaries, however, were less convinced. Three years after the publication of *The Historie of Tithes*, Richard Montagu (1577–1641), a controversialist and bishop who enjoyed the patronage of the king, published a reply to Selden entitled *Diatribæ upon the first part of the late History of Tithes*. Montagu challenged Selden's claims to empiricism, reminding him that 'a meere Narration, is a plaine Relation, nothing else. *History* disputeth not *Pro*, or *Con*; concludeth not what should be, or not be; Censureth not what was well done, or done amisse: But proposeth Accidents, and Occurrences as they fall out: examples and Precedents unto Posterity . . . [whereas] . . . you . . . make your Selfe a Party, which no *Historian* doth, at least should doe'.[100] Montagu was not the only commentator to respond to Selden's tract; its publication prompted a whole series of incensed replies.

Selden's 'meer narration' was, in fact, a contribution to an ongoing controversy about tithes that had begun in the early sixteenth century. With the dissolution of the monasteries, a large amount of church property came under the control of lay administrators, and throughout the sixteenth century church revenues steadily declined. Under Elizabeth, ecclesiastic and lay authorities had been jointly responsible for the jurisdiction of tithe cases, an arrangement which by the end of the sixteenth century had remained relatively unquestioned.[101] As relationships between king, Parliament and church came under increasing strain during the reign of James I, however, this system of joint jurisdiction began to break down. Bishops exacerbated the situation further by claiming that the High Commission had overall authority for trying tithe cases, whereas Common Law judges denied its competence in this matter.[102] Invariably, those who the most vocal supporters of Common Law, including John Selden, also sat in Parliament, and there they attempted to restrict the clergy's power to collect tithes. The debate about tithes had a wider significance, therefore, than the purely financial: it represented a contest between the church, in conjunction with the monarchical establishment, and supported by Canon and Civil Law, and Parliament, supported by Common Law. At the beginning of the seventeenth century, lawyers such as Edward Coke emphasised the historic association between Common Law and 'the people', Parliament and the English nation, and claimed that Canon and Civil Law served the agenda of the church establishment.[103] Their opponents responded by arguing that tithes were due by divine right.

The controversy prompted by Selden's *Historie of Tithes*, therefore, from 1618 onwards, was the culmination of mounting tension over the issue.[104] In 1619, Sir James Sempill (1566–1625) dedicated his *Sacrilege sacredly handled* to James I, advertising his commitment to the monarchy.[105] Richard Tillesley (1582–1621), archdeacon of Rochester, responded to Selden in the same year, with his *Animadversions upon M. Selden's History of Tithes*, also dedicated to the King.[106] Montagu's *Diatribœ* appeared in 1621. William Sclater (1575–1626), rector of Pitminster, produced, in 1623, *The Quæstion of Tythes Revised*, which was an expansion of an earlier essay, *The Minister's Portion* (1612). Finally, Stephen Nettles (fl. 1644), the controversialist and minister, published his *Answer to the Jewish Part of Mr. Selden's History of Tithes* in 1625.[107] Lying behind arguments for the divine right of tithes was the argument for the divine right of kings: Montagu identified opposition to tithe-paying with both religious and political dissent: 'Hath any appeared opposite of late, that was not a Schismaticke marked out?'[108]

John Selden knew, perhaps, that his tract was rather more controversial than the words 'meer Narration' might suggest; the *Historie* was, after all, directed at 'the rable of late Canonists' with their 'lazie ignorance',[109] and its publication attracted strong official disapproval. Selden was summoned before members of the High Commission and the Privy Council, and ordered to write a statement of regret about the publication of the tract, although he stood by its contents. Selden was forbidden from publishing a reply to his respondents, and he was questioned on the matter by James I himself. This response cannot have come as much of a surprise: Selden was a committed

52 *Judaism without Jews*

Parliamentarian, serving as a member in 1624, 1626 and during the Long Parliament, and he headed the Erastian faction of the Westminster Assembly during the 1640s, which lobbied for the church to exist under the jurisdiction of the state. Along with other MPs, Selden was imprisoned in the Tower in 1629 for speaking in the Lords against Charles I's methods of raising money.[110]

In this context, Selden's Jewish scholarship was not disinterested; in *The Historie of Tithes*, Jewish precedents were employed in the service of a critique of the divine right of tithes. Selden surveyed a large quantity of biblical and post-biblical Jewish history for proof that tithes were instituted as a result of historically specific customs and laws, thereby implying that they were not guaranteed by divine right; he argued that Jewish tithes were not a universal and fixed entity, but were subject to alteration over time. During a discussion of *'whether any certaine Quantitie were obserued in the Offerings of* Cain *and* Abel', Selden uses the contrast between Cain and Abel's offerings to argue that tithes were contingent and variable:

> *Abel* brought of his first fruits, but *Cain* only of his fruit of the ground; the one giuing the Lord a portion of the best, the other not regarding of what time, what worth it were, so it were of his fruit. So, here is not any quota pars [fixed quota], or any certain quantitie noted, but . . . of the mind only of him that offered, and the qualitie of the oblation'.[111]

Selden's opponents accused him of a disproportionate reliance on Jewish history. Stephen Nettles claims that 'the Historian himselfe and many others, led rather with affection, then judgement, doe still much magnifie among the rest, the Iewish part of that History, (as though some hidden matters of importance were involued therein)'.[112] Nettles particularly objects to the fact that Selden relies on post-biblical Jewish sources as well as biblical ones, stating that 'these and such like are the expositions and glosses of some of those grand Rabbies, on whose testimony the History of Tithes is principally grounded'.[113] Richard Tillesley denigrates Selden's use of 'the latter [later] barbarous Rabbins',[114] and Montagu declares 'these are the Rabbines, your great Patriarkes, Master *Selden*, the best Flowers in your garland, and stakes in your hedge for Iewish *Tithes*, that so sencelesly blaspheme aginst the great type of our Eternal High Priest'.[115] Montagu rails against '*Gemaraes*, upstart Punyes of after-Ages . . . the mis-borne Imps of miscreant Dotards [imbeciles]', implying that Talmudic interpretation of scripture can be compared to precocious (and misshapen) infants.[116] Montagu even claims that Selden trusts Jewish sources more than Christian ones: 'you are strangely besotted upon these Hags, that Christians can carry no greater sway or credit with you'.[117] Like Hugh Broughton before him, Selden's Jewish learning rendered him, in the eyes of his opponents, both partisan and heretically Jewish.

Since the divine right of tithes was explicitly associated with the divine right of kings, moreover, Selden's book was considered even more controversial; and indeed *The Historie of Tithes* was, in fact, an expression of Selden's belief in mixed monarchy.[118] James Sempill criticises Selden for attacking the divine right of kings under the guise of an objective historian, and indicates the dangers of this strategy: 'Though M. *Selden* hath given us *veram Historiam* [a true history/story] as he found it recorded; yet, *haec ipsa Historia non est vera*: [this history/story is not true], but leaveth dangerous insinuations, and preiudicial impressions in *Ius diuinum* [divine right]'.[119] Selden's opponents are, after all, committed monarchists: Tillesley's preface claims, for example, that the payment of tithes and support for the monarch are mutually dependent:

> And so much the rather for that *Kings* as they are in their power *the Image of God*, who sayd, *The Tythe is mine*: so in the right of their sustentation have the proportion of God, *Tenths*: which quantity in Tribute was so usuall amongst the Grecians, that . . . to tithe and pay Tribute, were as properly *Synonymaes*, as . . . to tithe and consecrate. So that to assume the protection of Gods challenged Tenth assigned to his ministers, is indeed to strengthen the reason of that right of Tribute allowed to your selfe.[120]

In other words, because the Greeks were accustomed to paying tribute to their rulers in the form of a tenth of their goods, and since ten is 'God's number', both customs were effectively performed in one act.

It was Selden's methodology, as well as his subject matter, furthermore, which was considered contentious, since it was the grounds on which he distanced himself from Canon lawyers. Selden claims that his own work is far superior to the scriptural digests and summaries which are employed by Canonists: his *Historie* is 'not of the Pitch of the Doctrine of the Breuiarie, or within the compasse of Pocket-learning'.[121] Since the Common Law was so closely associated with Erastianism, which desired secular control over the church, Selden's opponents interpreted his contribution to the debate, correctly, as a challenge to the power of ecclesiastical authorities. And since the Common Law was, through the continental tradition of Beza, Grotius and Scaliger, associated with Jewishness, form and content were combined in the same political project. After all, it was the cumulative, legalistic accretion of rabbinic commentary and debate which Selden was mirroring in his own work. Selden's invocation of Jewish precedents, via the methodology of Common Law, carried connotations of Parliamentarianism, Erastianism, and opposition to both ecclesiastical and monarchical supremacy. In later years, Selden would become associated with other Erastian Parliamentarians; in 1648, the Commons bought a large number of Hebrew books, and the transaction was arranged by John Lightfoot and John Selden.[122] Lightfoot, and another Erastian member of the Assembly, Thomas Coleman (1598–1647), were so closely linked, in the minds of contemporaries, with the study of Hebrew that they were known as 'Rabbi'.[123] Selden's use of Jewish sources provoked animosity, therefore, not only because those sources were perceived as heterodox, but also because their application implied a form of political subversion; and Selden's respondents characterised him as a Judaizer because it enabled them to imply that he held anticlerical and even antimonarchist sympathies.

III

Judaizing in practice: Sabbath and Passover

Puritans not only developed proficiency in Jewish scholarship in the early modern period; they also went as far as to practise Jewish customs. At times, allegations of Judaizing behaviour were simply slanders, but they also contained an element of truth. One of the most widespread and well-documented instances of Christian Judaizing in the early modern period was Sabbatarianism, the keeping of the Sabbath on Sundays, or, more controversially, on Saturdays. Sabbatarianism is an unusual doctrine, in that it was associated with a variety of Christian denominations during the Long Reformation: some Conformist, some Nonconformist. Sabbatarianism began as a Roman Catholic ritual, was taken up under James I as an official Anglican duty, but in the seventeenth century became a characteristically Puritan practice. Whereas Roman Catholics had regarded the practice as a holy ceremony, linked to saints' days, the rise of Sabbatarianism among Protestants was associated with their commitment to Old Testament scripturalism. The Ten Commandments were at the core of the Old Testament, and most were easily assimilable to Christianity; the injunction against murder, theft, adultery and so on. But the fourth commandment, to observe the

Sabbath, seemed to be more of a specifically Jewish law than the others. Sabbatarianism became, therefore, a bone of contention between Christians, as to whether it should be observed as a moral law, which applied to Christians as well as Jews, or whether it retained the taint of ceremonial Judaism.[124] Furthermore, some Christians began to argue that the Sabbath should be observed on the Saturday rather than the Christian Sunday. The more contentious Saturday-Sabbatarianism, with even stronger connotations of Judaizing, gradually gained acceptance in the build-up to the Civil War.[125]

The ambivalent nature of Sabbatarianism, split between a universal precept that could be applied to Christians, and a specifically Jewish one which was therefore abrogated, is reflected in the modern historical literature on the subject. Sabbatarianism has received very different treatment in the field of ecclesiastical history on the one hand, and Jewish history on the other; whereas ecclesiastical historians have regarded Sabbatarianism as an aspect of purely Christian history, Jewish historians tend to focus on the Judaizing connotations of the practice.[126] However, early modern Christians were prone to imagining that even relatively 'mild' examples of Judaizing behaviour, such as Sabbatarianism, were, as it were, the thin end of the wedge; there was a sliding scale, in polemical writing, between what seemed like general biblical precepts, and ones which were suspiciously heterodox and Jewish. This blurring phenomenon can be observed, for instance, in the case of one of the most prominent Judaizers of the sixteenth and seventeenth centuries: the preacher John Traske (1585?–1636?). The seventeenth-century ecclesiastical historian, Thomas Fuller, writes that 'Of the Broakers of Judaisme, John Thraske was a principall',[127] and the Jesuit John Falconer (1577–1656) refers to '*Iohn Traske* in his nouell obseruance of the Iewish Sabaoth, abrogated by the Apostles themselues'.[128] Traske was influenced by a tailor called Hamlet Jackson, who persuaded him that the Mosaic law applied to Christians as well as Jews; Jackson later converted to Judaism in Amsterdam.[129] Traske was regarded as the indirect inspiration for many other Judaizers, including the minister Theophilus Brabourne,[130] and in 1618 was brought before the Court of High Commission, where he was sentenced to confinement for life in order 'that hee might not infecte others'.[131] Traske's sentence also specified that he be barred from the ministry, that his ear should be nailed to the pillory at the Palace of Westminster, and the letter 'I' branded on his forehead 'in token that hee broached Jewish opynions'.[132]

Traske was associated, in fact, with a whole range of Jewish customs, Saturday Sabbatarianism among them. The bishop and scholar Lancelot

Andrewes's 1619 speech against Traske in the Star Chamber accuses him of Sabbatarianism, circumcision and Kosher dietary laws, condemning all of them as 'anathema'.[133] The Conformist heresiographer Ephraim Pagitt (1575?–1647) refers to 'the *Traskites*, who would have us observe many Jewish ceremonies'.[134] It was characteristic of anti-Puritan rhetoric to imply that one form of Judaizing led inevitably to others, and while Traske's Judaizing activities have been well documented, his reputation as a political subversive is less well-known. Pagitt describes Traske arriving in London 'zealously affected, and in the path of *non conformity*',[135] and that 'as the manner of sectaries is, after they had made choice of their several Novelties, or private opinions to maintain; so he, after this resolution taken, as he had done before concerning meats, so now concerning the Sabbath'.[136] Falconer portrays him, likewise, as 'a Puritan minister lately grown halfe a Iew in his singular opinions concerning the old Saboath, and Moysaical difference of meates'.[137] In fact, a spectrum of Judaizing behaviour was constructed by both Conformists and Roman Catholics; at the beginning of the spectrum lay scripturalism, proficiency in Hebrew, and preference for the Old Testament; further along the spectrum was the study of Talmud and other heterodox Jewish material, and further along still was the observance of Jewish customs. At the end of the spectrum was the imagined conversion from Christianity to Judaism.

The name 'Traske' came to be associated not only with 'Traskites', his immediate followers, but also with sectarianism in general.[138] James I himself presents Traske as a link in a chain which connected Judaizing and Puritanism in his 1619 *Meditation Upon The Lords Prayer*:

> Hold fast therefore your profession . . . trust not to that priuate spirit or holy ghost which our *Puritans* glory in; for then a little fiery zeale will make thee turne *Separatist*, and then proceed still on from *Brownist* to some one Sect or other of *Anabaptist*, and from one of these to another, then to become a Iudaized *Traskite*, and in the ende a profane *Familist*.[139]

'Private' worship was associated with both schism and Judaizing; taking one step away from the established church, the King declares, may result eventually in an entropic degradation: 'letting slippe the holde of the true Church . . . according to our *Puritans* doctrine, it is easy to fall and slide by degrees into the *Chaos*, filthy sinke and *farrago* of al horrible heresies'.[140] It is, in fact, these associative rhetorics which 'fall and slide into the *Chaos*', since it is in James's ideological interest to portray

Judaizing as a suggestive indicator of Puritanism. Edward Norice describes Traske, likewise, as a dangerously indeterminate figure:

> a man well knowne by common fame, and yet not knowne according to his manifold deceits but of a few, turning and winding himselfe like another *Proteus*, into so many formes as that he could not easily be discerned to be the same individuall, but descryed only by his unconstancy to be none other, because therein he had not his like: this man falling from one errour to another, and pursuing all with equall vehemency.[141]

It is this evocation of the Protean nature of Traske's heresy which precisely characterises Conformist ideas about Puritan Judaizing. In Norrice's description, Traske's Jewish practices are notorious and publicised ('well knowne by common fame'), they are more numerous than is at first apparent ('not knowne according to his manifold deceits but of a few'), his nature, like his activities, remain elusive ('he could not easily be discerned to be the same individuall'), and he passes 'from one errour to another'.[142]

This indeterminacy was also exploited by the Puritan side. Figures like Traske were not necessarily practicing Jewish customs because they believed in them, but rather, because such alignments allowed them to signal a political identification whose roots stretched right back to the early church. Yet another instance of Judaizing behaviour in this period was the observance of the Jewish Passover. Falconer reports, for instance, that Traske's fellow prisoners observed with his encouragement the 'Iewish manner of keeping Easter', and attempted to conduct a Passover meal.[143] In the preface to his 1618 *Briefe Refutation of Iohn Traske's Ivdaical and Novel Fancyes*, Falconer writes:

> By reading in *Eusebius* history . . . how Saint *Policarpe* and other holy Bishops of Asia observed the Iewes time of keeping Easter, he and his disciples are lately therein resolued to imitate them. And that which he neuer read of S. Policarpe or any Christian Doctor before him, he hath added to his Easter the festiuall obseruance of Azimes [the Jewish Passover], as is probably guessed by all his fellow prisoners, seing him and his disciples after the fourteenth of March moone to eate contrary to their custome at other times, white vnleauened loaues, and seeming in his speaches to allow of the obseruance of that festiuity, albeit of the manner he be something doubtfulll, as peraduenture, whether it must be with a Pascall Lambe eaten &c.[144]

Falconer is incensed by Traske's 'Iudaisme & Hereticall innouation',[145] suggesting that keeping the Jewish Passover is tantamount to actually becoming a Jew:

> And not contented with this hereticall temerity of renewing the Quartodeciman heresy, he surpasseth *Blastus* himself in his Iewish manner of keeping Easter. For as I haue touched in my Preface, he by his eating of unleauened bread seven days together after the 14. of March-Moon, and by sundry speeches uttered to some of his fellow prisoners, hath given great suspicions that lately he hath observed the feast of *Azimes*, [the Jewish Passover] together with his disciples. The next year peradventure they will have profited in Judaism so far, as to sacrifice a Paschal Lamb also. And lastly it is to be feared, that falling more and more from their Christian profession, they will with . . . other Puritan Divines finally forsake Christ, and embrace Judaism, or Turkism, the fearful sequel and just punishment of such fantastical spirits, as will embrace no Religion but of their own devising, nor be obedient children to any Church, but of their owne raising.[146]

In order to understand what the early church, Saint Policarp, Blastus, Eusebius and the Quartodeciman controversy have to do with early seventeenth-century Judaizing, it is necessary to look back at the earliest forms of Christianity in England, and one of the longest running ecclesiastical controversies of all time: the attempt to find a stable and universal date for Easter.[147]

In the second century AD, Rome attempted to stamp out the practice, in some Asian churches, of celebrating Easter on the Jewish date of Passover; a practice which was known as the Quartodeciman heresy. Quartodecimanism was eventually suppressed, but the issue did not go away; Easter had drifted away from the Vernal equinox, and different churches throughout Christendom were employing varying systems of calendrical compensation in an attempt to stabilise the date. In the year 325AD, the Council of Nice announced a universal formula for the dating of Easter, which was designed to end the church's reliance on Jewish calendrical systems.[148] The Nicaean decree was so hostile to Jewish influence that it stipulated that if the date of Easter, as calculated according to the correct formula, happened to fall on the date of the Jewish Passover, it had to be transferred to the following Sunday.[149] Despite the imposition of a universal formula, Quartodecimanism continued, not only in outlying Asian churches, but also in England; papal missionaries arriving in the country in the eighth century found that the date for Easter was still being calculated differently to Rome.[150]

The reason why the Easter controversy was so fiercely contested was that the very origin of Christianity appeared to be at stake. Easter was considered to be the festival closest to the point at which Christianity broke off from Judaism: the name of Easter, the paschal feast, is derived from the Passover paschal lamb, and the Last Supper was a Passover meal.[151] Easter therefore became an important ground for determining the apostolic origins of Christianity, and the definition of the English church's relationship to Rome.[152] While writers identifying themselves as Protestant often attempted to connect themselves to a pre-Roman Catholic form of religion – Judaism – those who identified as Roman Catholics invariably denounced Judaism as heretical and emphasised the Roman origins of Christianity.

The Easter controversy was revived in the sixteenth century, as different factions debated the apostolic origins of the English church.[153] The story of the controversy in the early church was recounted by John Bale and John Foxe, the influential sixteenth-century historians, in their intensely Protestant accounts, and countered by Roman Catholics such as Robert Persons who was, in turn, answered by the Protestant minister Matthew Sutcliffe.[154] The debate was also exacerbated by two developments: the proposed reform of the Julian calendar, and the construction of a new Protestant historical tradition. In return, the driving force behind calls for calendar reform became the desire to celebrate Easter at the 'correct' time.[155] By the late sixteenth century, the relatively crude Julian calendar had failed to prevent the Vernal equinox from slipping ten days ahead of the calendrical equinox, by which the date of Easter was calculated.[156] When the mathematician and astronomer John Dee wrote his 'Playne discourse' to Queen Elizabeth in 1593, his advice on whether to adopt the Gregorian calendar, he included a passage describing the formula for the calculation of Easter.[157] But as well as these tangible considerations, the pressure for reform had an unambiguously Roman Catholic origin, and was discussed in great detail at the Council of Trent.[158] It was Pope Gregory XIII who was instigating the reform, and its potential adoption by England was regarded as a return to pre-Reformation times.

The new Protestant tradition included its own calendar, which was designed to replace the Roman Catholic calendar of saints. Structured around the lives of Protestant martyrs, the new calendar helped to create an emergent sense of English national culture. The Book of Common Prayer established a timetable of devotion, which greatly reduced the number of festival days and focused those remaining on the life of Christ. In the last quarter of the century, an additional calendar was created in order to commemorate the birthdays and accessions of England's Protestant monarchs, and to reflect significant events in English history.[159] It was John Bale, followed by John Foxe, who spearheaded this new Protestant historiography, in which reformers were portrayed as engaged in an apocalyptic struggle against popery.[160] Bale argued that the prefiguration of Protestantism in the early church could be demonstrated by chronicling the suffering of martyrs at the hands of (Roman) church authorities.[161] Bale wrote his *Illustrium Maioris Britanniae Scriptorium . . . Summarium* in 1548, in which he attempted, under the patronage of figures such as Matthew Parker, to create an inventory of historical books and manuscripts after the destruction of academic and monastic libraries in the 1530s.[162] It was Foxe's 'Book of Martyrs', however, which became the archetypal work of Protestant historiography; it quickly became mainstream Protestant propaganda, with a copy kept in every cathedral in the country.[163] Since the ecclesiastical histories of Bale and Foxe were explicitly intended to replace Roman Catholic calendars and historiography, Roman Catholic commentators such as Robert Persons were predictably incensed.[164] The English Jesuit missionary Robert Persons wrote *Three Conversions* to prove that Britain had been Roman Catholic from the very birth of Christianity in the country.

When Foxe, Persons and Sutcliffe narrated the early church controversy, therefore, they did so in the context of their current responses to Roman Catholic proposals for calendar reform, and efforts to create a new Protestant calendar. For sixteenth-century commentators, the Gregorian calendar reform was implicitly connected to the Easter controversy in the early church. Discussing what he considers to be the correct formula for the dating of Easter in the context of the early church controversy, Robert Persons inserts an approving reference to the contemporary Georgian reform, thus reflecting the connection in the minds of contemporaries:

> this 14. day of the moone must be that, which falleth Upon the very day of the spring equinoctiall or immediatly followeth the same (which equinoctium was obserued by the Councell of *Nice* to be in those dayes Upon the 21. of Marche, though since that time it fell backe by little and little to the eleuenth day, for correction whereof *Pope Gregory* the 13. was forced to make his reformation from the yeare 1582. by detracting ten dayes as all men know).[165]

Protestant opponents of the Gregorian reform also slip easily between discussing the controversy of the present and that of the past. In the middle of a refutation of Persons's claim that the first English church was Roman, Matthew Sutcliffe inserts a reference to 'Gregorie the 13's seditious, rayling and outragious Buls' and a critique of 'the Popes of Rome of this time'.[166]

In one of the documents accompanying the English bishops' written decision to hinder the reform, moreover, an explicit connection is made with the early church controversy: 'if it should be stablished here by a synod without the consent of other Churches reformed it would breed a schisme as was betwixt the east and west Churches about the passover'.[167]

Early modern commentators drew attention to the fact that the Easter controversy in the early church had been as much to do with the imposition of Rome's authority over outlying churches, as with the details of calendrical calculation, and they were thus able to place themselves in an established paradigm of opposition.[168] Protestant historians tended to favour the Quartodecimans, while Roman Catholic historians favoured the Roman imperialists who attempted to suppress the practice. The former argued that the Quartodeciman custom originated in the Eastern Orthodox church, and was imported from there into England, thereby proving that English Christianity did not have a Roman origin. The latter resisted this interpretation, asserting instead that the Quartodeciman heresy was a belated corruption of the Roman church in England.

While Bale, Foxe and Sutcliffe provided sympathetic accounts of the Quartodecimans, therefore, Persons praised the actions of the Roman missionaries sent to bring them back into line. For example, Bale dismisses the anti-Quartodeciman Wilfrid, abbot of Ripon in his *Illustrium Maioris Britanniae Scriptorum . . . Summarium* as a fool.[169] Foxe represents those in England who resisted the Roman edicts as heroic defenders of the faith against Popery: three Scottish bishops, for example, 'held with the Britons against the Romish order for the keeping of Easter-day'.[170] Persons refers to his enemies as 'sectaries', in the sense that they approve of this early church opposition to the edicts of Rome:

> we may not omitt . . . the small piety or religion of these sectaries of our dayes. Who care not what they graunt, deny, or say, soe they say somwhat against Rome, her Bishops or religion, euen in the first ages or primitiue Church. For to this end, and with this good mynd, you shall see them heere preferre in effect the forsaid Easterne custome of celebrating Easter used by the Britans and Scotts, before the Cath[olic] custome of Rome.[171]

The opposition between Roman authority and the independence of Eastern or British churches was reinforced – in the sixteenth century as in the early church – by manipulating the particularly contentious Jewish aspect of the debate. As well as locating the origins of the Quartodeciman custom in the Eastern church, Persons also associates it with Judaism, complaining, for example, that 'Iohn Bale defendeth the Iewish keeping of Easter'.[172] Part of the reason why Quartodecimanism was associated with Jewishness is that, according to the Protestants, Simon the Zealot, one of the Jewish rebels who opposed the imperial dictums of Rome, was instrumental in converting England to Christianity. Persons denigrates Jewishness as another plank in the Protestant argument that Christianity did not originate in Rome:

> the Reader maye see, how good an argument it is, which the Magdeburgians and Iohn Foxe doe use and urge so muche: to witt. That for so muche, as this Greeke or Asian custome of celebrating Easter with the Iewes, was fownde among the Scotts & some Britans in Saint Bedes tyme and afterward: *Ergo* it is likelie, that the first preachers of Britanie came not from Rome, nor were not of the Romane Religion, but rather of the Easte partes.[173]

For sixteenth-century commentators, the Quartodeciman custom was associated with the Eastern church, opposition to Rome, a dissident inclination, and Judaism; and while Protestants approved of this set of characteristics, Roman Catholics did not.[174] In these debates, a positive portrayal of Jewish customs signalled a rejection of the influence of the Roman church. If Roman Catholics invoked the heterodox connotations of Judaizing in order to criticise resistance to Rome, their opponents reinforced England's Protestant identity by asserting its Jewish origins.

It is this long-standing sectarian context which informs John Falconer's accusations that John Traske and his followers are keeping the Jewish Passover. In turn, seemingly arcane disagreements such as those about Easter, with their references to Judaism, were inflected by live contemporary debates. These historical contexts throw light on what are often represented as eccentric, enthusiastic and unmotivated instances of Puritan Judaizing. Robert Persons accuses his opponents not only of siding with the Judaizing Quartodecimans, but also of actually resurrecting the long-dead heresy: 'Albeit they well know how many ages gone [the Quartodeciman practice] hath byn condemned not only for error, but also for heresy. Yea though themselues do practise the contrary custome at this day in England and Germany'. A printed marginal note besides these lines reads, 'The sectaries of our time allow of the celebrating Easter with the Iewes'.[175] It should now be clear why Falconer criticises not only Traske's Judaizing, but also his partisan history of the controversy in the early church.[176]

Falconer writes, referring to Traske, that 'by reading in *Eusebius* history . . . how Saint *Policarpe* and other holy Bishops of Asia observed the Iewes time of keeping Easter, he and his disciples are lately therein resolued to imitate them' and that 'not contented with this hereticall temerity of renewing the Quartodeciman heresy, he surpasseth *Blastus* himself in his Iewish manner of keeping Easter'.[177] For Falconer, Traske's Judaizing is inextricably linked to a long-standing Christian debate, and for his Puritan opponents, Judaizing is part of a strategy of studied opposition to Popery.

***

Sixteenth- and seventeenth-century Puritans learned Hebrew, studied post-biblical Jewish literature and history, and even practised Jewish customs, for specific reasons. Hebraic and Talmudic scholarship, and Judaizing practices, were employed by dissenting Protestants as indicators of denominational identity, and in turn were regarded as such by Conformists and Roman Catholics, who used accusations of Judaizing as an effective way of arguing with their opponents. Puritan Judaizing was not necessarily, therefore, an expression of straightforward appreciation of Judaism or Jews. After all, Puritans were, in a fundamental sense, *against* Jews. Discussions about the Hebrew language, for example, were characterised by a standard anti-Jewish prejudice: in the middle of recommending the Old Testament and the Hebrew language to his readers, William Fulke was in the habit of inserting derogatory descriptions of Jews. He describes one fault in the Latin Vulgate as 'a Iudaical additio[n]',[178] and refers to the evidence of 'a Popishe Iewe'.[179] For all his use of Jewish and Hebrew sources, Hugh Broughton was clearly not fond of contemporary Jews: he calls them 'dogg Iewes',[180] 'blasphemous Iewes',[181] and 'wicked Cabalistes'.[182] John Selden also perceived Jews as religious heretics, and at times denigrated the evidence of rabbis whom elsewhere he cited with respect; he refers to a certain Rabbi Jarchi as having 'rash and idle fancies'.[183] Even John Traske and his followers were determinedly anti-Jewish; their argument was simply that Old Testament Mosaic laws applied to Christians. Many Anglo-Jewish historians acknowledge that Puritan philosemitism was often merely the flipside of an age-old Judeophobia; but taken out of historical context, Christian attitudes exist in something of a vacuum, alternating opaquely and unpredictably between sympathy and antipathy. Seen in context, however, Puritan philosemitism takes on an added dimension: that of triangulated opposition to Conformity.

3
Anglicans and Judaism: From Ceremony to Legalism

The poem 'Sion' (1633) by George Herbert, part of his cycle 'The Temple', encapsulates both the attraction and the danger of Old Testament Judaism:

> Lord, with what glorie wast thou serv'd of old,
> When Solomons temple stood and flourished!
>   Where most things were of purest gold;
>   The wood was all embellished
> With flowers and carvings, mysticall and rare:
> All show'd the builders, crav'd the seers care.
>
> Yet all this glorie, all this pomp and state
> Did not affect thee much, was not thy aim;
>   Something there was, that sow'd debate:
>   Wherefore thou quitt'st thy ancient claim:
> And now thy Architecture meets with sinne;
> For all thy frame and fabrick is within.[1]

If this passage evokes the beauty of the biblical Jewish temple, it also suggests that this beauty is superficial, and not suitable for Christians. The 'purest gold', 'flowers' and 'carvings' from the first stanza become 'pomp and state' in the second; the material worship of the ancient Israelites has been replaced, with the coming of Christ, by true, inward Christianity: 'for all thy frame and fabrick is within'. Yet despite this transformation, the ambivalence of Herbert's poem suggests that the vestiges of external ritual have continued to exert an influence over Christian worship.

The continuation of outward ritual had an additional resonance, however: the revival of aspects of pre-Reformation Roman Catholicism.

During the 1630s, Archbishop Laud instituted a series of reforms, which made church ceremony respectable again. 'Sion' dramatises the opposition between Laud's followers, who were known as ceremonialists, and the anti-ceremonialists who accused them, as this chapter will reveal, of being both Jewish and popish. Laud's followers were not only interested in beautiful church interiors, however. The period witnessed a reassertion of the church's Episcopal hierarchy. Broadly speaking, ceremonialists took the place of Conformists, and anti-ceremonialists opposed them as Puritans had done before.[2] This resulted in intense debates, in the course of which it was Anglicans, not Puritans, who invoked Old Testament precedents to justify their practices, and who were, therefore, accused of Judaising by their Puritan opponents. In fact, during the first half of the seventeenth century, Anglicans made use of Jewish precedents to justify not only their opposition to Puritan 'plainness', but also their religious rituals, their form of church administration, and even the broader question of the relationship between church and state. This chapter not only explores the Anglican use of Jewish precedents in the 1630s; it also traces the use of the Sanhedrin, the Jewish court, to define the Anglican constitution from the late sixteenth century onwards.

As Chapter 1 illustrated, the history of Jews and Judaism in England has been dominated by the association with Puritanism. The speeches at the Tercentenary celebration of readmission referred to the 'intense interest taken in the Old Testament by the Puritan movement',[3] Vivian Lipman describes how 'the Puritans had a devotion to the Old Testament',[4] Robert Paul reminds us that 'we should not forget that the Old Testament played a very important part in seventeenth-century Puritanism',[5] and, referring to readmission in a study of toleration, John Coffey writes that 'the roots of this remarkable development lie in the philo-semitic strain within English Puritanism'.[6] However, as this chapter will demonstrate, Christian interest in Judaism in the early modern period was not restricted to Puritans.[7] The shift from Puritan Judaizing to Anglican Judaizing was, to some extent, a consequence of wider historical change. During the transition from the Elizabethan to the Jacobean era, the Conformist 'establishment' increasingly appropriated arguments drawn from scriptural authority. Jacobean Conformists were concerned that Archbishop Whitgift's emphasis on *adiaphora*, on the freedom of church authorities to develop solutions to questions of church government, did not provide the church with sufficiently fundamental guarantees for its policies. These early seventeenth-century Conformists attempted to underpin their policies, therefore, by giving them the status of divine ordinances. In doing so, however, they frequently and unwittingly mimicked the scriptural fundamentalism of Elizabethan Puritans.[8] But if the emergent tradition of Conformist Judaizing was, like the Puritan one that preceded it, based on scripturalism, it was also highly ceremonial. The ceremonialist Judaizing of the Anglican community was, in this sense, different in character from Puritan Judaizing; and this reflected a split in the nature of Judaism itself, as it was perceived by Christians. On one hand, Judaism was the original touchstone of Christianity; the Old Testament was the universal text for Jews and Christians alike. On the other, Judaism was legalistic and ritualistic: it was 'carnal' as opposed to spiritual.[9] This was partly a function of the different texts which make up the Jewish canon; in addition to the Old Testament, the post-biblical commentaries of the Talmud were designed to codify practices and behaviours and were suspected, by Christians, to be heretical annexations.

The debates about ceremonialism suggest that factions were reinforced through doctrinal disagreement. In *A Fresh Suit* (1633), a reply to the minister John Burges, the Puritan theologian William Ames (1576–1633) cites Burges as claiming: 'the tearming of our Cerem[ony] Popish, is done out of faction'. Ames replies: 'where is that body, into which the Non-conformitants gather them selves?' Burges reportedly answers: 'they draw (as fast as they can) into a body of themselves, ingrossing [adopting] aforehand, the name of brethren, The Godly, the Church, the good Christians'.[10] These religious divisions were, furthermore, mapped onto the factional divisions of the previous century. The ceremonialist clergyman John Pocklington associates his enemy, John Williams with the Puritan William Ames, and also with Elizabethan Puritans such as Thomas Cartwright: 'we can . . . point you to the time of your coming in. You *Cartwright*, and your brood came in, as most *Sabbatarians* did, under Arch-Bishop *Whitguift*; and you *Ames* . . . came in under Archbishop *Bancroft*'.[11] Likewise, another supporter of Laudian ceremony, the theologian and historian Peter Heylyn (1660–1662) places Williams in the same category as the vestiges of Elizabethan Puritanism, embodied in the notorious trinity of anti-ceremonialists Henry Burton (1578–1648), author of many anti-Laudian tracts and sermons, the anti-Episcopalian controversialist John Bastwick (1593–1654) and William Prynne (1600–1660).[12] He suggests that Williams is 'some remainder of that scattered company, which hitherto hath hid his head, and now thrusts out with *Bastwick*, *Prinne*, and *Burton*, to disturbe the State'.[13] These texts were polemical as well as descriptive, therefore, and they served to exacerbate the factionalism of the period.

I

Ceremonialism and Jewish precedents

Debates about outward ceremony versus inward prayer, aesthetics versus plainness, and Episcopacy versus Presbyterianism, were a central feature of Protestant culture in the early seventeenth century. These debates reached their peak during the 1630s, but their origins can be traced back to the previous century. Concerns about ceremonial worship began to circulate during the reign of Elizabeth, with the authors of *An Admonition to the Parliament* (1572) protesting that earlier church reforms had not gone far enough, and that, in practice, the English church still contained 'the prieste in his surplesse, singing gospels, and making crosses'.[14] The ceremonialist position had been articulated by Conformists such as Richard Hooker in his *Of the Lawes of Ecclesiastical Polity* (1593), but never instituted as official policy,[15] and the debates continued into the seventeenth century with James I's efforts to reverse the neglect of ceremonies.[16] Tensions began to increase when Charles I facilitated the rise of William Laud, who became Bishop of London in 1628 and Archbishop of Canterbury in 1633. Laud set about instituting in the English church an emphasis on architectural and artistic ornamentation, kneeling and bowing, altars and music. These reforms were designed to endorse 'the beauty of holiness', an emphasis on the physical performance of prayer, and a sense of religious community. Laud's reforms became the dominant form of worship in the 1630s, and the suppression of Nonconformists gathered strength, culminating in the notorious trial and punishment of Prynne, Burton and Bastwick in 1637, for writing anti-Episcopal pamphlets. Ceremonialism did not survive in the religious and political climate of the last years of Charles's reign, however, and Laud was executed as a traitor in 1645; but for a time, it held sway.[17]

In 1572, the authors of *An Admonition to the Parliament* declared:

> We should be to long to tell your honoures of Cathedrall churches, the dennes aforesaide of all loytering lubbers, wher . . . the cheefe chauntor, singing men speciall favourers of religion, squeaking queresters, organ players, gospellers . . . live in great idlenesse . . . if you would knowe whence all these came, we can easely answere you, that they came from the Pope.[18]

Puritans had always disapproved of church ceremonies, but whereas in the Elizabethan period they associated ceremonies with popery; in the 1630s, they came to associate them with Judaism. This is because ceremonialists increasingly justified their promotion of physical, architectural and aesthetic forms of worship by appealing to Jewish precedents. Puritans even accused ceremonialists of an excessive reliance on scripture: the Puritan William Ames rather pedantically suggests that his opponent, Thomas Morton, 'should not in stead of *Testimonie* of Scripture, haue put *Warrant* of Scripture', suggesting an acute awareness of the ways in which ceremonialists were using the Bible.[19] This was an ironic reversal, given that scripturalism had been the grounds, in the previous century, for so many accusations of Puritan Judaising.

Ceremonialists combined a reliance on biblical precedents with the ongoing strategy of justifying church ceremonies by defining them as *adiaphora*, a situation which Peter Lake describes as Laudians attempting 'to have their polemical cake and eat it'.[20] The Puritan side also attempted to have it both ways, characterising both the Conformist use of scriptural fundamentalism, and their use of *adiaphora*, as forms of Judaising. Their justification for doing so was that, first, scripturalism was easily identifiable with Judaism because of associations with the Old Testament, and, second, that *adiaphora* represented the freedom to innovate new ceremonies, and since these were ordained by humans rather than by God, they resembled the legalistic rituals of the Jews, as the anti-ceremonialist William Ames argues: 'no humane inventions are lawfull parts of Gods Worship'.[21] Invention, or innovation, a Jewish characteristic, was posited in contrast to natural laws which were binding on Christians as well as Jews.[22] Judaism was a particularly productive site for Christian controversy about ceremonialism because it embodied 'originality' in both senses of the word: it signified both authenticity and innovation. Christian controversy about ceremony was, therefore, paradigmatic of a wider ambivalence about Judaism. Jewish 'invention' was also linked, associatively, with human invention; surfacing, in literary texts of the period such as Herbert's 'The Temple', as anxiety about the use of human artistic creation in praise of God.[23]

The interpretation of seventeenth-century Conformist–Nonconformist debates in terms of Jewish precedents throws light on an issue which has long preoccupied historians of this period. Modern historiography of the Laudian church has been concerned, to a large extent, with the question of whether the Archbishop's reforms represented an innovation of radical Arminianism or a lapse back into the traditional Conformist values of order and uniformity.[24] Christopher Hill and Kevin Sharpe have resisted the notion that there was 'a rise of Arminianism', arguing that the

Laudian controversy was rather a continuation of the well-worn Anglican–Puritan opposition, with Charles I and Archbishop Laud taking the places of Elizabeth I and Archbishop Whitgift, respectively.[25] 'Revisionists', on the other hand, led by Nicholas Tyacke, have presented Calvinism as the dominant Protestant ideology in the period and have therefore regarded Laudianism as a theological innovation; an Arminian revolution. Indeed, such was the scale of the change, in Tyacke's view, that 'Arminians . . . not only rejected Calvinist orthodoxy – they also transformed the issue of Protestant non-conformity'.[26] A third group of historians including Kenneth Fincham and Peter Lake have sought a compromise between the two positions.[27]

While this debate is valid, it tends to downplay both the Jewish and the rhetorical aspects of early seventeenth-century Christian debate. When anti-ceremonialists called their opponents 'innovators', this label carried the connotations of Jewish legalism as well as Arminian innovation. But they also called ceremonialists old-fashioned, in an attempt to suggest that ceremonialists were resurrecting the popery of the pre-Reformation era. These shifting temporalities can be seen in the words of the Puritan minister Henry Burton, who labels ceremonialists both 'Innovators' and 'Backe-sliders into Popery' and describes 'Popery' as 'a religion of Changes, as from antiquity of truth to novelty of error'.[28] Burton's definition of ceremonialism is paradoxical because he presents it as a regression back to a position ('Popery') which is itself innovatory; and this kind of multivalent formulation was facilitated by the multivalent nature of Judaism in the eyes of Christians. It is this polemical ambiguity, mediated by references to Judaism, which complicates the historiographical model of continuity versus change.

During Elizabethan ecclesiastical controversies, Conformists such as John Whitgift argued for the abrogation of Jewish laws, while Puritans such as Thomas Cartwright defended their continued application. In the Laudian controversy, these positions were reversed: ceremonialists were now in favour of the application of Jewish laws, and anti-ceremonialists against. Many of the arguments about Conformist Judaizing can be found in a network of controversial texts concerned with the question of whether churches should have an altar or a communion table, and where it should be positioned. These were particularly contentious issues during the Laudian debates, because they were regarded as a measure of the degree to which the church in question was 'low church', and therefore inclusive of the congregation, or 'high church', and exclusive. Efforts to place the table at the upper end of the chancel, often at the east end of the church, and to surround it with rails, were interpreted as an attempt to convert the table into an altar, restrict congregational access and therefore encourage idolatry.[29] In 1628, a dispute arose in the church at Grantham after the vicar decided to move the altar to the east end. The parishioners appealed the decision to John Williams, bishop of Lincoln and archbishop of York (1582–1650), who ruled that the altar should be kept at the east end, but moved further down the church for communion. The dispute was resurrected during the debates of the 1630s, prompting a complex printed controversy between John Williams, Peter Heylyn, John Pocklington, William Prynne, Robert Shelford and Edmund Reeve.[30]

The altar was justified using Jewish precedents, with John Pocklington and Peter Heylyn arguing that the ceremonial function of the altar, the communion – itself prefigured by the Jewish Tabernacle sacrifice – guaranteed the use of a physical altar. Pocklington quotes his opponent John Williams, who had claimed that 'the Sacrifice of the Altar being abolished, these (call them what you will) are no more Altars, but Tables of Stone or Timber', and counters 'that *Altar*, and that *Sacrifice*, must continue alwaies'.[31] Heylyn agrees:

> A *Sacrifice* there was among the *Iewes*, shewing forth *Christs* death unto them, before his coming in the flesh: a *Sacrifice* there must bee amongst the *Christians*, to shew *forth the Lords death till he* come in judgement. And if a *Sacrifice* must bee, there must also be *Priests* to doe, and *Altars* whereupon to doe it.[32]

Heylyn is careful to discriminate between the literal Jewish and the metaphorical Christian sacrifice, but he is concerned, too, that his opponent Williams may be downplaying the physical reality of altars and ceremonies:

> your purpose is, to shew unto your credulous Readers, that there is no *materiall Altar* to be used in a Christian Church: and for a proof thereof, you make a muster of all those severall *Metaphors* and *Allegories*, which you have met with in old Writers, concerning *Altars* . . . I hope you will not think that there was no such thing, as the Garden of *Eden*; no such particular Vestments for the *Priests*, or sacrifices for the people; because the ancient Writers, some of them at least, have drawn them into Allegories; or can afford you at first word, a Metaphoricall *Ephod*, a Metaphoricall *Pasch*, or a Metaphoricall *Paradise*.[33]

Heylyn is arguing that just because church fathers have derived allegorical significance from biblical events or places, this does not mean they never existed.

During this controversy, Conformists took the bold step of advocating not just the continuation of natural or moral law, but even suggested that the Mosaic law applied to Christians as well as Jews. For example, Edmund Reeve (d. 1660), who was a ceremonialist divine, Hebrew teacher and strong supporter of Laud, attempted to enlarge the definition of moral laws to include some Mosaic injunctions. In his 1635 text, *The Communion Booke Catechisme Expounded*, Reeve moves smoothly from the laws against incest and murder to the law of ceremonial worship established in Solomon's Tabernacle:

> whereas some say, that now in our temples no such ceremonies or rites are to be used, which were of use in Solomons Temple; but that all were forever abolished, when CHRISTS Ministration was established by the holy Ghost in the Apostles time, Such consider not, that no where in the holy Scriptures there is declared, that there was an utter abolishing of all ceremonies.[34]

On the other side, the Puritan William Ames asserts the complete abrogation of all Jewish laws, including ceremonies:

> all religious use of Circumcision, for Ceremonie, &c is now after due publication of the Gospel, unlawfull or *deadly* . . . our Divines are so confident of this, that from the unlawfulnesse of Circumcision, they usually dispute against other humane Ceremonies.[35]

In a section where he claims that his ceremonialist opponents, Thomas Morton (1564–1659), bishop of Lichfield and Coventry, and John Burges (1563–1635) defend circumcision, Ames expresses a fear that the observation of some Jewish ceremonies will encourage the observation of others:

> Circumcision cannot be esteemed more lawfull to be instituted for a significant Ceremonie, then a *Paschall* [Passover] *lambe*: and they two being brought into the Churche, what shall hinder (if it please our Convocation house) but the greatest part of the olde Ceremoniall law, may in like manner follow?'[36]

Ironically, Ames's fears here resemble those of the earlier Conformist Ephraim Pagitt and the Jesuit John Falconer, who, as the previous chapter described, feared that the Puritan observance of Passover would lead to many other Judaizing offences.

The ceremonialists' invocation of Jewish examples was not restricted to the biblical precedents of the Israelites; they also invoked Jews' current religious habits in order to reinforce the argument against abrogation. The biblical scholar and Hebraist Joseph Mede (1586–1638), for example, who initially inclined towards Puritanism but then came to support Episcopacy, cites the '*Seder Tephiloth* [prayer book] or Forme of prayer used by the Jewes of Portugal' as an authority for his observation that contemporary Jews still hold communal services, even though some material aspects of the synagogue have changed:

> the Jews at this day continue the like opinion of their moderne places of worship: namely, that the blessed Angels frequent their assemblies, and praise and laud God with them in their Synagogues: notwithstanding they have no other memoriall of his there, than an imitative one onely; to wit, a Chest with a volume or roll of the Law therein, in stead of the Ark with the two Tables.[37]

Mede's implication is that if the Jews imitate Moses's tablets of stone by using a prayer scroll in their services, Christians therefore ought to imitate the Jews' Temple services in their churches.

Mede's description of contemporary Jewish customs centres on 'discalceation', or the custom of removing shoes before entering a holy place: 'Among the Jews and other Nations, of the Orient especially, that rite of Discalceation, or putting off their shooes, still used and continued amongst them unto this day, when they come into their Temples and sacred places'.[38] Mede argues that this tradition is not restricted to 'the Jews, and those Nations of the Orient, which agreed with them in this custome',[39] but is also continued in Jewish communities closer to home:

> It is further confirmed by their modern practice in their Synagogues; even here in these Westerne and colder parts of the world: where though no such custome be in use, as in the Orient, nor our manners with conveniencie capable thereof; yet they stil observe it, as farre as the guise of the West will permit them; an argument it descends unto them by a strong and rooted tradition from their forefathers.[40]

The fact that the custom of taking off one's shoes in holy places has survived the cold climate of the North, the lack of wider cultural legitimation (as in the Orient) and the religious restrictions of their hosts which necessitate disguise, serves as additional proof for Mede that such traditions should be perpetuated, rather than abrogated.

Laudian appropriation of Jewish examples extended, furthermore, towards approving references to post-biblical Jewish sources as well as customs. A certain 'R.T.', writing approvingly about the Israelites' temple, cites the Jewish historian Flavius Josephus and the Jewish philosopher Philo Judaeus on numerous occasions.[41] The Laudian scholar and controversialist Robert Shelford cites Josephus in his argument in favour of priestly vestments,[42] and the author of *The Originall of Popish Idolatrie* writes 'if any man desire to know more at large, the multitude and varietie of sacrifices: let him reade the bookes of *Philo* the Iew; and of *Iosephus* in his Antiquities of the Iewes, according as *Moses* hath expressely written in the bookes of *Leviticus*, & *Numbers*'.[43] Puritans were aware of this ceremonialist predeliction: during a discussion of how rabbinical sources can prove that the (ceremonialist) altar is called an (anti-ceremonialist) table in the book of Ezekiel, John Williams simultaneously disowns such sources altogether, consigning 'these Rabbies' derogatively to 'Rabbi Coal', a reference to his opponent in the altar controversy, Peter Heylyn and his 1636 tract *A coale from the Altar*:

> I will adde to these and other Testimonies of the most *ancient Fathers* . . . the conceits of two *Iewish Rabbins*, somewhat tending to our purpose . . . it is thus written, *And he said unto me, This is the Table before the LORD*: Meaning (without doubt) *the Altar of Incense*. The Question then grows, why the *Altar* is here call'd a *Table*, I have heard this given as a Reason of it, saith R. *Shelomo, That at this day the* Table *performs what the* Altar *was wont to do*. R. *Iohanan* and R. *Eliezer* give the like reason, *That while the Temple stood, the* Altar *of God but sithence the destruction therof, the* Table of man, *is become the place of Sacrifice and propitiation*. But I leave these *Rabbies* to *Rabbi Coal's* consideration, whether he shall reject them, for their concept of the *Table*.[44]

Observing that some ceremonialists fear being identified as Judaizers for drawing such parallels, 'R.T.' draws reassurance from the notion that the laws which governed the Jews' behaviour were natural, universal ones: 'some people are so wise, as they feare lest to build a Christian Church so like *Salomons* Temple, bee directly to bring in Judaisme. But wiser men than they, know that all which the Jewes did, was not Judaisme, Let them remember that for their comfort'.[45] R.T.'s words resemble those of the Puritan Foulke Robarts (1580?–1650), who argued that 'we must not call every thing Iewish or Leviticall, which is done by a Iew or a Levite: no more then we terme every thing Popish which is done by a Papist'; at this moment, the transformation from Puritan to Anglican Judaizing was complete.[46]

Beauty and prayer

Laudians defended their construction of aesthetically pleasing and ornate churches by appealing to the precedent of both the biblical Jewish Tabernacle, the tent-like structure in which the Jews prayed during their wanderings in the desert and in the first years of settlement in Palestine, and Solomon's temple at Jerusalem. 'R.T.' describes how the Tabernacle was the model for the temple at Jerusalem: 'The Jewes, before Salomons Temple was built, had their Tabernacle . . . the Jewes Tabernacle had the forme of a Temple, but was made as the Tents and Tabernacles wherein the Jewes dwelt at that time when Moyses built it.[47] Both buildings were regarded as prefigurations of the Christian church; as Robert Shelford writes: 'Gods house is set forth in the old law by the Tabernacle . . . Gods' house is described by the Temple at Jerusalem'.[48] Shelford indulges in a rich description of the Tabernacle's decorative interior, drawing a parallel between the Jews' creation of an earthly model of the beauties of heaven, and the Christians' duty to do the same:

> This holinesse respective to Gods house consisteth of certain holy offices. The first is, To adorn and beautifie it fit for his greatnesse, as himself gave pattern in beautifying his tabernacle: there was gold and silver, precious stones, silks, with all precious colours, the most choice woods, and all things framed with the best cunning that God inspired *Bezaleel* and *Aholiab*, and all the wise-hearted of that time . . . shall we look for glorious mansions in the kingdome of heaven, and will we not prepare comely mansions in the kingdomes of the earth? Doth not God challenge us where he challengeth his chosen people?[49]

'R.T.' argues that the word 'Tabernacle' is ultimately derived, via the Greek, from 'the Hebrew word *Naghan*, which signifies beauty, since nothing ought to be so beautifull, as the Temple,' thereby guaranteeing aesthetic worship through Hebrew etymology.[50] The scholar and parson Alexander Read uses a similar tactic, albeit with some rather anxious qualification:

> When [God] platform'd out his own Tabernacle & inspired *Solomon* to his own Temple, we see how glorious they were. Not only the

buildings, but even the lowest utensils, the snuffers and snuffe-dishes . . . all of pure gold . . . though we are not bound to take this as a law from God, to make all our Te[m]ple by; yet we shal do wel to make him our pattern. At least to learn thence, what manner of Temples distast him not. And if we acquit our selves from the cost-lines & gloriousnes; yet may we not free our selves from the decency & comelines. Though *God* shun not a *cottage*, yet *men* must think him *worthy* of a *palace*.[51]

The ceremonialist John Pocklington goes as far as to declare, in one of his chapter headings, that 'The whole of the Christian Church was framed by the patterne of the Jewish Church',[52] and he boldly states:

> there is not any one ancient Father that ever I see, who doth not derive the polity of the Christian Church, and take their patterne in laying downe the platforme thereof from Gods Church among the Iewes, as well before *Moses*, as after: as well in externall Rites and Ceremonies, as in the internall, spirituall and essentiall parts of Gods service.[53]

Ceremonialists invoked the Tabernacle as a precedent for prayer and ritual as well as the physical form of the church. Foulke Robarts, for example, presents Jewish prostration as a precedent for Christian kneeling. Other rituals which were guaranteed through Jewish precedent included standing at certain points in the service, bowing at the name of Jesus, using a ring in the marriage ceremony, the wearing of the surplice, making the sign of the cross and kneeling to receive communion.[54] Ceremonialists such as Edmund Reeve were in favour of following a calendar of festivities as a structured ritualisation of prayer, and employed not only the example of the biblical Israelites but also that of Jesus Christ and the apostolic Christians who emulated certain Jewish festivals:

> Our godly forefathers were zealous in the keeping of them, though wee now for the most part doe little consider of them. Was not the LORD CHRIST in the dayes of his flesh here on earth present at the feasts celebrated by the Jews? Doth not Saint Paul say, speaking concerning Easter . . . Let us keepe that feast, &c. Doth not Saint Jude tell us, that the Christians of the primitive Church, as well Gentiles as Jews, had their feasts of charitie?[55]

Indeed, for the Laudian commentator, church architecture and church ceremonies were analogically related. As well as both being manifestations of material worship, they were also connected through the festival of the anniversary of church dedication. 'R.T.', for example, lists precedents for this Christian ceremony in the dedication of Jewish altars, Tabernacles and finally the Temple at Jerusalem:

> the solemnities used by the Jewes, at the Dedication of their Altars, before the written Law, are copiously set downe in the sacred Scriptures. In them we also read of the great gifts and oblations offered by the Hebrew Princes under the Law, at the Dedication of their Tabernacle, when it was anointed all over with an oyntment of a most fragrant smell . . . above all, the rites and solemnities used by the Jewes, those used by Salomon, at the first Dedication of the Temple, are most remarkable.[56]

The awed tone with which the ceremonialists describe the past habits of the Jews is revealing.

Puritan opposition to the use of Jewish precedents to justify church ceremonies was intense during this period. William Ames complains that his opponents' arguments rely heavily on 'the doctrine and practise of the Apostles about the Jewish ceremonies. Now all the force of this reason doth depend upon that paritie or equalitie which is supposed to be betwixt our ceremonies and the Jewish . . . so that if this paritie faileth, the whole argument falleth'.[57] The Puritan minister Henry Burton accuses ceremonialists of idolatry, and equates their emulation of the Israelites' behaviour with the worst excesses of popish ceremony. After a sarcastic rehearsal of Laudian reforms, including the installation of altar-rails, Burton asks if churches will now contain images of God to which Christians, like the idolatrous worshippers of the Golden Calf, will pray:

> Well now, what's the next? Thus farre wee now see Popery, like a thiefe, stollen in upon us step by step, when wee, as men asleep in our beds, suspected no danger. And perhaps, the next degree will bee the placing of their God-Almighty in the Host or Pix visibly and conspicuously upon the Altar, and a Masse with the piping of the Organs, chanted unto it, as the Israelites did about their Calfe.[58]

The equation of Jewish with Popish ceremonies is a frequent device in anti-ceremonialist polemic, designed to cheapen and denigrate what ceremonialists present as the beautiful, ancient precedents of the Old Testament.

Church discipline

Peter Heylyn's stipulation that 'if a *Sacrifice* must bee, there must also be *Priests* to doe, and *Altars* whereupon to doe it' underwrites the role of prelates as much as it does the physical apparatus of the altar.[59] Indeed, the Episcopal subtext of the ceremonialist emphasis on material and communal forms of worship was one of the main topics of complaint in anti-ceremonialist rhetoric. The apparatus of ceremony emphasised the status and grandeur of the officiating clergy, and parallels with the Jewish Tabernacle supported comparisons between the Jewish High Priests, revered by the community, and contemporary prelates. In 1636, William Prynne declares 'in all regards then you see how the Iewish high Priests, and Lordly Prelates are direct Parallels, and so in verity their undoubted Successors'.[60] Prynne provides detailed lists of similarities between prelates and Jews: both build, consecrate and bow to the altar. Moreover, Laudians derive their 'costly pontificall Robes, ornaments, and attires, whereby they were differenced from other men' from the Jews. Both preach just once a year to their congregation.[61] Prynne draws a lengthy parallel between the oppression of Puritans, in his own time as well as under Elizabeth, and the oppression of rebels such as St Paul by the Jewish high priests:

> The Iewish high Preist . . . accused St. *Paule* before *Felix* the Governour, for a Pestilent fellow, a mover of sedition among all the Iewes throughout the world, and a ring-leader of the Sect of the *Nazarens* . . . the selfe same accusation haue the Lord Prelates laid to our Ministers charge in former ages, and to our zealous godly Ministers and Preachers now adayes, accusing them to the King and his Counsell, and persecuting yea, suspending: imprisoning them everywhere as pestilent, factious, sedicious persons, and ringleaders of Sects and Schisme; as many late examples, and some now in agitation evidence.[62]

A printed marginal note by the side of this passage reads, 'Witnes M. Henry Burton now charged by them, with sedition: with many others, as was B. Latimer, and all our Martyrs of old'.[63]

Puritan claims that ceremonialists were invoking the example of Jewish high priests to strengthen the status of bishops were not unfounded: the dean of Rochester, Walter Balcanquhall describes how 'the rites of consecration in the Iewish Church were ever performed by the Priests; in the Christian by the Bishops',[64] and John Pocklington defensively rejects

Prynne's observation that 'the Iewish high Priests, and Lordly Prelates are direct Parallels':

> he which saies, *Altars crept into the Church by a kinde of complying with the people of the Iewes*, may with as good reason say, that the orders of *Archbishops, Bishops, Priests and Deacons*, with their severall offices and degrees, with their attyre, habits, and vestments, together with oblations, tythes, glebe lands, and maintenance, crept into the Christian Church by a kinde of complying with the Iewes, and are therefore alike, and altogether to bee cast out of the Church, as Iudaicall Ceremonies.[65]

Edmund Reeve is less cautious: he draws a line of apostolical succession from the Israelites to contemporary bishops: 'even as the Shepheards of Israel (according to Gods commandment) humbled themselves under the High Priesthood, and afterward the Elders or Priests of the inferiour order did unto the Apostleship; So is it the duty of Pastours unto the Bishoprick the succession of the Apostleship'.[66] Ceremonialist Judaizing had a political, as well as an aesthetic, dimension.

II

Jewish precedents and the Conformist constitution

The Temple and Tabernacle were not the only ancient Jewish institutions emulated by Christians in the sixteenth and seventeenth centuries. From the mid-sixteenth century onwards, a variety of Christian denominations set about redefining the relationship between the church and state, and they frequently invoked the Sanhedrin, the Jewish court, as a useful precedent. The following chapter will describe how Puritans in the Civil War period employed the idea of the Jewish commonwealth in order to articulate a new religious and political constitution. But in the late sixteenth century, it was Anglicans who first used an ancient Jewish model as a template for England. The idea that the church was a department of the state, supported by evidence from Jewish history, was in circulation from the beginning of the Reformation, but it was articulated most famously by the Swiss theological and medical scholar, Thomas Erastus (1524–1583).[67] The idea became known as Erastianism, and was propagated throughout Europe: Erastus's Latin *Theses* on excommunication were published in London in 1589, and translated into English as *The Nullity of Church-Censures* in 1659.[68] Born at Baden, Switzerland, Erastus was appointed Professor of Medicine at Heidelberg in 1558.[69] His *Theses* contributed to an ongoing tradition of applying biblical Jewish models of religious administration to contemporary problems of church government. Similar texts by the Dutch jurist Hugo Grotius and the Hebraists Joseph Justus Scaliger and Johannes Buxtorf circulated in Geneva, Frankfurt and Basle, filtering across the Channel via the interest of Conformist writers in the sixteenth century, and Common lawyers such as John Selden in the seventeenth.[70] Selden's tract on the Sanhedrin, for example, his *De Synedriis* (1653) cites a range of continental and Jewish sources.[71] James Harrington's utopian *The Common-wealth of Oceana* (1656), as well as Thomas Hobbes's *Leviathan* (1656), contain references to the Jewish commonwealth, and were both influenced by Selden.[72] Continental texts on this subject also appeared in English versions: as well as Erastus's 1659 treatise, Grotius's *True religion explained And defended* appeared in 1632,[73] and Petrus Cunæus's *Republica Hebraeorum* (1632) was translated by the Royalist Clement Barkesdale (1609–1687) and published in London as *Of the Common-Wealth of the Hebrews* in 1653.[74] English commentators had access, therefore, to a range of biblical, post-biblical and continental sources which provided accounts of the Sanhedrin and its potential application to the Christian church and state.

Although these commentators drew on both biblical and post-biblical Jewish sources, the former was traditionally considered more reliable. The relationship between the two sources was already complicated, however, by the notion that the Mosaic council of 70 elders in the Old Testament prefigured the 71 members of the Sanhedrin as described in the Talmud, thus blurring the boundary between biblical and post-biblical example.[75] In his 1584 account of the administration of biblical Israel, *The Scepter of Iudah*, Edmund Bunny (1540–1618), the theological writer and chaplain to Edmund Grindal, bishop of York explains his reluctance to refer to Talmudic commentaries. He claims to have restricted his interpretation to biblical laws alone 'both for the better understanding therof; and bicause that most of them are altogither abolished to us, but so far as in sense and spirit, we are to take instruction of them'.[76] Bunny is loath to discuss the post-biblical government of the Jews:

> For as touching those others, that afterward grew to be in use and practise among them, such as their kings from time to time thought good to ordain, they do not appertain to our purpose: for that we seek not what was done among them; but whereunto by the law of God they were directed.[77]

Bunny believes that biblical injunctions apply in a certain sense to Christians as well as Jews, but he is reluctant to take example from post-biblical Jewish history. He is also unwittingly revealing, here, an inherent ambiguity in textual sources about the Sanhedrin: whether they constitute actual or ideal descriptions of the council. This ambiguity runs right through the Christian appropriation of these Jewish sources, since a universal precept advocated by God in the Bible was considered far preferable to the empirical practices of post-biblical, and therefore heretical, Jews.

There was an additional ambiguity, too: it was not clear exactly how the Sanhedrin had been constituted at all; and this made it an especially fertile topic for debate and opposition, as different factions offered rival interpretations. The term 'Sanhedrin', taken from the Greek word for council (*synedrion*), had been applied to a range of administrative bodies in New Testament Palestine. It became associated with the Supreme Court at Jerusalem, but it also designated local or regional councils. In turn, a variety of religious, political and judicial functions were ascribed to the Sanhedrin. In the writings of the Jewish historian Flavius Josephus, it had a political and judicial role, and was administered by the high priest in his joint capacity as civil ruler. According to the Talmud, however, it was primarily a religious legislative body, but, confusingly, with some political functions. Scholarly opinion was also divided: some believed that there were two Sanhedrins, one political and one religious, while others believed that its religious and political functions were inseparable and therefore combined in a single body. The former position was adopted, in late sixteenth-century England, by Presbyterians, and the latter by Conformist Erastians.

The relationship between church and state featured regularly in controversies between Archbishop Whitgift and the Puritan leader, Thomas Cartwright, in the last years of the sixteenth century. Whereas Whitgift believed that all citizens should be subject to the authority of the national church, Cartwright was committed to opposing what he regarded as an oppressive imposition; Whitgift believed in the conjunction of church and state, Thomas Cartwright argued for their separation. Whitgift applied state controls to the maintenance of religious uniformity, was instrumental in enforcing Elizabeth's role as head of the church, including her Thirty-nine Articles, and argued that religious disunity would be a threat to law and order in the state. He was the first Archbishop of Canterbury to be admitted a member of the Privy Council, in 1586, and in 1593 he appealed to the Queen to pass an act of Parliament censuring ministers who attended unauthorised prayer meetings rather than Anglican services. Cartwright, on the other hand, believed in the institution of an independent Presbyterian church government, free from the influence of the national church, which elected its own ministers and followed the Genevan prayer book. Along with other Puritan leaders, including John Field and Thomas Wilcox, Cartwright resisted Whitgift's efforts to enforce uniformity.[78]

Whitgift used a variety of argumentative strategies to counter his Puritan opponents; one of which was to legitimise the conjunction of church and state through appeals to Jewish law. This strategy coexisted, however, with a reluctance to apply Jewish laws to the Christian state, and Whitgift developed, therefore, a concept of Jewish law which could accommodate his resistance to Jewish legalism: he asserts that the biblical Jews 'had not onely the morall and ceremoniall, but the iudiciall [judicial] law also'.[79] This notion of 'iudiciall law' signified for Whitgift both civil government and 'outward' or material aspects of religious worship. Cartwright and his Nonconformist allies rejected the notion of an 'outward' church as Popish and ceremonial. But Whitgift argued for a marriage of material and spiritual aspects of worship at the same time as he united civil and ecclesiastical government:

> Christ is the head of the Churche, and spiritually governeth the same in the conscience, but bicause it hath also an outwarde and visible forme, therefore it requireth an outwarde and visible government, whiche Christ dothe execute aswell by the civill Magistrate, as he dothe by the ecclesiasticall minister, and therefore the government of the Churche, in the respect of the externall and visible forme of it, is not onely spirituall.[80]

On the other side, Cartwright declares in 1577 that 'it is unlawful in an established estate of the church, that a Minister of the church should bear civil office. And thus much against the Ministers, which have one foot in the church, and an other in the common wealth'.[81] Perhaps aware of the irony of earlier having accused Cartwright of 'play[ing] the Jew', and now invoking Jewish legal precedents himself, Whitgift reemphasised the association between Puritans and Judaizing. In his 1575 answer to Whitgift, Cartwright refers to an occasion when Whitgift accused the Presbyterians of deriving from the Jews the principle that 'seing the church and common wealth, are distinguished aswel under a Christian Prince, as under an unchristian . . . the principal autority belo[n]geth unto the the ministery'.[82] Cartwright uses the opportunity to suggest that it is in fact Conformists who are making use of Jewish precedents:

> We are not afraid to confes, that we consent in some point, with the Iues and Turkes, or they rather with us. But yow are fou[n]d in divers places, in their private orcheyardes, gathering your frute of trees, which their handes did first plant: and from thence yow bring your stockes, which yow would place in the lords vineyard.[83]

Thomas Morton, bishop of Chester, Lichfield and Durham, also utilises the concept of the 'judicial' law, but he is very ambivalent about the extent to which it applies to Christians. On the one hand, he asserts that the Jewish commonwealth was the only system which was 'instituted by God himselfe, or at the least approved by him . . . in the which respectes we cannot doubt, but that the true and perfect knowledge of it doth greately belong to the Church and to all the members of it'. On the other, however, he claims that

> the iudiciall lawes of the commonwealth or of the kingdome of *Israel* doe not belong to the Church. Neyther yet doe we affirme this kingdome to be the most excellent and convenient state, and that which christians according to the example of this people shoulde earnestly desire and seeke after: wishing rather that everie one be content with that government which is already established in the place where he liveth, not thinking of any alteration which is verie dangerous and bringeth with it, as alwaies great troubles, so often a finall overthrow to the people . . . onely we purpose to make a bare and historical narration of the state of this kingdome.[84]

Morton is here contradicting his own previous statement, and implying that a transformation in government along the lines of the biblical Jewish kingdom would pose a threat to the stability of his own. Jewish laws appear to have inherently suspect connotations for Morton: he uses the same phrase, 'bare and historical narration', which Selden used in his *Historie of Tithes* to qualify the application of Jewish historical precedents to the Christian state. William Ames satirises Morton's uncomfortable equivocations, observing that Morton has 'excused Jewish Rites, if they were used without Iewish opinion', and quoting Morton's statement that *'the use of some Iewish rite, without any Iewish opinion, is not damnable: instancing in circumcision and Easter'*.[85] Ames claims to be mystified by Morton's distinction: 'he should haue told us, how a Iewish rite can bee used, without some part of a Iewish opinion?'[86] Ames seems relieved that, for once, it is his opponent who has to deal with the consequences of invoking Jewish precedents.

The theologian and priest Richard Hooker (1554?–1600), the author of the highly influential Anglican manifesto, *Of the Lawes of Ecclesiastical Polity*, was one of the most important architects of the Anglican church.[87] Hooker's aim was to put an end to the factional disagreements so manifest in the controversies between Whitgift and Cartwright, and to defuse Nonconformist challenges to the Episcopal – and in Conformist eyes, the monarchical – establishment. Hooker was an Erastian; he argued that since church and state were comprised of the same population, they were therefore symbiotic entities: 'We hold that . . . there is not any man of the church of England but the same man is also a member of the commonwealth; nor any man a member of the commonwealth which is not also of the church of England'.[88] He believed, moreover, that religious and civil administration should be exercised by the same leaders: 'Civil and Ecclesiastical Functions may be lawfully united in one and the same Person'.[89] Hooker attempted, in the *Lawes*, a balancing act in which the role of the state in church affairs was as important as the place of the clergy in the commonwealth.[90] Hooker cited precedents for this arrangement in Old Testament Israel:

> Unto the *Jews* [God] so revealed the truth of Religion, that he gave them . . . Laws, not only for the administration of things spiritual, but also temporal. The Lord himself appointing both the one and the other in that Common-wealth, did not thereby distract it into several independent Communities, but institute several Functions of one and the self-same Communitie: Some Reasons therefore must there be alledged why it should be otherwise in the Church of Christ.[91]

Hooker was an implicit advocate of 'mixed government' by monarch, Parliament and nobility, but he felt that the authority of the monarch needed special protection from the unrest plaguing the English church.[92] He drew on the example of biblical Israel in order to argue that the monarch should derive power from being head of the church:

> it was not thought fit in the *Jews Commonwealth*, that the exercise of *Supremacy Ecclesiastical* should be denied unto him, to whom the exercise of *Chiefty Civil* did appertain; and therefore their Kings were invested with both . . . according to the pattern of which example,

the like power in causes Ecclesiastical is by the Laws of this Realm annexed unto the Crown.[93]

Thomas Morton, who was a friend and associate of Hooker, also wrote in favour of an Erastian unity of church and state in the 1590s. His *Salomon, or A treatise declaring the state of the kingdome of Israel, as it was in the daies of Salomon* (1596) applied the model of Old Testament kingship to contemporary England. He dedicated his tract to the Queen, and declares in the preface: 'We have annexed to this treatise of the kingdome of *Israell*, a treatise of the right manner of framing or building the Church, as it were ioyning the Church and the commonwealth into one bodie under one head, as we are perswaded that they are not two but one onely bodie'.[94] Morton believes that the two institutions are incomplete on their own: 'The Church is not heere a perfect bodie by it selfe but maketh the civil body more excellent & happie'.[95] He notes that opposition to Erastianism has originated in the assumption that the state, if combined with the church, would pollute it; but argues that this assumption is mistaken.[96]

Not only did Anglicans justify the idea of an Erastian constitution in England by invoking Old Testament precedents, but also directly invoked the example of the Sanhedrin. Thomas Bilson (1547–1616), bishop of Winchester, was one such advocate; in *The Perpetual Government of Christes Church* (1593) he explores in detail 'the points in question at this day; Touching the Iewish Synedrion'.[97] In the context of a discussion about the relative powers of the Jewish and Roman authorities in the New Testament era, a popular topic in church history,[98] Bilson argues that the Sanhedrin had sufficient 'iudiciall' or civil authority to function as a court with sentencing powers: 'whatsoever power the Romanes limitted or enlarged to the Elders of the Jewes after they were lordes over them, I greatly force not: this is evident, they were Magistrates by *Moses* lawe, and had the sword from God to execute his iudiciall ordinances'.[99] Richard Bancroft (1544–1610), a staunch opponent of Puritanism and archbishop of Canterbury from 1604, wrote *A Survay of the Pretended Holy Discipline* against Cartwright in 1593; it contains an assurance that the Sanhedrin 'had to do as well in civile causes, as ecclesiasticall'.[100]

Hooker, Morton, Bilson and Bancroft not only believed in joint religious and civil government, they also believed in a relatively inclusive church, open to Christians of different denominations. Strategically, this was an attempt to diminish the threat of Nonconformists by extending them, as it were, an invitation. There was also a more tendentious motive at work: Conformists were opposing the strict Presbyterian discipline, which excommunicated the ungodly, as well as opposing sectarians who separated themselves from the national church.[101] Presbyterians denounced, in return, what they regarded as heretical inclusiveness; a reaction which can be observed in the reply to Hooker and his Anglican associates which eventually appeared in 1599: the anonymous *A Christian Letter*.[102] In this tract, the authors defend Presbyteriansim, expressing a desire for English Christians to 'thinke the better of Maister Calvin and the cause of discipline'.[103] They object to Conformist Erastian attempts to bring Presbyterian discipline under the control of civil government, challenging Hooker to 'declare unto us, what moved that Reverend and learned man Mai[ster]. D[r]. *Whitgeeft* to spende so manie leaves to shewe that the partes of Discipline might be altered by the civill Magistrate'.[104] Not only is their true church set apart from the civil state, but the authors of *A Christian Letter* are angered by the idea that Hooker and Morton might include Roman Catholics in the national church.[105] Moreover, they fear that not only Roman Catholics would be allowed into Hooker's church, but even more exotic groups: 'and heere we crave your judgement of the Turke, how your rule fitteth them'.[106] The authors fear that if Hooker has his way, 'all religions shalbee tollerated'.[107] Here it is Anglicanism, rather than Puritanism, which was considered – even feared – to be a tolerant religion.

By invoking the post-biblical Sanhedrin, as well as the commonwealth of Old Testament Israel, Elizabethan Anglicans attracted accusations of Judaizing from their Presbyterian opponents. The authors of *A Christian Letter*, for example, disingenuously portray themselves as being in a dilemma as to whether or not the use of Jewish precedents to support the conjunction of church and state was endorsed by early Reformers: 'we are in a streight except you helpe us out. For if we beleeve you, we must thinke our reverend Fathers to have misledd us all this while; either of malice, or ignorance; if wee beleeve them we must thinke that Mai. *Hoo.* is verie arrogant and presemptuous to make him self the onelie Rabbi'.[108] The word 'Rabbi' implies, of course, disapproval of Hooker's use of Judaism.

III

If the examples of Anglican Judaising described so far in this chapter run counter to the prevailing association between Puritanism and Judaism, the following chapter explores controversies between Erastians and Presbyterians in the seventeenth century in which the use of Jewish precedents shifted between different religious and political factions. In fact, there were moments in the early modern period when Anglicans and Puritans actually swapped positions on a particular Jewish issue, depending on the position they were adopting at the time. Three brief examples illustrate this point: the Quartodeciman controversy in the 1630s, the tithes controversy in 1659, and the Sabbatarian controversy at various points during the early modern period.

The Quartodeciman controversy in the 1630s

During the Laudian debates of the 1630s, the factional positions taken on the subject of Easter observance and Quartodecimanism, as with other aspects of Judaising, reversed entirely. Whereas in the late sixteenth century, as the previous chapter demonstrated, it was the Puritans who favoured the Quartodecimans against the Roman church, in the early seventeenth century it was the Puritans who now disapproved of the Quartodeciman heresy. In 1622, the Puritan William Ames wrote in reply to the ceremonialist bishop, Thomas Morton:

> the Councel of Nice decreed that Christians might not keep the feast of Easter at the time, or in the manner as the Iewes did. Not . . . *that it was alwayes unlawful so to do*, which question I will leave to them that are skilful in human traditions, but 1. *for hatred of the Iewes.* 2. *because of the Iewes insultation.* 3. *for vniformitie.* The last of these causes doth not agree: for vniformitie might as well haue followed, if all Christians could have been drawn to the same time with the Iewes. The other two agree wel to our ceremonies. For we are to hate the idolatrous supersititions of the Papists with a perfect hatred.[109]

Ames rejects the Jewish Quartodeciman custom as he rejects popery, and draws parallels between Quartodecimanism and Laudian ceremony. Ames even denies that the Quartodeciman custom was widespread amongst Christians, claiming that if it did at times appear, this was simply a circumstantial anomaly:

> the feast of Easter . . . was never generally observed at the same time with the Iewes, nor ever so appointed by any decree or canon of Councel: if it had, yet that had been but an agreement in a circumstance of time, and the translation of it to another time, did shew, they liked of no conformitie of Iewes . . . circumcision, he sayth, was

continued under many Christian Bishops of Ierusalem. But let him shew that those Christian Bish[ops] allowed of any such thing.[110]

Ames is particularly critical of what he presents as repeated attempts on the part of his opponent, Thomas Morton, to invoke early church Quartodecimanism, and indeed circumcision, as justifications of contemporary Laudianism. Reading Morton's text, Ames is annoyed by the repeated references to Quartodecimanism, 'which now the fourth time is brought upon the stage by [Morton] in vain'.[111] Here it is a Conformist, Morton, who is referring to the Quartodecimans as 'godly Bishops, and Martyrs of the Church of *Asia*', a description which would fit perfectly in the texts of Foxe and Bale in the previous phase of the controversy.

The tithes controversy in 1659

The controversy over the payment of tithes, explored in the previous chapter, never fully disappeared after the furore over Selden's *Historie*, and because the issue was essentially a microcosm of power struggles between monarch, church and Parliament, it intensified during the Civil War.[112] In the 1650s, the anti-clericalism of the Quaker movement, bolstered by radicals such as John Milton, was expressed in the refusal to pay tithes. By this time, the place of the Jacobean prelates had been taken by the Presbyterians, now dominant in the ecclesiastical hierarchy. These Presbyterians were now arguing, ironically, for an Erastian conjunction of church and state – what the Presbyterian commentator Robert Baillie calls 'a lame Erastian Presbytery'.[113] In 1659, the anti-tithe lobby came to a head: a petition of 15,000 signatures was presented to the Rump Parliament in June, and in the following month, another petition was signed by 7,000 Quaker women.[114] The comments of the Quaker John Canne (d. 1667?), writing in reply to the Presbyterian William Prynne, indicate the ubiquity of the issue in contemporary debate: 'at this time, the great Controversie is about *Tythes*, and that there is so much writing *Pro* and *Con*'.[115]

In the debates of 1659, it was the Quakers who argued for the abrogation of the Jewish law of tithing, against the Presbyterians who used Jewish precedents to justify the payment of tithes. John Selden had used Jewish precedents in entirely the opposite way: to argue against their payment. William Prynne supported John Selden in the Westminster Assembly debates of the 1640s, but on the issue of tithing in 1659 he was opposed to Selden's position. Prynne challenges his opponents to 'answer all the Arguments . . . produced by' those who wrote against Selden in the earlier controversy: Tillesley, Sempill, Nettles, Montagu and Sclater.[116] Another Presbyterian commentator, Immanuel Bourne (1590–1672), likewise cites Jacobean arguments in favour of the divine right of tithes: those by Tillesley and Sclater.[117] Prynne goes one step further than the Jacobean commentators in promoting the practices of the Jews. He asks 'whether it be not a most arrogant, high, inexcusable presumption for a few *giddy-pated Innovators* in this Age, to condemn, censure . . . the practise, wisedom, piety of *Abraham, the Father of the Faithfull*, and all the people of God in the Old Testament, before and under the Law'.[118] Prynne wrote these apparently philosemitic words just three years after his famously anti-Jewish *Short Demurrer*, which argues against proposals to readmit the Jews to England.

John Milton, supporting the Independent side which included the Quakers, claims that corrupt church authorities have 'brought back again priests, altars and oblations; and in many other points of religion had miserably Judaiz'd the church'.[119] Milton, like Selden, argues that since the Jews themselves stopped paying tithes after the destruction of the temple, it would be perverse for Christians to resurrect the practice:

> the Jewes ever since thir temple was destroid, though they have Rabbies and teachers of thir law, yet pay no tithes, as having no Levites to whom, no temple where to pay them, no alter wheron to hallow them; which argues that the Jewes themselves never thought tithes moral, but ceremonial only. That Christians therefor should take them up, when Jewes have laid them down, must needs be very absurd and preposterous.[120]

Milton, who learned a great deal about Judaism from the works of John Selden, was nevertheless here against the application of that Jewish knowledge to Christian England.

In the earlier controversy, it was John Selden and those who opposed the payment of tithes who were accused of Judaizing, but in this later one it was the supporters of tithes who were now criticised for being excessively interested in the Jews. The Independent John Canne labels the national church 'carnal',[121] and declares that the Papacy and their equivalents, the Presbyterian ministry, have resurrected ceremonial Jewish practices, such as tithe-collecting:

> No sooner sits the man of sin in the Temple of God, and had set up an Antichristian Priesthood, calling himselfe the high Priest, and the

Priests, the *Tribe of Levi*, and Gods inheritance . . . and commanded the people to pay Tythes to his Priests, and his Priests to pay first fruits, and tenths or tythes to him, after the manner of the Jewish people, and *Levites* to *Aaron* under the Law.[122]

In Canne's eyes, 'to retein tythes, is to keepe up and give honour to the Jewish shadowes, which by Christs death were taken away'.[123] The Presbyterian Immanuel Bourne complains about 'a proud peremptory Quaker, who called me *Old Jew*, because I justified that it was lawful for the Ministers of Christ to take Tythes, and that they were justifiable by the written Word of God, when he thought them onely a Jewish Ceremony. But it is evident that Tythes are not onely Jewish, or paid by the Jews onely'.[124] In the Jacobean controversy, opposition to tithes was considered Jewish; in 1659, it was considered Jewish to support them.

The Sabbath

Sabbatarianism was associated with Puritan Judaizing in the early seventeenth century, but at the same time, in the context of the controversy over the payment of tithes, it was Conformists who were in favour of the Sabbath.[125] John Selden's opponents drew direct parallels between the payment of tithes and the observance of the Sabbath. William Sclater claims at the end of his tract that 'scarce is there any Argument bent against moralitie of Tithing, but strikes with keenest edge against moralitie of Sabbath', and he constructs a table of parallels between the Sabbath and tithes. One of these parallels states that those who declare tithes to have been abrogated by Christ also claim that the Sabbath is a culpable resurrection of Jewish ceremonialism.[126] James Sempill draws a parallel between the numerical value of one day of rest in seven working days, with the numerical value of a tenth to be given as tithes. The continuation of the Jewish Sabbath is allied with the continuation of Jewish tithe-payments:

> and so the Morall (*Time*) yet remaineth, A Sabbath, though not the same Indiuiduall day from the Creation.
> Obiect. *And why may we not also haue still a Maintenance, though not the same meanes, and* quotum.
> Answ. If yee admit of my ground, the same *quotum* kept in the Sabbath, will binde the same *quotum* in Maintenance. Still a seventh day, though not the same seventh: so still a tenth, though not a Legall, Iudaicall, or Leuiticall tenth.[127]

Sempill is careful here to stipulate that he is not advocating the slavish emulation of the Jews under the Law, as revealed by the final phrases in the quotation above. He is referring to Sunday Sabbatarianism, not the more contentious Saturday Sabbatarianism practised by Judaizers such as John Traske. And yet, the Conformist recruitment of the divine right argument for the defence of ecclesiastical tithing, and here their adoption of Sabbatarianism, laid Conformists open to charges of Judaizing. It is precisely these accusations that Sempill's defensive caveat is designed to deflect.[128]

During the Laudian controversy of the 1630s, the ceremonialist side was, rather surprisingly, against Sabbatarianism, despite their support for other rituals and festivals. The unbroken succession of religious practice from Jews to Christians was emphasised by Laudian writers such as Joseph Mede, Walter Balquancall, Foulke Robarts and Peter Heylyn, but the Sabbath stood out as a dividing line between the Jewish past and the Christian present. On this issue alone, ceremonialists broke with their endorsement of festivals and ceremonies, emphasising the abrogation of the Jewish law, and contradicting the position on the Sabbath held by earlier Conformists.[129] Peter Heylyn sets out his anti-Sabbatarian views in *A History of the Sabbath* (1636).[130] Edmund Reeve, discussing the fourth commandment, writes

> Q. Doth the holy Catholike and Apostolike Church of JESUS CHRIST now observe that seaventh naturall day of every weeke, which the Church of the Jewes was required to keepe holy, and which that nation celebrateth unto this present time?
> A: In no wise.[131]

Reeve does concede that the first day of the week is indeed the Lord's Day. But when it comes to the issue of Sabbatarian observance, including abstinence from labour, 'ceremonial' becomes a dirty word, and he emphasises the power of the church to select its rites.[132] Francis White (1564?–1638), bishop of Ely and dean, from 1625, of Sion College, a centre for Talmudic learning, explicitly connects Sabbatarianism with anti-ceremonialism. He accuses his opponents of hypocrisy; of denying the validity of altars because the word 'altar' does not appear in scripture, but advocating Sabbatarianism even though the word 'Sabbath' is likewise absent:

> I desire the Reader to observe the perverse disposition of our novell Sabbatarians. *For* they will not permit that the Communion Table

shall be named an *Altar*, no, not by an allusion or similitude, because it is not so called in holy Scripture: *And* because the *Romists* have been superstitious in their doctrine and practise concerning the Masse: *And* because of the perill of Idolatrie.

But againe, on the other side, they stile the *Lord's* day, the Sabbath day: although this name is not given it in holy Scripture: *Or* by any of the godly Fathers of the Church: *And* although the Sabbath, and the *Lord's* day, are so different, as that one is legall, and the other Evangelicall: *And* notwithstanding the perill of *Iewish super*stition, and the heresie of Iudaizants.[133]

White is willing to invoke scriptural precedents in order to justify the altar, but disowns them in the case of the Sabbath. His own scriptural ceremonialism, moreover, is just as likely as the Sabbatarianism of his opponents to attract suspicions of 'the perill of *Iewish super*stition'. Anti-ceremonialists were quick to observe the anomaly presented by the Laudian exclusion of Sabbatarianism from their catalogue of legitimate ceremonies. In a printed marginal note, the Puritan Henry Burton refers to several recent attacks on Sabbath observance by Peter Heylyn, Francis White and John Prideux, and comments 'though they condemne the very name of Sabbath, as Iewish, yet they are all characterised with that name and title'.[134]

***

Throughout the late sixteenth and early seventeenth centuries, a variety of different religious factions adopted shifting positions regarding the relationship between Christianity and Judaism. Puritans were in favour of Judaism in the context of their enthusiasm for learning Hebrew, but they were against it when it came to the issue of church ceremony and ritual. Conformists were in favour of Judaism when it suited their arguments on ceremony and ritual, but at the same time they were against it in relation to the Sabbath, despite the fact that just a few years earlier, Conformists had justified their observance of the Sabbath through the use of Jewish precedents. This apparently contradictory evidence illustrates how easy it was for trenchantly opposed factions to, nevertheless, realign over time. In such a contentious and unstable atmosphere, Christians sincerely attempted, once and for all, to banish doctrinal disagreements by using Jewish precedents to prove the other side wrong; but in the process, the Christian consensus was refracted further.

4
Religious Toleration: Jews and Jewish Precedents in the Christian Church and State

If factionalism and controversy dominated the religious landscape of the late sixteenth and early seventeenth centuries, the mid-seventeenth century is thought to have seen the emergence of a desire to encourage religious freedom; an attempt, on the part of many English Christians, to transform denominational intolerance into religious toleration. The birth of the tolerationist movement in the 1640s has been well documented, beginning with the development of the patriotic idea, in the Victorian era, that tolerance was a uniquely English virtue, and the resulting efforts to trace its genealogy.[1] Later on, as fascism swept across Europe, the recovery of a tolerant past became an even more pressing task: W.K. Jordan's *The Development of Religious Toleration in England* was published between 1932 and 1940, at the same time as the American historian William Haller's *Tracts on Liberty*, a collection of seventeenth-century texts on toleration, and A.S.P. Woodhouse's collection, *Puritanism and Liberty*.[2]

According to the tradition of Anglo-Jewish history established in the late nineteenth century, Cromwell's readmission of the Jews was a consequence of Puritan tolerationism. The Catalogue from the exhibition of Anglo-Jewish art and history at the Victoria and Albert Museum, organised as part of the Tercentenary celebrations, laid emphasis on 'the part played by the Jews in English life, where they have breathed freely since the Commonwealth in a climate of tolerance and deep reverence for the Bible'.[3] In a speech at the Tercentenary banquet, the historian Edgar Samuel told the story of 'the firm establishment of the Jewish community in England, and of its increase in prosperity and numbers under the tolerant protection of successive English rulers'.[4] Speaking of the special services taking place in synagogues around the country, Lord Cohen described how 'the Anglo-Jewish Community not only expressed its gratitude for the ever-increasing measures of toleration which have been shown to its ancestors over the past 300 years but also recorded its determination for the future to be, as they hope they have been in the past, good Jews and good citizens of the British Commonwealth'.[5] Both philosemitism and toleration were conceptualised as the expression of benevolent idealism, and the roots of both were located in the seventeenth century.

Revisionist historians have since pointed out that, in the early modern period at least, religious toleration was more often considered to be a vice than a virtue, and there were limits to toleration imposed by both religious and political circumstances. Puritans were often highly intolerant of other religious groups, and the liberalism of Cromwell has been overstated.[6] However, echoes of a more traditional approach to the history of toleration can still be found; and the desire to follow a trajectory from the first stirrings of Nonconformist toleration to secular liberty and modern tolerance has, even in modern historiography, proven hard to resist.[7] As far as the study of the toleration of Jews is concerned, the revisionist approach has hardly made any impact at all. If tolerationist statements towards other Christian groups have been interpreted, within the revisionist strain of early modern history, in the context of the political and religious context of the time, statements in favour of the toleration of Jews tend to be read at face value; as straightforwardly benign. The traditional assumption is that Puritans, inclined as they were towards toleration, extended that sentiment to Jews, and that this was the ground on which later calls for the readmission of the Jews to England were based.[8]

If previous chapters have located Christian interest in Jewish ideas in the context of internecine Christian concerns, this one addresses the question of whether that context retains its significance when Christians were exploring not only Jewish ideas, but also ideas about Jews. Instead of regarding tolerationist ideas in the seventeenth century as a progressive innovation, furthermore, this chapter places them in the context of debates about the religious and political constitution which had been active since the late sixteenth century, and which were discussed in the previous chapter. The historical context for the later, seventeenth-century debates, was different, but many of the issues were the same: the question of whether the inclusion of diverse religious groups could be resolved politically, by separating church from state, or whether this move was inherently subversive and heretical. Like the earlier debates, these ones made frequent use of Jewish history, especially the composition of the Sanhedrin. If there has been too great an emphasis, in the existing literature, on the connection between tolerationist thought and the toleration of Jewish people, there has, at the same time, been too little emphasis on the extent to which the development of religious toleration was built on Jewish ideas. An analysis of Jewish ideas in these debates illustrates the continuity between Elizabethan church–state debates and seventeenth-century tolerationist debates, demonstrating both that seventeenth-century toleration was less of a radical departure than its subsequent representation sometimes suggests, and also that references to the toleration of Jews followed in the same tradition as Christian polemical discourse written in a much earlier period, when the very idea of Jews in Christian England was almost entirely theoretical.

Toleration in the seventeenth century

The upheavals of the early to mid-seventeenth century – religious, political and military – did create a climate in which diverse opinions began to be expressed, and radical groups began to make their presence felt. It is no accident that historians of toleration have tended to locate the first flourishings of religious liberty in the 1640s; it was at this moment that dissident Christians began, it seems, to resist religious uniformity more vocally than ever before. Roger Williams (1604?–1683) was one of the most well-known advocates of toleration in the seventeenth century; and in addition to Williams, there were many others who wrote in defence of religious minorities in the 1640s and 1650s. John Goodwin (c. 1594–1665) was a popular London preacher, political and religious polemicist and, eventually, a supporter of the regicide; he opposed the persecutory tendencies of Presbyterianism and publicly defended religious liberty and freedom of conscience, as did the Levellers Richard Overton and William Walwyn. Calls for religious toleration echoed on the Continent in the works of Sebastian Castellio and Hugo Grotius.[9] Radical dissenters of the period sometimes went as far as announcing an intention to extend religious toleration towards Jews: the merchant and writer, Henry Robinson, argued that the Jews should 'be suddenly recalled, and encouraged to continue by a Liberty of Conscience',[10] and the heresiographer Thomas Edwards was moved to complain in his 1646 edition of *Gangraeana* that

> The sectaries being now hot upon the getting of a Toleration, there were some meetings lately in the City, wherein some persons of the severall sects, some Seekers, some Anabaptists, some Antimonians,

some Brownists, some Independents met; some Presbyterians also met with them, . . . some professing at one of the meetings, it was the sin of this Kingdom that the Jews were not allowed the open profession and exercise of their religion amongst us; only the Presbyterians dissented and opposed it.[11]

There is evidence, moreover, of increasing contact between Christians and Jews during this period: the number of Jews in England was increasing, and Christians met with Jews during their travels on the Continent; there was also more indirect contact, too; the Hebraist John Lightfoot and the travel writer Thomas Coryat corresponded, for example, with the Venetian rabbi Leon Modena.[12]

Roger Williams is renowned for being the founding protagonist of both English and American tolerationism. After his ordination as a minister, Williams became disaffected with the Anglican church and fled England in 1630 on grounds of religious persecution, first to Massachusetts and then, after being expelled by the government there for his separatist views, to Rhode Island, where he founded the settlement of Providence. Throughout the 1640s and 1650s, Williams participated in controversies about toleration and the religious constitution, and his 1644 tract, *The Bloudy Tenent, of Persecution*, which argued that religion should be free from the control of civil government and that churches should be independent organisations, was burned by order of the Long Parliament; Williams subsequently fled England again, but returned to England in 1651; throughout this period he added contributions to the controversy.[13] In 1652, Roger Williams produced a commentary on a paper submitted to the parliamentary Committee for the Propagation of the Gospel, which considered the question of 'whether it be not the duty of the Magistrate to permit the Jews, whose conversion we look for, to live freely and peaceably amongst us?'[14] Williams answers, 'I humbly conceive it to be the Duty of the Civil Magistrate to break down that superstitious wall of separation (as to Civil things) between us Gentiles and the Jews, and freely (without their asking) to make way for their free and peaceable Habitation amongst us'.[15] In *The Bloudy Tenent, of Persecution*, Williams writes that, since the coming of Christ, the most '*Paganish, Jewish, Turkish* or *Antichristian consciences* and *worships*' should be allowed, and only challenged with the Word.[16] These are indeed extraordinary statements, but their meaning is not self-evident; elsewhere in *The Bloudy Tenent*, Williams uses the word 'gentile' in a different context: he argues for 'the *permission* of divers and contrary *consciences*, either of *Iew* or *Gentile*'.[17] It is not immediately clear what the word 'Gentile' means; in the quotation from the

1652 commentary, 'Gentile' means 'Christian'; here it could mean 'heathen', but it has a biblical resonance, suggesting that the word 'Jew' also carries a timeless, metaphorical significance.

Furthermore, Williams' desire that 'the most *'Paganish, Jewish, Turkish* or *Antichristian consciences* and *worships'* should be allowed, closely resembles similar utterances which can be found in religious texts throughout the early modern period. They appear, for example, in The Book of Common Prayer:

> Mercifull God, who hast made all men, and hatest nothing that thou hast made, nor wouldest the death of a sinner, but rather that he should be converted and live, have mercie upon all Jewes, Turkes, Infidels, and Heretikes, and take from them all ignorance, hardnesse of heart, and contempt of thy worde: and so fetch them home, blessed Lord, to thy flocke, that they may bee saved among the remnant of the true Israelites, and bee made one fold under one shepheard, Jesus Christ our Lord.[18]

The formula of 'Jewes, Turkes, Infidels' and so on was employed, furthermore, by a variety of Christian writers protesting against religious persecution, even in a much earlier period. In 1612, the Baptist leader Thomas Helwys writes in support of toleration in his *Short declaration of the mistery of iniquity*:

> Our lord the King is but an earthly King, and he hath no aucthority [sic] as a King but in earthly causes, and if the Kings people be obedient & true subjects, obeying all humane lawes made by the King, our lord the King can require no more: for mens religion to God, is betwixt God and themselves; the King shall not answere for it, neither may the King be iugd betwene God and man. Let them be heretickes, Turks, Jewes, or what soever it apperteynes not to the earthly power to punish them in the least measure.[19]

Helwys's words appear progressive and forward-looking, but it is important to interpret his reference to 'heretickes, Turks [and] Jewes' in context. As the phrase 'or what soever' suggests, the use of these groups is, to some extent, rhetorical. Helwys is protesting against state interference in the matter of private religious belief, and the reference to heretical groups helps to strengthen his argument. Even if they are heretics, Helwys says, the state should not be interfering with their consciences; this does not mean, however, that he necessarily approves of them.

Furthermore, these lists of epithets ('heretickes, Turks, Jewes, or what soever') also frequently appeared in inverted form throughout the period. In 1593, Richard Hooker, setting out his plans for the Anglican church, reluctantly admits that only those who are 'signed with this marke, *One Lord, one faith, one baptisme*' can be counted a Christian; 'for want of these it is that Saracens, Iewes, and Infidels are excluded out of the bounds of the church'.[20] Likewise, Thomas Morton declares in his 1596 treatise on the ideal English church that

> The nation of the Iewes having reiected Christ, is by that meanes reiected of God from being his people: neyther are they to be accounted members of the Church, although they serve God with never so great zeale *Rom*. II. The same account we are to make of the *Turkes, Saracens, Moores,* and all those nations which professe the religion of *Mahomet*.[21]

The subtitle of the Elizabethan translator Arthur Golding's version of Phillipe de Mornay's *Woorke concerning the Trewnesse of the Christian Religion* (1587) explains that Mornay's *Woorke* is written 'against Atheists, Epicures, Paynims, Iewes, Mahometists, and other infidels'.[22] The easy reversal of the formula serves as a reminder that statements in favour of toleration should not be taken entirely at face value; that they are, to some extent, part of a long tradition of listing categories of various 'others' in rhetorics of inclusion or exclusion.

The Westminster Assembly debates

So much for the diachronic context for Roger Williams's words, then; what about the synchronic context in which they were written and read? During the 1640s and 1650s, the turbulent years of the Civil War and interregnum, English political and religious leaders set about reformulating the English constitution. Printed discussions circulated rapidly about the relationship between the King – or, after Charles I's execution, the Lord Protector – and Parliament, and the relationship between church and state: whether there should be a national church, in which the religious and the political spheres were combined, or whether the church should be entirely separate from the state.[23] These issues were debated by the Westminster Assembly of Divines, an advisory council set up by the Puritan Long Parliament in order to draw up proposals for the reform of the Church of England, based on the Root and Branch petition of 1640, which had called for the abolition of episcopacy.[24] The Assembly met between 1643 and 1648 in Westminster

Abbey, and although the Scottish Kirk and other Presbyterian churches north of the border adopted the Assembly's recommendations, they made little impact on the English church. The sessions were important, however, because they were the occasion for a great deal of debate about England's religious and political future.[25]

At first, there were two main factions in the Westminster Assembly: Erastians and Presbyterians. The Presbyterian party wanted to institute in the English church a hierarchical system of strict Scottish church discipline, whereas the Erastian party feared that this would remove Parliamentary control over religious affairs.[26] In the first years of the debates, Erastians such as the controversialist pamphleteer William Prynne (1600–1669) and John Lightfoot (1602–1675), the Cambridge Hebraist, were pitched against Presbyterians George Gillespie (1613–1648), the Scottish minister, and Robert Baillie (1599–1662), also a Scottish minister and scholar.[27] Throughout the early 1640s the Presbyterians steadily rose in power, until in 1645 the Assembly decided in favour of adopting the Scottish system of church government. The MPs in the Assembly were against this, but Parliament was offered the consolation that although a system of Presbyterian church government would be put in place, Parliament would be granted control over religion, a situation which the Presbyterian Robert Baillie labelled 'a lame Erastian Presbytery'.[28]

In the later years of the Westminster Assembly debates, a radical Christian affiliation known as the Independents became dominant; they took the place of the Erastians in their opposition to the Presbyterian party. In these later debates, it was the Independents who were now arguing for the separation of church and state, so that they could practise their dissident form of religion unhindered by state powers. Presbyterians, on the other hand, were arguing for the conjunction of church and state, because by this time Presbyterianism had effectively become the national religion. In this second phase, Independents Roger Williams, Thomas Goodwin (1600–1680) and the Leveller Richard Overton (fl. 1646), were pitched against supporters of the national church including William Prynne, Robert Baillie and the New England Presbyterian John Cotton (1584–1652). John Cotton, a prominent Puritan commentator and pastor of the Boston church, engaged in a back-and-forth controversy with Roger Williams about the religious and political constitution of both England and New England.

The broader context for the Westminster Assembly debates was the proliferation of religious groups in this period, and the new questions their existence posed. What was to be the status of these churches, and in order to accommodate them, was England required to separate church from state, so that a variety of religious denominations could become, as it were, separate islands of faith within civil society? Presbyterians in the Assembly argued that their church should be the national church, continuous with the state, and were unwilling to countenance the existence of smaller, more radical churches, regarding them as subversive institutions. The representatives of those churches in the Assembly, the loose conglomeration of Baptists, Congregationalists, Levellers and other groups who made up the constituency of the Independents, had a shared agenda: opposition to the idea of a national church. The Independents wanted to share a civic identity only with members of other churches, and they particularly objected to the potential power of the national church, reinforced by the authority of the magistrate, to excommunicate dissenters – especially since those dissenters potentially included themselves. It was in response to the factional debates in and around the Westminster Assembly that many statements in favour of toleration were uttered, and it is this context – the network of tracts and pamphlets which were produced as a written accompaniment to the Westminster debates – which sheds a rather different light on the development of religious toleration in the seventeenth century. After all, religious toleration was often defended in the course of internecine controversy. William Prynne describes toleration, indeed, as a negative polemical strategy when he denounces 'these *New furious Sectaries*: who to engage all sorts of people in their *Quarrell*, proclaim a free *Toleration* and *Liberty of Conscience*, to all *Sects*, all *Religions* whatsoever, be it *Judaisme, Turcisme, Arianisme, Popery*; (as all their Pamphlets manifest)'.[29]

In the complex and intricate religious politics of the Civil War period, factions frequently changed sides. For example, although William Prynne argued from an Erastian standpoint in the Presbyterian–Erastian debate, prompting the complaint from Robert Baillie that 'Mr. Prynne and the Erastian lawyers are now our remora [obstacle]',[30] in the later Presbyterian–Independent debate he changed sides, throwing his weight behind the institution of a Presbyterian national church. Equally contradictory was the position of Robert Baillie, who had been strongly in favour of a separation of church and state in the early debates, but later on argued, against the Independents, in favour of the intervention of the magistrate in ecclesiastical affairs. These commentators also changed their minds about the use of Jewish precedents. As long as they supported the Presbyterian cause, George Gillespie and Robert Baillie were opposed to the idea of an Erastian state church, and opposed to the use of Jewish precedents such as the Sanhedrin as a model for Christian church government. Their Parliamentary Erastian opponents, John Selden and John Lightfoot, were in favour of using Jewish precedents such as the Sanhedrin. But as the Presbyterians gained power, Baillie and Gillespie became Presbyterian Erastians, and were now in favour of applying the Jewish precedent of the Sanhedrin.

The Bloudy Tenent, of Persecution

If Roger Williams's 1644 tract *The Bloudy Tenent* remains one of the most lauded tolerationist manifestos, it also exemplifies the bitter arguments between Presbyterians and Independents. *The Bloudy Tenent* was widely condemned in its own time;[31] George Gillespie answered it in 1645 with *Wholesome severity reconciled*, and a printed exchange developed between Williams and the Presbyterian John Cotton.[32] An additional reply to *The Bloudy Tenent* appeared anonymously in 1646 under the title *Hell broke loose: or, A catalogue of many of the spreading Errors, Heresies and Blasphemies of these Times*.[33] As an Independent, Williams was concerned to prove that church and state should remain distinct, an argument which recurs frequently throughout his account. For example, drawing on metaphors from the *Song of Songs*, he writes:

> As the *Lilie* is amongst the *Thornes*, so is Christs *Love* among the *Daughters*: and as the *Apple-tree* among the *Trees* of the *Forrest*, so is her *Beloved* among the Sons: so great a difference is there between the *Church* in a Citie or Country, and the *Civill state, City* or Country in which it is.
> No lesse [far] then . . . are they that are truly *Christs* (that is, anointed truly with the Spirit of *Christ*) from many thousands who love not the *Lord Iesus Christ.* and yet are and must be permitted in the World or Civill State, although they have no right to enter into the gates of *Jerusalem* the *Church* of God.[34]

If church and state are separate, Williams's argument goes, then diverse religions can exist in the state, without polluting the church.[35] The title of Williams's tract refers to the blood of souls whose religious belief is threatened by the civil interference of the Presbyterian national church; 'tenent' is an obsolete form of 'tenet'.[36] Williams includes in his tract a lengthy analysis of Matthew 13:24–30, the parable of the wheat and the tares, which is often employed in debates about toleration: '*Christ* commandeth to let alone the *Tares* to grow up together with the *Wheat*, until the *Harvest*'.[37] The parable was modified in these debates by presenting tares, or weeds, as a metaphor for sinners or non-Christians, and wheat as a metaphor for the Godly. Controversialists then argued over whether the field represented the church or the state.

The notion that the field represented the state provided tolerationists such as Roger Williams with a way of demarcating a sphere in which heathens could exist without affecting the church: 'the field in which the these *Tares* are sowne, is not the *Church*. Again affirmatively: First, the *Field* is properly the *World*, the *Civill State* or *Common-wealth*'.[38] In order to emphasise that faith is entirely separate from civil society, Williams appeals to the most exotic and extreme scenarios, in which true Christians would be allowed to exist under the civil jurisdiction of authorities who were members of very different faiths: 'Who doubts but *Gods people* may appeal to the Romane *Caesar*, an Egyptian *Pharaoh*, a Philistinian *Abimelecke*, an Assyrian *Nabuchadnezzar*, the great *Mogol*, *Prester Iohn*, the great *Turke*, or an Indian *Sachim*?' The printed marginal note reads: 'Lawfull appeales in civill things to Civill Magistrates'.[39] Williams is deliberately referring to those who are farthest from Christianity in order to make a structural point. John Cotton disputes the existence of a civil sphere distinct from the spiritual one, qualifying Williams's argument by writing that 'it is true, Christ expoundeth the Field to be the world . . . but he meant not the wide world, but (by an usuall Trope) the Church scattered throughout the world'.[40] Cotton believes, furthermore, that state rulers should have jurisdiction in religious affairs: 'the Magistrate need not to feare, that he should exceede the bounds of his Office, if he should meddle with the spirituall affairs of the Church in Gods way'.[41]

Williams's publications contributed to the English debate between Presbyterians and Independents, but they were also engaged with the religious and political administration of the New World. Another target of Roger Williams's polemic was the Puritan theocracy of Massachusetts – in which church and state were closely combined – and its apologist John Cotton. But Williams was able to draw more positive comparisons with his (somewhat idealised) impression of the treatment of Native Americans in New England. The Puritans who were engaged in setting up the New England community were preoccupied by the relationship between the new church and state, and whether Native Americans ought to be members of either. Williams uses the example of the Native Americans in New England as a useful parallel to the plight of heretics (and Jews) in England:

> In *New England* it is well known that they not onely *permit* the *Indians* to continue in their unbeliefe . . . but they also permit or tolerate

them in their *Paganish worship*, which cannot be denied to be a *worshipping* of *Devils*, as all false Worship is.

And therefore consequently . . . not onely the *Indians*, but their *Countrymen, French, Dutch, Spanish, Persians, Turkes, Iewes,* &c should also be permitted in their *Worships*, if correspondent in *civill obedience*.[42]

The example of New England is helpful to Williams, because, aside from Massachusetts, it is a place where the church is not established, and where a variety of faiths can practise their own religion undisturbed; he argues that the 'heathens' who make up civil society at large should be allowed to worship freely and are not to be forcibly converted, even if their form of religion amounts to devil worship.[43] By contrast, John Cotton is in favour of establishing a national church in New England, and is (albeit coyly) in favour of the conversion of the Native Americans so that they can enter it: 'we doe not say that it is a part of the Magistrates duty, to see all his Subjects to become Christians, if they were Pagans before: though wee say, it is his Duty to neglect no good meanes to help them onward to the knowledge and faith of Christ Jesus'.[44] Williams's wish that diverse groups and religions be tolerated on both sides of the Atlantic is in part, tendentious; he employs references to Jews, Turks and Native Americans as theoretical limit cases, deliberately extreme guarantees, as it were, of the toleration of Nonconformist Christians.

An Apologeticall Narration and The Arraignment of Mr. Persecution

Williams's *Bloudy Tenent* was one of a series of tolerationist texts precipitated by the debates of the Westminster Assembly. Another was a tract jointly written by several Independent members of the Assembly: Thomas Goodwin, Philip Nye, Sidrach Simpson, Jeremiah Burroughs and William Bridge. These men were dissenters from the Laudian era who had been living in exile in the Low Countries, and, returning to England, found that they had a new enemy: the centralised authority of the Presbyterian majority. Their *Apologeticall Narration* was published in 1643, prompting a flood of responses, including two tracts by William Prynne: *Twelve Considerable Serious Questions* (September 16) and *Independency Examined* (September 26).[45] Like Roger Williams, the authors of *An Apologeticall Narration* proposed the toleration of non-Christians, as long as they existed in a separate civil state. Prynne and the Scottish commissioners, however, ignored their opponents' emphasis on this condition and regarded the idea of including these 'heretic' groups as 'dangerous' and *'Licentious'*. Quoting Williams, Prynne wonders if the final result of Independency

> ... (as Master *Williams* in his late dangerous *Licentious Booke* determines) will not really resolve it selfe into this detestable conclusion. *That every man, whether he be Jew, Turk, Pagan, Arminian, Anabaptist, &c ought to be left to his owne free liberty of conscience, without any coertion or restraint, to embrace & publikely to professe what Religion, Opinion, Church-Government he pleaseth, & conceiveth to be truest, though never so erronious, false seditious, detestable in it selfe?*[46]

Prynne's use of the word 'Jew' here is clearly intended for exaggerated effect.

Another Independent tract in favour of religious liberty was *The Arraignment of Mr. Persecution*, written in 1645 by the Leveller Richard Overton. Dedicated to the Westminster Assembly, *The Arraignment* dramatises its critique of Presbyterianism in the form of a court hearing in which the character 'Persecution' is found guilty of curtailing religious liberty. He is defended by 'Sir Symon Synod' and 'Sir John Presbyter', and the jury consists of 'Mr Good-samaritane' (explicitly alluding in the text to William Walwyn) and 'Mr Trueth-and-peace' (explicitly alluding to Roger Williams). The publishing details are given as 'Martin Claw Clergie, Printer to the Reverend Assembly of Divines, and are to be sould at his Shop in Toleration Street, at the Signe of the Subjects Liberty, right opposite to Persecuting Court'. *The Arraignment* was published under the pseudonym 'Martin Marpriest', alluding to the 1580s Marprelate controversy, with its opposition between Elizabethan Conformists and Nonconformists.[47] *The Arraignment* is disapprovingly attributed to Henry Robinson in Prynne's *Fresh Discovery*,[48] and Thomas Edwards argues against it in his 1645 catalogue of heresies and sects, *Gangraeana*.[49]

Richard Overton's tract contains one of the most explicit statements in favour of tolerating Jews in this period. In the course of the character Liberty-of-Conscience's interpretation of the parable of the tares, Overton remarks that Mr Persecution 'depriveth the *Jewes* (as much as in him lieth) of their deliverance according to the Covenant God made with their Father from this their Captivity . . . yea, his nature is not to leave a man of them to pisse against the wall'.[50] Overton complains that the authorities of his day do not allow Jews to live among Christians, and he holds these restrictions responsible for the state in which Christians now find themselves:

> this Incendiary hath caused our Kings, and our Rulers, our Bishops and our priests not to suffer a Jew by authority to live amongst them; how then can we complaine of the vengance that is at this time upon us & our children, that have been so cruel, so hatefull, so bloody minded to them and their children? We have given them the *cup of trembling*, surely we must *tast of the dregges*: Hearken therefore no longer to those which teach this bloody doctrine of persecution.[51]

Although Overton's statements are striking, he nevertheless desires the conversion of the Jews, and blames Persecution for obstructing this aim:

> Now what hindreth their salvation and deliverance so much as persecution, for they are even led captive by PERSECUTION, and made slaves to him even to this day? And how shall they beleive, if they shall have no time given them to beleive? This *divelish Spirit* gives them not a minute, he will not suffer a Jew to live amongst the Christians, or come neare him: what hopes then is there the Jewes should be converted, where this Tyrant is in force?[52]

Overton discusses Jews and Jewishness in a manner fairly typical of seventeenth-century Christians – in terms of conversion and the abrogation of Jewish law – but he also mentions contemporary Jews and the possibility of their 'liv[ing] amongst' Christians. However, Overton's primary focus is '*the* Presbyterian *fist of wickednesse*', his opponents in the Westminster Assembly. Far from being a free-standing manifesto, Overton's text is intimately connected to those which are answering and defending it.[53] Moreover, by dramatising his tract in the form of a play and animating the participants in the controversy, Overton is emphasising its oppositional character. His pro-Jewish statements are, therefore, pragmatic as well as idealistic.

'A parallel made with the Jewish Sanhedrin'[54]

Common to all these tracts and pamphlets was an attempt to define the relationship between church and state, a dimension which has been underplayed in the later reception of these texts. This relationship was hammered out with the help of Jewish ideas, to an even greater extent than in the debates of the sixteenth century. In 1653, the Fifth Monarchist John Rogers suggested a plan to model the new Parliament on the Sanhedrin, with its 70 members, and the idea appeared in the manifesto of the Fifth Monarchy rebels in 1657.[55] Like the Anglican theologians Richard Hooker and Thomas Morton in the late sixteenth century, in the seventeenth it was the Erastians who most commonly invoked the example of the Sanhedrin to advance their vision of church government. The Presbyterians responded either by disputing the Erastian interpretation of the Sanhedrin's composition and jurisdiction, or by disallowing the use of Jewish precedents altogether. At stake was the question of whether or not the kings of Israel had held responsibility for both Tables of the Law – both the religious and the civil injunctions of the Ten Commandments – and whether these functions were combined in the Sanhedrin.

Before the Presbyterians adopted the role of the national church, George Gillespie wrote in opposition to the Erastians. In a tract entitled *A late dialogue betwixt a Civilian and a Divine* (1644), he refutes the Erastian claim that the Sanhedrin had control over spiritual affairs by claiming that his opponents simply confuse civil and religious institutions. Gillespie employs in this tract a dialogue format in which a curious citizen is progressively enlightened by a (Presbyterian) divine. The uninformed civilian tells his interlocutor that 'I have heard it asserted by some learned men, that among the Jewes . . . there was no such distinction as Church and State, but that the Jewish Church was the Jewish State, and the Jewish State the Jewish Church' and he goes on to wonder 'if it was so among them (whose formes you take in many particulars for patterns) I would fain know why it may not be so among us'. The divine enlightens the citizen by differentiating between the roles of church and state under the Law:

> Though the Iewish Church and Common wealth were for the most part not different materially, the same men being members of both, even as in all Christian republikes, yet they were formally different one from another, in regard of distinct Acts, Lawes, Courts, Officers, Censures, and Administrators. For, I. The Ceremoniall law given was given to them as a Church, the Judicial law given to them as a State. 2. They did not worship, doe sacrifice, pray, praise, &c. as a State; nor did they kill malefactors with the sword as a Church.[56]

Gillespie is here employing his idea of the Jewish commonwealth as evidence that Parliament should not interfere in religious affairs. This leads him to portray, for effect, the extreme scenario which he imagines would result from the adoption of the Jewish combination of civil and religious government:

> Must Ministers have vote in Parliament? Must they be civill Lawyers? Must all criminal and capitall Judgements be according to the Judiciall Law of *Moses*, and none otherwise? Must there be no civill punishments, without previous admonition of the offender? Must Parliaments sit, as it were in the Temple of God, and interpret Scripture, which sence is true, and which false, and determine controversies of faith and cases of conscience, and judge of all false doctrines? Yet all this must be, if there be a parallel made with the Jewish Sanhedrin.[57]

Although Gillespie displays his knowledge of Jewish precedents, he disavows them by invoking the absurd and 'Judaicall' state of affairs which, he believes, will be the consequence of drawing 'a parallel . . . with the Jewish Sanhedrin'. Gillespie is uncomfortable with the invocation of Jewish ideas in general:

> Now, if our opposites could prove that the Jewish Church was nothing but the Jewish State, and that the Jewish Church-government, was nothing but the Jewish State-government, and that the Jewes had never any supreame Sanhedrin but one onely, and that civil, and such as had the temporall coercive power of Magistracy (which they will never be able to prove) yet there are divers considerable reasons, for which that could be no president to us.[58]

Gillespie cites, as his sole reason for addressing these Jewish examples at all, the fact that they are mentioned by the other side. Like John Selden's opponents, who reluctantly admit that they have 'trod the pathes of *Mr. Seldens* Historie of Tithes',[59] Gillespie must follow the rules of pamphlet controversy:

> Observing that very much of *Erastus* his strength, and much of his followers their confidence, lieth in the old Testament, and Jewish Church, which (as they averre) knew no such distinction, as Civill Government, and Church Government; Civill Justice, and Church Discipline; I have thought good, first of all, to remove that great stumbling-block, that our way afterward lie fair and plain before us.[60]

Gillespie's evident failure to transcend the Jewish subject-matter of his opponents is transformed, positively, into an opportunity to label Erastians as Judaizers. Robert Baillie writes in a similar vein in 1645:

> The most of the house of Commons are downright Erastians: they are lyke to create us much more woe than all the sectaries of England . . . L'Emperour promised to write against Selden, for the Jewish ecclesiastick Sanhedrim, and their excommunication. This man is the head of the Erastians: his glory is most in the Jewish learning; he avows every where, that the Jewish State and Church was all one, and that so in England it must be, that the Parliament is the Church.[61]

Another tract by George Gillespie, *Aarons Rod Blossoming* (1646), received an answer later the same year in the form of an anonymous Erastian tract entitled *Nil Probas*. The author, who refers to Gillespie as 'our Presbyter', recommends that civil leaders take responsibility for the spiritual guardianship of their citizens.[62] He asks 'were not Priests and Levites Ministers of their *State* too? And their Judges *Church Officers* also? When *they* officiated in matters criminall, and *these* judged matters of the Lord?'[63] The author takes his examples not only from the Sanhedrin, but also from the Old Testament kings: 'those Levites did judge also IN THE SERVICE OF THE KING, I Chron. 26.30,32. And was not this judging, *of the same kind, in the same manner, or for the same ends*, with the Civill Rulers?'[64] *Nil Probas* concludes with a final answer to Gillespie: 'I doubt not but you already are convinc't of the unsatisfactorinesse of our Author his Arguments toward the proote of an *Ecclesiasticall Jewish Sanhedrin*', in other words, a Sanhedrin with religious jurisdiction alone.[65] The Erastian Hebraist John Lightfoot was also in favour of using Jewish precedents to prove the conjunction between church and state. During a discussion about whether or not it was possible to distinguish between different administrators in the Sanhedrin, in which he marshals quotations from both John Selden and Talmudic discussions of the Sanhedrin, Lightfoot writes that 'I grant, indeed, that there were elders in the Sanhedrin that were not priests or Levites, but withal they were civil magistrates, as our Parliament'.[66]

As these sources suggest, the association between Erastianism and Judaism was strong during this period; indeed, as the second chapter of this book illustrated, Parliament was associated during the Civil War with the Hebrew language. Erastianism, Judaism, Parliament and the work of continental scholars such as Hugo Grotius, Joseph Justus Scaliger and Jean Bodin were associated themes in this period; and writers like

Selden were their English proponents. Selden published his voluminous treatise, *De Synedriis et Praefecturis Juridicis Veterum Ebraorum* in the early 1650s; it described the constitution of Jewish administrative bodies such as the Sanhedrin, and argued that they had both religious and secular functions.[67] Presbyterians in the Assembly disapproved of this Erastian Hebraism. In Gillespie's *A late dialogue*, which argues against Selden's denial of ecclesiastical excommunication in the Jewish commonwealth, Gillespie couples Selden with the Hebraist Hugh Broughton, denouncing their acquaintance with Jewish history and literature: they are both 'most exquisitely acquainted with those studies'.[68]

During the debates between Presbyterians and Erastians in the early to mid-1640s, therefore, it was apparent that Erastians were enthusiastic consumers of Hebrew, Jewish history and rabbinic scholarship, and Presbyterians denied the relevance of this Jewish knowledge to the English Christian commonwealth. But with the consolidation of Presbyterianism as the national church, those, like George Gillespie and William Prynne, who had previously denied the application of Jewish precedents, were now strongly in favour of them, because they provided justification for the extension of the Presbyterian church's remit into the civil sphere. The Independents, who opposed the rise of the Presbyterian national church, were therefore now against the use of Jewish precedents, even while they advocated the toleration, in principle, of religious minorities such as Jews. This resulted, unexpectedly, in a situation in which those commentators who were in favour of the application of Jewish precedents were against the toleration of Jewish people.

For example, in spite of the tolerant stance adopted by Roger Williams on the treatment of dissident Christians and Jews, he was against the application of Jewish precedents to seventeenth-century England. This is because he reluctantly accepted that the religious and the political functions of the Sanhedrin had been combined, and this contradicted his belief in their ideal separation. Both sides, therefore, tended at times to agree that the Sanhedrin included within it both religious and political functions. But commentators such as Roger Williams rejected such Jewish precedents as appropriate ones for Christians to follow, declaring that the Sanhedrin, like other Jewish institutions, had been abrogated by the coming of Christ. Referring to the early church habit of retaining some Jewish practices for a period of time as a sign of respect to the Jews, Williams argues that this should not be used as a justification for tolerating corruption in the seventeenth-century church. Since he is advocating the separation of church and state, however, he is not so concerned if such corruption surfaces in civil society.

A printed marginal note in his *Bloudy tenent* draws a parallel between ancient Jewish practices and contemporary Popery: 'Toleration of Jewish ceremonies for a time upon some grounds in the Jewish Church, proves not toleration of Popish and Antichristian Ceremonies in the Christian Church, although in the State'. Williams elaborates this theme in the main body of the text:

> Can we thinke that because the tender Consciences of the *Iewes* were to be tendred in their *differences* of *meats*, that therefore persons must now bee tolerated in the *Church* (for I speake not of the *Civill State*) and that to the worlds end, in superstitious forbearing and forbidding of *flesh* in *Popish Lents*, and *superstitious Fridays* . . . in the observation of Popish *Christmas, Easter, Whitsontide*, and other superstitious Popish *Festivals*?[69]

For Williams, the precedent of ancient Israel is '*figurative* and *ceremoniall*' and no pattern for England to follow,[70] and the use of the word 'ceremoniall' here indicates Williams's disapproval of Jewish legalism; it is associated with Roman Catholic ceremonialism. If Williams is reluctant to draw inspiration from an institution which combined, as he is forced grudgingly to concede, both religious and political powers, he is also unwilling to employ the precedent of ancient Israel because of its Popish overtones.

Williams's opponents, by contrast, were in favour of applying the precedent of the Sanhedrin, even though they were against the toleration of Jews. As Williams observes, 'Persecutors seldom plead Christ but Moses for their author'.[71] With the rise of the Presbyterian national church, George Gillespie came to believe that the Sanhedrin was in fact an Erastian body, and that the power of the Jewish leader in the Sanhedrin should be retained by the head of the Christian state. This led Gillespie to argue, therefore, for the continuation of Jewish laws into Christianity: 'If God would have the Morall law transmitted from the Jewish people to the Christian people; then he would also have the Judiciall law transmitted from the Jewish Magistrate to the Christian Magistrate'.[72] This position was in marked contrast to the one he had held during his earlier debates with Erastians such as Prynne and Lightfoot. Despite calling for the retention of Jewish laws in Christian England, however, Gillespie opposed the toleration of Jewish people: he stridently refutes Williams's belief in religious liberty.[73]

It was not only Gillespie who disputed the interpretation of biblical Israel with Roger Williams. A similar exchange occurred when Prynne replied to Williams in his *Twelve Considerable Serious Questions* (which was also a reply to *An Apologeticall Narration*). Prynne was answered in turn by John Goodwin and his associates in *Certaine briefe observations and antiquaeries: On Master Prin's twelve questions about church-government* (October 4, 1644). Prynne countered with his *Full reply* (October 19, 1644), and so on.[74] Prynne's eighth and ninth questions, in his *Twelve Considerable Serious Questions* concern 'whether the concession of one *Catholike Church throughout the world*, denied by none: the . . . *Nationall Assemblie*, and Church of the *Israelites* under the Law . . . be not an infallible proofe and Justification of Nationall Churches; of a common Presbyterian, Classical government, to which particular Congregations persons ought to be subordinate, & an apparent subversion of the Novell Independent Invention?'[75] John Goodwin replied to Prynne, attacking his Presbyterian Erastianism, and complaining that 'you thinke Church-government must be ordered according to civill State, and be cast into that mould'.[76] Prynne, quoting his opponent correctly, objects to the fact that Goodwin disallows the Jewish precedent:

> To the eighth *Quere* he gives a negative Answer, First in generall, next in particular to some instances. First he grants, *that there was a Nationall Church* (yea Nationall assemblies, Parliaments, determining church-affaires,) *of the Jewes, but these* (saith he) *cannot be a pattern for us now, because the covenant of the Gospell is not made with any one particular Nation, as with the Jewes, but to all Nations that embrace the Gospel, and beleeve in Christ; you have no promise nor prophesie of any Nation to be holy to God but the Jewes Nation, when they shall bee called againe.*[77]

In other words, Prynne is pointing out that Goodwin himself admits there was a national church under the Jews, even if, according to Prynne, he mistakenly believes that this precedent cannot apply to the Christian world. Here it is Prynne who is in favour of using Jewish ideas.

In a final twist, Independents like Goodwin looked for alternative precedents in biblical Israel, precedents which would reinforce their own vision of the English religious and political constitution: they found one such example in the Tabernacle, the portable tent-like shrine in which the Israelites worshipped during their wanderings in the wilderness. Prynne scorns this strategy:

> Independents have not the least precept or example for any solemne Covenant made betwixt God and men, *to walke in the wayes of God, &c.*

> but onely in the *old Testament, and Church of the Israelites, and that no private congregationall, but publike Nationall covenant, prescribed by the supreme temporall Magistrate and Assembly*, not by the Priests or private Synagogues . . . the pattern of it [the National Church of the Israelites] under the Law a better president for the Church under the Gospel, (of which it was a type and fore-runner) then *the pattern of the Tabernacle shewed in the Mount* (so frequent in your Lips and Books) a president for your *Independent Modell*, to which it hath no analogy.[78]

In other words, Prynne is arguing that no precedent exists in the Old Testament, which would corroborate the Independents' style of church government; the only applicable model is that of the national church or Temple. The Independents were indeed keen to use the Tabernacle as a precedent for their church, because it embodied more effectively than the Temple at Jerusalem the Independents' vision of the true church, existing against the odds as an island of true faith within the civil state.

In these debates, references to the Israelites' Temple, Tabernacle and Sanhedrin were passed back and forth between Presbyterians, Erastians and Independents without, it seems, much awareness that such ideas may have been related to the toleration of contemporary Jews. These Christians did not even appear to regard biblical Judaism as part of the same coherent genealogy as 'real' Jews, or realise that their employment of Jewish precedents might result in sympathy towards the Jewish people. A text such as Williams's *The Bloudy Tenent* is full of references to the 'Old and New Israel', by which he means biblical Israelites and contemporary Christians, respectively. In his typological discourse, Old Testament Israel is sublimated time and again into Christianity, leaving little room for contemporary Jews. Invoking the great wars of the Old Testament for his own troubled times, Williams writes:

> What State, what Kingdome, what warres and combats, victories and deliverances can parallel this people, but the Spirituall and mysticall *Israel* of *God* in every *Nation* and *Country* of the *World*, typed out by that small typicall handful, in that little spot of ground the land of *Canaan*? The *Israel* of *God* now, men and women, fight under the Great *Lord Generall*, the Lord *Iesus Christ* . . . they are Spirituall *conquerours* . . .[79]

In other words, contemporary Christians are spiritual, rather than legalistic or material warriors, as the biblical Jews were. The 'small typicall handful' no longer exists for Williams, raising the question of who it was, exactly, that Christians contemplated readmitting to England in the following decade?

***

This chapter has considered tolerationism in the light of broader, ongoing debates about the relationship between church and state. Like the earlier, sixteenth-century debates, these ones were highly dependent on Jewish sources. Presbyterians, Erastians and Independents fought over the interpretation of the ancient Jewish commonwealth in an attempt to articulate their favoured English religious constitution. Although Independents such as Roger Williams were in favour of toleration, at times extending the idea, at least on paper, to Jews, such statements were often more figurative than they appear; and these commentators were against the application of Jewish precedents to Christian England. Their Presbyterian opponents, on the other hand, were in favour of invoking Jewish sources, but they opposed the toleration of dissident Christians or Jews.

The final chapter of this book explores the controversy over the proposed readmission of the Jews; during this controversy, the clergyman William Hughes argued against applying the example of religious toleration in Amsterdam to England. Hughes writes that 'Reason of State makes the Dutch-men tolerate all Religions but the Popish. From whence shall it not presently be concluded, that all their neighbours should do the like'.[80] In other words, political pragmatism has prompted the authorities in Amsterdam to allow a variety of religious groups to co-exist in the city state. Arguing the opposite position, an anonymous pamphlet published in 1609 had used the same formula: 'It standeth with the reason of State to allow the Toleration desired by us'. The 'reason of state' argument may appear odd to the modern reader, accustomed to regarding religious toleration as a matter of principle rather than pragmatism. But, as this chapter has argued, those who promoted toleration in the seventeenth century did so for a reason: they were in favour of a particular arrangement of church and state which would allow religious minorities to practise their faith undisturbed. Tolerationists posited the most extreme examples of religious inclusion they could imagine as limit cases: church and state should be so separate, they argued, that even Jews could live amongst us.

5
Contesting Readmission: Common Law and the English Constitution

On 14 December 1656, John Evelyn recorded in his diary: 'Now were the *Jewes* admitted'.[1] Soon after, the clergyman and writer Alexander Ross, who had already displayed his interest in the Jews by writing a four volume study on Jewish history, *Rerum Judaicarum memorabilium*, set about preparing his fellow citizens for the influx of Jews to England by explaining their religion and customs:

> I am confident Reader, thou canst not be Ignorant, of that which is so commonly reported: namely the coming in of the Jewes to live amongst us: wherefore I conceive it must needs yeeld some satisfaction to thee, to know with what kind of people we shall have to do. This is the motive, by which I am induced to present unto thee, this present work; wherein thou hast plainly deciphered, their Lawes, Rites, customes, and manners both ecclesiastical and civill. From whence I shall not here draw any conclusion, either pro, or con, but leave it to thy more serious judgment.

Although the Whitehall Conference ended in failure, it prompted a great deal of speculation and comment; and it appeared that, for the first time, English Christians were finally taking the existence of contemporary Jews seriously. The previous chapter described how tolerationist statements were less literal and benign than they sometimes appear; this one considers whether, in 1656, Christians were now at last considering the plight of the Jewish people; because, if readmission did not actually happen, the debates around it certainly did. As this chapter will reveal, however, those debates were also concerned with matters far removed from the welfare of Jews.

Motives for and against readmission

Two accounts of the Whitehall Conference were written; one by the Baptist preacher Henry Jessey; the other by Nathaniel Crouch, who wrote under the name of Robert or Richard Burton. As these accounts record, the Whitehall Conference set out to answer two questions: first, whether the Jews had any legal right to live in England, and second, if they did have that right, how their resettlement should be managed. The first question emerged from the confusion which surrounded the expulsion of the Jews in the thirteenth century: there was considerable disagreement about the circumstances of the expulsion, its ramifications and even the date on which it occurred. Medieval chroniclers recorded the date as 1290, but the seventeenth-century legal historian Edward Coke argued that since no expulsion order had been found, the Jews probably left England voluntarily as a result of the statute banning usury in 1275, which was ordered by Edward I, and signed by Parliament. According to Coke, there was no law against the Jews returning to England, as long as they did not practise usury. Other seventeenth-century historians, such as John Stow, came to a slightly different conclusion: Stow claimed that Edward I had expelled them personally, by royal prerogative, because the Jewish merchants living in the country at the time were draining the country's assets. Since the King's ruling applied only to Jews who were living in England in 1290, Stow argued, there was no law forbidding the Jews' return to England now.[2] A number of lawyers in the Conference took a similar view: the eighteenth-century historian, D'Blossiers Tovey, who draws on seventeenth-century accounts, writes that 'to the first point the *Lawyers* answer'd very briefly, that if their Return was judg'd convenient for the *State*, they knew of no *Law* that oppos'd it'; others, however, disagreed.[3]

Notwithstanding the eventual outcome of the Conference, Anglo-Jewish historians have long speculated about the reasons why some Christians were in favour of readmission at all; and two factors are generally cited: millenarianism and mercantilism.[4] There was a popular belief in the early to mid-seventeenth century that the return of the Jews to England, along with their conversion, would hasten Christ's Second Coming.[5] Since the biblical Flood had occurred in 1656 BC, many Christians thought that the Apocalypse was scheduled for 1656 AD. Furthermore, these Christians noted that in Deuteronomy it was prophesied that the Second Coming would be preceded by the dispersal of the Jews to the ends of the earth. According to medieval Jewish literature, the French name 'Angleterre' meant 'the extreme angle or end of the earth', suggesting that if the Jews were readmitted there, the millenarian prophecy would be enacted. But first the Jews had to be found; and accordingly, there was an upsurge of interest in the ten lost tribes of Israel: many speculated for example, that the American Indians were descended from one of the tribes; hence the testimony of Antonio de Montezinos.[6] Commentators who wrote about the readmission of the Jews invariably returned to the themes of millenarianism, the fear that God would punish the English for mistreating the Jews, and hopes for their speedy conversion. Millenarian beliefs were, after all, becoming common currency across Europe, and these beliefs fuelled the prospect of readmitting the Jews; Menasseh ben Israel himself made use of them in his attempts to persuade Cromwell's government.

Many Christian commentators referred to the Jews' harsh treatment in medieval times, particularly their expulsion in 1290. These commentators stressed the Christian virtue of harbouring strangers, and warned that God would punish those who did not show mercy to the Jews. They discussed the fact that the Jews were expelled under Edward I because they practised usury, and pointed out that usury was currently practised in many European countries, including England; and they referred to fears that Christians would be seduced by and converted to Judaism, offering assurances that this would not happen. One of the participants in the Conference, Joseph Caryll, cites the example of the 'many Protestants who were persecuted in the Reign of Q Mary, and since have been kindly received as Strangers in other countries', and argues that

> We should the more pity and harbour our fled Strangers, especially persecuted Jews. That the cruel Injuries and Inhumanities used towards that Nation (that intruded not, but were invited into England) by our Kings and Government, whereby multitudes of them were kill'd & drowned in the Thames, & the Sea, &c. might still lye as a Sin upon these Kingdoms, which our kindness to their Survivors and Successors may make some kind of amends and satisfaction for.[7]

The millenarian writer and agent for Cromwell, John Dury, writes that 'taking Jews as they are, that is, men of a strange Nation; Who are banished from the Country of their inheritance, and made pilgrims and wanderers through the world; A People in misery and distress, and so an Object of hospitality, there is no doubt, but they may lawfully be received into any civil Societie of men, to live and have a being therein, as strangers'.[8] Henry Jessey calls attention to the fact that Jews have been in 'very great streighs in many places; multitudes in *Polonia, Lithuania,* and *Prussia* . . . also the Jews in *France, Spain, Portugal,* & in the *Indies,* under the *Spanish,* &c. if they are professed Jews, must wear a badge of it; & are exposed to so many violencies, mocks, & cruelties; which to avoid, many dissemble themselves to be Roman Catholicks'.[9] Like Joseph Caryll, he reminds his readers that 'Many of the good people here, being persecuted in Queen *Maries* dayes, and under the Prelates since, have been kindly harboured as strangers in other Lands; and therefore should the[y] more pity and harbour persecuted strangers, especially the persecuted Jews'.[10]

However, the very same writers who called attention to the harsh treatment of the Jews demonised them according to standard anti-Jewish stereotypes. For example, although Edward Spencer, a Member of Parliament who replied to Menasseh ben Israel's *Hope of Israel,* was complimentary towards Menasseh and ostensibly supportive of his project, addressing him as 'my deare brother Menasseh Ben Israel, the Hebrew Philosopher', he also writes: 'Seeing you would yet have us love you more and more, I will tell you what is the true bond of Love & the greatest obligation, even true Religion, wherein because you fall short, I cannot yet love you so much as I would, but I doe abundantly pitty you, that you yet live I darkenesse and the shadow of death, and will not entertain the light which your Adonai and ours hath sent into the world.'[11] Spencer goes on,

> For examine your selves in what is revealed: have not all of you a bloody issue about your bodies . . . and doe not the Italians say, *they smell a Jew before they discerne him with their eyes*? Did not your forefathers say, *His blood be upon us and our children*? Was not his prophesie fulfilled in the *destruction of your Temple,* and the dispersion of the reliques of your nation? . . . O brethren, be not wilfully blinde. My consent ye shall have, that you and your people shall live in *England,* and have meeting places to worship *Adonai,* but no place for sacrifices, for that were to deny Christ, as your owne Countryman . . . And ye all bee allowed to expound the Old Testament, and Christians shall be admitted to heare you, and you shall admit them to teach you.[12]

As far as the reality of readmission is concerned, Spencer lays down certain conditions which he believes must be met before the Jews can be allowed back: Jews should not be allowed to circumcise their sons, and if they do, half the parents' estate should be confiscated. When they die, unless they have converted to Christianity, they should leave only a third of their estate to their children, giving a third to the state and a third 'to the maintenance of converted Jews'.[13] They should be made to pay double taxes, and be barred from forming any Guilds or corporations. John Dury, one of the most outspoken supporters of readmission, also describes the Jews' 'covetous practices and biting usury, and other subtilties in trade'.[14] Alexander Ross explains his motives for writing a descriptive account of the Jews thus:

> That so having before your eyes their sensuall stupidity, and obdurate incredulity, together with the great wrath and severity of God against them, we may be put in serious remembrance of the wonderfull bounty and goodnes of God unto us, and so be stirred up to render him due praise and glory, lest for our ungratefulnesse the light of the Gospel should be taken from us, and we involved in our pristine darkness.[15]

Invariably, therefore, those who were in favour of tolerating and readmitting the Jews were also in favour of converting them to Christianity. For example, in reply to Menasseh's *The Hope of Israel*, Edward Spencer argues that Nonconformist Christianity and Judaism share many similarities: both religions adhere to the Old Testament, abhor idolatry, and uphold the Sabbath. But Spencer goes on to berate Menasseh and other Jews for not giving up their faith, admitting that 'truely my bowells yearne for your conversion'.[16] Alongside his support for readmission, John Dury emphasises that 'the intention of the State in admitting of them, is not to have profit or temporall advantages by them; (which may be had aswell by our owne industry, and perhaps better, without theirs) but rather out of Christian love and compassion towards them, and in witness of our thankfulness to God, for the good which hath been derived from them to us; and for the hope which we have, that all his goodness shall be fulfilled both in them and us, when the Messiah shall returne in his Glory'.[17] Likewise, the Baptist preacher Thomas Collier writes that the objections against the Jews' readmission have prompted him 'to write a few lines in their behalf, not to vindicate them in their practice or profession; but in bowels of compassion towards them in their dark estate, believing that God will (according to his promises in the Scriptures of truth) in his appointed time cause the true light to shine unto them'.[18] An anonymous writer known as 'Philo-Judaeus', who refers in flattering terms to Edward Spencer, announces in his Epistle to Menasseh his hope that Cromwell will readmit the Jews: 'I do submissively propose, that the Supreme Authority of this Nation would be pleased to hearken to those Propositions which intend their admission into England'.[19] However, Philo-Judaeus's ultimate aim is, once again, the Jews' conversion: he continues, 'I shall use all the strong motives that my weak capacity will afford me, by the which I would excite all my native Countrymen to use much study in the safe-guarding and bringing home this poor straid sheep of Israel'.[20] The conversionary motivation behind millenarian Christians' desire to readmit the Jews does not negate that desire, but it does complicate it.

Mercantilism is often cited as the other primary motivation behind pro-readmission sentiments.[21] England's trading activities during this period, particularly the attempt to compete with the Dutch, were indeed significant, and the Jews' trading connections with the East Indies meant that they were attractive agents. Many of the participants in the readmission debates cited mercantile interest as their pragmatic (and often reluctant) motive for supporting Jewish readmission. In 1647, the Independent army chaplain Hugh Peter (1598–1660) recommends in his pamphlet *A Word for the Armie* that 'Merchants may have all manner of encouragement, the law of Merchants set up, and strangers, even *Jewes* admitted to trade, and live with us'.[22] Other commentators, however, argued the opposite case, fearing that Jewish merchants would provide harmful competition: Henry Jessey records that during the Whitehall Conference, 'The *Merchants* said; *such an in-let would be to enrich Forreigners, and impoverish English Merchants*'.[23] Millenarianism and mercantilism were significant factors in the discussions about readmission, but they were not the only ones.

As the first chapter of this book illustrated, Anglo-Jewish historians have tended to emphasise the informal nature of readmission; but this traditional evocation of a characteristically English act – one which was practical and benign, based on empirical facts rather than a prescription from above – does not resonate with the intensely legalistic, hair-splitting nature of the debates about readmission that took place in and around the Whitehall Conference: John Thurloe, Secretary of State between 1652 and 1658, reported that the matter of readmission was 'debated with much candour and ingenuitye, and without any heat'.[24] Indeed, the precise conditions of citizenship which could be granted to 'aliens' resident in England were of great importance in seventeenth-century England; and the failure of the Whitehall Conference to determine the status of English Jews led not only to a great amount of confusion, but also to constant threats to the Jews' livelihood and very existence as a community, in the second half of the seventeenth century and after. Frequent attacks were made on the Jews' continued residence in England, on the grounds of their ambiguous legal status.[25]

If, as chapter 1 described, readmission is understood to have been an informal event, the motives of millenarianism, mercantilism and religious toleration sufficiently explain the motivations of English Christians, because they pertain to the existence of a Jewish presence in England, whether formally readmitted or not. But in D'Blossiers Tovey's account of the Whitehall Conference, he writes that 'The *Preachers* kept pelting one another so furiously, with *Texts of Scri*pture, and spent so much Time in turning their Bibles for *Proofs*, and wiping their *Spectacles*, that the Debates continu'd for four Days; tho' very little was said on the second Question'.[26] The Conference was primarily concerned with the first question it set out to resolve, that of whether the Jews had any legal right to live in England, rather than the 'second Question', about the process by which the Jews' readmission could be achieved; in other words, with the question of formal, rather than practical, readmission. As this chapter will argue, it was the exact circumstances of the Jews' expulsion under Edward I, and the legal possibility of readmitting them under Cromwell, which were subject to detailed, even pedantic, debate; because it was these issues which had ramifications for English commentators at the time.[27] The first clue to the existence of this wider context is that the debate about readmission extended well beyond the texts normally discussed – the accounts of the Whitehall Conference and the millenarian pamphlets which accompanied it. In fact, the issue of readmission appears in a larger network of polemical tracts and pamphlets, which are not ostensibly concerned with the Jews at all; and, moreover, those who supported readmission, and those who rejected it, came from opposing sides of a pre-existent political divide.[28]

Readmission and Common Law

In 1656, the prolific Puritan controversialist, William Prynne, produced yet another addition to the mountain of tracts and pamphlets published during the turbulent years of the Civil War and Interregnum. Running to more than 250 pages, it was rather misleadingly entitled *A short demurrer to the Jewes Long discontinued remitter into England. Comprising, An exact Chronological Relation of their first Admission into, their ill Deportment, Misdemeanors, Condition, Sufferings, Oppressions, Slaughters, Plunders, by popular Insurrections, and regal Exactions in; and their total, final Banishment by Iudgement and Edict of Parliament, out of England.*[29] The first part of Prynne's title referred to the fact that Jews had not been permitted to live in England since Edward I expelled them in 1290. As the second part indicates, Prynne's tract was a detailed history of the Jews from the time of William the Conqueror until their expulsion. Despite his claim that he was offering *'an exact Chronological Relation'* of the history of the Jews, Prynne's *Demurrer* is highly tendentious. His aim is to demonstrate that the Jews' diabolical behaviour throughout the medieval era justified their expulsion, and proved that they should never be allowed to return to England again. It was no accident that Prynne's tract appeared in the mid-1650s: it was first circulated during the Whitehall Conference,[30] and its intervention is cited by numerous historians as a decisive factor in the Conference's failure.[31] *A Short Demurrer* is certainly Judeophobic; but what has escaped comment is the fact that it was written in reply to another tract: a treatise on governance and domestic policy, printed in 1651 by Hugh Peter, and entitled *Good work for a good magistrate*. Prynne was not alone in replying to Peter; later that year the lawyer Rice Vaughan (fl. 1650) also responded to Peter in the form of a treatise on legal methodology, *A Plea for the Common-Laws of England*.

Hugh Peter was one of the ministers appointed to discuss readmission with the Committee of the Council of State when Menasseh ben Israel presented his petition in 1655. He stated his pro-readmission views as early as 1647 in a pamphlet entitled *A Word for the Armie*, where he recommended that 'strangers, even *Jewes* admitted to trade, and live with us'.[32] Hugh Peter's greater interest, however, was in the reform of the law. Hugh Peter lived in Massachusetts between 1635 and 1641, and in 1636, the colony appointed a committee to draft a new set of laws, which included Peter and John Cotton. Peter became minister at Salem in 1636, taking over the post from Roger Williams. He returned to England in 1641, and in January 1652 was included on the committee to reform the law appointed by Parliament; he later became chaplain to the army. A contemporary of Peter's, Nathaniel Ward (1578–1652), trained as a lawyer in London, and in 1629, fled to New England to escape Archbishop Laud. Like Peter, Ward was also involved in drawing up laws for the colony of Massachusetts, a few years later than Peter, and his 'Body of Liberties' found more favour in the colony than Peter's proposals had done. Ward's proposals were a great influence on *The Lawes and Liberties of Massachusetts*, which were finally adopted in 1644, and which combined biblical precepts with Common Law precedents. When Peter returned to England, he brought with him a preference for the codification and simplification of the law in line with biblical principles, while Ward, who returned in 1646, believed that some Common Law should be retained. After all, it was easier to codify the law in a small, new colony in Massachusetts, but harder in the context of England's ancient legal system. While Ward and Peter appeared to have disagreed about the ideal ratio of Old Testament commandments to historical precedents in the law in Massachusetts, therefore, this debate became a feature in England too, as the committee for legal reform set up by Parliament made reference to the New England law code.[33] The disagreement between Ward and Peter fed into a wider seventeenth-century controversy, therefore, between those who advocated the application of Canon or Civil law, also known as 'natural' or 'moral' law, and those who advocated Common Law, or the use of accumulated historical precedents.[34] It is this controversy which features in the exchanges between Hugh Peter, William Prynne and Rice Vaughan, and which intersects with the issue of readmission.[35]

Peter's legal interests are reflected in his *Good Work for a good magistrate*, where he reveals his lack of enthusiasm for the methodology of Common Law. He suggests that the historical records kept in the Tower of London, useful to common lawyers in compiling lists of precedents, should be burned, being merely 'monuments of tyranny'. Peter goes on to criticise the common lawyers' habit of assembling copious amounts of historical evidence to support legal recommendations:

> For a Bodie of Laws, I know none but such as should bee the result of sound reason, nor do I know anie such reason, but what the God of wisdom hath appointed. Therefore the Moral Law (that short Law called ten words) is doubtles best; to which *Moses's* judicials added, with *Solomon's* Rules and experiments, will be compleat. I wish our Lawyers would urge these for Law; and not those obsolete presidents, which will hardly prove, or make a Sea man's suit to fit our occasions. *Neccesitie* is the mother, and *ill manners* together, of the best Laws.[36]

By favouring the brevity of the Ten Commandments over Common Law, therefore, Peter is making an implicit attack on the lawyers' profession and habits: why accumulate precedents, he argues, when moral guidance from the Bible can suffice?

Prynne and Vaughan react angrily to Peter's attack on their historicist method. Prynne's 1656 *Short Demurrer*, after all, relies on records kept in the Tower: 'the first Records of our former Kings now extant (except some few Charters, and Exemplifications of them in *Leiger-books*, Records, and Histories) are those of King *Iohn* preserved in the Tower of London, and *Exchequer*'.[37] Peter's proposal that the records be burnt is just one suggestion contained in his *Good Work*, among a varied raft of reforms, including those regarding matters of religion, the poor, the navy and merchandising. But Vaughan, in his reply to Peter's text, chooses to focus on this proposal only. Vaughan acknowledges this selectiveness in the subtitle of his text: '*Or, An Answer to a Book entituled, a good work for a good Magistrate:. . . (Published by Mr. Hugh Peters:) So far as concerns his Proposals touching the said Laws*'. In his introduction, Vaughan foregrounds the attack on Common Law in Peter's tract by claiming that 'the dint [main thrust] of Mr Ps. Book is against my own Profession'. The book, which contains Peter's statements in favour of readmission, is not *Good Work for a good magistrate*, but his earlier *A Word for the Armie* (1647). Peter's comments on readmission are brief compared to his treatment of other topics, and when Nathaniel Ward replies to Peter, he ignores the reference to readmission, focusing instead on Peter's attack on 'the fundamentall Laws of the Land', as well as his infringement of 'the Authority of Parliament'.[38] In his reply to Peter, Ward is concerned, not with the matter of readmission, but with the legal and constitutional content of Peter's text. Prynne's reply to *Good Work for a Good Magistrate*, by contrast, refers back to the short passage on readmission from *A Word for the Armie* and uses it as the pretext for a blistering, two-volume attack on the presence – past and future – of the Jews in England.

At first sight, Prynne's tract appears to be simply an outpouring of virulent hatred towards the Jews. But curiously, it should be remembered that it is not *A Word for the Armie* that Prynne's *Short Demurrer* is replying to, but rather his later text, *Good Work*, which contains nothing on the subject of Jewish readmission. Moreover, a close reading of Prynne's text reveals the presence of a further purpose: he is deliberately employing Common Law methodology to record in cumulative detail the history of the Jews in England. Prynne's account catalogues what he regards as the Jews' abominable behaviour throughout the history of England, implying that if they were unprofitable to the state before 1290, it was inadvisable to readmit them now; his notion of the law is historical: what was good for the English in the thirteenth century should be enforced in the seventeenth. In reply to *Good Work for a Good Magistrate*, Prynne responds to Peter's suggestion that the records in the Tower should be burned, and in doing so he reveals, crucially, the function of his attack on the readmission of the Jews: it is an illustrative example of the benefits of Common Law:

> I hope *the God of the Spirits of all flesh*, will in this stupid, selfish, degenerated age, raile up some heroick active publike *English* Spirits of all these rankes, not only to preserve our precious antient Records from *Hugh Peters* designed *Martyrdom*, but likewise diligently to study and extract such useful collections out of them, as I have hinted, for the benefit, honor of their Native country, and advantage of succeeding ages, of which I have here given them a *leading president* in these *Historical, Legal, Chronological collections* relating only to our *English Iews*.[39]

Although Prynne's treatise is ostensibly about the history of the Jews, its form is as important as its content. In other words, the book is a performative exemplification of the use of history in legal argument. While *A Short Demurrer* explicitly argues against readmission, therefore, it also operates as a worked example of this legal methodology, in which Jewish readmission is simply the chosen subject-matter, the *'leading president'*; as signified by the phrase 'relating only to our *English Iews'*. Indeed, Prynne declares that the reason he has restricted himself to the history of the Jews is that his years of imprisonment in the Tower for seditious pamphleteering have kept him from wider study. Prynne has provided the nation with this *'leading president'* because 'the transcendent malice of my former causelesse Enemies, in *debarring me . . . from all accesse to the Tower Records* . . . so much impoverished, so far disabled me from these *Noble Undertakings* . . . that I must recommend the pursuite of them to some other Gentlemen of lesser years'.[40] Prynne thus picks up on one of Peter's suggested reforms for England, the readmission of the Jews, and feeds it into a much broader intervention about the law, which, as the following pages will illustrate, was an issue with profound Parliamentary and proto-nationalist resonance.

An anonymous commentator, 'D.L.', wrote in defence of Hugh Peter against Prynne. D.L. regards it as unreasonable that Prynne interprets Peter's wish that the records in the Tower be burned, as an attack on Common Law: 'The second thing that inflames his spirit so to rage and rant it *ad random in folio*, is (as he says) that *Mr. Peters* should desire and would have all the ancient Records of the Nation to be burn'd, and that makes him bestir himself for fear least the common Law Records should be included in the Number'. Yet at this point D.L. himself embarks upon an extended digression about styles of law, continuing for several pages.

He regards the records in the Tower as 'Monuments of Tyranny', and agrees that they should be burned, and refers to 'the common Law it self honoured and indeed idolized by Mr. *Prynn*'.[41] D.L. evokes the spectacle of lawyers 'searching old rotten Records,'[42] and objects to the way in which the historical precedents which comprise Common Law are being presented as 'unalterable'; he believes the law should, instead, be able to respond to changing circumstances: 'We know the very constitution of men in several ages to differ . . . must it needs be so, also now, and of force binding for the *future*? Because there stands an old House built by [William] the *Conqueror*, may it not be *altered*, or if this age thinks and findes it fitting, utterly pull'd down?'[43] D.L. employs a sympathetic reference to the Jews as a way of criticising Prynne further: 'But how would he have had matter to have so inveigh'd against the noble Nation of the *Jews*, had not he been furnish'd with the *old Records* (as he calls them) of *Friers* and P*opish Legends* to make his Book to swell?'[44] Although D.L. refers to the Jews as 'noble', his words illustrate nevertheless how they have become a legal precedent in a wider debate.

Parliament and the expulsion of the Jews

The second term in Ward's answer to Peter's *A Word for the Armie*, the 'Authority of Parliament', signals the next issue with which readmission was intertwined. Ever since the beginning of the seventeenth century, Common Law had been associated with Parliament, and, as the Civil War got underway, it was allied contentiously with the Parliamentary faction. Rice Vaughan's *Plea for the Common-Laws of England* (1651) is addressed, for example, to 'the Parliament of England, The Supream Power of this Common-Wealth'.[45] The Parliamentary faction had a stake in the issue of readmission because the Common Law was being threatened by the supporters of readmission; but they also had a more substantive interest. There was a great deal of discussion during the Whitehall Conference about who had exiled the Jews in the first place, and whether or not there had been an act of Parliament for their banishment. There was a drive to establish the facts of the expulsion, indeed, not only to debate the proposals to readmit the Jews, but also because those facts served other argumentative purposes altogether.

As well as narrating the conduct of Jews in England's history, Prynne's *Short Demurrer* also discusses at length the circumstances surrounding the expulsion of the Jews in 1290, as does a 1656 treatise by the minister William Hughes entitled *Anglo-Judaeus* and written in reply to

Menasseh ben Israel's plea for readmission.⁴⁶ According to these accounts, Edward I is said to have returned home from Gascony, France, in 1289 with large debts, which he attempted to repay with a tax he obtained by bargaining with Parliament. In return for agreeing to raise the tax, Parliament demanded the expulsion of the Jews from England. As James Shapiro, and before him Kenneth Stow and Robert Stacey, argued, the expulsion in 1290 was best understood in the context of power struggles between king and Parliament; indeed, during a major alteration in the constitution of England.⁴⁷ The obvious parallels with contemporary politics made the events of 1290 irresistible fodder for mid-seventeenth-century controversialists. During the interregnum, the idea that Edward I might have expelled the Jews by exercising the royal prerogative took on particularly negative connotations. Predictably, some commentators regarded the act as an abuse of royal power; others, like William Prynne, denied that the King had acted on his own, arguing instead that '[the Jews'] banishment was by the unanimous desire, judgment, edict, and decree both of the King and his Parliament, and not by the King alone'. This banishment was 'total . . . and likewise final: never to return into England'.⁴⁸

Those in favour of Parliament, therefore, resurrected and reinterpreted the historical precedent of the expulsion in order to argue in favour of the legislative powers of Parliament in this new, analogous case. They believed that the specific jurisdiction which had ordered the expulsion in the first place was the body that had the power to overturn the decision now. According to Prynne, 'None once banished the Realm by judgement or Act of Parliament, can, may, or ought, by the fundamental and known common Laws of *England*, to be restored and recalled again, but only by a like judgement, Act, and Restitution in full Parliament'.⁴⁹ Prynne refers to the expulsion, in other words, as a way of denouncing the arbitrary power of kings, and he disapproves of readmission – to a large extent – because he believes that his Parliamentary ancestors played an important part in expelling the Jews in the first place. Understandably, Prynne is galled by the inconvenient fact that he cannot locate the actual thirteenth-century Parliamentary decree of expulsion, as he reluctantly admits in his *Short Demurrer*.⁵⁰

At times, Prynne's history of the Jews in England degenerates into simple diatribe; he claims for example that medieval Jews

> were so exceeding execrable and detestable to the people in all places where they resided, both for their infidelity, blasphemies, apostacies, enmity to Christ and Christianity, circumcising and crucifying

Christian Children, clipping of coin, falsifying of Charters, extortion, brokage, usury, frauds, unconscionable Jewish cut-throat dealing, and discrepancy of maners from the English, that many places and ports opposed their coming over, other Towns . . . purchased exemptions or removals of them.[51]

By appealing to traditional prejudices about Jews – their murdering of Christian children, their financial greed and so on – Prynne is able to bolster his argument against readmitting the Jews through recourse to age-old prejudices. But Prynne's derogatory attitudes also serve a political purpose, too: his representation of medieval Jews works to vindicate Parliament's role in their expulsion. In the same vein, he invokes the liberal treatment of the Jews by English kings through the ages as a way of strengthening his critique of the monarchy. He refers, for example, to the conciliatory stance taken by King John, who during his thirteenth-century reign granted 'large Liberties and Charters . . . to the Jewish High Priests and Jews throughout his Dominions'.[52] The expulsion narrative provides Prynne, therefore, with a way of reinforcing the role of Parliament in England's history, while at the same time denouncing monarchical supremacy. For commentators such as Prynne and Hughes, the thirteenth-century events were ripe for interpretation according to current polemical needs, and the expulsion and readmission of the Jews offered ideal pretexts for contributions to a constitutional debate.

English nationhood

The debates about expulsion and readmission were connected with a further dimension, too: an evolving story about the English nation. Since the beginning of the seventeenth century, legal experts such as Edward Coke had emphasised the association between Common Law, Parliament and English national sentiment, an association which was reinforced by Prynne, Vaughan and Ward. As Richard Helgerson has noted, 'the common law was quintessentially English',[53] and the reputation of Parliament as a long-standing English institution was bolstered by its supporters' historical accounts. Prynne believed that both the practice of Common Law and the writing of English history were important nation-building exercises. His *Short Demurrer* contains an extensive eulogy of historical records which represents them as directly beneficial to the nation:

> these old Records which he [Hugh Peter] would have burnt, contain in them all the antient Rights, Titles, Evidences, Charters, Agreements,

Leagues, Compacts of the Kings, Kingdom, Nation and people of *England*, to all their pristine and present Dominions, Jurisdictions, Prerogatives, Preheminences, Priviledges, Hereditaments and enjoyments . . . as they are a Kingdom, Nation, Republike & body Politick in general; whose ancient undoubted Rights, Titles to all or any of our Dominions, Territories, Jurisdictions, Royalties, cannot otherwise be cleared & judicially evidenced . . . but by our old Records, the only publike evidences of the whole Kingdom and English Nation.[54]

According to Prynne, English history, as recorded in these documents, should be in the control of his beloved Parliament: he suggests that they be 'faithfully transcribed and methodologically digested into a *Parliamentary Chronicle'*, which would 'far excell all other Abridgements, collections, Reports, Institutes . . . as the richest Diamond exceeds the basest pibble [pebble], and bring more honour, benefit to the English Nation, than all the *Shepheards Calendars'*.[55]

An important foundational era for proto-nationalist historians of England was that of the Anglo-Saxons, and Prynne takes pains to erase, as far as possible, the notion that there were Jews living in England at this time:

That they were setled in our Island in the *Saxons time*, is collected, onely from that Law inserted by (*g*) *Hoveden*, and (*h*) *Spelman* amongst *Edward the Confessors*, here cited . . . but there being no mention of the Jews in any of our *Saxon Kings Raigns, Councils, Decrees, Laws*, before the *Confessor* . . . I cannot but reject it as counterfeit.[56]

If the Jews were not present in that significant era, Prynne does not want them in the country now, when England is going through a period of transformation and establishment defined, in turn, by reference to Anglo-Saxon history.[57]

Jews have restricted entry, then, into Prynne's version of England's past, and by implication, Prynne is against their readmission to England in his own lifetime. Moreover, there are hints in these texts at a final objection to Menasseh's proposal: that not only would readmission bring Jews into the country, but also that the proposal itself was a distinctly foreign import. William Hughes frequently cites English Protestant chroniclers John Stow, Raphael Holinshed and John Foxe, and is disappointed in Menasseh ben Israel for his ignorance (on account, perhaps, of being both Jewish and foreign) of their accounts: 'the Rabbi appears to be utterly ignorant of our Histories (though a learned man)'.[58] Prynne goes further: in his eyes Menasseh is 'inquiring after a *convenient Summer-house*, intending to settle himself at least, if not his *exiled Nation*, here among us'.[59] As the previous chapter noted, William Hughes was opposed to the idea of England adopting the example of liberal yet expedient Amsterdam, writing that 'Reason of State makes the Dutch-men tolerate all Religions but the Popish. From whence shall it not presently be concluded, that all their neighbours should do the like'.[60]

As well as being an expression of anti-Jewish feeling, then, opposition to Jewish readmission was grounded in the notion that their presence would threaten an evolving sense of English nationhood, as distinct from Amsterdam and the Continent at large. During the interregnum, a fledgling confidence in the possibilities of the English nation was juxtaposed with insecurity about the instability of the times. According to Nathaniel Crouch's account of the Whitehall Conference, some of the participants feared 'If [the Jews] should return that many would be seduced and cheated by them, and tho' they heartily desir'd the Conversion of the Jews, yet they feared greatly it would prove the subversion of many here, because People at this time were so soon drawn aside to new Opinions'.[61] By contrast, those in favour of readmission frequently argued that inviting the Jews back to England would encourage God to bestow favour on the English nation, and reassured their opponents that the presence of Jews would not adversely affect national interests. D.L. insists that the Jews will not 'come Rushing in, as an overflowing floud, to drown all *Religion, Laws,* and all our *Privileges*, nor yet to be such *Hors-leaches,* and Spunges of our Treasure, and transport it away; nor to usurp upon any mans *Birthright,* nor yet to Cozen, oppress, poll, pill, defraud, fleece, and squeeze the *English* Nation'.[62] It was concern for the English nation, rather than for the Jewish people, which lay uppermost in these commentators' minds.

***

In his *Short Demurrer*, William Prynne summarises his objections to the readmission of the Jews: 'Reasons against their re-admission into *England* they are divers, Theological, Political, and mixt of both'.[63] This chapter has argued that the motives for both supporting and rejecting readmission were more diverse, and more political, than their traditional portrayal has suggested. The idea that Christians were seriously contemplating the readmission of the Jews to England should not be underestimated, but neither should the context in which that possibility was imagined. As in the controversy about toleration between Roger Williams and John Cotton, the context for the readmission debates straddled the Atlantic between old and New England. It concerned conflicting traditions of legal methodology, the relative powers of Parliament and king and the evolving character of the English nation; issues which, in turn, were themselves interrelated. The readmission debate reflected and refracted the administrative and political turmoil brought about by the Interregnum; and even when Christians appeared, finally, to recognise the Jews as a people, they were still recruited, as an idea, into political, constitutional and legal controversy. At times, even, the rejection of the opposite Christian faction was as much of a priority as the rejection (or acceptance) of Jews. As 'D.L.' says of Prynne: 'He is not onely bitter but superlative invective against the Jews, but he drives as furiously against his brethren and Countreymen, and he is unwilling the Jews should come In; so he would be as much pleased if some of his Country men were turn'd Out'.[64]

Conclusion

In 1612, the Hebrew scholar Hugh Broughton found himself in a quandary: he was relying on the work of Talmudic scholars to help him write his commentaries on the Old Testament, but he was aware that, being Jews, they were not to be trusted. According to Broughton, Jewish scholars held the key to the true interpretation of the Hebrew scriptures, but they were in the habit of deliberately obscuring that truth in order to mislead Christians; one of the worst culprits, in Broughton's eyes, was the fifteenth-century Jewish philosopher and biblical exegete, Isaac Abravanel:

> some *Iewes* of malice study to peruert all Christians doctrine: as this man *Abrabbaneel*, or *Barbinel*, a Rabbine of great paines & witte, but not of grace: and only to be followed, when he clearely is on our side. Without them our age can not search al things: and much they deceiue the unacquainted with them.[1]

Broughton's admission that 'without them our age can not search al things' exemplifies the centrality of Jewish ideas and scholarship to early modern Christians, something which this book has attempted to illustrate; and his insistence that Abravanel should only be 'followed, when he clearely is on our side' is suggestive of another central claim of this book. For Broughton and other Christian writers of the early modern period, Jews were only to be followed when they were clearly on their side; Judaism was, in their eyes, a contingent, malleable resource which could be co-opted in the service of Christian truth. There is, furthermore, an additional resonance to Broughton's qualification: Broughton's 'side' is not only Christian truth, but also his 'side' of an argument about Christianity; because although Broughton may appear, like other Christian Hebraists, to be a curious, disinterested scholar, his employment of the Hebrew language and Jewish ideas was, as Chapter 2 illustrated, motivated by historically specific polemical concerns.

It was the inescapably contentious quality of references to Judaism which John Selden's opponents in the early seventeenth-century controversy about the payment of tithes recognised when they derided Selden's claim that his *Historie of Tithes* was 'a meer Narration'. But

Selden's attempt to have his cake and eat it, to interpret the Jewish past tendentiously and, at the same time, as a neutral, universal precedent, was facilitated by the essential ambivalence which Judaism possessed for early modern Christians. For Puritans, Judaism embodied the origins of scripture and the archetype of the Old Testament Chosen; but also the earthly ritual and corrupt materiality of the insufficiently reformed English church. For Anglicans, Judaism represented the prototype of aesthetic forms of worship and the authentic performance of prayer, but its emulation was also potentially subversive and heretical. As far as Roman Catholics were concerned, Judaizing was further evidence of the schismatic character of all forms of Protestantism; and for a variety of factions in the early modern period, both Puritan and Anglican, ancient Israel prefigured either the ideal constitution of the state, or the constitution to be avoided at all costs. Indeed, as several chapters in this book have demonstrated, Judaism was used as a political football as well as a religious pivot; and in some cases, it was invoked in order to accuse the opposing religious faction of political subversion. Because it could signify either perfection or corruption, Judaism was ideally suited to religious and political controversy, because it could be used both to bolster one's own arguments, and to destroy those of the opposition.

If the synchronic analysis of triangulated relationships between different Christian factions and Judaism has illustrated the oppositional nature of early modern religio-political discourse, therefore, it has also revealed that the removal of religious difference was, if anything, an even more pressing priority. The Reformation gave rise to an unprecedented splitting of the religious consensus in England, which, as the seventeenth century got underway, became both more acute and more political. The emerging realisation that not only different forms of Christianity, but also different religions altogether, could exist in England, was deeply unsettling to Christian commentators who were still thoroughly wedded to the maintenance of religious unity. If Judaism provided a way of contesting rival claims to religious truth, it could also be made to function as the denial of religious difference *per se*, through the invocation of its foundational, proto-Christian aspect. Hugh Broughton's belief that Judaism exemplified biblical truth mitigated, therefore, his anxious dismissal of post-biblical Jews as heretics. Judaism provided a safe vehicle, in other words, in which to explore and contain the possibility of religious alterity; and, viewed in this light, Christian Judaizing can be understood as a performative investigation of the fault line between different conceptions of religion. Even while Christians postulated the 'thin end of the wedge' argument to warn against the observance of Jewish rituals such as the Sabbath and Passover, they were able to retreat into the notion that if Christians could turn Jewish that easily, Judaism did not really exist at all.

Towards the middle of the seventeenth century, as the religious landscape became even more fractured, and there was increasing contact between Christians and other religious groups such as Jews, anxieties about religious difference only intensified. When the question of tolerating and readmitting the Jews came into view, Christians found it difficult to countenance them as a people rather than as an idea; in fact, as Chapter 4 demonstrated, those who were in favour of employing Jewish ideas were against the toleration of Jewish people. The idea of tolerating the Jews was not imagined primarily in terms of practical coexistence, informal readmission or facts on the ground; it hinged on precise, detailed and fraught considerations, but also about the relationship between church and state. If Christians countenanced the possibility of opening up a space outside the church where other religions could exist, then that meant admitting the possibility of religious difference; although the purity of the church would thereby be protected. If, on the other hand, church and state were to remain intertwined, then religious heresy could be excluded with the added force of secular authority, but the church was now in danger of being polluted by the coexistence of other religions. As this book has argued, the development of tolerationist ideas in seventeenth-century England was bound up, to a large extent, with these detailed, constitutional and, intractably, intolerant considerations.

It is not hard to understand why Jewish historians of Victorian England, writing in the context of mass immigration and rising antisemitism, would have wanted to cultivate a positive tradition of Anglo-Jewish history. Their priority was the recovery of a body of evidence which pointed to the progressively tolerant attitude of early modern English Christians towards Jews. Those nineteenth-century pressures may have disappeared, but they have left a lasting legacy; and the modern emphasis on the celebration of multiculturalism and religious identity fosters a view of the past which is similarly essentialist and teleological. This book has attempted to articulate a more differentiated and paradoxical interpretation of the meaning of Judaism for early modern Christians; to understand how – as Hugh Broughton's comments about Talmudic scholarship illustrate – it was possible to take the ideas and leave the people behind.

Notes

Introduction

1. The year of commemoration was also marked by the fashioning of a 'Tercentenary Medal', featuring portraits of Cromwell and Menasseh ben Israel. See 'Calendar of Events' in Vivian Lipman, ed., *Three Hundred Years: A Volume to Commemorate the Tercentenary of the Re-settlement of the Jews in Great Britain 1656–1956* (London: Vallentine, Mitchell & Co., 1956), 135 and Tony Kushner, 'The End of the "Anglo-Jewish Progress Show": Representations of the Jewish East End, 1887–1987' in Kushner, ed., *The Jewish Heritage in British History: Englishness and Jewishness* (London: Frank Cass, 1992), 78–105 at 85–9.
2. ' "Three Hundred Years", a Broadcast by Lord Samuel, Broadcast on April 15, 1956' in Lipman, ed., *Three Hundred Years*, 143–6 at 144.
3. Lucien Wolf, 'The Whitehall Conference: Celebration of the 250th Anniversary', *Transactions of the Jewish Historical Society of England*, (hereafter referred to as *TJHSE*) 5 (1908), 276–98 at 281 and 278–9, respectively.
4. Menasseh ben Israel, *Vindiciae Judaeorum, or a Letter in Answer to certain Questions propounded by a Noble and Learned Gentleman, touching the reproaches cast on the Nation of the Jewes; wherein all objections are candidly, and yet fully cleared* ([London]: R.D., 1656), E4v–Fr.
5. [Henry Jessey], *A Narrative Of the late Proceeds at White-Hall, concerning the Jews: Who had desired by R. Manasses an Agent for them; that they might return into England, and Worship the God of their Fathers here in their Synagogues, &c. Published for satisfaction to many in several parts of England, that are desirous, and inquisitive to hear the Truth thereof* (London: Printed for L. Chapman, at the Crown in Popeshead-Alley, 1656), 10.
6. D'Blossiers Tovey, *Anglia Judaica: Or the History and Antiquities of the Jews in England, Collected from all our Historians, both Printed and Manuscript, as also from the Records in the Tower, and other Publick Repositories* (Oxford: J. Fletcher, 1738). Tovey may have been influenced by another history of the Jews, written by Jacques Basnage de Beauval and translated into English by Thomas Taylor. It appeared in 1708 and was entitled *The History of the Jews, from Jesus Christ to The Present Time: Containing, Their Antiquities, their Religion, their Rites, the Dispersion of the Ten Tribes in the East, And the Persecutions this Nation has suffer'd in the West* (London: J. Beaver and B. Lintot et al., 1708).
7. Tovey, *Anglia Judaica*, 274. See also H.S.Q. Henriques, who concluded in 1905 that 'his mission had proved an utter failure'. Henriques, *The Return of the Jews to England: Being a Chapter in the History of English Law* (London: Macmillan and Co., 1905), 44.
8. Wolf, 'The Whitehall Conference', 279.
9. Cecil Roth, *A History of the Jews in England* (Oxford: Clarendon Press, 1941).
10. Roth, *A History of the Jews in England*, vii. For further exploration of the motivations of early Anglo-Jewish historians, see James Shapiro, *Shakespeare and the Jews* (New York: Columbia University Press, 1996), 60–8.

11. David Katz, *The Jews in the History of England 1485–1850* (Oxford: Clarendon Press, 1994), 74.
12. See David Katz, 'The Marginalization of Early Modern Anglo-Jewish History', *Immigrants & Minorities*, X (1991), 60–77 and Shapiro, *Shakespeare and the Jews*, 65–6.
13. Katz, *Philo-Semitism and the Readmission of the Jews to England, 1603–1655* (Oxford: Clarendon Press, 1982); and Katz, *Sabbath and Sectarianism in Seventeenth-Century England* (Leiden: E.J. Brill, 1988).
14. See, for example, Katz, The Jews in the History of England, 138, and Katz, 'The Phenomenon of Philo-Semitism', *Studies in Church History*, xxix (1992), 327–361 at 334. Notable examples of David Katz's successful integration of Judaism and English history are two chapters in *The Jews in the History of England*, namely, Chapter 1, 'The Jewish Advocates of Henry VIII's Divorce' and Chapter 4, 'The Jews of England and the Glorious Revolution'; 15–48 and 145–89 respectively.
15. Shapiro, *Shakespeare and the Jews*, 225–6.
16. Tony Kushner, 'Heritage and Ethnicity: An Introduction', in Cesarani and Kushner, eds, *The Jewish Heritage in British History*, 1–28 at 7.
17. Although the term 'philosemitism' is anachronistic when applied to the early modern period, since attitudes towards Jews as a (Semitic) race were only properly formulated in the nineteenth century, this book uses it nonetheless as a convenient label to denote Christians' enthusiastic interest in Judaism, rather than the rather unwieldy 'philo-Judaism'. Furthermore, the word philosemitism is primarily used in this book in terms of the need to contextualise it. 'Judeophobia' is used instead of 'antisemitism', however, because the latter term carries, for historical reasons, an even stronger sense of an attitude based on race rather than religion. Since the terms 'philosemitism' and 'antisemitism' refer to a preference for, and an antipathy towards, an imagined racial category, they remain uncapitalised throughout this book. For the use of the terms 'philosemitism' and 'antisemitism' and their relation to the historical past, see Robert Chazan, *Medieval Stereotypes and Modern Antisemitism* (Berkeley, CA: University of California Press, 1997), Chapter 8; Gavin Langmuir, *History, Religion and Antisemitism* (London: Tauris Press, 1990) and Langmuir, *Toward a Definition of Antisemitism* (Berkeley, CA: University of California Press, 1990).

Chapter 1 Anglo-Jewish history and early modern England

1. Wolf continues, more explicitly: 'There is no question that it saved us from the Ghetto system then in force all over Europe. We consequently owe to it, in a very large measure, the fact that our social assimilation with our non-Jewish fellow-citizens is, and has always been, far more complete in this country than in any other country, and that, as a result, the baleful wave of anti-Semitism which has swept across the Continent, has dashed impotently against our shores' (Lucien Wolf, 'The Whitehall Conference: Celebration of the 250th Anniversary', *TJHSE*, 5 [1908], 276–98 at 281–2).
2. Wolf's words were mirrored by members of the English establishment; although Prime Minister Arthur Balfour did not attend the 250th anniversary celebrations of 1906, he wrote to Wolf, stressing the importance of readmission in providing a philosemitic exception to the antisemitism of Europe: 'Had Continental Europe followed the example set by this country for the last

two hundred and fifty years its history would not be stained by many crimes and many injustices which now stand on record as a perpetual reproach to Christian civilisation. That in this country there is no Jewish question, that race prejudices and religious prejudices, which elsewhere play so disastrous a part in the social organisation, are unheard of here, is due in no small measure to the fact that the Jews have shown themselves entirely worthy of the rights and privileges which they enjoy as citizens of this country, and that those rights and privileges have been granted to them in full measure' (Letter from Arthur Balfour, as cited in Wolf, 'The Whitehall Conference', 278–9).
3. All sixteenth- and seventeenth-century dates have been modernised.
4. For histories of antisemitism, see for example Bernard Glassman, *Anti-Semitic Stereotypes Without Jews: Images of the Jews in England 1290–1700* (Detroit: Wayne State University Press, 1975); Paul E. Grosser and Edwin G. Halperin, *The Causes and Effects of Anti-Semitism: The Dimensions of a Prejudice. An Analysis and Chronology of 1900 Years of Anti-Semitic Attitudes and Practices* (New York: Philosophical Library, 1978); Shmuel Almog, ed., *Antisemitism Through the Ages* (Oxford: Pergamon Press, 1988); Dan Cohn-Sherbok, *The Crucified Jew: Twenty centuries of Christian Anti-Semitism* (London: Fount, 1993).
5. See Kenneth Stow, *Alienated Minority: The Jews of Medieval Latin Europe* (Cambridge, MA: Harvard University Press, 1992), 285–6 and 295; Robert Stacey, '1290–1260: A Watershed in Anglo-Jewish Relations?', *Historical Research*, 61 (1988), 35–50 and Stacey, 'The Conversion of the Jews to Christianity in Thirteenth-Century England', *Speculum*, 67 (1992), 263–83.
6. For Lopez, see Alan Stewart, 'The Birth of a National Biography: The Lives of Roderigo Lopez, Solomon Lazarus Levi and Sidney Lee', EnterText [e-journal], 3:1 (2003), 183–203; David Katz, *The Jews in the History of England 1485–1850* (Oxford: Clarendon Press, 1994), 49–106; Arthur Dimock, 'The Conspiracy of Dr. Lopez', *English Historical Review*, 9 (1894), 440–72; Martin A.S. Hume, *Treason and Plot: Struggles for Catholic Supremacy in the Last Years of Elizabeth* (London: James Nisbet & Co., 1901), Chapter 5; Hume, 'The so-called conspiracy of Dr Ruy Lopez', *TJHSE*, 6 (1908), 32–55; Max J. Kohler, 'Dr. Rodrigo Lopez, Queen Elizabeth's Jewish Physician, and his Relations to America', *Publications of the American Jewish Historical Society*, 17 (1909), 9–25 and John Gwyer, 'The Case of Dr Lopez', *TJHSE*, 16 (1952), 163–84.
7. For Jews in seventeenth-century England, see for example, Katz, *The Jews in the History of England*, Chapter 3; Todd Endelman, *The Jews of Britain, 1656–2000* (Berkeley, CA: University of California Press, 2002), 15–20; James Shapiro, *Shakespeare and the Jews* (New York: Columbia University Press, 1996). For Jews in Elizabethan England, see for example, Sidney Lee, 'Elizabethan England and the Jews', *Transactions of the New Shakespeare Society*, I (1887–1892), 143–66; Lucien Wolf, 'Jews in Elizabethan England', *TJHSE*, 11 (1928), 1–91 and Wolf, 'Jews in Tudor England' in Cecil Roth, ed., *Essays in Jewish History by Lucien Wolf* (London: JHSE, 1934), 71–90.
8. See Jonathan Israel, 'Menasseh ben Israel and the Dutch Sephardic Colonization Movement of the Mid-Seventeenth Century (1645-1657)', in Yosef Kaplan, Henry Mechoulan and Richard H. Popkin, eds, *Menasseh ben Israel and His World* (Leiden: E.J. Brill, 1989), 139–65 at 153.
9. James Howell to R. Lewis, 3 January 1655, as cited in Todd Endelman, *The Jews of Britain*, 18–9.

10. 'Paul Isaiah', *The Messiah of the Christians, and the Jewes; Held forth in a discourse between a Christian and a Iew obstinately adhering to his strange opinions, & the forced interpretations of Scripture* (London: William Hunt, 1655), B3r. See Shapiro, *Shakespeare and the Jews*, 58. See also Katz's observation that in 1655 Abraham de Mercado and his son David Raphael were permitted to emigrate to Barbados, where the father was given permission to practise medicine by Cromwell himself. Mercado was officially noted to be a 'Hebrew'. David Katz, *Philo-Semitism and the Readmission of the Jews to England, 1603–1655* (Oxford: Clarendon Press, 1982), 197, citing Calendar of State Papers, Domestic, 1655, 583.
11. For communication between Christians and Jews for millenarian purposes, see Claire Jowitt, '"The Consolation of Israel": The Representation of Jewishness in the Writings of Gerrard Winstanley and William Everard', *Prose Studies*, 22 (1999), 83–99; Jowitt, '"Inward" and "Outward" Jews: Margaret Fell, Circumcision and Women's Preaching', *Reformation*, 4 (1999), 139–68; Cecil Roth, 'Leona da Modena and England', *TJHSE*, 11 (1928), 206–25; Roth, 'Leone da Modena and his English Correspondents', *TJHSE*, 17 (1953), 39–43 and Bonnelyn Young Kunze, *Margaret Fell and the Rise of Quakerism* (Basingstoke: Macmillan, 1994), Chapter 11.
12. Menasseh ben Israel, *The Hope of Israel: Written by Menasseh, An Hebrew Divine, and Philosopher. Newly extant, and Printed at Amsterdam, and Dedicated by the Author, to the High Court the Parliament of England, and to the Councell of State* (London: R.I. for Hannah Allen, 1650).
13. Thomas Thorowgood, *Iewes in America, or, Probabilities That the Americans are of that Race. With the removal of some contrary reasonings, and earnest desires for effectuall endeavours to make them Christian* (London: Printed by W.H. for Thomas Slater, 1650). For the Montezinos story, see for example, Katz, *Philo-Semitism*, 141–9 and Harold Pollins, *An Economic History of the Jews in England* (East Brunswick, NJ: Associated University Presses, 1982), 31.
14. For the mid-seventeenth century Sephardi colonisation movement, see Jonathan Israel, *European Jewry in the Age of Mercantilism 1550–1750* (Oxford: Clarendon Press, 1985), 130.
15. *The Petition of the Jewes For the Repealing of the Act of Parliament for their banishment out of England. Presented to his Excellency and the generall Councell of Officers on Fryday Jan. 5. 1648* (London: Printed for George Roberts, 1648–9), 3.
16. See Lucien Wolf, 'Cromwell's Jewish Intelligencers', in Roth, ed., *Essays in Jewish History*, 91–114 at 104–7 and Katz, *Philo-Semitism*, 195–6. Katz highlights the importance of the Dormido episode, at the same time as he cautions against drawing any firm conclusions from it.
17. Robles was acquitted not, therefore, as is often claimed because he declared himself openly to be a Jew, but because they could not determine his identity. See Katz, *The Jews in the History of England*, 136–7, citing *State Papers* 18/127, f. 83: report of Admiralty commissioners, 14 May 1656. See also Roth: 'As a Spanish Catholic his position had been open to question. As a refugee Jew he was safe' (Roth, *The History of the Jews*, 166), as well as Endelman, *The Jews of Britain*, 26 and Pollins, *An Economic History*, 34.

18. Menasseh ben Israel, *To his Highnesse the Lord Protector of the Common-wealth of England, Scotland, and Ireland. The humble addresses of Menasseh Ben Israel, adivine, and doctor of physick, in behalfe of the Jewish nation* (London, 1655).
19. For the Whitehall Conference, see for example, Katz, *Philo-Semitism*, Chapter 6 and Nathan Osterman, 'The Controversy over the Proposed Readmission of the Jews to England (1655)', *Jewish Social Studies*, 3 (1941), 301–28.
20. [Nathaniel Crouch], '*The Proceedings of the Jews in England in the Year 1655*' in *Two Journeys To Jerusalem . . . Collected by R.B. and Beautified with Pictures* (London: Printed for Nathaniel Crouch, 1715), 167–74 at 172–4.
21. [Crouch], *Proceedings*, as cited by Claire Jowitt in '"Inward" and "Outward" Jews'.
22. State Papers 18/25, f. 169, as cited in Katz, *Philo-Semitism*, 236.
23. Pepys to Edward Montagu, 3 December 1659, as cited in Katz, *Philo-Semitism*, 242, Greenhalgh to Thomas Crompton, 22 April 1662, reprinted in *TJHSE*, 10 (1924), 49–57 and Wilfred Samuel, *The First London Synagogue of the Resettlement (Founded in 1657, Enlarged in 1674)* (London: Published by Spottiswoode, Ballantyne and Co ltd, for the JHSE, 1924), Appendix, 49–57.
24. See Katz, *Philo-Semitism*, 241. See also William Godwin, *History of the Commonwealth of England, from its commencement, to the Restoration of Charles the Second* (London: Printed for Henry Colburn, 1828), 250–1. For the cemetery lease, See also A.S. Diamond, 'The Cemetery of the Resettlement', *TJHSE*, 19 (1960), 163–90.
25. See Katz, *Philo-Semitism*, 3 and 241 and R.D. Barnett, ed., 'The Burial Register of the Spanish and Portuguese Jews, London 1657–1735', in *Miscellanies of the Jewish Historical Society of England*, VI, (1962), 1–72.
26. See Pollins, *An Economic History*, Chapter 2; Jonathan I. Israel, 'Menasseh ben Israel and the Dutch Sephardic Colonization Movement of the Mid-Seventeenth Century (1645–1657)' in Kaplan et al., eds, *Menasseh ben Israel and his World*, 139–63; Pollins, *An Economic History*, 43; Wilfred Samuel, 'The First Fifty Years' in V.D. Lipman, ed., *Three Centuries of Anglo-Jewish History* (Cambridge: Published for the JHSE by W. Heffer and Sons, 1961), 27–44 at 28; Todd Endelman, *Radical Assimilation in English Jewish History 1656–1945* (Bloomington, Indiana: Indiana University Press, 1990), 10 and Endelman, *The Jews of Britain*, 29.
27. See Pollins, *An Economic History*, 47 and Charles Wilson, 'New introduction' to W.A. Cunningham, *Alien Immigrants in England* (London: Cass, 1969), xv.
28. Calendar of State Papers, Domestic, 1663–4, 672, as cited in Katz, *Philo-Semitism*, 243.
29. See Katz, *The Jews in the History of England*, 150, 140–4 and 149–51; Pollins, *An Economic History*, 38–9 and Endelman, *The Jews of Britain*, 27–9.
30. Thomas Violet, *A Petition Against the Jewes, Presented to the Kings Majestie and the Parliament* (London: n.p., 1661), 2.
31. Violet, *A Petition Against the Jewes*, 3.
32. Violet, *A Petition Against the Jewes*, 7.
33. See Katz, *Philo-Semitism*, 179–80. Lucien Wolf refers to hostile petitions against the Jews as evidence that Cromwell readmitted them to England. Referring to a passage in a petition presented to the King by the Lord Mayor and Aldermen, complaining about the 'admission of Iewes to a free cohabitation and trade in these dominions', Wolf writes, 'this statement by an official body that the Jews

were admitted by Cromwell finally disposes of the contention of [D'Blossiers] Tovey and others, which has recently been adopted by Dr. Gaster, that Charles II was the first to grant that privilege' (Wolf, 'Cromwell's Jewish Intelligencers', n. 120 and n. 121). Dr Moses Gaster (1856–1939) was the leader of the Spanish and Portuguese Jews' Congregation in England, and a prominent scholar.
34. Violet, *A Petition Against the Jewes*, 3.
35. Violet, *A Petition Against the Jewes*, 6.
36. Thomas Barlow, *Several Miscellaneous and Weighty Cases of Conscience, Learnedly and Judiciously Resolved By the Right Reverend Father in God, Dr. Thomas Barlow, Late Lord-Bishop of Lincoln* (London: Mrs. Davis, 1692), 6.
37. Barlow, *Several Miscellaneous and Weighty Cases of Conscience*, v, 14, 30.
38. As recognition of this, the Anglo-Jewish community used to celebrate Charles II's readmission of the Jews to England. See Wolf, 'American Elements in the Resettlement', *TJHSE*, 3 (1899), 85–93.
39. D'Blossiers Tovey, *Anglia Judaica: Or the History and Antiquities of the Jews in England, Collected from all our Historians, both Printed and Manuscript, as also from the Records in the Tower, and other Publick Repositories* (Oxford: J. Fletcher, 1738), 279–80.
40. Anon, *An Apology for the Naturalization of the Jews . . . By a True Believer* (London: Printed for M. Cooper, 1753), 29.
41. Anon, *An Historical Treatise Concerning Jews and Judaism, in England* (London: Printed for R. Baldwin, 1753).
42. Anon, *An Historical Treatise*, 1.
43. [William Romaine], *An Answer to a PAMPHLET, entitled, "Considerations on the bill to permit persons professing the Jewish religion to be naturalized"* (London: H. Cooke, 1753), 7.
44. See Thomas Perry, *Public Opinion, Propaganda, and Politics in Eighteenth-Century England: A Study of the Jew Bill of 1753* (Cambridge, Mass: Harvard University Press, 1962); Katz, *The Jews in the History of England*, Chapter 6 and Shapiro, *Shakespeare and the Jews*, Chapter 7.
45. Elijah Blunt, *A History of the Establishment* (London: Printed for Saunders and Benning, 1830).
46. See Tovey, *Anglia Judaica*, 279–80.
47. Their titles included *The History of the Jews, From the Taking of Jerusalem by Titus to the Present Time: Comprising, A Narrative of their Wanderings, Persecutions, Commercial Enterprises, and Literary Exertions; with an Account of the Various Efforts Made for Their Conversion* by James Huie (Edinburgh: Oliver & Boyd, 1840); James Hosmer, *The Jews: In Ancient, Medieval and Modern Times* (London: T. Fisher Unwin, 1886) and Jack Myers, *The Story of the Jewish People, Being a History of the Jewish People since Bible Times* (London: Kegan Paul, Trench, Trubner & Co., 1909). In 1887, Lucien Wolf and Joseph Jacobs published *Bibliotheca Anglo-Judaica*, a catalogue of sources relating to Jewish history in Britain; it was enlarged and updated by Cecil Roth in 1937. The *Bibliotheca* contains a large cluster of works of Anglo-Jewish history published between the early nineteenth century and 1887. See Cecil Roth, *Magna Bibliotheca Anglo-Judaica* (London: Published for the JHSE, 1937).
48. The first Jew to be knighted was Solomon de Medina, in 1700.
49. See William D. Rubinstein and Hilary L. Rubinstein, *Philosemitism: Admiration and Support in the English-Speaking World for Jews, 1840–1939*

(Basingstoke: Macmillan, 1999), Chapter 1; Katz, *The Jews in the History of England*, Chapter 8 and Endelman, *The Jews of Britain*, Chapter 3.
50. Huie, *The History of the Jews*, v–vi.
51. Myers, *The Story of the Jewish People*, Dedication.
52. Hosmer, *The Jews: In Ancient, Medieval and Modern Times*, iv.
53. For the philosemitic desire to convert the Jews, and its interpretation, see Michael Ragussis, *Figures of Conversion: "The Jewish Question" and English National Identity* (Durham: Duke University Press, 1995); Rubinstein and Rubinstein, *Philosemitism*, especially Chapter 7 and Bryan Cheyette and Nadia Valman, eds, *The Image of the Jew in European Liberal Culture, 1789–1914* (London: Vallentine Mitchell, 2004), Introduction.
54. See Jacob Katz, *From Prejudice to Destruction: Anti-Semitism, 1700–1933* (Cambridge, MA: Harvard University Press, 1980), 260–1; David Cesarani, *Reporting Anti-Semitism: The "Jewish Chronicle" 1879–1979*, The Parkes Lecture 1993 (Southampton: University of Southampton, 1993), 3; Colin Holmes, *Anti-Semitism in British Society 1876–1939* (London: Edward Arnold, 1979), Chapter 1 and Cesarani, *The "Jewish Chronicle" and Anglo-Jewry, 1841–1941* (Cambridge: Cambridge University Press, 1994), 82 and 70–88.
55. See David Feldman, 'Jews in London, 1880–1914' in Raphael Samuel, ed., *Patriotism: The Making and Unmaking of British National Identity*, (London: Routledge, 1989), II, 207–229 at 208–9 and David Cesarani, 'The Changing Character of Citizenship and Nationality in Britain' in Cesarani and Mary Fulbrook, eds, *Citizenship, Nationality and Migration in Europe* (London: Routledge, 1996), 57–73.
56. James Picciotto, *Sketches of Anglo-Jewish History* (London: Trubner & Co., 1875). The *Sketches* were originally printed in the *Jewish Chronicle*, and later revised by Israel Finestein and reissued in 1956. For more on Lucien Wolf and his work, see his *Essays in Jewish History*, edited by Roth.
57. See for example, Lee, 'Elizabethan England and the Jews', 143–66.
58. See David Cesarani, 'Dual Heritage or Duel of Heritages': Englishness and Jewishness in the Heritage Industry', in Cesarani and Tony Kushner, eds, *The Jewish Heritage in British History: Englishness and Jewishness* (London: Frank Cass, 1992), 29–41 at 35.
59. Israel Abrahams, 'The Science of Jewish History', *TJHSE*, 5 (1908), 193–201 at 199. See Cesarani, 'Dual Heritage or Duel of Heritages?' 32–4 and Tony Kushner, 'Heritage and Ethnicity: An Introduction' in Cesarani and Kushner, eds, *The Jewish Heritage*, 1–28 at 7–8.
60. Abrahams, 'The Science of Jewish History', 199.
61. See Shapiro, *Shakespeare and the Jews*, 64–5.
62. In 1887, Lucien Wolf concluded his published lecture, 'The Middle Age of Anglo-Jewish History (1290–1656)' by declaring that 'this, roughly, is the story of the Jews in England, from their expulsion by Edward I, to their readmission by Cromwell'. Lucien Wolf, *A Lecture Delivered at the Anglo-Jewish Historical Exhibition, Royal Albert Hall, 12th May 1887* (London: Wertheimer & Co, 1887), 29.
63. See Kushner, 'Heritage and Ethnicity', 18; Pollins, *An Economic History*, 40 and Cesarani, 'Dual Heritage or Duel of Heritages', 35. Cesarani sheds light on the memorialisation of 'readmission', but he does not question the notion that readmission took place.

64. Raphael Samuel, 'The Discovery of Puritanism, 1820–1914: A Preliminary Sketch' in Jane Garnett and Colin Matthew, eds, *Revival and Religion since 1700* (London: The Hambledon Press, 1993), 201–48 at 205. For earlier representations of Cromwell, see Laura Lunger Knoppers, *Constructing Cromwell: Ceremony, Portrait and Print 1645–1661* (Cambridge: Cambridge University Press, 2000).
65. See Blair Worden, *Roundhead Reputations: The English Civil Wars and the Passions of Posterity* (London: Penguin, 2001), 294.
66. Godwin, *History of the Commonwealth*, as cited in Samuel, 'The Discovery of Puritanism'.
67. See for example, Antonia Fraser, *Cromwell, Our Chief of Men* (London: Weidenfeld and Nicolson, 1973), 568. Even Sigmund Freud is said to have named one of his sons Oliver in recognition of what Cromwell had done for the English Jews; see Fraser, *Cromwell*, n. 567.
68. According to Blair Worden, 'no English centenary . . . has produced a more prodigious intensity of sentiment than the three hundredth anniversary, in 1899, of the birth of Oliver Cromwell . . . he was described frequently as the greatest of Englishmen, sometimes as the greatest figure, or one of the greatest figures, in the history of the world' (Worden, *Roundhead Reputations*, 215). See also Timothy Lang, *The Victorians and the Stuart Heritage: Interpretations of a Discordant Past* (Cambridge: Cambridge University Press, 1995), 184.
69. See Samuel, 'The Discovery of Puritanism', 204–5, referring, among other sources, to George Crabbe, *Tales* (London, 1812).
70. Carlyle, *Letters and Speeches of Oliver Cromwell*, as cited in Samuel, 'The Discovery of Puritanism', 215, see also 221.
71. See Lang, *The Victorians*, 93 and 206.
72. See Lang, *The Victorians*, 166–8, and Worden, *Roundhead Reputations*, 258.
73. During a speech at the 250th anniversary celebrations, the MP James Bryce addressed his Jewish audience thus: 'Sixty years ago, when Alderman Salomons and Baron Lionel de Rothschild were fighting for the admission of the Jews to Parliament, the Liberal Party, led by Lord John Russell, and true to the principles of religious liberty, fought for your admission, and ever since there has been a general feeling of satisfaction and pleasure that that liberty was given to you'. James Bryce, as cited in Wolf, 'The Whitehall Conference', 284.
74. See Lang, *The Victorians*, 98–103.
75. H.S.Q. Henriques, *The Return of the Jews to England: Being a Chapter in the History of English Law* (London: Macmillan and Co., 1905), 47–8. On the limits of Cromwell's toleration, see Blair Worden, 'Toleration and the Cromwellian Protectorate' in W.J. Sheils, ed., *Persecution and Toleration* (Oxford: Blackwell, 1984), 199–234 at 201. For Cromwell's pragmatic motivations, see Major-General Whalley, reported in T. Birch, ed., *The State Papers of John Thurloe* (London: Printed for the Executor of the late Mr. Fletcher Gyles; Thomas Woodward, 1742), IV, 308. See also Pollins, *An Economic History*, 37.
76. According to Roth, the toleration of the Jews was 'wholly dependent upon the benevolence of one man [Cromwell]' (Roth, *The History of the Jews*, 169), and see also Endelman, *The Jews of Britain*, 28. For an excellent account of James II's motives in tolerating the Jews, see Katz, *The Jews in the History of England*, 152.

77. Rather surprisingly, given his views, Henriques became the fifteenth President of the Jewish Historical Society of England. When Henriques died in 1925, Lucien Wolf published his obituary in the Society's *Transactions*, affectionately commenting on Henriques's controversial views: 'Before he joined the Society he had been much interested in the controversy which had arisen as to the date and circumstances of the foundation of the Anglo-Jewish community as it now exists. New evidence had been discovered which seemed to show conclusively that the resettlement of the Jews in this country was the work of the Commonwealth. Henriques opposed this view, at first on the ground that the evidence was insufficient and unconvincing. But in truth he had a deeper reason for his opposition, and to-day, when the controversy is at an end, it is only right that an effort should be made to understand the views he held. They were the outcome of his strong conservative opinion in regard to the sanctity of constitutional law . . . to him the Commonwealth was an illegal Government, and it had no power whatever to change the law as it then existed. Thus he held that, while the statement of the law in regard to the Jews by the Whitehall Conferences was valid because it was a mere reaffirmation of the legal situation which existed independent of the Commonwealth, any new concessions for the protection of the Jewish settlers which ran counter to the existing law in regard to Judaism had no legal value. Hence his conclusion that there was no resettlement of the Jews in a constitutional sense during the Commonwealth'. Lucien Wolf, 'Henry Straus Quixano Henriques, K.C., 1866–1925', *TJHSE*, 2 (1928), 247–51 at 248–9. Wolf is arguing that Henriques's interpretation of 1656 was determined by his political attitude towards Cromwell, as compared to Charles II. However, neither Henriques nor the more traditional Anglo-Jewish historians were claiming that there had been a change in the law during the Commonwealth, which either would or would not be valid depending on one's view of the legitimacy of the regime; Henriques's critique was directed at the idea of an informal readmission.
78. Henriques, *The Return of the Jews to England*, 51. See also 65–66.
79. Interestingly, Henriques cites a recent legal case concerning Jewish citizenship, in which the date of readmission was key: 'For a period of more than three and a half centuries Jews were not permitted to live in England, nor is the date when they were first allowed to settle here by any means certain. However, in considering the course of legislation, so far as it concerns the Jews, the time of the legal recognition of their resettlement is of great importance, and was much discussed in the recent case of De Wilton v. Montefiore, where Mr. Justice, now Lord Justice Sterling, decided it to be November 13, 1685' (Henriques, *The Return of the Jews to England*, 1). The case which Henriques is referring to, and which was heard in 1900, concerned a woman referred to as Mrs de Wilton who was Jewish by birth but had a Christian marriage; her daughter Eugenie was brought up as a Christian. In 1876, Eugenie became engaged to her maternal uncle Joseph Gompertz Montefiore who was, like Eugenie, a British subject domiciled in England. They were married in both a civil and a Jewish ceremony in Germany, and had five children. Eugenie died in 1893, and her mother revoked the trusts in her will in favour of Eugenie and her children. Although the marriage had been valid in Germany and performed according to Jewish law, it was decided that those

who were both Jewish and domiciled British subjects were governed, where marriage was concerned, by English law, and therefore that the marriage was not valid. Accordingly, Eugenie's mother's funds were distributed on the basis of her daughter having died without having had children. In this case, the date of Jewish readmission was decided, not as 1656, but as the date on which Charles II gave the Jews permission to practice their faith. In the realm of the law, it appeared that Cromwell was not yet considered to have first readmitted the Jews to England.

80. For assertions of the idea that informal readmission was more beneficial to the Jews than formal readmission, see Cecil Roth, *A History of the Jews in England* (Oxford: Clarendon Press, 1941), 166 and 172; Vivian D. Lipman, *A History of the Jews in Britain since 1858* (Leicester: Leicester University Press, 1990), 4; Endelman, *The Jews of Britain*, 27; Katz, *Philo-Semitism*, 244 and Katz, 'The Phenomenon of Philo-Semitism' in Diana Wood, ed., *Christianity and Judaism: Papers Read at the 1991 Summer Meeting and the 1992 Winter Meeting of the Ecclesiastical History Society* (Oxford: Published for the Ecclesiastical History Society by Blackwell, 1992), 327–62 at 335.

81. Cecil Roth, 'The Middle Period of Anglo-Jewish History (1290–1655) Reconsidered', *TJHSE*, XIX (1960), 1–12 at 12. In a lecture the following year, Roth described the informality of the readmission as 'the key to the specific quality of the modern period of Anglo-Jewish history, rooted like the history of the English people in a tradition of freedom'. Roth, 'The Resettlement of the Jews in England in 1656' in Lipman, ed., *Three Centuries*, 1–26 at 21. See also Roth, *Catalogue of an Exhibition of Anglo-Jewish Art and History: In Commemoration of the Tercentenary of the Resettlement of the Jews in the British Isles* (Published by the East and West Library for the Tercentenary Council and printed by the Shenval Press, London, Hertford and Harlow), 6.

82. Cromwell's 'verbal assurance' can be traced to an exchange of letters between the Grand Duke of Tuscany and his envoy in London, Francesco Salvetti. Salvetti wrote in January 1656 that since Cromwell had not pursued the question of readmission since the Whitehall Conference, 'it is not believed that he will declare [readmission] so soon as they desire, since it is a matter of great consequence, and such as to cause general disgust in this nation'. The following week Salvetti wrote another letter, suggesting that Cromwell would 'postpone action while conniving in the meantime at religious exercise in their private houses, as they do at present' in lieu of granting the Jews permission to establish a public synagogue. Salvetti to the Grand Duke, 11/21 Jan 1956, as cited in Katz, *Philo-Semitism*, 228 and Roth, 'New Light on the Resettlement', *TJHSE*, 11 (1928), 112–42 at 131 and 140–1. The idea of the verbal assurance, therefore, originates in a supposition recorded in a private letter; and it refers, not to readmission or even to public worship, but to a continued sanctioning of the habit of unofficial worship in private houses which had existed prior to 1656. It may also originate in Thomas Burton's *Diary* (London: Henry Colburn, 1828) first published under the editorship of J.T. Rutt in 1828. Wilfred Samuel writes, commenting on the date of the anniversary of readmission: 'In point of fact, February 4, 1658 was simply the date on which Cromwell dissolved his Parliament, and there is no ground at all for affixing this date to the oft-quoted passage which states that "the Jews, those able intelligencers . . . he

(Cromwell) now conciliated by a seasonable benefaction to their principal agent resident in England". Nor is this familiar passage in the words of the seventeenth-century diarist [Burton]; they are his nineteenth-century editor's words [Rutt], and thus have no especial historical significance'. Samuel, *The First London Synagogue of the Resettlement*, 37–8.

83. Lucien Wolf, *The Resettlement of the Jews in England* (London: The Jewish Chronicle, 1888), 12. Wolf's formulation encapsulates the paradoxical nature of the interpretation of Cromwell's actions. Although the assurance was 'oral', and therefore open to potential doubt, it was 'doubtless oral'; and even though Cromwell's assurance was informal, it apparently gave the Jews 'precise terms' as to what they could and could not do. These 'precise terms', unfortunately, 'have not been preserved', suggesting that they were not in fact oral, but rather written, in the form of a material document which has been lost.

84. Roth, *The History of the Jews*, 166.

85. Roth, 'The Resettlement', 13–6. The italics are Roth's. For a comment on the irony of Roth's discovery see Shapiro, *Shakespeare and the Jews*, 58. See Henriques on the 'verbal assurance' in *The Return of the Jews to England*, 49–50. Henriques observed that 'some few writers assert that, though the Conference was a failure, the Protector subsequently formally gave the Jews a legal right of settlement in the country, and permitted them to establish a synagogue here. A statement to this effect was made by Godwin . . . and of recent years much has been written by Jewish writers, and especially by Mr. Lucien Wolf, attempting to prove this statement' (49). For Godwin's statement, see Godwin, *History of the Commonwealth*, IV, 249–50. For more early references to the 'verbal assurance', see Roth, *A History of the Jews*, 166, Wolf, *A Lecture Delivered at the Anglo-Jewish Historical Exhibition*, 27 and Samuel, *The First London Synagogue of the Resettlement*, 3. For the afterlife of the 'verbal assurance' in more recent accounts, see for example, *Catalogue of an Exhibition*, 18; Endelman, *The Jews of Britain*, 19 and 27; Endelman, *Radical Assimilation*, 10; Pollins, *An Economic History*, 15, 29 and 34 and Glassman, *Anti-Semitic Stereotypes Without Jews*, 132.

86. William Godwin's account of his efforts to prove the readmission are suggestive; he writes: 'To bring the question [of whether readmission occurred in 1656] . . . to a still greater degree of evidence, I applied to the Rulers of the Spanish and Portuguese Synagogue in Bevis Marks, and by their permission, Mr. Almosnino, their secretary, obligingly went over with me some of their oldest records. Among them I found . . . an agreement in 1674, to enlarge, alter and improve the synagogue in Cree Church Lane, St Catherine Cree, London'. Godwin, *History of the Commonwealth*, 250–1. For the continued pairing of the synagogue and cemetery in modern accounts of readmission, see Pollins, *An Economic History*, 15 and 34 and Endelman, *The Jews of Britain*, 27.

87. Samuel, *The First London Synagogue of the Resettlement*, 3.

88. Samuel, *The First London Synagogue of the Resettlement*, 3.

89. Samuel, *The First London Synagogue of the Resettlement*, n. 25. See also 24–26, and appendix on 77, and Katz, *Philo-Semitism*, 242, citing *Miscellanies of the Jewish Historical Society of England*, II (1935), n. 26.

90. Samuel, *The First London Synagogue of the Resettlement*, 20–2. See also Roth, *A History of the Jews in England*, n. 166.

91. Cecil Roth wrote that 'it was at one time believed that he [Cromwell] gave an affirmative reply to the petition (if only by word of mouth) at the beginning of February, and the romantic Anglo-Jewish antiquarians of half a century ago introduced a new commemorative anniversary into their Calendar on 4 February as "Resettlement Day"'. Cecil Roth, 'The Resettlement of the Jews in England in 1656' in Lipman, ed., *Three Centuries*, 1–26 at 11, also cited in Pollins, *An Economic History*, 33.
92. Samuel, *The First London Synagogue of the Resettlement*, 37–8.
93. Wolf, *A Lecture Delivered at the Anglo-Jewish Historical Exhibition*, 27.
94. Wolf, *A Lecture Delivered at the Anglo-Jewish Historical Exhibition*, 4. The use of the words 'blanks' and 'thread' indicates Wolf's keenness to plot a continuous trajectory of Jews in the history of England. A similar continuity pre- and post-1656 can be observed in more modern accounts, such as those by Todd Endelman. Endelman writes of the Jewish community in London in the 1640s that 'despite this awareness [that there were Jews living there] government and religious authorities did not molest the converso community', and after 1656 that 'although [the Westminster] assembly failed to endorse resettlement, Cromwell apparently assured the leaders of the tiny crypto-Jewish colony already in London that they might live there unmolested, worshipping freely as Jews'. The difference between the two situations is slight, as signalled by the repeated use of the word 'molested'. Todd Endelman, *The Jews of Britain*, 19; see also Endelman, *Radical Assimilation*, 10.
95. As an example of this phenomenon, see, for example, David Katz, who, despite his own evidence of official awareness of Jews in England prior to Menasseh's arrival, writes elsewhere that 'throughout the entire public debate about the Jews that preceded the arrival of Rabbi Menasseh ben Israel in London in September 1655, the very existence of a Jewish community in an eastern corner of London was completely unknown to the English authorities . . . the origins, therefore, of the Jewish community in London are not to be found among the first Sephardi pioneers who came to England during the reign of Henry VIII, nor in the circle of Dr Roderigo Lopez' (Katz: *The Jews in the History of England*, 108). See also Endelman, *The Jews of Britain*, 18–9.
96. Indeed, contemporary historians sometimes go even further than their predecessors in emphasising the definitive quality of readmission; as early as 1941, Cecil Roth had pointed out that 'notwithstanding the accepted view, Cromwell did *not* authorize the resettlement of the Jews in England, however much he desired to do so' (Roth, *A History of the Jews in England*, 166; see also 149–72). Roth continues: 'the general impression that he did is due to the cumulative effect of eighteenth-century vituperation and nineteenth-century quasi-beatification, both of which laid especial stress, in accordance with the fashion of the day, on his treatment of the Jews'. In other words, that fluctuating attitudes towards Cromwell had used an overly decisive account of his actions towards the Jews in order to either praise or demonise him. David Katz's interpretation of Cromwell's actions is articulated in comparatively dramatic terms: 'That Jews were readmitted to that country in that period is not entirely surprising in itself, given the contemporary phenomenon of intellectual and even religious philo-Semitism. What is startling is that this was done openly and in full public view, an extreme example of political philo-Semitism . . . [compared to the rest of Europe] Oliver

Cromwell's strategy of admitting Jews to England by means of a public conference was therefore eccentric in the extreme, a bizarre event'. Katz, 'The Phenomenon of Philo-Semitism', 335.

97. For example, A.N. Wilson, writing in the *Daily Telegraph* on 6 May 2002, referred to 'one of the most interesting, and some of us would say the most glorious, moments in English history: namely, the readmission of Jews to London, after their long exile since the Middle Ages'. Michael Hoffman wrote in the *Independent on Sunday* on the 6 January 2003 that 'all the Jews had been expelled by Edward I in 1290. Oliver Cromwell, as Lord Protector, readmitted them in 1656, and one of the first groups to settle were Spanish and Portuguese refugees from the Inquisition', and according to Jonathan Romain (*The Times*, 1 June 2002) 'there were officially no Jews in England for almost four centuries until their return in 1656 under Cromwell. He readmitted them from a mixture of motives'. On the website for the *New Dictionary of National Biography*, published in 2004, the editors write that 'the official readmission of Jews into the country in the 1650s has been recognized with a clutch of new rabbis, merchants, and war financiers'. On BBC Radio 4's 'Thought for the Day' in December 2005, the Chief Rabbi, Jonathan Sacks, referred to readmission as 'one of the great reversals of all time'.

98. This is suggested, for example, by the title of Todd Endelman's *The Jews of Britain, 1656–2000* (2002). Paul Johnson lists in his table of contents in *A History of the Jews* (London: Weidenfeld and Nicolson, 1987): 'Menasseh ben Israel and the Jewish return to England' (ix). David Katz's interpretation of the ambiguous Robles case is emblematic; Katz writes that 'an open Anglo-Jewish community was thus a reality after the end of the Robles case', and 'a new era had begun for Jews in England'. See Katz, *The Jews in the History of England*, 136–7 and 138.

99. There are only two exceptions: H.S.Q. Henriques's *The Return of the Jews to England* and Shapiro's *Shakespeare and the Jews*. For the continuing problems in Anglo-Jewish history, see Cesarani, 'Dual Heritage or Duel of Heritages', 35.

100. See for example, Pollins, *An Economic History*, 9. Katz displays his awareness, at times, of the Whiggish tendency in Anglo-Jewish history, observing that those who, in the past, were engaged in writing this history 'saw the writing of Anglo-Jewish history as an act of testimony, reflecting their dual wish to praise their people and their country. Almost any subject that was liable to place the Jewish community in a negative light was self-censored, and any twist of interpretation which might spark gentile anger was banished and buried. As a result, Anglo-Jewish historiography has always been patriotic, conservative and Whig, that is, ends-orientated, written with one eye on the final destination of the history train, the End of Anglo-Jewish History – 'Emancipation' (Katz, 'The Marginalization of Early Modern Anglo-Jewish History', *Immigrants & Minorities*, X [1991], 60–77 at 61).

101. See for example, Lipman, *A History of the Jews in Britain*, 3; Robert S. Paul, 'Oliver Cromwell and the Jews' in Vivian Lipman, ed., *Three Hundred Years: A Volume to Commemorate the Tercentenary of the Re-settlement of the Jews in Great Britain 1656–1956* (London: Vallentine, Mitchell & Co., 1956), 9–14 at 9; Charles Webster, ed., *Samuel Hartlib and the Advancement of Learning*

(Cambridge: Cambridge University Press, 1970), 9–16 at 39; Katz, 'The Phenomenon of Philo-Semitism', *Studies in Church History*, xxix (1992), 327–61 at 334; Katz, *Philo-Semitism*, 198–9 and 208; Katz, *The Jews in the History of England*, 110 and 138 and Katz, 'English Redemption and Jewish Readmission in 1656', *Journal of Jewish Studies*, 34 (1983), 73–91.

102. Kabbalah is excluded from the scope of this book, since it does not lend itself well to analysis in terms of Christian controversy. For Christian appropriations of Kabbalah, see, for example, Joseph Dan, ed., *The Christian Kabbalah: Jewish Mystical Books and their Christian Interpreters* (Massachusetts: Harvard College Library, 1997); Joseph Blau, *The Christian Interpretation of the Cabala in the Renaissance* (New York: Columbia University Press, 1944); Hilary Gatti, *The Renaissance Drama of Knowledge: Giordano Bruno in England* (London: Routledge, 1989); Bernard McGinn, 'Cabalists and Christians: Reflections on Cabala in Medieval and Renaissance Thought' and Allison P. Coudert, 'The Kabbala Denudata: Converting Jews or Seducing Christians', in Richard H. Popkin, ed., *Jewish Christians and Christian Jews: From the Renaissance to the Enlightenment* (Dordrecht: Kluwer Academic Publishers, 1994), 11–35 and 73–97, respectively.

103. For discussions of Jewish ideas in sixteenth- and seventeenth-century Christian writing, see, for example, Achsah Guibbory, *Ceremony and Community from Herbert to Milton: Literature, Religion and Cultural Conflict in seventeenth-century England* (Cambridge: Cambridge University Press, 1998); Jason P. Rosenblatt, *Torah and Law in Paradise Lost* (Princeton: Princeton University Press, 1994), Chapter 2; Jonathan R. Ziskind, trans. and ed., *John Selden on Jewish Marriage Law: The* Uxor Hebraica (London: E.J. Brill, 1991), Introduction; Sharon Achinstein, 'John Foxe and the Jews', *Renaissance Quarterly*, 54 (2001), 86–120; Frank E. Manuel, *The Broken Staff: Judaism through Christian Eyes* (Massachusetts: Harvard University Press, 1992) 115–28; Jowitt, '"The Consolation of Israel"', Jowitt, "Inward" and "Outward" Jews' and Achsah Guibbory, 'Conversation, Conversion, Messianic Redemption: Margaret Fell, Menasseh ben Israel, and the Jews' in *Literary Circles and Cultural Communities in Renaissance England*, ed., Claude J. Summers and Ted-Larry Pebworth, 210–34 (Columbia, MI: University of Missouri Press, 2001).

104. William Sclater, *The Quæstion of Tythes Revised. Arguments for the Moralitie of Tything, Enlarged, and cleared. Obiections more fully, and distinctly answered. Mr Seldens Historie, so farre as Mistakers haue made it Argumentatiue against the Moralitie, ouer-ly viewed* (London: John Legatt, 1623), A2r–v.

105. William Prynne, *A short demurrer to the Jewes Long discontinued remitter into England. Comprising, An exact Chronological Relation of their first Admission into, their ill Deportment, Misdemeanors, Condition, Sufferings, Oppressions, Slaughters, Plunders, by popular Insurrections, and regal Exactions in; and their total, final Banishment by Iudgement and Edict of Parliament, out of England* (London: Edward Thomas, 1656), 2:R2r.

106. For Christian Judaizing, see, for example, Shapiro, *Shakespeare and the Jews*, Chapter 1, Katz, *Philo-Semitism* and Katz, *Sabbath and Sectarianism in Seventeenth-century England* (Leiden: E.J. Brill, 1988).

107. The word 'Judaize' is glossed in the *Oxford English Dictionary* as both 'to play the Jew; to follow Jewish customs or religious rites; to follow Jewish practice'

and 'to make Jewish; to imbue with Jewish doctrines or principles'. The first use is given as the Rheims New Testament (1582) 'Gal ii:14. How doest thou compell the Gentils to Iudaize?' *OED*, VIII, 291.

108. For representations of Jewish-Christian conversion (in both directions), see Shapiro, *Shakespeare and the Jews*, Chapter 5; Michael Ragussis, *Figures of Conversion: "The Jewish Question" and English National Identity* (Durham: Duke University Press, 1995) and Perez Zagorin, *Ways of Lying: Dissimulation, Persecution, and Conformity in Early Modern Europe* (Cambridge, MA: Harvard University Press, 1990), Chapter 3.

109. Accordingly, this book does not explore in detail Christian representations of Jews in the early modern period; for this see Katz and Shapiro as cited above, as well as Glassman, *Anti-Semitic Stereotypes Without Jews*, Jowitt; 'The Consolation of Israel' and Emily C. Bartels, *Spectacles of Strangeness: Imperialism, Alienation, and Marlowe* (Philadelphia: University of Pennsylvania Press, 1993), Chapter 4.

Chapter 2 Puritans and Judaism: From scholarship to sedition

1. George Gillespie, *Aarons Rod Blossoming. Or, The Divine Ordinance of Church-Government Vindicated, So as the present Erastian Controversie concerning the distinction of Civill and Ecclesiastical Government, Excommunication, and Suspension, is fully debated and discussed, from the holy Scripture, from the Jewish and Christian Antiquities, from the consent of latter Writers, from the true nature and rights of Magistracy, and from the groundlesnesse of the chiefe Objections made against the Presbyteriall Government in point of a domineering arbitrary unlimited power* (London: E.G. for Richard Whitaker, 1646), Epistle to the reader, A4r.
2. Richard Montagu, *Diatribæ upon the first part of the late history of tithes* (F. Kyngston for M. Lownes, 1621), K2v–K3r.
3. Thomas Goodwin, Philip Nye, Sidrach Simpson, Jeremiah Burroughs and William Bridge, *An Apologeticall Narration, Humbly Submitted to the Honourable Houses of Parliament. By Tho: Goodwin, Philip Nye, Sidrach Simpson, Jer: Burroughes, and William Bridge* (London: Robert Dawlman, 1643), E2v.
4. Gillespie, *Aarons Rod Blossoming*, Epistle to the reader, A4r. See also Hugh Peters, *A word for the Armie and two Words to the Kingdome, to cleare the one and cure the other. Forced in much plainness and brevity from their faithfull servant H. Peters* (London: M. Simmons for Giles Calvert, 1647), A2r and Nathaniel Ward, *A Word to Mr. Peters, and Two Words for the Parliament and Kingdom. Or, An Answer to a scandalous Pamphlet, entituled A Word for the Armie, and two Words to the Kingdom: subscribed by Hugh Peters* (London: Fr: Neile for Tho: Underhill, 1647), Br.
5. Certain 'great' figures are normally exempted from the representation of the early modern period as a 'Controversiall age': as Richard Helgerson has noted in a discussion about the Conformist theologian Richard Hooker, historians such as Alfred Pollard have lifted Hooker's tract *Of the Lawes of Ecclesiastical Polity* out of 'the timebound scuffle of Elizabethan ecclesiastical controversy and into the realm of ideas'. Pollard had claimed that Hooker went 'beyond the bickering world of wrangling about ecclesiastical power and scriptural

interpretation into the majestic realm of eternal verity'. See Richard Helgerson, *Forms of Nationhood: The Elizabethan Writing of England* (Chicago: University of Chicago Press, 1992), 279 and 347, n. 49. Pollard is quoted by Rudolph Almasy, 'The Purpose of Richard Hooker's Polemic', *Journal of the History of Ideas*, 39 (1978), 251–70 at 251. The reputation of John Selden has undergone a similar hagiographical decontextualisation. See, for example, Eric Fletcher's speech to the Selden Society in 1969, printed in *John Selden 1584–1654: Selden Society Lecture Delivered in the Old Hall of Lincoln's Inn, July 9th 1969 by The Right Hon. Sir Eric Fletcher, MP, President of the Society* (London: Bernard Quaritch, 1969), 3. Likewise, John Milton is not often described as one of the contributors to the controversy over the payment of church tithes in 1659; but he wrote, among other controversial pamphlets, *Considerations touching The likeliest means to remove Hirelings out of the church. Wherein is also discourc'd Of Tithes, Church-fees, Church-revenues; And whether any maintenance of ministers can be settl'd by law* (London: T.N. for L. Chapman, 1659). For more on Milton's tendentiousness, see William Lamont, 'The Puritan Revolution: a historiographical essay' in J.G.A. Pocock, ed., *The Varieties of British political thought, 1500–1800* (Cambridge: Cambridge University Press, 1993), 119–46 at 122–3 and John N. King, *Milton and Religious Controversy: Satire and Polemic in Paradise Lost* (Cambridge: Cambridge University Press, 2000).
6. For example, during the Jacobean controversy over the payment of church tithes, William Sclater admits reluctantly that he has 'trod the pathes of *Mr. Seldens* Historie of Tithes', and another of John Selden's opponents, James Sempill, speculates 'perhaps its expected I should trace M. *Selden* in his storie': William Sclater, *The Quæstion of Tythes Revised. Arguments for the Moralitie of Tything, enlarged, and cleared. Obiections more fully, and distinctly answered. Mr Seldens Historie, so farre as Mistakers haue made it Argumentatiue against the Moralitie, ouer-ly viewed* (London: John Legatt, 1623), Gg2r; James Sempill, *Sacrilege sacredly handled. That is, According to Scripture onely. Diuided into two parts: 1. For the Law. 2. For the Gospell* (London: William Iones, for Edmund Weaver, 1619), Xr. For the rules of animadversion, see Joad Raymond, *Pamphlets and Pamphleteering in Early Modern Britain* (Cambridge: Cambridge University Press, 2003), 206–14; see also Lamont, 'The Puritan Revolution: a historiographical essay', 124. As Lamont observes, ecclesiastical controversy was both constituted by, and also produced binary oppositions since 'political and religious polemic thrived on the assimilation of one's opponent to a discredited polarity' (124).
7. William Prynne, *A Full Reply To certaine briefe Observations and Anti-Queries on Master Prynnes twelve Questions about Church-Government: Wherein the Frivolousnesse, Falsenesse, and grosse Mistakes of this Anonymous Answerer (ashamed of his Name) and his weak grounds for Independency, and Separation, are modestly discovered, reselled* (London: Michael Sparke Senior, 1644), B3v.
8. The advent of printing, and, later, the relaxation of censorship laws in 1641, helped propagate these debates; they culminated in the prolific textual production of the period between 1640 and 1660, the results of which were collected by the bookseller George Thomason in 1640–1 and became known as the Thomason Tracts. For printed controversy and pamphlet culture, see Raymond, *Pamphlets and Pamphleteering*. For the relationship between print culture and political and religious polemic, see for example, Michael Questier,

Conversion, Politics and Religion in England, 1580–1625 (Cambridge: Cambridge University Press, 1996), 12–40; Jesse Lander, *Inventing Polemic: Religion, Print, and Literary Culture in Early Modern England* (Cambridge: Cambridge University Press, 2006), Introduction; Thomas N. Corns, ed., *The Literature of Controversy: Polemical Strategy from Milton to Junius* (London: Frank Cass, 1987), Introduction and Alexandra Halasz, *The Marketplace of Print: Pamphlets and the Public Sphere in Early Modern England* (Cambridge: Cambridge University Press, 1997).

9. Although the distinction between spiritual and secular realms was not clear, it was nevertheless asserted, in part because early modern commentators used words such as 'politique' and 'polititian' derogatively to denote arguments which were considered ungodly and pragmatic, and the word 'spiritual' positively to denote those which manifested inner religious commitment; furthermore, such distinctions were made in debates about the relationship between church and state. In these debates, which are explored in the following chapters, those who desired the separation of church and state complained that spiritual leaders who interfere in civil affairs are acting in a way that would 'far better become *Polititians*, then *Ministers*'. See William Walwyn, *The Compassionate Samaritan, unbinding The Conscience, and powring Oyle into the wounds which have been made upon the Separation: recommending their future welfare to the serious thoughts, and carefull endeavours of all who love the peace and unity of Commonwealths men* ([London]: n.pub., 1644), A5r.

10. For example, there has been considerable debate about whether labels such as 'Conformist', 'Anglican' and 'Puritan' should be used to describe Protestant denominations, or whether such labels obscure their indeterminate nature. For the use of this terminology, see Patrick Collinson, *The Elizabethan Puritan Movement* (Oxford: Clarendon Press, 1990), 12–3; Peter Lake, *Anglicans and Puritans? Presbyterianism and English Conformist Thought from Whitgift to Hooker* (London: Unwin Hyman, 1988), 7–11; Kenneth Fincham, ed., *The Early Stuart Church, 1603–1642* (Basingstoke: Macmillan, 1993), 3–4 and Christopher Hill, *The English Bible and the Seventeenth-Century Revolution* (London: Penguin, 1993), 35. The use of the term 'Anglican' is, arguably, anachronistic; but it is employed here as a convenient marker.

11. Anon [William Prynne], *A Quench-coale. Or, A briefe Disquisition and Inquirie, in what place of the Church or Chancell the Lords-Table ought to be situated, especially when the sacrament is administered, written against Robert Shelford, Edmond Reeve, John Pocklington, and 'A late Coale from the Altar'* ([Amsterdam: Richt Right Press], 1637), B3r and Montagu, *Diatribæ upon the first part of the late history of tithes*, L6v.

12. For these elisions see Tony Claydon and Ian McBride, 'The Trials of the Chosen Peoples: Recent Interpretations of Protestantism and National Identity in Britain and Ireland' in Claydon and McBride, eds, *Protestantism and National Identity: Britain and Ireland, c.1650–c.1850* (Cambridge: Cambridge University Press, 1998), 3–33 at 13–4. For the construction of factional stereotypes in print, see Nicholas McDowell, *The English Radical Imagination: Culture, Religion, and Revolution, 1630–1660* (Oxford: Clarendon Press, 2003), especially Chapter 2. For the polemical strategies of English Catholics, see for example, Ceri Sullivan, *Dismembered Rhetoric: English Recusant Writing, 1580–1603* (London: Associated University Press, 1995).

13. Anon [John Goodwin], *Certaine briefe observations and antiquaeries: On Master Prin's twelve questions about church-government. Wherein is modestly showne, how un-usefull and frivolous they are; How bitter and unchristian in censuring that way; whereas there are no Reasons brought to contradict it. By a well-wisher to the Truth, and Master Prin.* ([London]: 1644?), A2v. As long as there was a national church, challenges to it could be interpreted as challenges to the state. For the seditious connotations of Puritanism, see for example, Andrew McRae, *Literature, Satire and the Early Stuart State* (Cambridge: Cambridge University Press, 2004), Chapter 6 and Anthony Milton, *Catholic and Reformed: The Roman and Protestant Churches in English Protestant Thought 1600–1640* (Cambridge: Cambridge University Press, 1995), 515–23. For fears that the common people would learn Hebrew and thereby gain direct access to the interpretation of scripture, rejecting clerical authority, see Nicholas McDowell, 'The Stigmatising of Puritans as Jews in Jacobean England: Ben Jonson, Francis Bacon and the Book of Sports Controversy', *Renaissance Studies*, 19 (2005), 348–63 at 353.
14. See Thomas Rogers, *The faith, doctrine, and religion, professed, & protected in the Realme of England, and Dominions of the Same: Expressed in 39 Articles, concordably agreed upon by the reverend Bishops, and Clergie of this Kingdome, at two severall meetings, or Convocations of theirs, in the yeares of our Lord, 1562, and 1604* (Cambridge: Iohn Legatt, 1607), ¶¶¶2v. Rogers refers to 'our English Sabbatarians' as 'demi-Iewes' (Bb4r).
15. These patterns of triangulation were also constructed between Christians, Jews and Turks. For triangulation between Jews, Christians and Turks in *The Jew of Malta*, see Emily C. Bartels, *Spectacles of Strangeness: Imperialism, Alienation, and Marlowe* (Philadelphia: University of Pennsylvania Press, 1993), Chapter 4. For religious triangulation involving Turks more generally, see Nabil Matar, *Turks, Moors and Englishmen in the Age of Discovery* (New York: Columbia University Press, 1999), especially Chapter 3; Matthew Dimmock, *New Turkes: Dramatising Islam and the Ottomans in Early Modern England* (Aldershot: Ashgate, 2005); Daniel J. Vitkus, *Turning Turk: English Theatre and the Multicultural Mediterranean* (New York: Palgrave, 2002) and Anthony Milton, *Catholic and Reformed: The Roman and Protestant Churches in English Protestant Thought 1600–1640* (Cambridge: Cambridge University Press, 1995), 63.
16. Robert Davenport, *A Pleasant and Witty Comedy: Called, A New Tricke to Cheat the Divell* (London: John Okes, for Humphrey Blunden, 1639), F4v. For literary associations between Puritans and Jews, see for example, Paul N. Siegel, 'Shylock and the Puritan Usurers', in Arthur D. Matthews and Clark M. Emery, eds, *Studies in Shakespeare* (Florida: University of Miami Press, 1953), 129–39.
17. Ben Jonson, *Bartholomew Fayre: A Comedie, Acted in the yeare 1614. By the Lady Elizabeths Servants. And then dedicated to King Iames, of most Blessed Memorie* (London: I.B. for Robert Allot, 1631), in *The Workes of Benjamin Johnson. The Second Volume* (London: Richard Meighen, 1640), C4r. The word 'Brethren' here indicates his Nonconformist affiliation.
18. This book does not aim to contribute to the study of Christian Hebraism, except in terms of the significance of Hebraism in the context of Christian debate. For Christian Hebraism, see for example, Gareth Lloyd Jones, *The Discovery of Hebrew in Tudor England: A Third Language* (Manchester: Manchester University Press, 1983); Frank E. Manuel, *The Broken Staff: Judaism*

through Christian Eyes (Cambridge: Harvard University Press, 1992), 1–54 and 103–34; Jerome Friedman, *The Most Ancient Testimony: Sixteenth-Century Christian-Hebraica in the Age of Renaissance Nostalgia* (Ohio: The Kent State University Press, 1983) and Stephen G. Burnett, *From Christian Hebraism to Jewish Studies* (Leiden: E.J. Brill, 1996), 134.

19. See Lloyd Jones, *The Discovery of Hebrew in Tudor England*, 144–77.
20. John Udall, *Mafteach Leshon ha-Kodesh. That is the key of the holy language. Wherein is contained, first the Hebrew grammar (in a manner) woord for woord out of P. Martinius. Secondly A practize upon the first, the twentie fift and the sixtie eight Psalms, according to the rules of the same grammar. Thirdly, A short Dictionary conteining the Hebrue woords that are found in the Bible with their proper significations. All Englished for the benefit of those that (being ignoraunt in the Latin) are desirous to learn the holy tongue* (Leiden: Francis Raphelengius, 1593).
21. Conformists often twinned the Puritan tendency to derive arguments from the etymology of Hebrew words with the tendency to derive them from the heathen Classics. Bishop Bilson (1546/7–1616) complains of Hugh Broughton's use of Jewish sources along with his use of 'heathen writers', 'pagan Poets' 'prophane Philosophers' and 'your owne classical writers': Thomas Bilson, *The effect of certaine Sermons touching the full redemption of mankind by the death and bloud of Christ Jesus: wherein Besides the merite of Christs suffering, the manner of his offering, the power of his death, the comfort of his Crosse, the glorie of his resurrection, Are handled* (London: Peter Short for Walter Burre, 1599), Aaa4r–v.
22. For post-Reformation biblical translation, see Debora K. Shuger, *The Renaissance Bible: Scholarship, Sacrifice and Subjectivity* (Berkeley: University of California Press, 1994); Christopher Hill, *The English Bible and the Seventeenth-Century Revolution* (London: Penguin, 1993); Ilona N. Rashkow, *Upon the Dark Places: Anti-Semitism and Sexism in English Renaissance Biblical Translation* (Syracuse: Sheffield Academic Press, 1990), Chapters 1 and 2. For the problems of translating religious texts, see for example, David Jasper, ed., *Translating Religious Texts: Translation, Transgression and Interpretation* (Basingstoke: Macmillan Press, 1993). For an overview of English Renaissance translation, see Warren Boutcher, 'The Renaissance (c.1500–1650)' in Peter France, ed., *The Oxford Guide to Literature in English Translation* (Oxford: Oxford University Press, 2000), 45–54.
23. Edward Dering, *A bryefe and necessary Catechisme or Instruction. Very needefull to be knowne of al Housholders. Wherby they may the better teach and instructe theyr Families, in such pointes of Christian Religion as is most meete* (London: John Charlewood, 1577), Preface to the reader, A5v.
24. Anon, *A Seconde Admonition to the Parliament* (London: Christopher Barker, 1579), Biiiir–v.
25. Thomas Cartwright, *The Second replie of Thomas Cartwright: agaynst Maister Doctor Whitgiftes second answer/touching the Churche Discipline* ([Heidelberg: M. Schirat], 1575), Qv.
26. Gregory Martin, *A Discoverie of the manifold corruptions of the Holy Scriptures by the Heretikes of our daies, specially the English Sectaries, and of their foule dealing herein, by partial & false translations to the advantage of their heresies, in the English Bibles used and authorised since the time of Schisme* (Rheims: Iohn Fogny, 1582), a7r.

27. Broughton records his encounters: 'with three Iewes I had spech: At Amsteldem with Rabbi Farar a Physician: At Hanaw with the Synagogue Doctor Rabbi Wolf; At Basil, with a Rabbin most desirous of christianity'. Hugh Broughton, *A Require of Agreement to the Groundes of Divinitie studie: wherin great scholers falling, & being caught of Iewes, disgrace the Gospel: & trap them to destruction* (Middleburgh: R. Schilders, 1611), Dedicatory epistle to members of the Merchant Adventurer Company, Bv.
28. Hugh Broughton, *An Epistle to the Nobilitie of England with ancient warrant for euerie worde, vnto the full satisfaction of any that be of hart* (Middleburg: Richard Schilders, 1597), Aiiir. The word 'Hebrew' was thought to be derived from the name of Heber, or Eber as he is known in the Authorised Version, who was the great-grandson of Noah's son Shem. See David Katz, *Philo-Semitism and the Readmission of the Jews to England, 1603–1655* (Oxford: Clarendon Press, 1982), 60–1.
29. Ben Jonson, *The Alchemist* (London: Thomas Snodham, for Walter Burre, 1612), E2v. See James Shapiro, *Shakespeare and the Jews* (New York: Columbia University Press, 1996), 148. For Broughton, see for example, Lloyd Jones, *The Discovery of Hebrew*, 164–8. For a discussion of Broughton's scriptural ideas in relation to his apocalyptic ones, see Katharine R. Firth, *The Apocalyptic Tradition in Reformation Britain 1530–1645* (Oxford: Oxford University Press, 1979), 150–64.
30. Hugh Broughton, *Daniel his Chaldie visions and his Ebrew: both translated after the originall; and expounded both by reduction of heathen most famous stories unto the exact proprietie of his wordes (which is the surest certaintie what he must meane:) and by ioyning all the Bible, and learned tongues to the frame of his worke* (London: Gabriell Simson, 1597), *4v.
31. Broughton, *An Epistle*, B4v.
32. Broughton, *An Epistle*, Br.
33. Broughton writes: 'St Matthewes Gospell was written at the first, by that heavenly oratorious Greeke, which now we have; and if the holy Ghost had written it in the Iewes Ierusalem Ebrew, the holy learned of all time, would have kept it with more care, then Iewellers all precious stones' (Broughton, *An Epistle*, D3v.)
34. Broughton, *An Epistle*, Br.
35. Broughton, *An Epistle*, G2v. Broughton's phrase 'vowelled Ebrew' refers to the extensive controversy over vowel points in Hebrew script, which concerned whether the Bible was given to Moses on Mount Sinai with all the vowels in place, or whether they were added in by later rabbis, thereby rendering the text of the Bible in Hebrew untrustworthy. Broughton sided with the Jews against the Roman Catholics, claiming that vowels were in the original text of the Bible. This controversy foregrounded Christian preoccupations with the difference between authentic biblical and heretical post-biblical Jews. See J. Bowman, 'A Forgotten Controversy', *Evangelical Quarterly*, 20 (1948), 46–69 and Burnett, *From Christian Hebraism to Jewish Studies*, 203–40.
36. Hugh Broughton, *An Exposition on the Lords Prayer, compared with the Decalogue, as it was preached in a Sermon, at Oatelands: before the most Noble, Henry Prince of Wales. Aug. 13. Anno 1613. With a Postscript, to advertise of an error in all those that leave out the Conclusion of the Lords Prayer* ([Amsterdam: n.pub., 1613]), B4v.

37. Broughton, *An Epistle*, 3.
38. Hugh Broughton, *An Explication of the article κατῆλθε ὲις ἅδον, of our Lordes soules going from his body to Paradise; touched by the Greek, generally αδον, The world of Soules; termed Hel by the old Saxon, & by all our translations: with a defense of the Q. of Englands religion* ([Printed abroad], 1599), Preface, 2v, Ar.
39. See Collinson, *Godly People*, 336 and 370. Collinson writes of Field, 'in speaking of him, we are introducing the principal character in the drama': Collinson, *The Elizabethan Puritan Movement*, 86. See also Collinson, 'John Field and Elizabethan Puritanism' in *Godly People*, 335–71.
40. John Field, trans., *Thirteene Sermons of Maister Iohn Calvine* (London: Thomas Dawson for Tobie Cooke and Thomas Man, 1579), Dedicatory Epistle to the Earl and Countess of Bedford, A3v–A4r.
41. John Field, *A Caveat for Parsons Howlet, concerning his untimely flighte, and scriching in the cleare day lighte of the Gospell, necessarie for him and all the rest of that darke broode, and uncleane cage of papistes, who with their untimely bookes, seeke the discredite of the trueth, and the disquiet of this Church of England* (London: Robert Waldegrave, for Thomas Man, & Toby Smith, 1581), C4r–C6r.
42. For the use of Jewish sources in early modern biblical exegesis, see as a starting point Debora Kuller Shuger, *The Renaissance Bible: Scholarship, Sacrifice and Subjectivity* (Berkeley: University of California Press, 1994), 33–6.
43. Anon, *An Admonition, to the Parliament* ([Hemel Hempstead: J. Stroud], 1572), C3v.
44. See Patrick Collinson, *The Birthpangs of Protestant England: Religious and Cultural Change in the Sixteenth and Seventeenth Centuries* (Basingstoke: Macmillan Press, 1988), 3–11, 7–27; Collinson, 'Biblical Rhetoric: The English Nation and National Sentiment in the Prophetic Mode' in Claire McEachern and Debora Shuger, eds, *Religion and Culture in Renaissance England* (Cambridge: Cambridge University Press, 1997), 15–46 and Claydon and McBride, 'The trials of the chosen peoples'.
45. See for instance Field's preface to Henry Lord Huntingdon, introducing his translation of *Foure Sermons of Maister Iohn Calvin, Entreating of matters very profitable for our time, as may bee seene by the Preface: With a briefe exposition of the LXXXVII Psalme. Translated out of Frenche into Englishe by Iohn Fielde* (London: Thomas Man, 1579), → 2v.
46. Dering, *A bryefe and necessary Catechisme or Instruction*, Preface to the reader, B4r.
47. Anthony Gilby, *A Commentarye upon the Prophet Mycha. Written by Anthony Gilby* (London: John Daye, 1551), A6v.
48. Gilby, *A Commentarye upon the Prophet Mycha*, A3v.
49. Christopher Fetherstone, trans., *Haggeus, the Prophet, Haggeus, the Prophet. Where-unto is added a most plentifull commentary, gathered out of the publique lectures of D. Iohn Iames Gryneus, professor of Divinitie in the University of Basill, and now first published, Faithfully translated out of Latin into English, by Christopher Fetherstone student in Divinity* (London: John Wolfe for John Harrison the Younger, 1586), Dedicatory epistle to the Baron of Bletsoe, A3r. BL pressmark: 3166.aa.21. The word 'angle' also carries the sense of 'Anglo' or 'English'.
50. Whitgift, *The Defense of the Aunswere to the Admonition, against the Replie of T.C. by Iohn Whitgift Doctor of Divinitie* (London: Henry Binneman, for Humfrey Toye, 1574), Kvr.

51. Whitgift, *The Defense of the Aunswere*, K6v.
52. Cartwright, *A Replye to an answere*, Fiir.
53. Whitgift, *The Defense of the Aunswere*, Lr.
54. Cartwright, *The Second replie of Thomas Cartwright*, Miiiir.
55. For the Continent as a provider of Jewish knowledge, see for example, Lloyd Jones, *The Discovery of Hebrew*, Chapter 3 and 201–7; Rivkah Zim, *English Metrical Psalms: Poetry as Praise and Prayer 1535–1601* (Cambridge: Cambridge University Press, 1987), Chapter 4 and Manuel, *The Broken Staff*, 51–6.
56. The authors of *The Second Admonition* refer the reader to 'the examples of the best Churches beyonde the seas / as Geneva / Fraunce / &c' (Biir).
57. For the transmission into England of representations of the massacre, see Robert M. Kingdon, *Myths about the St. Bartholomew's Day Massacres 1572–1576* (Cambridge, MA: Harvard University Press, 1988), 'Introduction' and chapter 7; J.H.M. Salmon, *The French Religious Wars in English Political Thought* (Oxford: Clarendon Press, 1959) and Lisa Ferraro Parmelee, *Good Newes from Fraunce: French Anti-League Propaganda in late Elizabethan England* (New York: University of Rochester Press, 1996), 30–1. For French Protestants' political use of Jewish material, see Manuel, *The Broken Staff*, 51–6.
58. One of the most popular accounts was the Huguenot François Hotman's *De furoribus gallicis*, which appeared in several Latin and English editions. The Huguenot printer Thomas Vautrollier also published news from France in London, including the Puritan Arthur Golding's translation of a massacre pamphlet by Jean de Serres or Francois Hotman: *The Lyfe of the most godly, valiant and noble capteine . . . Iasper Colignie Shatilion* (1576). Sections of another tract, *Vindiciae, Contra Tyrannos* (1579), variously attributed to Philippe de Mornay and Hubert Languet, which justified armed resistance to tyranny, circulated in England from 1588. See George Garnett, ed., *Vindiciæ contra Tyrannos; a Defence of Liberty against Tyrants. Or, Of the lawfull power of the prince over the people, and of the people over the prince. Being a treatise written in Latin and French by Junius Brutus, and translated out of both into English* (Cambridge: Cambridge University Press, 1994).
59. John Stubbs, *The Discoverie of a gaping gulf whereinto England is like to be swallowed by another French marriage, if the Lord forbid not the banes by letting her majestie see the sin and punishment thereof* (London: H. Singleton for W. Page, 1579).
60. For the relationship between English Protestantism and Geneva, see N.M. Sutherland, 'The English Refugees at Geneva, 1555–1559' in Richard C. Gamble, ed., *Calvinism in France, Netherlands, Scotland, and England* (London: Garland, 1992), 271–80 and Robert M. Kingdon, *Church and Society in Reformation Europe* (London: Variorum Reprints, 1985), Chapters 5–9.
61. Philippe de Mornay, *A worke concerning the trewnesse of the Christian religion. Begunne to be translated by Sir P Sidney and finished by A Golding* (London: [J. Charlewood and G. Robinson] for T. Cadman, 1587), Hh8v–Iir. For the translation of this text, see for example, Louis Thorn Golding, *An Elizabethan Puritan: Arthur Golding the Translator of Ovid's Metamorphoses and also of John Calvin's Sermons* (New York: Richard R. Smith, 1937), 131.
62. Mornay, *A worke concerning the trewnesse*, Preface to the reader, ***v.

63. Anthony Gilby, trans., *The Psalmes of Dauid, truly opened and explaned by Paraphrasis, according to the right sense of euerie Psalme. With lage and ample Arguments before everie Psalme, declaring the true use thereof* (London: Henrie Denham, 1581), Epistle to the reader, A3r.
64. John Field, trans., *The Iudgement of a Most Reverend and Learned Man from Beyond the Seas, Concerning a Threefold Order of Bishops, With a Declaration of Certaine Other Waightie Points, Concerning the Discipline and Government of the Church* ([1580]).
65. For Sidney's continental contacts, see Blair Worden, *The Sound of Virtue: Philip Sidney's Arcadia and Elizabethan Politics* (New Haven: Yale University Press, 1996), 50–7; Martin N. Raitiere, *Faire Bitts: Sir Philip Sidney and Renaissance Political Theory* (Pittsburgh: Duquesne University Press, 1984), 7–9 and James M. Osborn, *Young Philip Sidney 1572–1577* (New Haven: Yale University Press, 1972).
66. See Diane Bornstein, 'The Style of the Countess of Pembroke's Translation of Philippe de Mornay's *Discours de la vie et de la mort*' in Margaret P. Hannay, ed., *Silent But for the Word: Tudor Women as Patrons, Translators, and Writers of Religious Works* (Athens, Ohio: The Kent State University Press, 1985), 126–49.
67. Franciscus Junius, *Grammatica Hebraeae Linguae* (Frankfurt: A. Wechel, 1580), Dedicatory Epistle, aijr–v. The translation is taken from Jan A. Van Dorsten, 'Sidney and Franciscus Junius the Elder', *The Huntington Library Quarterly*, 42 (1978), 1–13.
68. (Frankfurt: A. Wechel, 1575–1579). For Tremellius, see Lloyd Jones, *The Discovery of Hebrew*, 50–2.
69. Philip Sidney, *An Apologie for Poetrie. Written by the right noble, vertuous, and learned, Sir Phillip Sidney, Knight* (London: Henry Olney, 1595), C2v. For Protestant notions of the poetic or eloquent features of scripture, see Achsah Guibbory, *Ceremony and community from Herbert to Milton: Literature, religion and cultural conflict in seventeenth-century England* (Cambridge: Cambridge University Press, 1998); Barbara K. Lewalski, *Protestant Poetics and the Seventeenth-Century Religious Lyric* (New Jersey: Princeton University Press, 1979); Debora Shuger, *Sacred Rhetoric: The Christian Grand style in the English Renaissance* (New Jersey: Princeton University Press, 1988) and Hannay, ed., *Silent But for the Word*, Introduction.
70. For the political motivations of psalm translation, see Christopher Hill, *The English Bible and the Seventeenth-Century Revolution* (London: Penguin, 1993), 351–62; for Sidney's motivations in particular see Maureen Quilligan, 'Sidney and his Queen', in Heather Dubrow and Richard Strier, *The Historical Renaissance* (Chicago: Chicago University Press, 1988), 101–23 at 108.
71. For the Sidneian Psalms, see Zim, *English Metrical Psalms*, Chapter 5; Margaret P. Hannay, *Phillip's Pheonix: Mary Sidney, Countess of Pembroke* (Oxford: Oxford University Press, 1990), 91 and Hannay, ed., *Silent But for the Word*.
72. See Zim, *English Metrical Psalms*, Appendix, 211–60.
73. For the use of rabbinical literature in Christian biblical exegesis, see Burnett, *From Christian Hebraism to Jewish Studies*, 134 and Manuel, *The Broken Staff*, 128–41.
74. Martin, *A Discoverie*, Xv.

75. For the debate over Christ's descent to Hell see Dewey D. Wallace, 'Puritan and Anglican: The Interpretation of Christ's Descent into hell in Elizabethan Theology', *Archiv fur reformationsgeschichte*, 69 (1978), 248–88; James Hastings, eds, *A Dictionary of Christ and the Gospels* (Edinburgh: T. & T. Clark, 1906), I, 713–6; James Hastings et al., *A Dictionary of the Apostolic Church* (Edinburgh: T. & T. Clark, 1915), I, 289–92 and John Henry Blunt, ed., *Dictionary of Sects, Heresies, Ecclesiastical Parties, and Schools of Religious Thought* (London: Rivingtons, 1874), 226. The doctrine is derived from biblical passages such as Matthew 27:52 ff., Luke 23:43 and 1 Peter 3:18–20.
76. Bilson's *The effect of certaine Sermons* (1599) was answered by *A treatise of the sufferings and victory of Christ* (1598) by the Puritan minister Henry Jacob. Bilson replied in 1604 with *A Survey of Christs sufferings*, and both Bilson's works were also answered by Hugh Broughton in his *A Replie upon the R.R.F.TH. Winton for heads of his divinity in his sermon and survey: How he taught a perfect truth, that our Lord went he[n]ce to Paradise: But adding that he went thence to Hades, & striving to prove that, he injurieth all learning & Christianity* ([Amsterdam]: n.p., 1605).
77. For Rashi (Solomon ben Isaac [1040–1105]) and Midrash, see as a starting point Cecil Roth and Geoffrey Wigoder, eds, *Encyclopaedia Judaica*, 16 vols (Jerusalem: Keter Press, 1972), XIII, 1558–1566 and XI, 1507, respectively.
78. Broughton, *A Replie upon the R.R.F.TH. Winton*, B8r.
79. Broughton, *A Replie upon the R.R.F.TH. Winton*, Br.
80. Bilson, *The effect of certaine Sermons*, Xr.
81. Henry Jacob, *A Defence of a treatise touching the sufferings and victorie of Christ in the worke of our Redemption* (London: n.p., 1600), T4v.
82. Hugh Broughton, *Declaration of generall corruption of Religion, Scripture and all learning; wrought by D. Bilson. While he breedeth a new opinion, that our Lord went from Paradise to Gehenna, to triumph over the Devills* ([Middelburg: Richard Schilders], 1603), no sig.
83. Bilson, *The Survey of Christs sufferings*, Bbbr.
84. Thomas Bilson, *The Survey of Christs sufferings*, ¶3r.
85. Anon, *Master Broughtons Letters*, A3r.
86. See Henry Jacob, *A Treatise of the Sufferings and Victory of Christ, in the work of our redemption: Declaring by the Scriptures these two questions: That Christ suffered for us the wrath of God, which we maywell terme the paynes of Hell, or Hellish sorrowes* ([Middelburg: Richard Schilders],1598), D8r and K2v.
87. Broughton, *A Replie upon the R.R.F.TH. Winton*, Cv.
88. Broughton, *A Replie upon the R.R.F.TH. Winton*, Cr.
89. Broughton, *Declaration of generall corruption*, no sig.
90. Anon, *Master Broughtons Letters*, C3v.
91. Anon, *Master Broughtons Letters*, C4v.
92. For Selden, see Jason P. Rosenblatt, *Renaissance England's Chief Rabbi: John Selden* (Oxford: Oxford University Press, 2006); Reid Barbour, *John Selden: Measures of the Holy Commonwealth in Seventeenth-Century England* (Toronto: University of Toronto Press, 2003); Edith Bershadsky, 'Controlling the Terms of the Debate: John Selden and the Tithes Controversy' in Gordon J. Schochet, Patricia E. Tatspaugh, and Carol Brobeck, eds, *Law, Literature and the Settlement of Regimes* (Washington: Folger, 1990), 187–220; Rosenblatt, *Torah and Law in Paradise Lost* (Princeton: Princeton University Press, 1994),

Chapter 2; Jonathan R. Ziskind, trans. and ed., *John Selden on Jewish Marriage Law: The Uxor Hebraica* (London: E.J. Brill, 1991); Richard A. Filloy, 'The Religious and Political Views of John Selden: A Study in Early Stuart Humanism', unpublished Ph.D. dissertation, University of California at Berkeley, 1977; A.L. Rowse, *Four Caroline Portraits: Thomas Hobbes, Henry Marten, Hugh Peters, John Selden* (London: Gerald Duckworth & Co., 1993), 125–55 and Paul Christianson, *Discourse on History, Law, and Governance in the Public Career of John Selden, 1610–1635* (Toronto: University of Toronto Press, 1996).

93. See Jonathan R. Ziskind, 'Petrus Cunæus on Theocracy, Jubilee and the Latifundia', in Abraham I. Katsh, ed., *The Jewish Quarterly Review*, 68 (1978), 235–55.

94. See Rosenblatt, *Renaissance England's Chief Rabbi*, Chapter 6 and Richard Tuck, *Philosophy and Government 1572–1651* (Cambridge: Cambridge University Press, 1993), Chapter 5. For the works of Scaliger (1540–1609), see Anthony Grafton, *Joseph Scaliger: A Study in the History of Classical Scholarship* (Oxford: Clarendon Press, 1983).

95. The *mos gallicum* was practiced by continental jurists such as the Huguenot Francois Hotman (1524–1590). For more on this methodology, see J.H.M. Salmon, *The French Religious Wars in English Political Thought* (Oxford: Clarendon Press, 1959), 58–69; Kevin Sharpe, *Politics and Ideas in Early Stuart England: Essays and Studies* (London: Pinter, 1989), Chapter 6 and Donald R. Kelley, 'The French School' in J.H. Burns, ed., *The Cambridge History of Political Thought 1450–1700* (Cambridge: Cambridge University Press, 1991), 78–80. Selden attempts to justify the importation of the *mos gallicum* to England: 'why may not equally a *Common Lawier of England* use this *Philologie?*': John Selden, *The Historie of Tithes. That is, The Practice of payment of them. The Positive laws made for them. The opinions touching the Right of them. A review of it is also annext, which both Confirmes it and directs in the Use of it* (London: n.pub., 1618), C4v.

96. Selden makes an explicit case for Jewish history to become the subject matter not only of Christian theology but also of the Common Law: 'nor is the *Practice* or *Laws* of Tithes among the *Iews*, as they are deliverd & interpreted by their Doctors, more indeed restraind to the course of *Diuinitie*, then of *Law* and *Historie*' (Selden, *The Historie of Tithes*, C4r).

97. See Rowse, *Four Caroline Portraits*, 140.

98. Selden, *The Historie of Tithes*, a3v–a4r.

99. Ziskind, *Selden on Jewish Marriage Law*, 10. See also F. Smith Fussner's eulogising portrait in *The Historical Revolution: English Historical Writing and Thought 1580–1640* (London: Routledge and Kegan Paul, 1962), 278–9 and see also Arthur B. Ferguson, *Clio Unbound: Perception of the Social and Cultural Past in Renaissance England* (Durham, NC: Duke University Press, 1979), 117–24. Frank Manuel writes about another of Selden's apparently disinterested projects, his *Uxor Ebraica* (Hebrew Wife; 1646): 'While the treatment of Jewish laws on marriage and divorce was an objective, scholarly rendition of Talmudic opinion, the deeper motive behind Selden's exhaustive analysis was to revamp contemporary British divorce laws' (Manuel, *The Broken Staff*, 81). Christianson is, likewise, aware of Selden's partiality; see his *Discourse on History, Law, and Governance*, 197–211.

158   Notes

100. Montagu, *Diatribæ upon the first part of the late history of tithes*, B8v. Another respondent, Stephen Nettles, sarcastically refers to his opponent as 'the *Historian*'.
101. See Christianson, *Discourse on History, Law, and Governance*, 65.
102. See D.R. Woolf, *The Idea of History in Early Stuart England: Erudition, Ideology, and 'The Light of Truth' from the Accession of James I to the Civil War* (Toronto: University of Toronto Press, 1990), 222.
103. For the rise of Common Law and its relationship to Civil and Canon law, see J.G.A. Pocock, *The Ancient Constitution and the Feudal Law: A study of English Historical Thought in the Seventeenth Century* (Cambridge: Cambridge University Press, 1987), Chapters 1–3; J.H. Baker, *The Legal Profession and the Common Law: Historical Essays* (London: The Hambledon Press, 1986); John Guy, 'The Henrician Age' in J.G.A. Pocock, ed., *The Varieties of British Political Thought, 1500–1800* (Cambridge: Cambridge University Press, 1993), 22–30; Ann Hughes, *The Causes of the English Civil War* (Basingstoke: Macmillan Press, 1998), 74–9 and J.H. Baker, *An Introduction to English Legal History* (London: Butterworths, 1979), 111–4.
104. From the 1590s onwards, a pamphlet war arose between advocates of ecclesiastical jurisdiction on one hand and parliamentary jurisdiction on the other, intensifying in 1605 when Richard Bancroft, Archbishop of Canterbury, and the chief justice of the Court of Common Pleas, Sir Edward Coke (1552–1634) became involved. The first commentator to assert the divine right of tithes in print was the bishop of Chichester, George Carleton (1559–1628), who published *Tithes examined and proved to bee due to the Clergie by a divine right. Whereby the contentious and prophane Atheists, as also the dissembling Hypocrites of this age, may learne to honour the Ministers and not to defraude them, and to Rob the Church* (London: T. Este for Clement Knight, 1606). Carleton's sentiments were endorsed by Thomas Ridley, a prominent Civil and Canon lawyer, the historian and antiquary Henry Spelman and the divine Foulke Robarts. For the tithes controversy of the early seventeenth century, see Christopher Hill, *Economic Problems of the Church: From Archbishop Whitgift to the Long Parliament* (Oxford: Clarendon Press, 1956), Chapter 5; Christianson, *Discourse on History*, 64; Bershadsky, 'Controlling the Terms of the Debate: John Selden and the Tithes Controversy' in Schochet et al., eds, *Law, Literature and the Settlement of Regimes*, 197 and Edith Bershadsky, 'Politics, Erudition and Ecclesiology: John Selden's Historie of Tithes', unpublished Ph.D. dissertation, University of Michigan, 1994.
105. James Sempill, *Sacrilege sacredly handled. That is, According to Scripture onely. Diuided into two parts: 1. For the Law. 2. For the Gospell. An appendix also added; answering some Objections mooued, namely, against this Treatise* (London: William Iones, for Edmund Weaver, 1619).
106. Richard Tillesley, *Animadversions upon M. Selden's History of Tithes, and his review thereof: Before which (in lieu of the two first Chapters purposely pretermitted) is premised a Catalogue of seuenty two Authours, before the year 1215* (London: John Bill, 1619).
107. Stephen Nettles, *An answer to the Jewish part of Mr. Selden's History of Tithes* (Oxford: J. Lichfield & W. Turner, 1625). Stephen Nettles goes as far as to assert that the refusal to pay tithes will result in 'the decay of learning, the

ruine of Religion, and stopping the mouth of the Gospell, the bane of hospitality, the desolation of the poore, the delapidation of Churches, the contempt of the ministry of the Church, and neglect of all goodnes, &c'. See Nettles, *An answer*, Av. There were many other written replies to Selden's tract. For these, see Bershadsky, 'Controlling the Terms of the Debate' 198 and G.J. Toomer, 'Selden's Historie of Tithes: Genesis, Publication, Aftermath', *Huntington Library Quarterly*, 65 (2002), 345–78.
108. Montagu, *Diatribæ upon the first part of the late history of tithes*, G3v.
109. Selden, *The Historie of Tithes*, S2r–v.
110. For more on Selden's life, see Bershadsky, 'Controlling the Terms of the Debate', Richard A. Filloy, 'The Religious and Political Views of John Selden: A Study in Early Stuart Humanism', unpublished Ph.D. dissertation, University of California at Berkeley, 1977 and A.L. Rowse, *Four Caroline Portraits: Thomas Hobbes, Henry Marten, Hugh Peters, John Selden* (London: Gerald Duckworth & Co., 1993), 125–55.
111. Selden, *The Historie of Tithes*, D3r, A4r.
112. Nettles, *An answer*, Xr.
113. Nettles, *An answer*, H2r.
114. Tillesley, *Animadversions*, C2v.
115. Montagu, *Diatribæ upon the first part of the late history of tithes*, N6v.
116. Montagu, *Diatribæ upon the first part of the late history of tithes*, Cc5v. The Gemara is the later part of the Talmud, comprised of Rabbinic commentaries. Montagu accuses Selden: 'you with your *Rabbins* and *Talmudists* haue mistaught us' (X2r), and discounts 'any Rabbine of the rabble of Talmuditicall Writers' (Y2v).
117. Montagu, *Diatribæ upon the first part of the late history of tithes*, Aav. The word 'Hag' carries connotations of both the ugly and the fabled. Montagu is referring here to Selden's invocation of Moses Maimonedes (1135–1204), the rabbinical authority and philosopher. See Roth et al., eds, *Encyclopaedia Judaica*, 11, 754–82.
118. The relationship between Parliament and crown became increasingly fraught during the reign of James. See Conrad Russell, *The Crisis of Parliaments: English History 1509–1660* (Oxford: Oxford University Press, 1971), 266–84; Barry Coward, *The Stuart Age: A history of England 1603–1714* (London: Longman, 1994), 94–6 and Stuart E. Prall, *Church and State in Tudor and Stuart England* (Arlington Heights, Illinois: Harlan Davidson, 1993), 106–11. For James I's efforts to prove the divine right of kings against the arguments of Common lawyers, see J.P. Sommerville, 'James I and the divine right of kings: English politics and continental theory' in Linda Levy Peck, ed., *The Mental World of the Jacobean Court* (Cambridge: Cambridge University Press, 1991), 55–71.
119. Sempill, *Sacrilege sacredly handled*, S3v.
120. Tillesley, *Animadversions*, ¶4r–v.
121. Selden continues: 'Nor will it, I think, looke like what were patcht up out of *Postils, Polyantheas*, common place books or any of the rest of such excellent Instruments for the aduancement of Ignorance and Lazinesse' (Selden, *The Historie of Tithes*, A4r–v). In other words, it is the piling up of precedents, rather than the use of trivialising summaries, which lends his arguments weight.
122. See Katz, *Philo-Semitism*, 175.

123. Lightfoot produced an edition of Hugh Broughton's works in 1662. See Shapiro, *Shakespeare and the Jews*, 243, n. 132 and Katz, *Philo-semitism*, 87. See also Crowley, who writes in 'Erastianism in the Westminster Assembly': 'It appears that Erastian success in the Assembly was closely tied to Hebrew proficiency' (56–8).
124. The accusation of Puritan ceremonialism was especially ironic given that ceremonialism was the grounds on which Puritans accused the Anglican church during the Laudian debates of the 1630s, the subject of the following chapter. On early modern Christians' dilemmas concerning the application of the Old Testament, see David Katz, *Sabbath and Sectarianism in Seventeenth-century England* (Leiden: E.J. Brill, 1988), xiii.
125. On Sabbatarianism, see for example, Katz, *Sabbath and Sectarianism*, Kenneth L. Parker, *The English Sabbath: A Study of Doctrine and Discipline from the Reformation to the Civil War* (Cambridge: Cambridge University Press, 1988); Christopher Hill, *Society and Puritanism*, Chapter 5 and Bryan W. Ball, *The Seventh-day Men: Sabbatarians and Sabbatarianism in England and Wales, 1600–1800* (Oxford: Clarendon Press, 1994).
126. See Katz, *Sabbath and Sectarianism*, 9.
127. Thomas Fuller, *The Church-History of Britain; From the Birth of Jesus Christ, Untill the Year M.DC. XLVIII. Endeavoured By Thomas Fuller* (London: John Williams, 1655), Kkkk2v–Kkkk3r. For Traske see Katz, *Philo-Semitism*, 18–34; H.E.I. Phillips, 'An Early Stuart Judaizing Sect', *Transactions of the Jewish Historical Society of England*, 15 (1946), 63–72; R.B. White, 'John Traske (1585–1636) and London Puritanism', *Transactions of the Congregational Historical Society*, 20 (1968), 223–33; David R. Como, 'The Kingdom of Christ, the Kingdom of England, and the Kingdom of Traske: John Traske and the Persistence of Radical Puritanism in Early Stuart England' in Muriel C. McClendon, Joseph P. Ward and Michael MacDonald, eds, *Protestant Identities: Religion, Society, and Self-Fashioning in Post-Reformation England* (Stanford, CA: Stanford University Press, 1999), 63–82 and Ball, *The Seventh-day Men*, Chapter 2.
128. D.B. [John Falconer], *A Briefe Refutation of Iohn Traskes Iudaicall And Novel Fancyes. Stiling himselfe Minister of Gods Word, imprisoned for the Lawes eternall Perfection, or Gods Lawes perfect eternity* ([Saint Omer: English College Press, 1618]), Fv, Br and Bv–B2r. See also Edward Norrice, *The new gospel not the true gospel, Or, A discovery of the Life and Death, Doctrin, and Doings of Mr. Iohn Traske, and the effects of all, in his Followers* (London: R. Bishop, for Henry Hood, 1638), A4r; see also Fuller, *History*, X, 76 and Katz, *Philo-Semitism*, 25.
129. See Pagitt, *Heresiography*, N8r; Katz, *Philo-Semitism*, 20–9.
130. Pagitt mentions 'one Theophilus Braborne', who 'endeavoured with [Traske] to bring back again the Jewish Sabbath, and to that purpose writ a book in the yeare 1632', and also 'had his doome in the Star-chamber' (Pagitt, *Heresiography*, Mr–v).
131. See C.H. Greene, 'Trask in the Star-Chamber 1619', *Transactions of the Baptist Historical Society*, 5 (1916–7), 8–11.
132. Norrice, *The new gospel not the true gospel*, A4v. The letter 'I' later became the letter 'J'. See also Pagitt, *Heresiography*, S3r.
133. See Pagitt, *Heresiography*, O8v.

134. Pagitt, *Heresiography*, A3r. A certain 'T.S.', writing a letter to Traske's wife, included in Pagitt's *Heresiography*, refers to a whole series of Jewish customs with which the tailor Hamlet Jackson is said to have influenced Traske: 'Hamlet Jackson draweth Mr Trask to points of Judaism, as to the observation of Laws touching Meat, Drink, Apparel, Resting, Working, Building, and many other matters' (Pagitt, *Heresiography*, N8r).
135. Pagitt, *Heresiography*, N4v. The italics are Pagitt's.
136. Pagitt, *Heresiography*, N8v.
137. [Falconer], *A Briefe Refutation*, 'The Preface', A2r.
138. In April 1634, the Commissioners for Ecclesiastical Causes wrote to all Justices of the Peace and Mayors encouraging them to suppress 'Brownists, Anabaptists, Arians, Traskists, Familists, and some other sorts' of sectarians. See Katz, *Philo-semitism*, 31 and McDowell, 'The Stigmatizing of Puritans', 350–5.
139. [James I], *A Meditation Upon the Lords Prayer, Written by the Kings Maiestie, For the benefit of all his subiects, especially of such as follow the Court* (London: Bonham Norton and Iohn Bill, Printers to the Kings most Excellent Maiesty, 1619), Cv.
140. [James I], *A Meditation Upon the Lords Prayer*, C2r. For more on the rhetoric of proliferation and degradation in polemical discourse, see Kristen Poole, *Radical Religion from Shakespeare to Milton: Figures of Nonconformity in Early Modern England* (Cambridge: Cambridge University Press, 2000), especially Chapters 4 and 5.
141. Norrice, *The new gospel not the true gospel*, A3r–v.
142. Norrice, *The new gospel not the true gospel*, A3r–v.
143. For other accusations of Passover observance, see Katz, *Philo-Semitism*, 17.
144. [Falconer], *A Briefe Refutation*, 'The Preface', Cr–v.
145. This is an example of the word 'Judaism[e]' being used to denote Jewish practice rather than the Jewish religion.
146. [Falconer], *A Briefe Refutation*, Hr. Similarly, Falconer attributes to Traske the argument that the observance of one Jewish custom legitimates the observance of others, in the same way that St Paul considered circumcision to entail the observation of every law of the Jewish covenant: 'the Apostle telleth the Galathians ... that whosoeuer circumciseth himselfe, maketh himselfe a debtour of the whole law, and Christs death profitteth him not: and so it may be proportionately auerred of Traske, that in teaching the festiuall obseruance of Azimes [the Jewish Passover] he is consequently also bound by the same reason, to obserue the entire Law of Moyses, & so cannot be longer a Christian'. [Falconer], *A Briefe Refutation*, H2r–v. Falconer is citing Paul's Epistle to the Galatians, 5:1–6: 'Behold, I Paul say unto you, that, if ye receive circumcision, Christ will profit you nothing. Yea, I testify again to every man that receiveth circumcision, that he is a debtor to do the whole law. Ye are severed from Christ, ye who would be justified by the law; ye are fallen away from grace'. Falconer misunderstands the particular significance of circumcision as the sign of the covenant, unlike the observance of Passover, which is one observance among many guaranteed by the covenant.
147. The bibliography of the calendar controversy is vast. The best accounts are Robert Poole, *Time's Alteration: Calendar Reform in Early Modern England*

(London: UCL Press, 1998) and J.D. North, 'The Western Calendar: "intolerabilis, horribilis, et derisibilis"', Four Centuries of Discontent', in G.V. Coyne, M.A. Hoskin and O. Pedersen, eds, *Gregorian Reform of the Calendar: Proceedings of the Vatican Conference to Commemorate its 400th Anniversary, 1582–1982* (The Vatican: Vatican Press, 1983), 75–117. See also Arno Borst, *The Ordering of Time: From the Ancient Computus to the Modern Computer* (Cambridge: Polity, 1993) and G.J. Whitrow, *Time in History: The Evolution of Our General Awareness of Time and Temporal Perspective* (Oxford: Oxford University Press, 1988).

148. The Council recommended that Easter be held on the Sunday after the fourteenth day of the Paschal moon, the Paschal moon being the calendar moon whose fourteenth day is the next after the Spring equinox, taken as 21 March. The Nicaean decree implicitly rejected, therefore, both the Quartodeciman practice, which was thought to be inherently Jewish in character, and also the Jewish method of calendrical compensation. See O. Pedersen, 'The Ecclesiastical Calendar and the Life of the Church', in Coyne, et al., eds, *Gregorian reform of the calendar*, 17–75 at 42.

149. See Poole, *Time's Alteration*, 42.

150. See O. Pedersen, 'Eusebius and the Paschal Controversy' in Harold W. Attridge and Gohen Hata, eds, *Eusebius, Christianity and Judaism* (New York: E.J. Brill, 1992), 311–26 at 313 and 317.

151. See the entry by Frederick G. Holweck in C.G. Herbermann, Edward A. Pace, Condé B. Pallen, Thomas J Shahan and John J Wynne, eds, *The Catholic Encyclopaedia*, 15 vols (New York: Robert Appleton Company, 1907–12), V, 224.

152. See Glynn Parry, 'John Foxe, "Father of Lyes", and the Papists' in David Loades ed., *John Foxe and the English Reformation* (Aldershot: Scolar Press, 1997), 295–306 at 296–7 and Lake, *Anglicans and Puritans?*, 18.

153. According to Robert Poole, the development of print culture may have revived interest in the calendar controversy, since the spread of printed almanacs in the period would have seeded the impression that the calendar contained errors. See Poole, *Time's Alteration*, 37.

154. John Bale, *Illustrium Maioris Britanniae Scriptorium, hoc est, Angliae, Cambriae, ac Scotiae Summariu[m], in quasdam centurias divisum, cum diversitate doctrinaru[m] recta supputatione per omnes aetates a Iapheto sanctissimi Noah filio, ad annum domini M.D.XLVIII* ([Wesel: D. van der Straten], 1548), John Foxe, *Actes And Monuments of matters most speciall and memorable, happening in the Church, with an universall history of the same* (London: Peter Short, 1596) (this edition was published immediately prior to Persons's reply in 1603), Robert Persons, *A treatise of three conversions of England from paganisme to Christian Religion. The first vnder the Apostles, in the first age after Christ: The second vnder Pope Eleutherius and K.Lucius, in the second age. The third, under Pope Gregory the Great* ([St. Omer: F. Bellet], 1603) and Matthew Sutfcliffe, *The Subversion of Robert Parsons His confused and worthlesse worke, entituled, A treatise of three Conversions of England from Paganisme to Christian Religion* (London: Iohn Norton, 1606). The issue seems to have preoccupied a variety of Renaissance readers: the manuscript jottings in the flyleaves of a 1577 edition, in the British Library, of Meredith Hanmer's translation of Eusebius's *Ecclesiasticall Histories*, are almost entirely concerned with the Easter controversy, and in particular its Jewish content. See Meredith

Hanmer, *The Auncient Ecclesiasticall Histories of the first six hundred yeares after Christ* (London: T. Vautrollier, 1577). BL pressmark: 4530.f.3. See R.C. Alston, *Books with Manuscript: A Short Title Catalogue of Books with Manuscript Notes in the British Library* (London: The British Library, 1993), 209. Alston does not identify the annotator.

155. See North, 'The Western Calendar', 76. See also Poole, *Time's Alteration*, 37.
156. This was due to the over-compensatory leap year system in the Julian calendar; the earth takes 365 and a fraction less than a quarter of a day to circle the sun, and the Julian leap year system had not taken this fraction into account.
157. John Dee, 'A playne Discourse and humble Advise for our Gratious Queen Elizabeth, her most Excellent Majestie to peruse and consider, as concerning the needful Reformation of the Vulgar Kalendar for the civile years and daies accompting, or verifyeng, according to the time truely spent' Bodleian Library Ashmole MS 1789, fols 1–62.
158. Robert Poole refers to the reform as 'an act of the counter-reformation'. See *Time's Alteration*, 38. See also August Ziggelaar, 'The Decree of 1582' in Coyne et al., eds, *The Gregorian Reform of the Calendar*, 201–30 at 227.
159. For the Protestant rejection of the festival calendar, see David Cressy, *Bonfires and Bells: National Memory and the Protestant Calendar in Elizabethan and Stuart England* (London: Weidenfeld and Nicolson,1989); Christopher Hill, *Society and Puritanism in Pre-Revolutionary England* (London: Secker and Warburg, 1964), Chapter 5; for an account of the development of a Protestant tradition of ecclesiastical history in relation to the chronicler Raphael Holinshed, see Annabel Patterson, *Reading Holinshed's Chronicles* (Chicago: University of Chicago Press, 1994), Chapter 7.
160. For Bale (1495–1563), see May McKisack, *Medieval History in the Tudor Age* (Oxford: Clarendon Press, 1971), 11–25; Peter Happe, *John Bale* (New York: G.K. Hall & Company, 1996), 1–57; John R. Knott, *Discourses of Martyrdom in English Literature, 1563–1694* (Cambridge: Cambridge University Press, 1993), 46–9 and Firth, *The Apocalyptic Tradition*, Chapter 2. For Foxe, see Loades, 'John Foxe, "Father of Lyes", and the Papists', 296–7, Firth, *The Apocalyptic Tradition*, Chapters 1–3; Tessa Watt, *Cheap Print and Popular Piety 1550–1640* (Cambridge: Cambridge University Press, 1991), 90–1 and 158 and Lander, *Inventing Polemic*, Chapter 1.
161. See Loades ed., *John Foxe and the English Reformation*, 'Introduction', 2; V. Norskov Olsen, *John Foxe and the Elizabethan Church* (Berkeley: University of California Press, 1973), 51 and Knott, *Discourses of Martyrdom*, 46–7.
162. See Timothy Graham and Andrew G. Watson, eds, *The Recovery of the Past in Early Elizabethan England: Documents by John Bale and John Joscelyn from the Circle of Matthew Parker* (Cambridge: Cambridge Bibliographical Society, 1998), 'Introduction', xiii.
163. For Foxe's historiography, see for example, Loades, ed., *John Foxe and the English Reformation*; Thomas S. Freeman, '"Great Searching out of Bookes and Autors": John Foxe as Ecclesiastical Historian', unpublished Ph.D. dissertation, Rutgers University, 1995; Warren W. Wooden, *John Foxe* (Cambridge, MA: G.K. Hall & Company, 1983); Knott, *Discourses of Martyrdom*, 2–32; V. Norskov Olsen, *John Foxe and the Elizabethan Church* (Berkeley: University of California Press, 1973); Firth, *The Apocalyptic Tradition*, 69–111 and William Haller, *Foxe's Book of Martyrs and the Elect Nation* (London: Jonathan Cape, 1963).

164. See for example, Persons, *A Treatise of Three Conversions*, II, †8v. Others included Thomas Harding and Nicolas Harpsfield. See Parry, 'John Foxe, "Father of Lyes", and the Papists', 295.
165. Persons, *A Treatise of Three Conversions*, I, Divr–v.
166. Sutcliffe, *The Subversion of Robert Parsons*, I, E3v.
167. 'The Popes Callendar', British Library Additional Manuscripts 32092, folios 26r–27v, printed in Sylvanus Urban, ed., *The Gentleman's Magazine*, 36 (1851), 451–9 at 456.
168. See Vincent Twomey, *Apostolikos Thronos: The primacy of Rome as reflected in the Church History of Eusebius and the historico-apologetic writings of Saint Athanasius the Great* (Munster: Aschendorff, 1982), 92–3.
169. Bale, *Illustrium Maioris Britanniae Scriptorum*, Mv–Miiv.
170. Foxe, *Actes and Monuments*, I, Cv.
171. Persons, *A Treatise of Three Conversions*, I, Div–Dvr. Persons contends that the Quartodeciman custom was transmitted into this country much later than Foxe and Bale claim, by Britons 'trauailing into the east cowntries, or others of those east cowntries comming to them' (Persons, *A Treatise of Three Conversions*, I, Diir).
172. Persons, *A Treatise of Three Conversions*, I, Dvr, printed marginal note. Jewishness is one of a range of heterodox labels which Persons attaches to the Quartodeciman heresy; others are 'Greeke', 'Asian', 'Easterne', 'from Asia and the east Church', as well as 'Iewish'.
173. Persons, *A Treatise of Three Conversions*, I, Cv–Dr. The Centuriators of Magdeburg were the authors of *Historia Ecclesiae Christi* (Basle, 1559–74), a polemical anti-Papal account of the origins and development of Christianity.
174. This was reflected, moreover, in the choice of historical sources on either side: whereas Protestants tended to favour Eusebius, Roman Catholics favoured Bede. Eusebius was in favour of the Quartodecimans, Bede against. Thomas Freeman and the historian of the early church, V.N. Olsen have demonstrated that Foxe's *Acts and Monuments* is heavily reliant on Eusebius's *Ecclesiastical History*. See Freeman, 'Great Searching out of Bookes and Autors'; Olsen, *John Foxe and the Elizabethan Church*, 23–4; Knott, *Discourses of Martyrdom* 33–9 and Wooden, *John Foxe*, 20, 26 and 52–3. Sutcliffe accuses Bede of 'flatter[ing] the Romanists' (Sutcliffe, *The Subversion of Robert Parsons*, Bviiir). As O. Pedersen observes, Eusebius is, in contrast to Bede, 'an Easterner, a champion of minority, "heterodox" opinions', who supports Constantinople against Rome, and foregrounds the Jewish origins of Christianity (Pedersen, 'Eusebius and the Paschal Controversy', 318). For Eusebius, see for example, Sabrina Inowlocki, *Eusebius and the Jewish Authors* (Leiden: E.J. Brill, 2006); William Adler, 'Eusebius' *Chronicle* and its legacy' in *Eusebius, Christianity, and Judaism*, 467–92 and Robert M. Grant, *Eusebius as Church Historian* (Oxford: Clarendon Press, 1980).
175. Persons, *A Treatise of Three Conversions*, I, Dvr.
176. [Falconer], *A Briefe Refutation*, Hr and H4r.
177. Persons, *A Treatise of Three Conversions*, I, Eiir–v. Blastus was an early church Quartodeciman, mentioned in the account of the heresy written by Robert Persons.
178. Fulke, *A Defense*, dr.
179. Fulke, *A Defense*, c6r.

180. Broughton, *An Epistle*, F2r.
181. Broughton, *Two little workes defensive of our Redemption, That our Lord went through the veile of his flesh into Heaven, to appeare before God for us. Which iourney a Talmudist, as the Gospell would terme, a going up to Paradise: But Heathen Greek, a going down to Hades, and Latin, Descendere ad infernos* ([Middelburg: Richard Schilders], 1604), no sig.
182. Broughton, *A Replie upon the R.R.F.TH. Winton*, A8r.
183. Selden, *The Historie of Tithes*, Av.

Chapter 3 Anglicans and Judaism: From ceremony to legalism

1. George Herbert, *The Temple. Sacred Poems and Private Ejaculations* (Cambridge: Thomas Buck and Roger Daniel, 1633), E2r. For Herbert's equivocations about Old Testament beauty and ritual, see Achsah Guibbory, *Ceremony and Community from Herbert to Milton: Literature, Religion and Cultural Conflict in Seventeenth-Century England* (Cambridge: Cambridge University Press, 1998), Chapter 3.
2. Like the terms 'Puritan' and 'Anglican', these ones describe patterns rather than distinct groups, but they are useful, nevertheless, in categorising the nature of religious opposition in the period. Anti-ceremonialists were keen to portray themselves, after all, as the descendants of sixteenth-century Puritans: William Prynne refers to his party as 'wee poore *Puritans*'. See [William Prynne], *A Quench-coale. Or, A briefe Disquisition and Inquirie, in what place of the Church or Chancell the Lords-Table ought to be situated, especially when the sacrament is administered, written against Robert Shelford, Edmond Reeve, John Pocklington, and 'A late Coale from the Altar'* (Amsterdam: Richt Right Press, 1637), B3r.
3. Preface by Lord Cohen, in Vivian Lipman, ed., *Three Hundred Years: A Volume to Commemorate the Tercentenary of the Re-Settlement of the Jews in Great Britain 1656–1956* (London, Vallentine, Mitchell & Co., 1956), xl–xli.
4. Vivian Lipman, *A History of the Jews in Britain since 1858* (Leicester: Leicester University Press, 1990), 3.
5. Robert S. Paul, 'Oliver Cromwell and the Jews' in *Three Hundred Years*, 9.
6. John Coffey, *Persecution and Toleration in Protestant England* (Harlow: Longman, 2000), 155.
7. One of the only books to note this phenomenon is Guibbory's *Ceremony and Community from Herbert to Milton*. 'Attacks on the "Judaizing" Laudian prelates, with their ceremonial worship', she writes, 'should make us rethink assertions that the puritans were favourably disposed to Jews' (32).
8. See Lake, 'Presbyterianism, the Idea of a National Church and the Argument from Divine Right' in Peter Lake and Maria Dowling, eds, *Protestantism and the National Church in Sixteenth-Century England* (London: Croom Helm, 1987), 193–225 at 211–2.
9. For this distinction, see Daniel Boyarin, *Carnal Israel: Reading Sex in Talmudic Literature* (Berkeley: University of California Press, 1993).
10. William Ames, *A Fresh Suit Against Human Ceremonies in God's Worship. Or A Triplication unto. D. Burgesse His Rejoinder For D. Morton* ([Amsterdam: The successors of G. Thorp], 1633), Ev–E2r.

11. John Pocklington, *Altare Christianum: Or, The dead Vicars Plea. Wherein the Vicar of Gr. Being dead, yet speaketh, and pleadeth out of Antiquity, against him that hath broken downe his Altar* (London: Richard Badger, 1637), F2v.
12. For Burton, Bastwick and Prynne, see Andrew McRae, *Literature, Satire and the Early Stuart State* (Cambridge: Cambridge University Press, 2004), Chapter 6 and Kevin Sharpe, *The Personal Rule of Charles I* (New Haven: Yale University Press, 1992), 758–67. See also Hugh Trevor-Roper's (unsympathetic) account of the trio in *Archbishop Laud, 1573–1645* (Basingstoke: Macmillan Press, 1988), 65 and 317–23. Bastwick produced anti-Episcopal tracts from the early 1630s onwards, and was summoned before the Star Chamber for producing *The Letany of Dr. John Bastwicke* (1637). At the same time similar proceedings were being taken against Prynne for his *Histrio-Mastix* (1633) and against Henry Burton for his sermons. The latter, published under the title *For God, and the King* in 1636, were answered by Heylyn, and were the catalyst for Burton's imprisonment in the Fleet in February 1636-7, where he was soon joined by Prynne and Bastwick. All three were sentenced to a fine, life imprisonment and the loss of their ears, but were released in 1640.
13. Peter Heylyn, *Antidotum Lincolniense. Or an Answer to a book entitled, the Holy Table, Name, & Thing, &c. Said to be written long agoe by a Minister in Lincolnshire, And Printed for the Diocese of Lincolne, 1637* (London: John Clark, 1637), A3v–A4r.
14. Anon, *An Admonition, to the Parliament* ([Hemel Hempstead: J. Stroud], 1572), Dv.
15. See Kenneth Fincham, ed., *The Early Stuart Church, 1603–1642* (Basingstoke: Macmillan, 1993), 14.
16. See John Fielding, 'Arminianism in the Localities: Peterborough Diocese 1603–1642' in Fincham, ed., *The Early Stuart Church*, 93–115 at 96–99; Kenneth Fincham, 'Episcopal Government 1603–1640' in Fincham, ed., *The Early Stuart Church*, 71–92 at 75.
17. For the Laudian reform of the church, see also Anthony Milton, 'The Church of England, Rome and the True Church: The Demise of a Jacobean Consensus', in Fincham, ed., *The Early Stuart Church*, 187–211; John Morrill, 'The Religious Context of the English Civil War' in Richard Cust and Ann Hughes, eds, *The English Civil War* (London: Hodder Headline, 1997), 159–81 at 165–8 and Sharpe, *The Personal Rule of Charles I*, 284–92, 328–33 and 360–3.
18. Anon, *An Admonition, to the Parliament*, Dr.
19. William Ames, *A Reply to Dr Mortons Generall Defence of Three Nocent Ceremonies. Viz. The Surplice, Crosse in Baptisme, and kneeling at the receiving of the sacramentall elements of Bread and Wine* ([Amsterdam: G. Thorp], 1622), C4r.
20. Peter Lake, 'The Laudians and the Argument from Authority' in Bonnelyn Young Kunze and Dwight D. Brautigam, eds, *Court, Country and Culture: Essays on Early Modern British History in Honor of Perez Zagorin* (New York: University of Rochester Press, 1992), 149–77 at 170–2. See also Roger Pooley, 'Anglicans, Puritans and the Plain Style' in Francis Barker, Jay Bernstein, John Coombes, Peter Hulme, Jennifer Stone and Jon Stratton, eds, *1642: Literature and Power in the Seventeenth Century: Proceedings of the Essex conference on the Sociology of Literature* ([Colchester]: University of Essex, 1981), 187–201.
21. Ames, *A Reply*, D2v. See Guibbory, *Ceremony and Community*, 16.
22. For Conformist fears of Jewish legalism, see for example, Hooker, *Of the Lawes of Ecclesiasticall Politie. Eyght Bookes* (London: John Windet, 1593), Or–v.

23. As Achsah Guibbory observes, 'the seductions of art, for Herbert, are associated not just with Catholic worship but ultimately with Jewish'. See Guibbory, *Ceremony and Community*, 57.
24. Arminianism is the anti-Calvinist Protestant doctrine which derives its name from James Harmensen (Latinized into 'Arminius') (1560–1609), a minister at Amsterdam who abandoned the common Calvinist belief in predestination and came to believe that Christ died for all people and not just an elect few.
25. For this position see also Richard Cust and Ann Hughes, eds, *Conflict in Early Stuart England: Studies in Religion and Politics 1603–1642* (London: Longman, 1989), 24.
26. Nicholas Tyacke, *Anti-Calvinists: The Rise of English Arminianism c.1590–1640* (Oxford: Clarendon Press, 1987), 246. See also Julian Davies, *The Caroline Captivity of the Church: Charles I and the Remoulding of Anglicanism 1625–1641* (Oxford: Clarendon Press, 1992), 50.
27. See Kenneth Fincham and Peter Lake, 'The Ecclesiastical Policies of James I and Charles I' in Fincham, ed., *The Early Stuart Church*, 23–51 at 23–4 and Lake, 'The Laudian Style: Order, Uniformity and the Pursuit of the Beauty of Holiness in the 1630s' in Fincham, ed., *The Early Stuart Church*, 161–187 at 164, 185. See also Lake's observation that early modern commentators saw the world in terms of binary oppositions: Lake, 'Calvinism and the English Church, 1570–1635', *Past and Present*, 114 (1987), 32–76. Julian Davies also attempts to find a 'third way', positing instead of radical Arminianism the more measured term of 'Carolinism' which captures the ways in which Charles I departed from the 'Jacobean consensus' on church government (Davies, *The Caroline Captivity*, 2 and 288–90). See also Peter White, 'The Rise of Arminianism Reconsidered', *Past and Present*, 101 (1983), 24–54. For a discussion of Arminianism as 'a football in the revisionist debate', see William M. Lamont, 'The Puritan Revolution: A Historiographical Essay' in J.G.A. Pocock, ed., *The Varieties of British Political Thought, 1500–1800* (Cambridge: Cambridge University Press, 1993), 119–46.
28. Henry Burton, *For God, and the King. The Summe of Two Sermons Preached on the fifth of November last in St Matthewes Friday-Streete* ([London: Felix Kingston], 1636), B4r and N2v. See also the recurrent use of the words 'Novellists' and 'Innovators' in [Prynne], *A Quench-coale*, V4r.
29. The historical literature on the altar controversy is extensive. See for example Sharpe, *The Personal Rule of Charles I*, 333–45; Tyacke, *Anti-Calvinists*, 199–216; Trevor-Roper, *Archbishop Laud*, 45–6 and 151–2; Davies, *The Caroline Captivity*, Chapter 6. For a distinction between the controversy over altars and that over altar rails, see Sharpe, *The Personal Rule*, 339.
30. The controversy between Peter Heylyn and John Williams had a political dimension, too: Heylyn had been charged by the king to inform against the embattled Williams while he was dean of Westminster and a staunch opponent of Archbishop Laud; they subsequently embarked on the controversy over altars. A letter by John Williams to John Pocklington, written in 1627, is answered by John Pocklington's *Altare Christianum* (1637) and Peter Heylyn's *A coale from the Altar* (1636). Pocklington's and Heylyn's texts, as well as *Five pious and learned discourses*, written in 1635 by Robert Shelford and Edmund Reeve's *The Communion Booke Catechisme Expounded* (1635) are

answered by William Prynne, in *A Quench-Coale* (1637). John Williams's *The Holy Table, Name and Thing* appears in 1637, professing to be written by a Lincolnshire clergyman, and goes through six editions in the same year. Williams is answering Heylyn's *A coale from the Altar* as well as his *Antidotum Lincolniense* (1637).

31. Pocklington, *Altare Christianum*, E2r–v.
32. Heylyn, *Antidotum Lincolniense*, Aa3v–Aa4r.
33. Heylyn, *Antidotum Lincolniense*, Eee2v. An Ephod is a Jewish ecclesiastical vestment made of linen and beaten gold, worn by the high priest.
34. Edmund Reeve, *The Communion Booke Catechisme Expounded, According to Gods holy Wod, and the established Doctrine of the Church. Written for the furtherance of youth and ignorant persons, in the understanding of the grounds and principles of the true Christian Religion* (London: Miles Flesher, 1635), X4r. See also Robert Shelford's 'A Treatise Shewing That Gods Law, now qualified by the Gospel of Christ, is possible, and ought to be fulfilled of us in this life' in Shelford, *Five pious and learned discourses, 1. A Sermon shewing how we ought to behave our selves in Gods house* (Cambridge: [T. Buck and R. Daniel], 1635), Rr–Xr. This book was published with accompanying poems by sympathetic Cambridge divines, including Richard Crashaw.
35. Ames, *A Fresh Suit*, Mmm2r.
36. Ames, *A Fresh Suit*, Mmm2v. John Burges was Ames's father-in-law from his first marriage; he had become a Conformist apologist for the church.
37. Joseph Mede, *The Reverence of Gods House. A Sermon preached at St. Maries in Cambridge, Before The Universitie on St. Matthies day, Anno 1635/6* (London: M.E. for Iohn Clark, 1638), D3r.
38. Mede, *The Reverence of Gods House*, Fr. Mede cites 'Maymonides' and a certain 'Rabbi Solomon'. The term 'discalceation' refers to the custom of certain religious orders whose members wear sandals, for example, the Carmelites, Trinitarians and Passionists. It was introduced into the Western church by St Francis of Assisi.
39. Mede, *The Reverence of Gods House*, F2v.
40. Mede, *The Reverence of Gods House*, F2r–v.
41. See for example, 'R.T.', *De Templis, A Treatise of Temples: Wherein is discovered the ancient manner of Building, Consecrating, and Adorning of Churches* (London: R. Bishop, for Thomas Alchorn, 1638), H9v–H10r.
42. Shelford, *Five Pious and Learned Discourses*, Fr.
43. Anon, *The Originall of Popish Idolatrie, or The Birth of Heresies. Published under the name of CAVSAUBON,* [in 1625] *And called-in the same yeare, upon misinformation. But now upon better Consideration Reprinted with ALOWANCE* ([Amsterdam: The successors of G. Thorp], 1630), Aivr.
44. John Williams, *The Holy Table, Name & Thing, more anciently, properly, and litterally used under the New Testament, then that of an Altar: Written long ago by a Minister in Lincolnshire, in answer to D Coal* [i.e. Peter Heylyn], *a judicious Divine of Q.Maries dayes* ([London]: Printed for the Diocese of Lincoln, 1637), Q3r–v and V2r–v. Williams's use of rabbinic testimony relies on mapping the Jewish transformation from the sacrificial Tabernacle service to the symbolic post-exilic equivalent, onto the transformation from the Jewish service to the Christian one.
45. 'R.T.', *De Templis*, D5r–v.

46. Foulke Robarts, *Gods Holy House and Service, According to the primitive and most Christian forme thereof, described by Foulke Robarts, Batchelor of Divinity, and Prebendary of Norwich* (London: Tho. Cotes, 1639), B2v–B3v.
47. 'R.T.', *De Templis*, B6r–v and L7v–L8r.
48. Shelford, *Five pious and learned discourses*, B2v–B4r. See also John Swan, *Profano-Mastix. Or, A Briefe and Necessarie Direction concerning the respects which wee owe to God, and his House, even in outward worship, and reverent using of Holy Places* (London: J. Dawson, 1639), Ev.
49. Shelford, *Five Pious and Learned Discourses*, C2r–v. Shelford is alluding to Exodus 31, where God tells Moses that he has commanded Bezaleel and Aholiab to build and adorn the Tabernacle.
50. 'R.T.', *De Templis*, C2r–v.
51. Alexander Read, *A Sermon preached April 8. 1635 at a Visitation at Brentwood in Essex. By Alexander Read, Doctor of Divinitie, late Fellow of Pembroke-Hall in Cambridge, now Parson of Fifield in Essex* (London: Iohn Clark, 1636), C4v. Other tracts which associate the Laudian church with Solomon's Tabernacle include Walter Balcanquhall, *The Honour of Christian Churches; and the Necessitie of frequenting of Divine Service and Publike Prayers in them* (London: George Miller for Robert Allot, 1633), A4v; 'R.T.', *De Templis*, D5r–v; Reeve, *The Communion Booke*, X4r; Swan, *Profano-Mastix*, B3r; Robarts, *Gods Holy House*, B3v–B4r; Heylyn, *A Coale from the Altar*, Ddr and Heylyn, *Antidotum Lincolniense*, Ee8v.
52. Pocklington, *Altare Christianum*, A3r.
53. Pocklington, *Altare Christianum*, Rv.
54. Robarts, *Gods Holy House*, I4r.
55. Reeve, *The Communion Booke*, R3v–R4r. Reeve is referring to 1 Corinthians 5:8.
56. 'R.T.', *De Templis*, E5v–E7r.
57. Ames, *A Reply*, A2r.
58. Burton, *For God, and the King*, Ev. The pix or pyx is the vessel in which the host is stored.
59. Heylyn, *Antidotum Lincolniense*, Aa3r–Aa4v.
60. [William Prynne], *A Looking Glasse for all Lordly Prelates. Wherein they may Cleerely behold the true divine Originall and laudable Pedigree, whence they are descended; together with their holy lives and actions laid open in a double Parallel* ([London, 1636]), Iv.
61. [Prynne], *A Looking Glasse*, G3r. Prynne complains that prelates emulate both Jews and Old Testament Pagans in their episcopal paraphenalia: 'our Novellers will needes imitate the Gentiles & Jewes in their Sanctum Sanctorums, Mercie-Seates, Copes, Miters, Aaronicall attires vestments, Organs, Singing-men, & a world of Jewish and Heathenish Ceremonies, Orders, Pastimes Festivals & Consecrations'. [Prynne], *A Quench-coale*, V4v.
62. [Prynne], *A Looking Glasse*, G3v–G4r. Prynne is referring to Acts 23.
63. [Prynne], *A Looking Glasse*, Hv–H2r. 'B Latimer' is Hugh Latimer (1485?–1555), bishop of Worcester. John Bastwick complains that congregations are 'every-where deprived by the Prelats of their faithfull and true honourable Pastors and diligent teachers', and that 'if they goe into any other parish to heare the word when they have none at home, then they hoyst them up into the high Commission, and there ruine and undoe them'. John Bastwick, *The Letany of John Bastwick, Doctor of Phisicke, Being now full of Devotion, as well in respect of*

the common calamities of plague and pestilence; as also of his owne patticular miserie: lying in this instant in Limbo Patrum ([Leiden: Willem Christiaens], 1637), 'The first part', C2r and 'The Fourth part', A3v.
64. Balcanquhall, *The Honour of Christian Churches*, B2v–C3r.
65. Pocklington, *Altare Christianum*, R4v–Sr.
66. Reeve, *The Communion Booke*, B2r.
67. For Christian references to the Sanhedrin, see Hugo Mantel, *Studies in the History of the Sanhedrin* (Cambridge, MA: Harvard University Press, 1961), 268–90 and Solomon Zeitlin, 'The Political Synedrion and the Religious Sanhedrin', *The Jewish Quarterly Review*, 36 (1945), 109–40. For the application of Jewish constitutional models to early modern church government more generally, see Reid Barbour, *John Selden: Measures of the Holy Commonwealth in Seventeenth-Century England* (Toronto: University of Toronto Press, 2003), James Shapiro, *Shakespeare and the Jews* (New York: Columbia University Press, 1996), 173–5, Frank E. Manuel, *The Broken Staff: Judaism through Christian Eyes* (Cambridge, MA: Harvard University Press, 1992), 115–28, Jonathan R. Ziskind, *John Selden on Jewish Marriage Law: The Uxor Hebraica* (London: E.J. Brill, 1991), 10; J.G.A. Pocock, *The Ancient Constitution and the Feudal Law: A Study of English Historical Thought in the Seventeenth Century* (Cambridge: Cambridge University Press, 1987), Chapters 5 and 6 and Richard Tuck, *Philosophy and Government 1572–1651* (Cambridge: Cambridge University Press, 1993), Chapter 5.
68. See Thomas Erastus, *Explicatio grauissimae quaestionis utrum excommunicatio, mandato nitatur diuino, an excogitata sit ab hominibus. Opus nunc recens editum. Adiectae sunt aliquot theologorum epistolae* ([London: J. Wolfe], 1589); Anon, *The Nullity of Church-Censures: Or A Dispute Written by that Illustrious Philosopher, Expert Physician, and Pious Divine Dr Thomas Erastus, Publik Professor in the University of Heidelberge, and Basil* (London: Printed for G.L., 1659). Since the church was a department of the state, this book argued, the church should not have the power to excommunicate.
69. See J. Neville Figgis, 'Erastus and Erastianism', *The Journal of Theological Studies*, 2 (1901), 66–101 and J.H. Burns, ed., *The Cambridge History of Political Thought 1450–1700* (Cambridge: Cambridge University Press, 1991): 'Religion, Civil Government and the Debate on Constitutions'.
70. See Shapiro, *Shakespeare and the Jews*, 277; S.B. Liljegren, *Harrington and the Jews* (Lund: C.W.K. Gleerups Forlag, 1932) and Liljegren, *James Harrington's Oceana* (Lund: C.W.K. Gleerups Forlag, 1924), 80.
71. John Selden, *De Synedriis et Praefecturis Juridicis Veterum Ebraorum* (London: Jacob Flesher, 1653). He refers to the Talmudic *Tractate Sanhedrin* (Yy2v); Maimonedes (e4r); Petrus Cunæus's *De Republica Hebreorum* (Hhh2r); Hugo Grotius (Dd2v); Josephus and Scaliger (r4R). See Richard Tuck, *Philosophy and Government 1572–1651* (Cambridge: Cambridge University Press, 1993), 218–9.
72. See Richard Tuck, *Hobbes* (Oxford: Oxford University Press, 1989), 31–2; Tuck, *Philosophy and Government*, Chapter 7; Cedric C. Brown, 'Great Senates and Godly Education: Politics and Cultural Renewal in some Pre- and Post-Revolutionary Texts of Milton' in David Armitage, Armand Himy and Quentin Skinner, eds, *Milton and Republicanism* (Cambridge: Cambridge University Press, 1995), 43–60 at 47–9 and 53; Patricia Springborg, 'Hobbes on Religion' in Tom Sorell, ed., *The Cambridge Companion to Hobbes*

(Cambridge: Cambridge University Press, 1996), 346–81; Mark Goldie, 'The Reception of Hobbes', and 'Erastianism, Toleration and the Power of the Church' in Burns, ed., *The Cambridge History of Political Thought*, 589–616 and 610–616, respectively. For Harrington's views on the Sanhedrin, see Liljegren, *James Harrington's Oceana*, 81–5 and J.G.A. Pocock, ed., *The Commonwealth of Oceana and A System of Politics* (Cambridge: Cambridge University Press, 1992), Introduction.

73. Anon [translated by Franciscus a Sancta Clara], *True religion explained And defended against ye Archenemies thereof in these times, in six Bookes* (London: [John Haviland] for Richard Royston, 1632). The fifth section is a detailed comparison of Judaism and Christianity. Grotius frequently refers to Josephus and Maimonedes, as well Talmudic exegeses on the Sanhedrin.

74. Clement Barkesdale, trans., *Petrus Cunæus, Of the Common-wealth of the Hebrews* (London: Printed for T.W. for William Lee, 1653). Petrus Cunæus, or Piet van der Cun, lived in Holland among fellow Hebraists Isaac Casaubon, Scaliger and Grotius, as well as Menasseh ben Israel, and on a visit to England in 1603 he met John Selden. See Jonathan R. Ziskind, 'Petrus Cunæus on Theocracy, Jubilee and the Latifundia', *The Jewish Quarterly Review*, 68 (1978), 235–55 at 236 and Tuck, *Philosophy and Government*, 167–9.

75. See Liljregren, *James Harrington's Oceana*, 83–5.

76. Edmund Bunny, *The Specter of Judah: or, what maner of Government it was, that unto the Commonwealth or Church of Israel was by the law of God appointed* (London: N. Newton & A. Hatfield, for Iohn Wright, 1584), A4v.

77. Bunny, *Specter of Judah*, I4r. A printed marginal note directs the reader to I Chronicles 27: 1–34.

78. See Anon, *An Admonition*, C4r: 'in that they have civill offices, ioyned to the Ecclesiasticall, it is against the woorde of God'. See Patrick Collinson, *The Elizabethan Puritan Movement* (Oxford: Clarendon Press, 1990), Part 7.

79. Whitgift, *The Defense of the Aunswere to the Admonition, against the Replie of T.C. by Iohn Whitgift Doctor of Divinitie* (London: Henry Binneman, for Humfrey Toye, 1574), K5v–K6r.

80. Whitgift, *The Defense of the Aunswere*, Sv.

81. Thomas Cartwright, *The Second replie of Thomas Cartwright: agaynst Maister Doctor Whitgiftes second answer / touching the Churche Discipline* ([Heidelberg: M. Schirat], 1575), D4r.

82. Cartwright, *The Second replie*, yr.

83. Cartwright, *The Second replie*, X4v.

84. Thomas Morton, *Salomon, or A treatise declaring the state of the kingdome of Israel, as it was in the daies of Salomon. Whereunto is annexed another treatise, of the Church: or more particularly, Of the right constitution of a Church* (London: Robert Robinson for Robert Dexter, 1596), A6r–A6v.

85. Ames, *A Fresh Suit*, Mmm3r.

86. Ames, *A Reply*, Gr. See also Ames, *A Fresh Suit*, Mmmr–v.

87. Books 1–4 of the *Lawes* were published in 1593, Book 5 in 1597. In 1648, Books 6 and 8 appeared, and in 1662, Book 7. See Stanley Archer, *Richard Hooker* (Massachusetts: G.K. Hall and Company, 1983), 15–8. For the character of Hooker's Anglicanism, see Archer, *Richard Hooker*; Lake, *Anglicans and Puritans?*; Deborah K. Shuger, '"Societie Supernatural": The Imagined Community of Hooker's Lawes' in Arthur Stephen McGrade, ed., *Richard Hooker and the*

Construction of Christian Community (Temple, Arizona: Arizona State University Press, 1997), 307–31 and Robert K. Faulkner, *Richard Hooker and the Politics of a Christian England* (Berkeley: University of California Press, 1981).
88. Richard Hooker, *Of the Lawes of Ecclesiastical Politie; The Sixth and Eighth Books. By Richard Hooker. A work long expected, and now published according to the most Authentique Copies* (London: Richard Bishop, 1648), VIII, S3r. See J.H.M. Salmon, 'Catholic resistance theory, Ultramontanism, and the Royalist response, 1580–1620)', in *The Cambridge History of Political Thought*, 219–54 at 245 and Richard Helgerson, *Forms of Nationhood: The Elizabethan Writing of England* (Chicago: University of Chicago Press, 1992), 276–7.
89. Richard Hooker, *Of the Lawes of Ecclesiastical Politie. Eight Bookes* (London: Andrew Crooke, 1666), VII, Lll4r.
90. See Peter Lake, *Anglicans and Puritans? Presbyterianism and English Conformist Thought from Whitgift to Hooker* (London: Unwin Hyman, 1988), 219.
91. Hooker, *Of the Lawes* (1648), VIII, S4r.
92. For 'mixed government', see Markku Peltonen, ed., *Classical Humanism and Republicanism in English Political Thought 1570–1640* (Cambridge: Cambridge University Press, 1995), especially 47 and Howell A. Lloyd, 'Mixed Constitution or Mixed Government' in Burns, ed., *The Cambridge History of Political Thought*, 273–9.
93. Hooker, *Of the Lawes* (1666) VII, Qqq2r–v. For the relative powers of monarch and Parliament in Hooker and Morton, see Thomas Morton, *Salomon, or A treatise declaring the state of the kingdome of Israel, as it was in the daies of Salomon* (London: Robert Robinson for Robert Dexter, 1596), E4r: 'so that monarchie is most safe and acceptable, the power whereof moderated and yoked with some other power of positive lawes or of parliamentes'. See also Lake, *Anglicans and Puritans?*, 206–12 and W.J. Torrance Kirby, *Richard Hooker's Doctrine of the Royal Supremacy* (Leiden: E.J. Brill, 1990).
94. Morton, *Salomon*, A5r. See also P2r: 'a publicke Church with the civill estate maketh one bodie under one head'.
95. Morton, *Salomon*, Gv.
96. Morton writes that Presbyterianism 'hath risen of a reverend, religious, yea as it proved at length, a superstitious opinion of the ecclesiasticall estate, with too base and vile an opinion of the civill state, the which hath seemed so prophane and unholy, as that it coulde not in any respect be ioyned with the other, without defiling and prophaning it' (Morton, *Salomon*, P2r.)
97. Thomas Bilson, *The Perpetual Government of Christes Church. Wherein are handled; The fatherly superioritie which God first established in the Patriarke for the guiding of his Church, and after continued in the Tribe of Levi and the Prophetes* (London: The Deputies of Christopher Barker, 1593), Titlepage.
98. For the relationship between the Passion narrative and the powers of the Sanhedrin in the New Testament, see for example, A.N. Sherwin-White, *Roman Society and Roman Law in the New Testament: The Sarum Lectures 1960–1961* (Oxford: Clarendon Press, 1963), 32–47; Hugo Mantel, *Studies in the History of the Sanhedrin* (Cambridge, MA: Harvard University Press, 1961), 268–90 and Solomon Zeitlin, 'The Political Synedrion and the Religious Sanhedrin', *The Jewish Quarterly Review*, 36 (1945), 109–40.
99. Bilson, *The Perpetual Government of Christes Church*, B4r.

100. Richard Bancroft, *A Survay of the pretended Holy Discipline. Contayning the beginnings, successe, parts, proceedings, authority, and doctrine of it: with some of the manifold, and materiall repugnances, varieties and uncertainties, in that behalfe* (London: Iohn Wolfe, 1593), Eee2v.
101. The power to excommunicate originated in the third tenet of Calvinist Presbyterian Discipline. See Hill, *Society and Puritanism in Pre-Revolutionary England* (London: Secker & Warburg, 1994), Chapter 6; Collinson, *The Elizabethan Puritan Movement*, 346–56 and John Henry Blunt, ed., *The Dictionary of Sects, Heresies, Ecclesiastical Parties, and Schools of Religious Thought* (London: Rivingtons, 1874), 452–63.
102. Hooker died shortly after its publication, and the defence of his work against *A Christian Letter* fell to Hooker's friend William Covell, who published *A Iust and Temperate Defence of the Five Books of Ecclesiastical Policie* in 1603 (London: P. Short for Clement Knight, 1603).
103. Anon, *A Christian Letter of certaine English Protestants, unfained favourers of the present use of Religion, authorised and professed in England: unto that Reverend and learned man, Mr. R. Hoo. requiring resolution in certaine matters of doctrine (which seeme to overthrow the foundation of Christian Religion, and of the church among us) expresslie contained in his five books of Ecclesiasticall Pollicie* (Middelburg: Richard Schilders, 1599), Fv.
104. Anon, *A Christian Letter*, E3v.
105. They write that 'seeing it is nowe made manifest to the world, that they [Papists] are departed from the doctrine of Christ & his Apostles, &c. you call them backe and say, we gladlie acknowledge them to be of the familie of Iesus Christ, and to be helde and reputed a parte of the house of God, and a limme of the visible church of Christ' (Anon, *A Christian Letter*, C2r).
106. Anon, *A Christian Letter*, C2r.
107. Anon, *A Christian Letter*, F2r.
108. Anon, *A Christian Letter*, C2r.
109. Ames, *A Reply*, K3v.
110. Ames, *A Reply*, K4r.
111. Ames, *A Reply*, K4r.
112. In the 1650s controversy, Anthony Pearson's *The Great Case of Tythes Truly stated* (1657) is answered by Immanuel Bourne's *A Defence and Justification of Ministers Maintenance by Tythes* (1659); John Canne's *The Second Voyce from the Temple* (1653) is answered by Prynne, *Ten Considerable Quaeries* (1659), which is in turn answered by Canne in *A Querie to William Prynne*, contained in the preface to the reader which opens John Osborne's *An Indictment Against Tythes* (1659).
113. See Coward, *The Stuart Age*, 194; Nicholas Tyacke, 'The "Rise of Puritanism" and the legalizing of Dissent, 1571–1719', in Ole Peter Grell, Jonathan I. Israel and Nicholas Tyacke, eds, *From Persecution to Toleration: The Glorious Revolution and Religion in England* (Oxford: Clarendon Press, 1991), 17–51 at 28–9 and William Haller, *Tracts on Liberty in the Puritan Revolution 1638–1647* (New York: Columbia University Press 1934), I, 5.
114. See Barry Reay, 'Quaker Opposition to Tithes 1652–1660', *Past and Present*, 49 (1980), 85–120 at 86 and 110; Marcus Nevitt, 'Agency in Crisis: Women and the Pamphlet Culture of Revolutionary England, c.1640–c.1660', unpublished Ph.D. dissertation, University of Sheffield, 1999, Chapter 5.

115. John Canne, *A Querie to William Prynne* in John Osborne, *An Indictment Against Tythes: or, Tythes no Wages for Gospel-Ministers* (London: Livewel Chapman, 1659), a2v. The Quaker Anthony Pearson (1628–1670?) observes likewise that 'there are many differing opinions, and of late yeers have been great disputes concerning the right of Tythes'. Anthony Pearson, *The Great Case of Tythes Truly stated, clearly opened, and fully resolved. By a Countreyman, A P* (London: Giles Calvert, 1657), a2r. For the tithes controversy in the 1650s, see Reay, 'Quaker Opposition to Tithes', 86 and 98–120; Reay, *The Quakers and the English Revolution* (Middlesex: Temple Smith, 1985), 38–9; Ronald Hutton, *The Restoration: A Political and Religious History of England and Wales 1658–1667* (Oxford: Clarendon Press, 1985), 47–9 and 85–6; Thomas N. Corns, *John Milton: The Prose Works* (New York: Twayne, 1998), 109–10; H.N. Brailsford, *The Levellers and the English Revolution* (London: Cresset Press, 1961), 134 and Margaret Sampson, '"Property" in Seventeenth-Century English Political Thought', in Gordon J. Schochet, ed., *Religion, Resistance and Civil War, Proceedings of the Folger Institute Centre for the History of British Political Thoughts, Vol 3* (Washington: Folger, 1990), 259–76. For an introduction to the Quaker movement in this period, see A. Cole, 'The Quakers and the English Revolution', in T.H. Aston, ed., *Crisis in Europe, 1560–1660* (London: Routledge & Kegan Paul, 1965), 341–58 and Christopher Hill, *The World Turned Upside Down* (London: Maurice Temple Smith, 1972), Chapter 10.
116. William Prynne, *Ten Considerable Quaeries concerning Tithes, the Present Petitioners and Petitions for their total abolition, as Antichristian, Jewish, burdensom, oppressive to the godly, consciencious People of the Nation; excited, incouraged thereunto by disguised Jesuits, Popish Priests, Friers, and Romish Emissaries, to starve, suppress, extirpate our Protestant Ministers, Church, Religion; and bring them all to speedy confusion* (London: Edward Thomas, 1659), A3r.
117. Immanuel Bourne, *A Defence and Justification of Ministers Maintenance by Tythes. And of Infant-Baptism, Humane Learning, and the Sword of the Magistrate; Which some Anabaptists falsely call Four Sandy Pillars, and Popish Foundations of our Ministry and Churches* (London: John Allen, 1659), G5v.
118. Prynne, *Ten Considerable Quaeries*, A3v.
119. John Milton, *Considerations touching The likeliest means to remove Hirelings out of the church. Wherein is also discourc'd Of Tithes, Church-fees, Church-revenues; And whether any maintenance of ministers can be settl'd by law. The author J.M.* (London: T.N for L. Chapman, 1659), Dr.
120. Milton, *Considerations*, B9r.
121. John Canne, *A Second Voyce from the Temple, to the Higher Powers. Wherein Is proved that the Decrees and Institutions of Popes, and Popish Counsels, which have been established by the Law of the Land, and have been continued and confirmed throughout divers Ages, by several Acts of Parliament, against Jesus Christ, in the way and order of the Gospel (the same yet standing) ought by the present supream Authority of this Nation to be taken away* (London: M. Simmons, 1653), B2v.
122. Canne, *A Second Voyce from the Temple*, C3r.
123. Canne, *A Second Voyce from the Temple*, C4r.
124. Bourne, *A Defence*, C3r–v.
125. See Kenneth L. Parker, *The English Sabbath: A Study of Doctrine and Discipline from the Reformation to the Civil War* (Cambridge: Cambridge University Press, 1988), especially Chapter 4.

126. William Sclater, *The Quæstion of Tythes Revised. Arguments for the Moralitie of Tything, enlarged, and cleared. Obiections more fully, and distinctly answered. Mr Seldens Historie, so farre as Mistakers haue made it Argumentatiue against the Moralitie, ouer-ly viewed. By William Sclater, D.D. and Minister of Pitminster, in Somerset* (London: John Legatt, 1623), Gg2v.
127. James Sempill, *Sacrilege sacredly handled. That is, According to Scripture onely. Diuided into two parts: 1. For the Law. 2. For the Gospell. An appendix also added; answering some Objections mooued, namely, against this Treatise: and some others, I finde in Iox. Scaligers Diatribæ, and Ioh. Seldens Historie of Tithes. For the vse of all churches in generall: but more especially for those of North-Britaine* (London: William Iones, for Edmund Weaver, 1619), Pr.
128. In the tithes controversy of 1659, Quakers denounced the Sabbath just as they denounced the payment of tithes. William Prynne asks of his opponents: 'how then they can now be reputed *consciencious Godly Saints . . . some of them (as the Quakers) beginning of late to work on the Lords day*, denying God *one day* in *seven*, as well as the *Tenth* of their annual increase, deeming both *Jewish* and *Antichristian*, as they deem *our Ministers*' (Prynne, *Ten Considerable Quaeries*, A4v). See also Milton, *Considerations*, D7r.
129. For this reversal see Fincham, *The Early Stuart Church*, 'Introduction', 14 and Lake, 'The Laudians and the argument from authority', 160 and 171. Historians disagree about the relationship between Sabbatarianism and factionalism during the Long Reformation. Kenneth Parker claims that Sabbatarianism was widely accepted throughout the sixteenth and early seventeenth centuries, until it was attacked by Laudians in the 1630s. David Katz believes that Parker overstates his position, arguing that although Sabbatarianism spread among Anglicans during the sixteenth century, those who observed this custom were often accused of Judaising. See Parker, *The English Sabbath*, especially Chapter 4, Parker, 'Thomas Rogers and the English Sabbath; the Case for a Re-appraisal', *Church History*, 53 (1984), 335–48; David Katz, *Sabbath and Sectarianism in Seventeenth-century England* (Leiden: E.J. Brill, 1988), 10–20; M.M. Knappen, *Tudor Puritanism. A Chapter in the History of Idealism* (Chicago: University of Chicago Press, 1939), 447–9; Christopher Hill, *Society and Puritanism*, Chapter 5 and Patrick Collinson, *Godly People: Essays on English Protestantism and Puritanism* (London: The Hambledon Press, 1983), 429–43.
130. Peter Heylyn, *The History of the Sabbath. In two bookes* (London: Henry Seile, 1636).
131. Reeve, *The Communion Booke*, P4r.
132. See Reeve, *The Communion Booke*, Q4v.
133. Francis White, *A Treatise of the Sabbath-Day. Containing, A Defence of the Orthodoxall Doctrine of the Church of England, against all Sabbatarian-Novelty. By Dr. Fr. White, L. Bihop of Ely* (London: Richard Badger, 1635), Dd4r. This treatise is written against the notorious Saturday Sabbatarian, Theophilus Braborne. See Lake, 'The Laudians and the Argument from Authority', 172.
134. Henry Burton, *A Divine Tragedie lately acted; or a Collection of sundrie memorable examples of God's judgements upon Sabbath-breakers, and other like libertines, in their unlawfull sports, hapning within the realme of England, in the compasse onely of few yeers last past* ([Amsterdam: J.F. Stam], 1636), A3r. See Katz, *Sabbath and Sectarianism*, 18.

Chapter 4 Religious toleration: Jews and Jewish precedents in the Christian church and state

1. For the history of toleration in the early modern period, see Henry Kamen, *The Rise of Toleration* (London: Weidenfeld & Nicolson, 1967); Joseph Lecler, *Toleration and the Reformation*, (London: Longman, 1960); John Coffey, *Persecution and Toleration in Protestant England, 1558–1689* (Harlow, Essex: Pearson, 2000); Perez Zagorin, *How Religious Toleration came to the West* (Princeton: Princeton University Press, 2004); Ole Peter Grell and Roy Porter, eds, *Toleration in Enlightenment Europe* (Cambridge: Cambridge University Press, 2000); Ole Peter Grell, Jonathan I. Israel and Nicholas Tyacke, eds, *From Persecution to Toleration: The Glorious Revolution and Religion in England* (Oxford: Clarendon Press, 1991); W.J. Sheils, ed., *Persecution and Toleration: Papers Read at the Twenty-Second Summer Meeting and the Twenty-Third Winter Meeting of the Ecclesiastical History Society* (Oxford: The Ecclesiastical History Society, 1984) and Adam Sutcliffe, 'Enlightenment and Exclusion: Judaism and Toleration in Spinoza, Locke and Bayle' in Tony Kushner and Nadia Valman, eds, *Philosemitism, Antisemitism and 'the Jews': Perspectives from the Middle Ages to the Twentieth Century* (Aldershot, Hampshire: Ashgate, 2004), 177–93.
2. W.K. Jordan, *The Development of Religious Toleration in England; From the Beginning of the English Reformation to the Death of Queen Elizabeth* (London: George Allen & Unwin Ltd, 1932). William Haller, *Tracts on Liberty in the Puritan Revolution 1638–1647* (New York: Columbia University Press 1934); A.S.P. Woodhouse, ed., *Puritanism and Liberty* (London, 1938). W.K. Jordan was not unaware of the limitations of toleration, particularly in the early modern period, and he stressed that toleration, unlike tolerance, 'in its very nature ... disapproves, if it does not disallow, the point of view which is to be tolerated. Toleration, therefore, falls considerably short of religious liberty ... it is to be questioned whether we have ever got much beyond the first concept; certainly no progress was made beyond it in England during the sixteenth and seventeenth centuries'. Yet Jordan's study was nonetheless teleological in its approach. Jordan, *The Development of Religious Toleration in England*, I, 17–8.
3. *Catalogue of an Exhibition of Anglo-Jewish Art and History: In Commemoration of the Tercentenary of the Resettlement of the Jews in the British Isles* (London, Hertford and Harlow: Published by the East and West Library for the Tercentenary Council), 3.
4. Vivian Lipman, ed., *Three Hundred Years: A Volume to Commemorate the Tercentenary of the Re-settlement of the Jews in Great Britain 1656–1956* (London, Vallentine, Mitchell & Co., 1956), 27–33.
5. Preface by Lord Cohen, xi–ii in *Three Hundred Years*. Lord Cohen describes how a Professor Butterfield had chosen "Toleration in History" as his subject for a lecture delivered under the auspices of the Council of Christians and Jews in October 1956. Cohen continues, 'In the course of that lecture he said that toleration in this country might be said to date from Oliver Cromwell. He associated that development, as did Viscount Samuel in his broadcast last April, with the intense interest taken in the Old Testament by the Puritan movement'.

6. As William Prynne himself points out, 'the *Liberty of conscience* [tolerationists] plead for, & pretend they grant to Presbyterians . . . is but a meere fiction, contradicted by their practise'. William Prynne, *A Fresh Discovery of some Prodigious New Wandering-Blasing-Stars, & Firebrands, Stiling themselves New-Lights. Firing our Church and State into New Combustions* (London: John Macock, for Michael Spark, 1646), A2r. Nicholas Tyacke has described the association between Puritanism and Toleration as part of 'the great Whig tradition which runs from Macaulay to Trevelyan, the latter opining that toleration was "the true road of Puritan development in England"'. Nicholas Tyacke, 'The "Rise of Puritanism" and the Legalizing of Dissent, 1571–1719' in Grell, Israel and Tyacke, eds, *From Persecution to Toleration*, 17–51 at 17. Blair Worden regards toleration *per se* as 'a Victorian subject, a monument to Victorian liberalism'. Blair Worden, 'Toleration and the Cromwellian Protectorate' in Sheils, ed., *Persecution and Toleration*, 199–235 at 199 and 200, citing Gardiner, *The First Two Stuarts and the Puritan Revolution: 1603–1660* (London: Longmans, Green and Co, 1878), 136. For an overview of the Whig and Revisionist approaches to toleration, see Coffey, *Persecution and Toleration*, 1–7. For further critique of the traditional history of toleration, see Cary J. Nederman and John Christian Laursen, eds, *Difference and Dissent: Theories of Toleration in Medieval and Early Modern Europe* (Lanham, Maryland: Rowman & Littlefield, 1996), Introduction and John Christian Laursen and Cary J. Nederman, eds, *Beyond the Persecuting Society: Religious Toleration before the Enlightenment* (Philadelphia: University of Pennsylvania Press, 1998), Introduction.
7. Michael Walzer, for example, regards Puritanism as a modernising, democratic force: 'Calvinist politics, indeed, radicalism in general, is an aspect of that broad historical process which contemporary writers call "modernization" . . . [Puritan organisation] was preparation also for the debates and elections, the pamphlets and parties of liberal politics'. See Michael Walzer, *The Revolution of the Saints: A Study in the Origins of Radical Politics* (London: Weidenfeld and Nicolson, 1966), 18 and 300–1. More recently, Perez Zagorin's study, *How Religious Toleration came to the West*, although encyclopaedic, is essentially a broadly chronological catalogue of the 'pioneers' of religious liberty.
8. For example, the tolerationist Roger Williams, who is discussed in more detail below, has been represented by Jewish and non-Jewish historians alike as benignly sympathetic towards Jews. See David Wootton, ed., *Divine Right and Democracy: An Anthology of Political Writing in Stuart England* (Harmondsworth: Penguin, 1986), 215 and David Katz, *Philo-Semitism and the Readmission of the Jews to England 1603–1655* (Oxford: Clarendon Press, 1982), 187. See also Thomas Seccombe's portrait of Williams as a 'pioneer of religious liberty' in *The Dictionary of National Biography*, 61, 445–50 and Perez Zagorin's portrayal of Williams as 'one of the towering personalities in early American history' and one of the 'most noted early fighters for toleration' (Zagorin, *How the Idea of Religious Toleration Came to the West*, 196–208). The introduction to a modern collection of essays on religious toleration refers to Williams's famous tolerationist statement, 'God wills that a permission of the most paganish, Jewish, Turkish or anti-Christian consciences and worships be granted to all men in all nations and countries', and comments that

'it is within this context that we need to understand the discussions in the 1650s about the readmission of the Jews to England. Radical Protestants had been calling for this regularly during the previous decade. More generally a philo-Semitic movement had been gathering strength since the early seventeenth century'. Grell, Israel and Tyacke, eds, *From Persecution to Toleration*, 7, citing Roger Williams, *The Bloudy Tenent, of Persecution, for cause of Conscience, discussed, in A Conference betweene Truth and Peace. Who, In all tender Affection, present to the High Court of Parliament, (as the Result of their Discourse) these, (amongst other Passages) of highest consideration* ([London], 1644), Aii(v). In his history of toleration, John Coffey includes a section on 'The Readmission of the Jews', suggesting that 'the relative openness of the Cromwellian regime is illustrated by the informal readmission of the Jews to England in the mid-1650s'. Coffey, *Persecution and Toleration*, 155.

9. Tolerationism continued beyond the chronological scope of this book: John Milton published his pro-toleration tract in 1659; entitled *A Treatise of Civil power in Ecclesiastical causes*, it argued against state intervention in religious affairs. See John Milton, *A Treatise of Civil power in Ecclesiastical causes: Shewing That it is not lawfull for any power on earth to compel in matters of Religion* (London: Printed by Thomas Newcomb, 1659).
10. Anon [Henry Robinson], *Liberty of Conscience: Or the Sole means to obtaine Peace and Truth* (n.p., 1643), 7, as cited in Katz, *Philo-semitism*, 172.
11. Thomas Edwards, *Gangraeana: Or a Catalogue and Discovery of many of the Errours, Heresies, Blasphemies and pernicious Practices of the Sectaries of this time, vented and acted in England in these four last years: As also, A Particular Narration of divers Stories, Remarkable Passages, Letters; an Extract of many Letters, all concerning the present Sects; together with some Observations upon, and Corollaries from all the fore-named Premisses* (London: Ralph Smith, 1645), 14–15. Edwards does, however, perceive the Independents' protestations of toleration as disingenuous, writing that 'all these severall sects were agreed and held together for pretended liberty of conscience' (15).
12. See Cecil Roth, 'Leon da Modena and England', *Transactions of the Jewish Historical Society of England*, 11 (1928), 206–25; Cecil Roth, 'Leone da Modena and his English Correspondents', *Transactions of the Jewish Historical Society of England*, 17 (1953), 39–43 and Claire Jowitt, '"The Consolation of Israel": The Representation of Jewishness in the Writings of Gerrard Winstanley and William Everard', *Prose Studies*, 22 (1999), 83–99.
13. See Grell et al., eds, *From Persecution to Toleration*, 'Introduction', 6.
14. *The Fourth Paper, Presented by Maior Butler, To the Honourable Committee of Parliament, for the Propagating the Gospel of Christ Jesus* (London: Giles Calvert, 1652), A2(r). See Katz, *Philo-semitism*, 186–8.
15. Williams, commentary on *The Fourth Paper*, C2(r). Williams goes on to discuss the Jews' inhumane treatment of the Jews under King Henry II, King John, Richard I and Edward I.
16. Williams, *The Bloudy Tenent*, A2v.
17. Williams, *The Bloudy Tenent*, Aii(v).
18. *The Booke of Common Prayer, and the Administration of the Sacraments, And other Rites and Ceremonies of the Church of England* (London: Robert Barker, 1604), H4r.

19. Thomas Helwys, *A short declaration of the mistery of iniquity* ([Amsterdam]: 1612), Fiijr. Helwys is answered by John Robinson's *Of Religious Communion, Private, & Publique* (1614). See also Anon, [Henry Jacob], *To the right High and mightie Prince, IAMES by the grace of God, King of great Britannie, France, and Irelande, Defender of the faith, &c.* ([Middleburg: R. Schilders], 1609), B2r, Fr.
20. Richard Hooker, *Of the Lawes of Ecclesiasticall Politie. Eyght Bookes* (London: John Windet, 1593), III, L4r–v.
21. Thomas Morton, *Salomon, or A treatise declaring the state of the kingdome of Israel, as it was in the daies of Salomon* (London: Robert Robinson for Robert Dexter, 1596), Dr–v. See also N3r–v.
22. Arthur Golding, trans., *A Worke concerning the trewnesse of the Christian Religion, written in French: Against Atheists, Epicures, Paynims, Iewes, Mahumetists, and other Infidels. By Philip of Mornay Lord of Plessie Marlie* (London: Thomas Cadman, 1587), Titlepage.
23. For more on the relationship between church and state in early modern Christian debate, see Kevin Sharpe and Steven N. Zwicker, eds, *The Politics of Discourse: The Literature and History of Seventeenth-Century England* (Berkeley: University of California Press, 1987), 5–7; Weldon S. Crowley, 'Erastianism in the Westminster Assembly', *The Journal of Church and State*, 15 (1973) I, 49–65 at 56–8 and Robert S. Paul, *The Assembly of the Lord: Politics and Religion in the Westminster Assembly and 'the grand debate'* (Edinburgh: T. & T. Clark, 1985).
24. See Nicholas Tyacke, 'Puritanism, Arminianism and Counter-revolution' in Richard Cust and Ann Hughes, eds, *The English Civil War* (London: Hodder Headline, 1997), 136–59 at 156.
25. On the significance of the Westminster Assembly debates, see Reid Barbour, *John Selden: Measures of the Holy Commonwealth in Seventeenth-Century England* (Toronto: University of Toronto Press, 2003), Chapter 5 and Barry Coward, *The Stuart Age: A History of England 1603–1714* (London: Longman, 1994), 179.
26. For the Erastian–Presbyterian debate in the Westminster Assembly, see Crowley, 'Erastianism in the Westminster Assembly', 56–8; Paul, *The Assembly of the Lord*; William Lamont, *Marginal Prynne 1600–1669* (London: Routledge & Kegan Paul, 1963), Chapter 7 and Jonathan R. Ziskind, trans. and ed., *John Selden on Jewish Marriage Law: The* Uxor Hebraica (London: E.J. Brill, 1991), 13–4.
27. Robert Baillie complains in his *Journal* about 'the Erastian heresy, which in this land is very strong, especially among the lawyers, unhappy members of this Parliament'. See David Laing, ed., *The Letters and Journals of Robert Baillie*, 3 vols (Edinburgh: Alex Lawrie & Co., 1841), II, 315–60. George Gillespie is identified as one of the foremost Presbyterians of the Assembly in the 'Epistle To the Reader' prefacing the 1569 translation of Erastus's *Theses, The Nullity of Church-Censures* (A3v–A4r): the anonymous author mentions the fact that 'Mr. *Beza*, Mr. *Catherwoods* . . . Mr. *Gilespy* in his *Aarons Rod Blossoming*' and 'the Divines of *London* in their *Jus Divinum*, have all written against Erastus. He continues, 'Pardon the Errors of the Presse in this Edition: for both my Amanuensis, and the Corrector are Presbyterians'.
28. See Coward, *The Stuart Age*, 194; Tyacke, 'The "Rise of Puritanism"', 28–9; Haller, *Tracts on Liberty*, I, 5. For factionalism during the Civil War, see

Grell et al., eds, *From Persecution to Toleration*, 'Introduction', 5–6; Christopher Hill, *The World Turned Upside Down: Radical Ideas during the English Revolution* (London: Maurice Temple Smith, 1972); Hill, *The Century of Revolution 1603–1714* (Walton-on-Thames: Thomas Nelson, 1980), 141–53; John Morrill and John Walter, 'Order and disorder in the English Revolution' in Cust and Hughes, eds, *The English Civil War*, 310–40 at 327–30; Nigel Smith, *Literature and Revolution in England 1640–1660* (New Haven: Yale University Press, 1994); Smith, *Perfection Proclaimed: Language and Literature in English Radical Religion 1640–1660* (Oxford: Clarendon Press, 1989); Tyacke, 'The "Rise of Puritanism"', 30–1 and Mark Kishlansky, 'The Emergence of Adversary Politics in the Long Parliament' in Cust and Hughes, eds, *The English Civil War*, 62–83 at 68–76.

29. Prynne, *A Fresh Discovery*, A2r.
30. See *The Letters and Journals of Robert Baillie*, II, 315–60.
31. As William Haller, editor of *Tracts on Liberty* notes, 'Baillie, Gillespie, Pagitt, Prynne and Edwards, all called anathema upon it'. Haller, ed., *Tracts on Liberty*, I, 59.
32. Cotton left England in 1633. Williams's *The Bloudy Tenent* (1644) is answered by Cotton's *The Bloudy Tenent, Washed* (1647) which is in turn answered by Williams's *The Bloody Tenent Yet More Bloody* (1652).
33. Anon, *Hell broke loose: or, a catalogue of many of the spreading error, heresies and blasphemies of these times, for which we are to be humbled* (London: Tho. Underhil, 1646).
34. Williams, *The Bloudy Tenent*, F3v–F4r. See Song of Songs, 2:2–3.
35. There is a rich ambiguity in this formulation: it is not clear if the church in question is the national church, in which case dissenting Christians can exist, as it were, in the state, or whether in fact the church here is the 'true' church.
36. See for example, Williams, *The Bloudy Tenent*, a2r: 'the *Doctrine* of *Persecution* for cause of *Conscience*, is proved guilty of all the *blood* of the *Soules* crying for *vengeance* under the *Altar*'.
37. Williams, *The Bloudy Tenent*, F4v. George Gillespie argues against Williams's interpretation of the parable of the tares in Gillespie, *Wholsome Severity reconciled with Christian Liberty. Or, The true Resolution of a present Controversie concerning Liberty of Conscience* (London: Christopher Meredith, 1644), C4r.
38. Williams, *The Bloudy Tenent*, H2v.
39. Williams, *The Bloudy Tenent*, L3v–L4r.
40. Cotton, *The Bloudy Tenent, Washed*, Gr.
41. Cotton, *The Bloudy Tenent, Washed*, Yv.
42. Williams, *The Bloudy Tenent*, O3v.
43. As H.C. Porter describes, Williams also attempted to argue that the Native Americans' religion did have some monotheistic elements, thus arguing on the one hand that heretics should be tolerated in the civil state, and on the other hand that Native Americans were not entirely heretical. See Porter, 'Anglicans, Puritans and American Indians: Persecution or Toleration?' in Sheils, ed., *Persecution and Toleration*, 189–98 at 193. Williams believed that the Native American had qualities of the Jew, the Roman and the Greek. For the early modern notion that Native Americans were of Jewish descent, see Claire Jowitt, 'Radical Identities? Native Americans, Jews and the English

Commonwealth' in Sian Jones et al., eds, *Cultures of Ambivalence and Contempt: Studies in Jewish-Non-Jewish Relations* (London: Vallentine Mitchell, 1998), 153–81.
44. Cotton, *The Bloudy Tenent, Washed*, K4v.
45. William Prynne, *Twelve Considerable Serious Questions touching Church Government: Sadly propounded (out of a Reall Desire of Unitie, and Tranquillity in Church and State) to all Sober-minded Christians* (London: F.L., for Michael Sparke Sr, 1644); Prynne, *Independency Examined, unmasked, refuted, by twelve new particular interrogatories* (London: F.L., for Michael Sparke, Sr, 1644). For the other replies, see Haller, ed., *Tracts on Liberty*, I, 51–2.
46. Prynne, *Twelve Considerable Serious Questions*, A4r. A printed marginal note reads 'Bloudy Tenent'.
47. Richard Overton, *The Arraignement of Mr. Persecution: Presented to the consideration of the House of Commons, and to all the common people of England wherein he is indicted, arraigned, convicted, and condemned of enmity against God, and all Goodnesse, of Treasons, Rebellion, Bloodshed, &c.* ([London], 1645). For references to the Marprelate controversy in the Civil War, see Smith, *Literature and Revolution in England*, 297–304.
48. Prynne, *A Fresh Discovery*, Cr.
49. See Edwards, *Gangraeana*, i3r.
50. The phrase 'to pisse against the wall' is biblical; it means to let a man exist in the most basic sense. See 1 Kings 14:10; 2 Kings 9:8; 1 Samuel 25:22.
51. Overton, *The Arraignement of Mr. Persecution*, D4r.
52. Overton, *The Arraignement of Mr. Persecution*, D4r.
53. Thomas Edwards' *Gangraeana* (1645) is directed at Overton, and also at Hugh Peters (K3r) and John Goodwin (L5r); it recommends Prynne's *Fresh Discovery* (N1v).
54. Gillespie, *Aarons Rod*, B2r.
55. See David Katz, *Sabbath and Sectarianism in Seventeenth-century England* (Leiden: E.J. Brill, 1988), 2 and Bernard Capp, *The Fifth Monarchy Men: A Study in Seventeenth Century English Millenarianism* (London: Faber and Faber, 1972), 63, 117–8.
56. George Gillespie, *A late dialogue betwixt a Civilian and a Divine, concerning the present condition of the Church of England* (London: Robert Bostock, 1644), C2v. Gillespie is replying to the Royalist John Maxwell's *An answer by letter to a worthy gentleman Who desired of a Divine some reasons by which it might appear how Inconsistent Presbyteriall government is with monarchy* ([Oxford: L. Lichfield], 1644).
57. Gillespie, *Aarons Rod*, B2r.
58. Gillespie, *Aarons Rod*, Br–v.
59. Stephen Nettles, *An answer to the Jewish part of Mr. Selden's History of Tithes* (Oxford: J. Lichfield & W. Turner, 1625), Xr.
60. Gillespie, *Aarons Rod*, Br–v.
61. See Baillie, *The Letters and Journals of Robert Baillie*, 2:265–6; see also Jason P. Rosenblatt, *Torah and Law in Paradise Lost* (Princeton: Princeton University Press, 1994), 119.
62. Anon, *Nil Probas: or a Discovery of the Extreame Unsatisfactorinesse, in a piece of Mr Gilespie's, one of the Scotch Commissioners, lately published; called, Aarons Rod Budding* (London: Giles Calvert, 1646), A3v.

63. Anon, *Nil Probas*, Av.
64. Anon, *Nil Probas*, A3r. See 1 Chronicles 26:30: 'And of the Hebronites, Hashabiah and his brethren, men of valour, a thousand and seven hundred, were officers among them of Israel on this side Jordan westward in all the business of the Lord, and in the service of the King'.
65. Anon, *Nil Probas*, D2r. See also B2v, where the author disputes the notion that 'now this was an Ecclesiasticall (not Civill) Sanhedrin'.
66. John Lightfoot, *Elias Redivivus: A Sermon preached Before the Honourable House of Commons, In the Parish of Satin Margarets Westminster, at the publike Fast, March 29, 1643* (London: R. Cotes, for Andrew Crooke, 1643), A3r.
67. (London: Jacob Flesher, 1650, 1653, 1655). See Rosenblatt, *Torah and Law*, 90–1.
68. Gillespie, *A late dialogue*, C3v–C4r. For Selden's views on excommunication, see Rosenblatt, *Renaissance England's Chief Rabbi: John Selden* (Oxford: Oxford University Press, 2006), Chapter 11.
69. Williams, *The Bloudy Tenent*, Gv.
70. Williams, *The Bloudy Tenent*, A2v.
71. Williams, *The Bloudy Tenent*, as cited in Zagorin, *How Religious Toleration came to the West*, 201.
72. George Gillespie, *Wholsome Severity reconciled with Christian Liberty. Or, The true Resolution of a present Controversie concerning Liberty of Conscience* (London: Christopher Meredith, 1644), Biv(r). Gillespie is upholding the power of the magistrate to excommunicate sinners from the church. In other words, if church and state are combined, the ruler has the power to excommunicate those who do not subscribe to the national church.
73. An analogous comparison can be made here with the work of John Milton. Milton made extensive use of Mosaic law in *Paradise Lost* and in his tracts of 1643–5, in particular his tract on divorce, *Doctrine and Discipline of Divorce*, arguing that the Jewish legal position on divorce had not been abrogated. Consequently, Milton is regarded as one of the most important Christian scholars of Judaism in the seventeenth century. However, other tracts, such as *Of Civil Power* (1659), which concerns the interference of civil authorities in ecclesiastical affairs, explicitly rejects these Jewish precedents. Just as his *De doctrina Christiana* emphasised the liberty of the Christian gospel from Jewish legalism, *Of Civil Power* argued for Christian freedom from both political control over religious affairs, and from Mosaic law. Thus his tract in favour of religious toleration was against the use of Jewish precedents. For Milton and Judaism, see for example, Rosenblatt, *Torah and Law in Paradise Lost*, Chapter 2; Ziskind, *John Selden on Jewish Marriage Law*, Introduction and Jeffrey S. Shoulson, *Milton and the Rabbis: Hebraism, Hellenism and Christianity* (New York: Columbia University Press, 2001).
74. See Haller, ed., *Tracts on Liberty*, I, 53–5.
75. Prynne, *Twelve Considerable Serious questions*, A2v.
76. [John Goodwin], *Certaine briefe observations and antiquaeries: On Master Prin's twelve questions about church-government* ([London], 1644), B2r.
77. Prynne, *A Full Reply*, Bv.
78. Prynne, *A Full Reply*, Bv. The 'pattern of the Tabernacle shewed in the Mount' is a reference to the idea that the description of the Tabernacle was written by a priestly source much later than Moses, and that it was modelled on the later example of Solomon's Temple on Mount Moriah in Jerusalem.

79. Williams, *The Bloudy Tenent*, Dd4v.
80. William Hughes, *Anglo-Judaeus, or the History of the Jews, whilst here in England. Relating their Manners, Carriage, and Usage, from their Admission By William the Conqueror, to their Banishment. Occasioned by a Book, written to His Highness, the Lord Protector (with a Declaration to the Commonwealth of England) for their Re-admission, By Rabbi Menasses Ben Israel. To which is also subjoyned a particular Answer, by W.H.* (London: T.N. for Thomas Heath, 1656), F2r. See also [Henry Jacob], *To the right High and mightie Prince*: 'it standeth with the reason of State to allow the Toleration desired by us' (Fr).

Chapter 5 Contesting readmission: Common law and the English constitution

1. [Henry Jessey], *A Narrative Of the late Proceeds at White-Hall, concerning the Jews: Who had desired by R. Manasses an Agent for them; that they might return into England, and Worship the God of their Fathers here in their Synagogues, &c. Published for satisfaction to many in several parts of England, that are desirous, and inquisitive to hear the Truth thereof* (London: Printed for L. Chapman, at the Crown in Popeshead-Alley. 1656), 8–9. See Esmond Samuel, ed., *The Diary of John Eveyln: Now Printed in Full from the Manuscripts belonging to Mr. John Evelyn* (Oxford: Clarendon Press, 2000), III, 163 and David Katz, *Philo-Semitism and the Readmission of the Jews to England, 1603–1655* (Oxford: Clarendon Press, 1982), 213.
2. For Stow's interest in medieval Jewry, see Antony Bale, 'Stow's Medievalism and Antique Judaism in Early Modern London' in Ian Gadd and Alexandra Gillespie, eds, *John Stow (1525–1605) and the Making of the English Past* (London: The British Library, 2004), 69–80.
3. D'Blossiers Tovey, *Anglia Judaica: Or the History and Antiquities of the Jews in England, Collected from all our Historians, both Printed and Manuscript, as also from the Records in the Tower, and other Publick Repositories* (Oxford: J. Fletcher, 1738), 269. See also Henry Jessey, who writes that 'The *Lawyers* said, *That there is no Law that forbids the Jews return into* England'; [Jessey], *A Narrative*, 9.
4. See for example, Katz, *Philo-Semitism*, Katz, 'English Redemption and Jewish Readmission in 1656', *Journal of Jewish Studies*, 34 (1983), 73—91; James Shapiro, *Shakespeare and the Jews* (New York: Columbia University Press, 1996), 55—62; Bernard Glassman, *Anti-Semitic stereotypes without Jews: Images of the Jews in England* (Detroit: Wayne State University Press, 1975), Chapter 5; Nathan Osterman, 'The Controversy over the Proposed Readmission of the Jews to England (1655)', *Jewish Social Studies*, 3 (1941), 301–28.
5. For millenarian arguments in particular, see Jonathan Israel and David Katz, eds, *Sceptics, Millenarians and Jews* (Leiden: E.J. Brill, 1990); Christopher Hill, 'Till the Conversion of the Jews' in Richard H. Popkin, ed., *Millenarianism and Messianism in English Literature and Thought 1650–1800* (Leiden: E.J. Brill, 1988), 12—37; Bernard Capp, *The Fifth Monarchy Men: A study in seventeenth century English Millenarianism* (London: Faber, 1972), 28–9 and 190–2 and Claire Jowitt, '"The Consolation of Israel": The Representation of Jewishness in the Writings of Gerrard Winstanley and William Everard', *Prose Studies*, 22 (1999), 83–99.

6. See Claire Jowitt, 'Radical Identities? Native Americans, Jews and the English Commonwealth', *The Seventeenth Century*, 10 (1995), 101–19.
7. [Nathaniel Crouch], 'The Proceedings of the Jews in England in the Year 1655' in *Two Journeys To Jerusalem . . . Collected by R. B. and Beautified with Pictures* (London: Printed for Nathaniel Crouch, 1715), [Crouch], *Proceedings*, 172.
8. John Dury, *A Case of Conscience, Whether it be lawful to admit Jews into a Christian Common-wealth? Resolved by John Dury: Written to Samuel Hartlib, Esquire* (London: Printed for Richard Wodenothe, 1656), 3.
9. [Jessey], *A Narrative*, 3.
10. [Jessey], *A Narrative*, 6.
11. Edward Spencer, *A Breife Epistle to the Learned Manasseh Ben Israel in Answer to His Dedicated to the Parliament* (London: Titlepage missing, 1650), 2.
12. Spencer, *A Breife Epistle*, 11.
13. Spencer, *A Breife Epistle*, 16.
14. Dury, *A Case of Conscience*, 8.
15. Alexander Ross, *A View of the Jewish Religion Containing the manner of Life, Rites, Ceremonies and Customes of the Iewish Nation throughout the World at this present time; Together With the Articles of their Faith, as now received* (London: Printed by T.M. for E. Brewster and S. Miller, 1656), Preface.
16. Spencer, *A Breife Epistle*, 12.
17. Dury, *A Case of Conscience*, 7.
18. Thomas Collier, *A Brief Answer To some of the Objections and Demurs Made against the coming in and inhabiting of the Jews in this Common-wealth. With a plea on their behalf, Or some arguments to prove it not only lawful, but the duty of those whom it concerns to give them their liberty and protection* (they living peaceably in this Nation) (London: Printed by Henry Hills, 1656 [MS amendation: 1655]), 2. See also 18.
19. Philo-Judaeus, *The Resurrection of Dead Bones, Or, the Conversion of the Jewes* (London: Printed for Giles Calvert, 1655), 91.
20. Philo-Judaeus, *The Resurrection of Dead Bones*, 3. This extensive tract is full of scriptural references.
21. For mercantile arguments in particular, see Edgar Samuel, 'The Readmission of the Jews to England in 1656, in the Context of English Economic Policy', *Jewish Historical Studies*, 31 (1988), 153–69; Jonathan Israel, *European Jewry in the age of Mercantilism 1550–1750* (Oxford: Clarendon Press, 1985), especially 184–90 and Todd Endelman, *The Jews of Britain, 1656–2000* (Berkeley and Los Angeles: The University of California Press, 2002), 25.
22. Hugh Peter, *A word for the Armie and two Words to the Kingdome, to cleare the one and cure the other. Forced in much plainness and brevity from their faithfull servant H. Peters* (London: M. Simmons for Giles Calvert, 1647), Bii(r).
23. [Jessey], *A Narrative*, Av.
24. T. Birch, ed., *The State Papers of John Thurloe* (London: Printed for the Executor of the late Mr. Fletcher Gyles; Thomas Woodward, 1742), IV, 321, as cited in Katz, *Philo-Semitism*, 211.
25. When Parliament threatened to introduce a special tax for the Jews in 1689, the Jewish community printed a petition, *The Case of the Jews Stated*, which attempted to claim that since they belonged to a homeless Jewish nation, they should therefore be given special rights as subjects. They tried, in other words, to articulate a claim for citizenship as a national, as well as a religious

group. But such efforts were met by continued resistance from English Christians; numerous tracts such as the 1703 *Historical and Law Treatise Against the Jewes and Judaism*, referred to the Jews as 'mere aliens'. See Shapiro, *Shakespeare and the Jews*, 189–93.
26. Tovey, *Anglia Judaica*, 269.
27. The wider context of the readmission debates is noted by James Shapiro, who suggests that the debates provided an opportunity to hammer out questions of constitutional authority by reference to the circumstances surrounding the expulsion of the Jews in the thirteenth century, and that, in turn, these discussions contributed to an emergent sense of English national identity. This chapter reveals, in addition, the network of texts which discuss this issue, and demonstrates a further issue: the emergent English legal system. See Shapiro, *Shakespeare and the Jews*, 46–62.
28. In 1647, before the readmission controversy got underway, Hugh Peter wrote *A Word for the Armie*, in which he suggests that Jews be allowed to live in England. Peter's *A Word for the Armie* was answered anonymously by the divine Nathaniel Ward in the same year. In 1651, Peter wrote another treatise, *Good work for a good magistrate*, and the same year the legal writer Rice Vaughan replied to it with *A Plea for the Common-Laws of England*. In 1656, William Prynne produced another reply to *Good work*: his *A short demurrer to the Jewes Long discontinued remitter into England*. In the same year, 'D.L.' then defended Peter against Prynne's reply, with his *Israel's cause and condition pleaded. Or, some arguments for the Jews admission into England . . . objections answered, cautions added, with a vindication of Mr Peters from . . . aspersions cast upon him by W. Prynn* (London: P.W. for W. Turner, 1656).
29. London: Edward Thomas, 1656.
30. Prynne's *Demurrer* was not the first book about the history of the Jews to appear in England. The lawyer and scholar John Selden wrote extensively on the government, laws and customs of the Jews in both biblical and post-biblical times. Selden was influenced, in turn, by the historical work of continental scholars such as Hugo Grotius, Joseph Justus Scaliger and Johannes Buxtorf. For the continental roots of Jewish scholarship see, for example, Richard Tuck, *Philosophy and Government 1572–1651* (Cambridge: Cambridge University Press, 1993), Chapter 5 and Jonathan R. Ziskind, 'Petrus Cunæus on Theocracy, Jubilee and the Latifundia', *The Jewish Quarterly Review*, 68 (1978), 4, 235–55.
31. See, for example, Katz, *Philo-Semitism*, 220–3.
32. Peter, *A word for the Armie*, Bii(r).
33. Samuel Highland, for example, who served on the committee set up by the Barebones Parliament in 1653, hoped that 'the great volumes of law would come to be reduced into the bigness of a pocket book, as it is proportionable in New-England and elsewhere' (L.D. [Samuel Highland], *An Exact Relation of the Proceedings and Transactions of the Late Parliament* [London: Printed for Livewell Chapman, 1653]). Dv. Highland's report provides a sense of how inflamed the debate about law reform had become. Opponents of a new body of laws were outraged 'as if it were intended to destroy the Law, and take away the Laws we had been fighting for all this while as our birth-right and inheritance. And such a noise was made about it, that made many believe that the House was modelized of Monsters, rather then men of reason and judgement' (C4r).

34. For the conflict between Common and Canon Law, see Austin Woolrych, *Commonwealth to Protectorate* (Oxford: Clarendon Press, 1982), especially Chapter 8 and J.H. Baker, *An Introduction to English Legal History* (London: Butterworths, 1979), 111–14. For the rise of Common Law, see J.G.A. Pocock, *The Ancient Constitution and the Feudal Law: A study of English historical thought in the seventeenth century* (Cambridge: Cambridge University Press, 1987), Chapters 1–3; William Klein, 'The ancient constitution revisited' in Nicholas Phillipson and Quentin Skinner, eds, *Political Discourse in Early Modern Britain* (Cambridge: Cambridge University Press, 1993), 23–44; J.W. Tubbs, *The Common Law Mind: Medieval and Early Modern Conceptions* (Baltimore: The Johns Hopkins University Press, 2000), especially Chapter 7; J.H. Baker, *The Legal Profession and the Common Law: Historical Essays* (London: The Hambledon Press, 1986); John Guy, 'The Henrician Age', in J.G.A. Pocock, ed., *The Varieties of British political thought, 1500–1800* (Cambridge: Cambridge University Press, 1993), 22–30 and Ann Hughes, *The Causes of the English Civil War* (Basingstoke: Macmillan Press, 1998), 74–9.
35. Controversies about legal method in the seventeenth century resonated with Jewish ideas in a number of other ways. The prominent legal writer John Selden was renowned, for example, for applying Common Law methodology to Jewish historical and exegetical texts, and, in turn, Selden's invocation of Jewish precedents carried connotations of Parliamentarianism and Common Law. Moreover, the association between continental jurisprudence (whence Common Law emerged) and Judaism was already in place via the works of continental jurists and scholars Joseph Justus Scaliger and Hugo Grotius, which provided Selden with information about Hellenic and post-biblical Jewish history and Talmudic literature. See Tuck, *Philosophy and Government*, Chapter 5 and Tuck, *Natural Rights Theories: Their origin and development* (Cambridge: Cambridge University Press, 1979), 163.
36. Hugh Peter, *Good work for a good magistrate. Or, A short Cut to great quiet. By Honest, homely plain English Hints given from Scripture, Reason, and Experience, for the regulating of most Cases in this Common-wealth* (London: William Du-Gard Printer to the Council of State, 1651), Civ(v).
37. Prynne, *A Short Demurrer*, 2:Aiv(r).
38. [Nathaniel Ward], *A Word to Mr Peters, and Two Words for the Parliament and Kingdom. Or, An Answer to a Scandalous Pamphlet, entituled, A Word for the Armie, and two Words to the Kingdom: Subscribed by Hugh Peters. Wherein The Authority of Parliament is infringed, The fundamentall Laws of the Land subverted; The famous City of London Blemished; and all the godly Ministers of the City scandalized* (London: Fr: Neile for Tho: Underhill, 1647), replying to Peter, *A word for the Armie*. As well as their disagreements over the law, Ward was opposed to the army's control over parliament; this made him a natural enemy of Hugh Peter, the army chaplain.
39. Prynne, *A Short Demurrer*, 2:Tiii(r).
40. Prynne, *A Short Demurrer*, 2:Tiii(r).
41. 'D.L.', *Israels Condition and Cause pleaded; Or some Arguments for the Jews Admission into England. Objections answered, Cautions added, with a Vindication of Mr. Peters from those foul and unjust Aspersions cast upon him by W. Prynn, Esq.* (London: William Larnar and Jonathan Ball, 1656), 84.
42. 'D.L.', *Israels Condition and Cause pleaded*, 87.

43. 'D.L.', *Israels Condition and Cause pleaded*, 85–6.
44. 'D.L.', *Israels Condition and Cause pleaded*, 89.
45. Rice Vaughan, *A Plea for the Common-Laws of England: Or, An Answer to a Book entituled, a good work for a good Magistrate: Or, a short Cut to a great quiet. (Published by Mr. Hugh Peters:) So far as concerns his Proposals touching the said Laws* (London: Francis Tyton, 1651), Aii(r). Note the conjunction of grievances in the long title of Nathaniel Ward's answer to Hugh Peter: 'The Authority of Parliament is infringed, The fundamentall Laws of the Land subverted' (Anon [Ward], *A Word to Mr Peters*, Titlepage).
46. William Hughes, *Anglo-Judaeus, or the History of the Jews, whilst here in England. Relating their Manners, Carriage, and Usage, from their Admission By William the Conqueror, to their Banishment* (London, 1656). See especially Diii(r).
47. See Shapiro, *Shakespeare and the Jews*, 46–55. Kenneth Stow believes that 'the Jews were expelled during what might be called a protracted constitutional crisis'; see Stow, *Alienated Minority: The Jews of Medieval Latin Europe* (Cambridge, MA: Harvard University Press, 1992), 285–6 and 295. For more on the constitutional aspect of the thirteenth-century events, see also Robert Stacey, '1290–1260: A Watershed in Anglo-Jewish Relations?', *Historical Research*, 61 (1988), 35–50; Stacey, 'The Conversion of the Jews to Christianity in Thirteenth-Century England', *Speculum*, 67 (1992), 263–83 and J.H.M. Salmon, *The French Religious Wars in English Political Thought* (Oxford: Clarendon Press, 1959), 60–2.
48. Prynne, *A Short Demurrer*, I:G(r–v). See also Shapiro, *Shakespeare and the Jews*, 52, and H.S.Q. Henriques, *The Return of the Jews to England: Being a Chapter in the History of English Law* (London: Macmillan and Co, 1905), 10–1.
49. Prynne, *A Short Demurrer*, 1:G(v).
50. Prynne, *A Short Demurrer*, 1:G(r).
51. Prynne, *A Short Demurrer*, 2:Rii(v).
52. Prynne, *A Short Demurrer*, 2:Bii(v).
53. Richard Helgerson, *Forms of Nationhood: The Elizabethan Writing of England* (Chicago: University of Chicago Press, 1992), 63–104 at 104. For the connection between the rise of English national identity and the Common Law, see also Pocock, *The Ancient Constitution*, 56. Pocock observes that Coke 'saw the law he idolized as the immemorial custom of England, and he imagined it as being immemorial purely within the island'.
54. Prynne, *A Short Demurrer*, 2:Sii(r).
55. Prynne, *A Short Demurrer*, 2:T(r).
56. Prynne, *A Short Demurrer*, 1:Aiv(v). Printed marginal notes beside this passage refer to charters and decrees collected from Anglo-Saxon history.
57. Edwin Jones, following the nineteenth-century historian F.W. Maitland, writes of the 'theme in English historiography in the late sixteenth and seventeenth centuries, which stated that the Common Law of England, together with its concomitant institutions of freedom (including Parliament), all developed continuously from their earliest origins in the primitive forest life of Germany, from where the Anglo-Saxons had come'. See Jones, *The English Nation: The Great Myth* (Stroud, Gloucestershire: Sutton, 1998), 94–114 at 94.
58. Hughes, *Anglo-Judaeus*, Aii(r–v).
59. Prynne, *A Short Demurrer*, 2:Aiv(r).

188 Notes

60. Hughes, *Anglo-Judaeus*, Fii(r). For more on the toleration of Jews in Amsterdam, see Henry Mechoulan and Gerard Nahon, eds, *Menasseh ben Israel, The Hope of Israel: The English Translation by Moses Wall, 1652* (Oxford: Oxford University Press, 1987), 1–22; Israel, *European Jewry in the Age of Mercantilism*, Chapter 15; Miriam Bodian, *Hebrews of the Portuguese Nation: Conversos and Community in Early Modern Amsterdam* (Bloomington, IN: Indiana University Press, 1997); Kaplan, *Menasseh ben Israel*; Peter Van Rooden, 'Conceptions of Judaism as a Religion in the Seventeenth-century Dutch Republic' in Diana Wood, ed., *Christianity and Judaism: Papers read at the 1991 Summer meeting and the 1992 Winter meeting of The Ecclesiastical History Society*, 299–309 and C. Berkvens-Stevelinck, Jonathan Israel and G.H.M. Posthumus Meyjes, eds, *The Emergence of Tolerance in the Dutch Republic* (Leiden: E.J. Brill, 1997).
61. Crouch, *Proceedings*,
62. 'D.L.', *Israel's cause and condition pleaded*, 106.
63. Prynne, *A short demurrer*, 1:H4r.
64. 'D.L.', *Israels Condition and Cause pleaded*, F6v.

Conclusion

1. Hugh Broughton, *Observations Upon The first ten fathers* (London: W. White, 1612), B5r.

Bibliography

Books published before 1700

Ames, William, *A Reply to Dr Mortons Generall Defence of Three Nocent Ceremonies. Viz. The Surplice, Crosse in Baptisme, and kneeling at the receiving of the sacramentall elements of Bread and Wine* ([Amsterdam: G. Thorp], 1622).

Ames, William, *A Fresh Suit Against Human Ceremonies in God's Worship. Or A Triplication unto. D. Burgesse His Rejoinder For D. Morton* ([Amsterdam: The successors of G. Thorp], 1633).

Anon, *An Admonition, to the Parliament* ([Hemel Hempstead: J. Stroud], 1572).

Anon, *A Seconde Admonition to the Parliament* (London: Christopher Barker, 1579).

Anon, *A Christian Letter of certaine English Protestants, unfained favourers of the present use of Religion, authorised and professed in England: unto that Reverend and learned man, Mr. R. Hoo. requiring resolution in certaine matters of doctrine (which seeme to overthrow the foundation of Christian Religion, and of the church among us) expresslie contained in his five books of Ecclesiasticall Pollicie* (Middelburg: Richard Schilders, 1599).

Anon, *The Originall of Popish Idolatrie, or The Birth of Heresies. Published under the name of CAVSAUBON,* [in 1625] *And called-in the same yeare, upon misinformation. But now upon better Consideration Reprinted with ALOWANCE* ([Amsterdam: The successors of G. Thorp], 1630).

Anon [translated by Franciscus a Sancta Clara], *True religion explained And defended against ye Archenemies thereof in these times, in six Bookes* (London: [John Haviland for] Richard Royston, 1632).

Anon, *Hell broke loose: or, a catalogue of many of the spreading error, heresies and blasphemies of these times, for which we are to be humbled* (London: Tho. Underhil, 1646).

Anon, *Nil Probas: or a Discovery of the Extreame Unsatisfactorinesse, in a piece of Mr Gilespie's, one of the Scotch Commissioners, lately published; called, Aarons Rod Budding* (London: Giles Calvert, 1646).

Anon, *The Nullity of Church-Censures: Or A Dispute Written by that Illustrious Philosopher, Expert Physician, and Pious Divine Dr Thomas Erastus, Publik Professor in the University of Heidelberge, and Basil* (London: Printed for G.L., 1659).

Anon, *An Apology for the Naturalization of the Jews . . . By a True Believer* (London: Printed for M. Cooper, 1753).

Anon, *An Historical Treatise Concerning Jews and Judaism, in England* (London: Printed for R. Baldwin, 1753).

Balcanquhall, Walter, *The Honour of Christian Churches; and the Necessitie of frequenting of Divine Service and Publike Prayers in them* (London: George Miller for Robert Allot, 1633).

Bale, John, *Illustrium Maioris Britanniae Scriptorium, hoc est, Angliae, Cambriae, ac Scotiae Summariu[m], in quasdam centurias divisum, cum diversitate doctrinaru[m] recta supputatione per omnes aetates a Iapheto sanctissimi Noah filio, ad annum domini M.D. XLVIII* ([Wesel: D. van der Straten], 1548).

Bancroft, Richard, *A Survay of the pretended Holy Discipline. Contayning the beginnings, successe, parts, proceedings, authority, and doctrine of it: with some of the manifold, and materiall repugnances, varieties and uncertainties, in that behalfe* (London: Iohn Wolfe, 1593).

Barkesdale, Clement, trans., *Petrus Cunæus, Of the Common-wealth of the Hebrews* (London: Printed for T.W. for William Lee, 1653).

Barlow, Thomas, *Several Miscellaneous and Weighty Cases of Conscience, Learnedly and Judiciously Resolved By the Right Reverend Father in God, Dr. Thomas Barlow, Late Lord-Bishop of Lincoln* (London: Printed and sold by Mrs. Davis in Amen-corner, 1692).

Bastwick, John, *The Letany of John Bastwick, Doctor of Phisicke, Being now full of Devotion, as well in respect of the common calamities of plague and pestilence; as also of his owne patticular miserie: lying in this instant in Limbo Patrum* ([Leiden: Willem Christiaens], 1637).

Bilson, Thomas, *The Perpetual Government of Christes Church. Wherein are handled; The fatherly superioritie which God first established in the Patriarke for the guiding of his Church, and after continued in the Tribe of Levi and the Prophetes* (London: The Deputies of Christopher Barker, 1593).

Bilson, Thomas, *The effect of certaine Sermons touching the full redemption of mankind by the death and bloud of Christ Jesus: wherein Besides the merite of Christs suffering, the manner of his offering, the power of his death, the comfort of his Crosse, the glorie of his resurrection, Are handled* (London: Peter Short for Walter Burre, 1599).

Bourne, Immanuel, *A Defence and Justification of Ministers Maintenance by Tythes. And of Infant-Baptism, Humane Learning, and the Sword of the Magistrate; Which some Anabaptists falsely call Four Sandy Pillars, and Popish Foundations of our Ministry and Churches* (London: John Allen, 1659).

Broughton, Hugh, *An Epistle to the Nobilitie of England with ancient warrant for euerie worde, vnto the full satisfaction of any that be of hart* (Middleburg: Richard Schilders, 1597).

Broughton, Hugh, *Daniel his Chaldie visions and his Ebrew: both translated after the originall; and expounded both by reduction of heathen most famous stories unto the exact proprietie of his wordes (which is the surest certaintie what he must meane:) and by ioyning all the Bible, and learned tongues to the frame of his worke* (London: Gabriell Simson, 1597).

Broughton, Hugh, *An Explication of the article κατήλθε εἰς ᾅδου, of our Lordes soules going from his body to Paradise; touched by the Greek, generally ᾅδου, The world of Soules; termed Hel by the old Saxon, & by all our translations: with a defense of the Q. of Englands religion* ([Printed abroad], 1599).

Broughton, Hugh, *Declaration of generall corruption of Religion, Scripture and all learning; wrought by D. Bilson. While he breedeth a new opinion, that our Lord went from Paradise to Gehenna, to triumph over the Devills* ([Middleburg: Richard Schilders], 1603).

Broughton, Hugh, *Two little workes defensive of our Redemption, That our Lord went through the veile of his flesh into Heaven, to appeare before God for us. Which iourney a Talmudist, as the Gospell would terme, a going up to Paradise: But Heathen Greek, a going down to Hades, and Latin, Descendere ad infernos* ([Middelburg: Richard Schilders], 1604).

Broughton, Hugh, *A Replie upon the R.R.F.TH. Winton for heads of his divinity in his sermon and survey: How he taught a perfect truth, that our Lord went he[n]ce to Paradise: But adding that he went thence to Hades, & striving to prove that, he injurieth all learning & Christianity* ([Amsterdam]: n.p., 1605).

Broughton, Hugh, *A Require of Agreement to the Groundes of Divinitie studie: wherin great scholers falling, & being caught of Iewes, disgrace the Gospel: & trap them to destruction* (Middleburgh: R. Schilders, 1611).

Broughton, Hugh, *Observations Upon The first ten fathers* (London: W. White, 1612).

Broughton, Hugh, *An Exposition on the Lords Prayer, compared with the Decalogue, as it was preached in a Sermon, at Oatelands: before the most Noble, Henry Prince of Wales. Aug. 13. Anno 1613. With a Postscript, to advertise of an error in all those that leave out the Conclusion of the Lords Prayer* ([Amsterdam: n.p., 1613]).

Bunny, Edmund, *The Specter of Judah: or, what maner of Government it was, that unto the Commonwealth or Church of Israel was by the law of God appointed* (London: N. Newton & A. Hatfield for Iohn Wright, 1584).

Burton, Henry, *A Divine Tragedie lately acted; or a Collection of sundrie memorable examples of God's judgements upon Sabbath-breakers, and other like libertines, in their unlawfull sports, hapning within the realme of England, in the compasse onely of few yeers last past* ([Amsterdam: J.F. Stam], 1636).

Burton, Henry, *For God, and the King. The Summe of Two Sermons Preached on the fifth of November last in St Matthewes Friday-Streete* ([London: Felix Kingston], 1636).

Canne, John, *A Second Voyce from the Temple, to the Higher Powers. Wherein Is proved that the Decrees and Institutions of Popes, and Popish Counsels, which have been established by the Law of the Land, and have been continued and confirmed throughout divers Ages, by several Acts of Parliament, against Jesus Christ, in the way and order of the Gospel (the same yet standing) ought by the present supream Authority of this Nation to be taken away* (London: M. Simmons, 1653).

Carleton, George, *Tithes examined and proved to bee due to the Clergie by a divine right. Whereby the contentious and prophane Atheists, as also the dissembling Hypocrites of this age, may learne to honour the Ministers and not to defraude them, and to Rob the Church* (London: T. Este for Clement Knight, 1606).

Cartwright, Thomas, *The Second replie of Thomas Cartwright: agaynst Maister Doctor Whitgiftes second answer/touching the Churche Discipline* ([Heidelberg: M. Schirat], 1575).

Collier, Thomas, *A Brief Answer To some of the Objections and Demurs Made against the coming in and inhabiting of the Jews in this Common-wealth. With a plea on their behalf, Or some arguments to prove it not only lawful, but the duty of those whom it concerns to give them their liberty and protection* (they living peaceably in this Nation (London: Printed by Henry Hills, 1656 [MS amendation: 1655]).

Covell, William, *A Iust and Temperate Defence of the Five Books of Ecclesiastical Policie* (London: P. Short for Clement Knight, 1603).

[Crouch, Nathaniel], 'The Proceedings of the Jews in England in the Year 1655', in *Two Journeys To Jerusalem . . . Collected by R.B. and Beautified with Pictures* (London: Printed for Nathaniel Crouch, 1715).

Davenport, Robert, *A Pleasant and Witty Comedy: Called, A New Tricke to Cheat the Divell* (London: John Okes for Humphrey Blunden, 1639).

Dering, Edward, *A bryefe and necessary Catechisme or Instruction. Very needefull to be knowne of al Housholders. Wherby they may the better teach and instructe theyr Families, in such pointes of Christian Religion as is most meete* (London: John Charlewood, 1577).

'D.L.', *Israels Condition and Cause pleaded; Or some Arguments for the Jews Admission into England. Objections answered, Cautions added, with a Vindication of Mr. Peters from those foul and unjust Aspersions cast upon him by W. Prynn, Esq.* (London: William Larnar and Jonathan Ball, 1656).

Dury, John, *A Case of Conscience, Whether it be lawful to admit Jews into a Christian Common-wealth? Resolved by John Dury: Written to Samuel Hartlib, Esquire* (London: Printed for Richard Wodenothe, 1656).

Edwards, Thomas, *Gangraeana: Or a Catalogue and Discovery of many of the Errours, Heresies, Blasphemies and pernicious Practices of the Sectaries of this time, vented and acted in England in these four last years: As also, A Particular Narration of divers Stories, Remarkable Passages, Letters; an Extract of many Letters, all concerning the present Sects; together with some Observations upon, and Corollaries from all the fore-named Premisses* (London: Ralph Smith, 1645).

Erastus, Thomas, *Explicatio grauissimae quaestionis utrum excommunicatio, mandato nitatur diuino, an excogitata sit ab hominibus. Opus nunc recens editum. Adiectae sunt aliquot theologorum epistolae* ([London: J. Wolfe], 1589).

[Falconer, John], *A Briefe Refutation of Iohn Traskes Iudaical And Novel Fancyes. Stiling himselfe Minister of Gods Word, imprisoned for the Lawes eternall Perfection, or Gods Lawes perfect eternity* ([Saint Omer: English College Press, 1618]).

Fetherstone, Christopher, trans., *Haggeus, the Prophet, Haggeus, the Prophet. Whereunto is added a most plentifull commentary, gathered out of the publique lectures of D. Iohn Iames Gryneus, professor of Divinitie in the University of Basill, and now first published, Faithfully translated out of Latin into English, by Christopher Fetherstone student in Divinity* (London: John Wolfe for John Harrison the Younger, 1586).

Field, John, *Foure Sermons of Maister Iohn Calvin, Entreating of matters very profitable for our time, as may bee seene by the Preface: With a briefe exposition of the LXXXVII Psalme. Translated out of Frenche into Englishe by Iohn Fielde* (London: Thomas Man, 1579).

Field, John, trans., *Thirteene Sermons of Maister Iohn Calvine* (London: Thomas Dawson for Tobie Cooke and Thomas Man, 1579).

Field, John, trans., *The Iudgement of a Most Reverend and Learned Man from Beyond the Seas, Concerning a Threefold Order of Bishops, With a Declaration of Certaine Other Waightie Points, Concerning the Discipline and Government of the Church* ([1580]).

Field, John, *A Caveat for Parsons Howlet, concerning his untimely flighte, and scriching in the cleare day lighte of the Gospell, necessarie for him and all the rest of that darke broode, and uncleane cage of papistes, who with their untimely bookes, seeke the discredite of the trueth, and the disquiet of this Church of England* (London: Robert Waldegrave for Thomas Man, & Toby Smith, 1581).

Foxe, John, *Actes And Monuments of matters most speciall and memorable, happening in the Church, with an universall history of the same* (London: Peter Short, 1596).

Fuller, Thomas, *The Church-History of Britain; From the Birth of Jesus Christ, Untill the Year M.DC. XLVIII. Endeavoured By Thomas Fuller* (London: John Williams, 1655).

Gilby, Anthony, *A Commentarye upon the Prophet Mycha. Written by Anthony Gilby* (London: John Daye, 1551).
Gilby, Anthony, trans., *The Psalmes of Dauid, truly opened and explaned by Paraphrasis, according to the right sense of euerie Psalme. With lage and ample Arguments before everie Psalme, declaring the true use thereof* (London: Henrie Denham, 1581).
Gillespie, George, *A late dialogue betwixt a Civilian and a Divine, concerning the present condition of the Church of England* (London: Robert Bostock, 1644).
Gillespie, George, *Wholsome Severity reconciled with Christian Liberty. Or, The true Resolution of a present Controversie concerning Liberty of Conscience* (London: Christopher Meredith, 1644).
Gillespie, George, *Aarons Rod Blossoming. Or, The Divine Ordinance of Church-Government Vindicated, So as the present Erastian Controversie concerning the distinction of Civill and Ecclesiastical Government, Excommunication, and Suspension, is fully debated and discussed, from the holy Scripture, from the Jewish and Christian Antiquities, from the consent of latter Writers, from the true nature and rights of Magistracy, and from the groundlesnesse of the chiefe Objections made against the Presbyteriall Government in point of a domineering arbitrary unlimited power* (London: E.G. for Richard Whitaker, 1646).
Golding, Arthur, trans., *A Worke concerning the trewnesse of the Christian Religion, written in French: Against Atheists, Epicures, Paynims, Iewes, Mahumetists, and other Infidels. By Philip of Mornay Lord of Plessie Marlie* (London: Thomas Cadman, 1587).
[Goodwin, John], *Certaine briefe observations and antiquaeries: On Master Prin's twelve questions about church-government. Wherein is modestly showne, how un-usefull and frivolous they are; How bitter and unchristian in censuring that way; whereas there are no Reasons brought to contradict it. By a well-wisher to the Truth, and Master Prin.* ([London]: 1644?).
Goodwin, Thomas, Philip Nye, Sidrach Simpson, Jeremiah Burroughs and William Bridge, *An Apologeticall Narration, Humbly Submitted to the Honourable Houses of Parliament. By Tho: Goodwin, Philip Nye, Sidrach Simpson, Jer: Burroughes, and William Bridge* (London: Robert Dawlman, 1643).
Hanmer, Meredith, *The Auncient Ecclesiasticall Histories of the first six hundred yeares after Christ* (London: T. Vautrollier, 1577).
Helwys, Thomas, *A short declaration of the mistery of iniquity* ([Amsterdam]: n.p., 1612).
Herbert, George, *The Temple. Sacred Poems and Private Ejaculations* (Cambridge: Thomas Buck and Roger Daniel, 1633).
Heylyn, Peter, *The History of the Sabbath. In two bookes* (London: Henry Seile, 1636).
Heylyn, Peter, *Antidotum Lincolniense. Or an Answer to a book entitled, the Holy Table, Name, & Thing, &c. Said to be written long agoe by a Minister in Lincolnshire, And Printed for the Diocese of Lincolne, 1637* (London: John Clark, 1637).
[Highland, Samuel], *An Exact Relation of the Proceedings and Transactions of the Late Parliament* (London: Printed for Livewell Chapman, 1653).
Hooker, Richard, *Of the Lawes of Ecclesiasticall Politie. Eyght Bookes* (London: John Windet, 1593).
Hooker, Richard, *Of the Lawes of Ecclesiastical Politie; The Sixth and Eighth Books. By Richard Hooker. A work long expected, and now published according to the most Authentique Copies* (London: Richard Bishop, 1648).

Hughes, William, *Anglo-Judaeus, or the History of the Jews, whilst here in England. Relating their Manners, Carriage, and Usage, from their Admission By William the Conqueror, to their Banishment. Occasioned by a Book, written to His Highness, the Lord Protector (with a Declaration to the Commonwealth of England) for their Re-admission, By Rabbi Menasses Ben Israel. To which is also subjoyned a particular Answer, by W.H.* (London: T.N. for Thomas Heath, 1656).

'Isaiah, Paul', *The Messiah of the Christians, and the Jewes; Held forth in a discourse between a Christian and a Iew obstinately adhering to his strange opinions, & the forced interpretations of Scripture* (London: William Hunt, 1655).

Jacob, Henry, *A Treatise of the Sufferings and Victory of Christ, in the work of our redemption: Declaring by the Scriptures these two questions: That Christ suffered for us the wrath of God, which we maywell terme the paynes of Hell, or Hellish sorrowes* ([Middelburg: Richard Schilders], 1598).

Jacob, Henry, *A Defence of a treatise touching the sufferings and victorie of Christ in the worke of our Redemption* (London: n.p., 1600).

[Jacob, Henry], *To the right High and mightie Prince, IAMES by the grace of God, King of great Britannie, France, and Irelande, Defender of the faith, &c.* ([Middleburg: R. Schilders], 1609).

[James I], *A Meditation Upon the Lords Prayer, Written by the Kings Maiestie, For the benefit of all his subiects, especially of such as follow the Court* (London: Bonham Norton and Iohn Bill, Printers to the Kings most Excellent Maiesty, 1619).

Jonson, Ben, *The Alchemist* (London: Thomas Snodham for Walter Burre, 1612).

Jonson, Ben, *Bartholomew Fayre: A Comedie, Acted in the yeare 1614. By the Lady Elizabeths Servants. And then dedicated to King Iames, of most Blessed Memorie* (London: I.B. for Robert Allot, 1631).

Junius, Franciscus, *Grammatica Hebraeae Linguae* (Frankfurt: A. Wechel, 1580).

Lightfoot, John, *Elias Redivivus: A Sermon preached Before the Honourable House of Commons, In the Parish of Satin Margarets Westminster, at the publike Fast, March 29, 1643* (London: R. Cotes for Andrew Crooke, 1643).

Martin, Gregory, *A Discoverie of the manifold corruptions of the Holy Scriptures by the Heretikes of our daies, specially the English Sectaries, and of their foule dealing herein, by partial & false translations to the advantage of their heresies, in the English Bibles used and authorised since the time of Schisme* (Rheims: Iohn Fogny, 1582).

Maxwell, John, *An answer by letter to a worthy gentleman Who desired of a Divine some reasons by which it might appeare how Inconsistent Presbyteriall government is with monarchy* ([Oxford: L. Lichfield], 1644).

Mede, Joseph, *The Reverence of Gods House. A Sermon preached at St. Maries in Cambridge, Before The Universitie on St. Matthies day, Anno 1635/6* (London: M.E. for Iohn Clark, 1638).

Menasseh, ben Israel, *The Hope of Israel: Written by Menasseh, An Hebrew Divine, and Philosopher. Newly extant, and Printed at Amsterdam, and Dedicated by the Author, to the High Court the Parliament of England, and to the Councell of State* (London: R.I. for Hannah Allen, 1650).

Menasseh, ben Israel, *To his Highnesse the Lord Protector of the Common-wealth of England, Scotland, and Ireland. The humble addresses of Menasseh Ben Israel, a divine, and doctor of physick, in behalfe of the Jewish nation* (London, 1655).

Menasseh, ben Israel, *Vindiciae Judaeorum, or a Letter in Answer to certain Questions propounded by a Noble and Learned Gentleman, touching the reproaches cast on the*

Nation of the Jewes; wherein all objections are candidly, and yet fully cleared ([London]: R.D., 1656).

Milton, John, *A Treatise of Civil power in Ecclesiastical causes: Shewing That it is not lawfull for any power on earth to compel in matters of Religion* (London: Printed by Thomas Newcomb, 1659).

Milton, John, *Considerations touching The likeliest means to remove Hirelings out of the church. Wherein is also discourc'd Of Tithes, Church-fees, Church-revenues; And whether any maintenance of ministers can be settl'd by law* (London: T.N. for L. Chapman, 1659).

Montagu, Richard, *Diatribæ upon the first part of the late history of tithes* (F. Kyngston for M. Lownes, 1621).

Mornay, Philippe de, *A worke concerning the trewnesse of the Christian religion. Begunne to be translated by Sir P Sidney and finished by A Golding* (London: [J. Charlewood and G. Robinson] for T. Cadman, 1587).

Morton, Thomas, *Salomon, or A treatise declaring the state of the kingdome of Israel, as it was in the daies of Salomon. Whereunto is annexed another treatise, of the Church: or more particularly, Of the right constitution of a Church* (London: Robert Robinson for Robert Dexter, 1596).

Nettles, Stephen, *An answer to the Jewish part of Mr. Selden's History of Tithes* (Oxford: J. Lichfield & W. Turner, 1625).

Norrice, Edward, *The new gospel not the true gospel, Or, A discovery of the Life and Death, Doctrin, and Doings of Mr. Iohn Traske, and the effects of all, in his Followers* (London: R. Bishop for Henry Hood, 1638).

Overton, Richard, *The Arraignement of Mr. Persecution: Presented to the consideration of the House of Commons, and to all the common people of England wherein he is indicted, arraigned, convicted, and condemned of enmity against God, and all Goodnesse, of Treasons, Rebellion, Bloodshed, &c.* ([London]: n.p., 1645).

Pearson, Anthony, *The Great Case of Tythes Truly stated, clearly opened, and fully resolved. By a Countrey-man, A P* (London: Giles Calvert, 1657).

Persons, Robert, *A treatise of three conversions of England from paganisme to Christian Religion. The first vnder the Apostles, in the first age after Christ: The second vnder Pope Eleutherius and K.Lucius, in the second age. The third, under Pope Gregory the Great* ([St. Omer: F. Bellet], 1603).

Peter, Hugh, *A word for the Armie and two Words to the Kingdome, to cleare the one and cure the other. Forced in much plainness and brevity from their faithfull servant H. Peters* (London: M. Simmons for Giles Calvert, 1647).

Peter, Hugh, *Good work for a good magistrate. Or, A short Cut to great quiet. By Honest, homely plain English Hints given from Scripture, Reason, and Experience, for the regulating of most Cases in this Common-wealth* (London: William Du-Gard Printer to the Council of State, 1651).

Philo-Judaeus, *The Resurrection of Dead Bones, Or, the Conversion of the Jewes* (London: Printed for Giles Calvert, 1655).

Pocklington, John, *Altare Christianum: Or, The dead Vicars Plea. Wherein the Vicar of Gr. Being dead, yet speaketh, and pleadeth out of Antiquity, against him that hath broken downe his Altar* (London: Richard Badger, 1637).

[Prynne, William], *A Looking Glasse for all Lordly Prelates. Wherein they may Cleerely behold the true divine Originall and laudable Pedigree, whence they are descended; together with their holy lives and actions laid open in a double Parallel* [London: n.p., 1636]).

[Prynne, William], *A Quench-coale. Or, A briefe Disquisition and Inquirie, in what place of the Church or Chancell the Lords-Table ought to be situated, especially when the sacrament is administered, written against Robert Shelford, Edmond Reeve, John Pocklington, and 'A late Coale from the Altar'* ([Amsterdam: Richt Right Press], 1637).

Prynne, William, *A Full Reply To certaine briefe Observations and Anti-Queries on Master Prynnes twelve Questions about Church-Government: Wherein the Frivolousnesse, Falsenesse, and grosse Mistakes of this Anonymous Answerer (ashamed of his Name) and his weak grounds for Independency, and Separation, are modestly discovered, reselled* (London: Michael Sparke Sr, 1644).

Prynne, William, *Independency Examined, unmasked, refuted, by twelve new particular interrogatories* (London: F.L. for Michael Sparke Sr, 1644).

Prynne, William, *Twelve Considerable Serious Questions touching Church Government: Sadly propounded (out of a Reall Desire of Unitie, and Tranquillity in Church and State) to all Sober-minded Christians* (London: F.L. for Michael Sparke Sr, 1644).

Prynne, William, *A Fresh Discovery of some Prodigious New Wandering-Blasing-Stars, & Firebrands, Stiling themselves New-Lights. Firing our Church and State into New Combustions* (London: John Macock, for Michael Spark, 1646).

Prynne, William, *A short demurrer to the Jewes Long discontinued remitter into England. Comprising, An exact Chronological Relation of their first Admission into, their ill Deportment, Misdemeanors, Condition, Sufferings, Oppressions, Slaughters, Plunders, by popular Insurrections, and regal Exactions in; and their total, final Banishment by Iudgement and Edict of Parliament, out of England* (London: Edward Thomas, 1656).

Prynne, William, *Ten Considerable Quaeries concerning Tithes, the Present Petitioners and Petitions for their total abolition, as Antichristian, Jewish, burdensom, oppressive to the godly, consciencious People of the Nation; excited, incouraged thereunto by disguised Jesuits, Popish Priests, Friers, and Romish Emissaries, to starve, suppress, extirpate our Protestant Ministers, Church, Religion; and bring them all to speedy confusion* (London: Edward Thomas, 1659).

Read, Alexander, *A Sermon preached April 8. 1635 at a Visitation at Brentwood in Essex. By Alexander Read, Doctor of Divinitie, late Fellow of Pembroke-Hall in Cambridge, now Parson of Fifield in Essex* (London: Iohn Clark, 1636).

Reeve, Edmund, *The Communion Booke Catechisme Expounded, According to Gods holy Wod, and the established Doctrine of the Church. Written for the furtherance of youth and ignorant persons, in the understanding of the grounds and principles of the true Christian Religion* (London: Miles Flesher, 1635).

Robarts, Foulke, *Gods Holy House and Service, According to the primitive and most Christian forme thereof, described by Foulke Robarts, Batchelor of Divinity, and Prebendary of Norwich* (London: Tho. Cotes, 1639).

[Robinson, Henry], *Liberty of Conscience: Or the Sole means to obtaine Peace and Truth* ([Leiden?]: n.p., 1643).

Robinson, John, *Of Religious Communion, Private, & Publique* (1614).

Rogers, Thomas, *The faith, doctrine, and religion, professed, & protected in the Realme of England, and Dominions of the Same: Expressed in 39 Articles, concordably agreed upon by the reverend Bishops, and Clergie of this Kingdome, at two severall meetings, or Convocations of theirs, in the yeares of our Lord, 1562, and 1604* (Cambridge: Iohn Legatt, 1607).

[Romaine, William], *An Answer to a PAMPHLET, entitled, "Considerations on the bill to permit persons professing the Jewish religion to be naturalized"* (London: H. Cooke, 1753).

Ross, Alexander, *A View of the Jewish Religion Containing the manner of Life, Rites, Ceremonies and Customes of the Iewish Nation throughout the World at this present time; Together With the Articles of their Faith, as now received* (London: Printed by T.M. for E. Brewster and S. Miller, 1656).

'R.T.', *De Templis, A Treatise of Temples: Wherein is discovered the ancient manner of Building, Consecrating, and Adorning of Churches* (London: R. Bishop for Thomas Alchorn, 1638).

Sclater, William, *The Quaestion of Tythes Revised. Arguments for the Moralitie of Tything, enlarged, and cleared. Obiections more fully, and distinctly answered. Mr Seldens Historie, so farre as Mistakers haue made it Argumentatiue against the Moralitie, ouer-ly viewed* (London: John Legatt, 1623).

Selden, John, *The Historie of Tithes. That is, The Practice of payment of them. The Positive laws made for them. The opinions touching the Right of them. A review of it is also annext, which both Confirmes it and directs in the Use of it* [London: n.p., 1618].

Selden, John, *De Synedriis et Praefecturis Juridicis Veterum Ebraorum* (London: Jacob Flesher, 1653).

Sempill, James, *Sacrilege sacredly handled. That is, According to Scripture onely. Diuided into two parts: 1. For the Law. 2. For the Gospell. An appendix also added; answering some Objections mooued, namely, against this Treatise: and some others, I finde in Iox. Scaligers Diatribæ, and Ioh. Seldens Historie of Tithes. For the vse of all churches in generall: but more especially for those of North-Britaine* (London: William Iones for Edmund Weaver, 1619).

Shelford, Robert, *Five pious and learned discourses, 1. A Sermon shewing how we ought to behave our selves in Gods house* (Cambridge: [T. Buck and R. Daniel], 1635).

Sidney, Philip, *An Apologie for Poetrie. Written by the right noble, vertuous, and learned, Sir Phillip Sidney, Knight* (London: Henry Olney, 1595).

Spencer, Edward, *A Breife Epistle to the Learned Manasseh Ben Israel in Answer to His Dedicated to the Parliament* (London: title page missing, 1650).

Stubbs, John, *The Discoverie of a gaping gulf whereinto England is like to be swallowed by another French marriage, if the Lord forbid not the banes by letting her majestie see the sin and punishment thereof* (London: H. Singleton for W. Page, 1579).

Sutcliffe, Matthew, *The Subversion of Robert Parsons His confused and worthlesse worke, entituled, A treatise of three Conversions of England from Paganisme to Christian Religion* (London: Iohn Norton, 1606).

Swan, John, *Profano-Mastix. Or, A Briefe and Necessarie Direction concerning the respects which wee owe to God, and his House, even in outward worship, and reverent using of Holy Places* (London: J. Dawson, 1639).

The Booke of Common Prayer, and the Administration of the Sacraments, And other Rites and Ceremonies of the Church of England (London: Robert Barker, 1604).

The Fourth Paper, Presented by Maior Butler, To the Honourable Committee of Parliament, for the Propagating the Gospel of Christ Jesus (London: Giles Calvert, 1652).

The Petition of the Jewes For the Repealing of the Act of Parliament for their banishment out of England. Presented to his Excellency and the generall Councell of Officers on Fryday Jan. 5. 1648 (London: Printed for George Roberts, 1648–9).

Thorowgood, Thomas, *Iewes in America, or, Probabilities That the Americans are of that Race. With the removal of some contrary reasonings, and earnest desires for effectuall endeavours to make them Christian* (London: Printed by W.H. for Thomas Slater, 1650).

Tillesley, Richard, *Animadversions upon M. Selden's History of Tithes, and his review thereof: Before which (in lieu of the two first Chapters purposely pretermitted) is premised a Catalogue of seuenty two Authours, before the year 1215* (London: John Bill, 1619).

Udall, John, *Mafteach Leshon ha-Kodesh. That is the key of the holy language. Wherein is contained, first the Hebrew grammar (in a manner) woord for woord out of P. Martinius. Secondly A practize upon the first, the twentie fift and the sixtie eight Psalms, according to the rules of the same grammar. Thirdly, A short Dictionary conteining the Hebrue woords that are found in the Bible with their proper significations. All Englished for the benefit of those that (being ignoraunt in the Latin) are desirous to learn the holy tongue* (Leiden: Francis Raphelengius, 1593).

Vaughan, Rice, *A Plea for the Common-Laws of England: Or, An Answer to a Book entituled, a good work for a good Magistrate: Or, a short Cut to a great quiet. (Published by Mr. Hugh Peters:) So far as concerns his Proposals touching the said Laws* (London: Francis Tyton, 1651).

Violet, Thomas, *A Petition Against the Jewes, Presented to the Kings Majestie and the Parliament* (London: n.p., 1661).

Walwyn, William, *The Compassionate Samaritan, unbinding The Conscience, and powring Oyle into the wounds which have been made upon the Separation: recommending their future welfare to the serious thoughts, and carefull endeavours of all who love the peace and unity of Commonwealths men* ([London]: n.p., 1644).

[Ward, Nathaniel], *A Word to Mr Peters, and Two Words for the Parliament and Kingdom. Or, An Answer to a Scandalous Pamphlet, entituled, A Word for the Armie, and two Words to the Kingdom: Subscribed by Hugh Peters. Wherein The Authority of Parliament is infringed, The fundamentall Laws of the Land subverted; The famous City of London Blemished; and all the godly Ministers of the City scandalized* (London: Fr: Neile for Tho: Underhill, 1647).

White, Francis, *A Treatise of the Sabbath-Day. Containing, A Defence of the Orthodoxall Doctrine of the Church of England, against all Sabbatarian-Novelty. By Dr. Fr. White, L. Bihop of Ely* (London: Richard Badger, 1635).

Whitgift, John, *The Defense of the Aunswere to the Admonition, against the Replie of T.C. by Iohn Whitgift Doctor of Divinitie* (London: Henry Binneman for Humfrey Toye, 1574).

Williams, John, *The Holy Table, Name & Thing, more anciently, properly, and literally used under the New Testament, then that of an Altar: Written long ago by a Minister in Lincolnshire, in answer to D Coal* [i.e. Peter Heylyn], *a judicious Divine of Q.Maries dayes* ([London]: Printed for the Diocese of Lincoln, 1637).

Williams, Roger, *The Bloudy Tenent, of Persecution, for cause of Conscience, discussed, in A Conference betweene Truth and Peace. Who, In all tender Affection, present to the High Court of Parliament, (as the Result of their Discourse) these, (amongst other Passages) of highest consideration* ([London], 1644).

Books published after 1700

Achinstein, Sharon, 'John Foxe and the Jews', *Renaissance Quarterly*, 54 (2001), 86–120.

Adler, William, 'Eusebius' Chronicle and its Legacy', in Harold W. Attridge and Gohen Hata, eds, *Eusebius, Christianity and Judaism* (New York: E.J. Brill, 1992), 467–92.

Almasy, Rudolph, 'The Purpose of Richard Hooker's Polemic', *Journal of the History of Ideas*, 39 (1978), 251–70.
Almog, Shmuel, ed., *Antisemitism Through the Ages* (Oxford: Pergamon Press, 1988).
Alston, R.C., *Books with Manuscript: A Short Title Catalogue of Books with Manuscript Notes in the British Library* (London: The British Library, 1993).
Archer, Stanley, *Richard Hooker* (Massachusetts: G.K. Hall and Company, 1983).
Baker, J.H., *An Introduction to English Legal History* (London: Butterworths, 1979).
Baker, J.H., *The Legal Profession and the Common Law: Historical Essays* (London: The Hambledon Press, 1986).
Bale, Antony, 'Stow's Medievalism and Antique Judaism in Early Modern London', in Ian Gadd and Alexandra Gillespie, eds, *John Stow (1525–1605) and the Making of the English Past* (London: The British Library, 2004), 69–80.
Ball, Bryan W., *The Seventh-Day Men: Sabbatarians and Sabbatarianism in England and Wales, 1600–1800* (Oxford: Clarendon Press, 1994).
Barbour, Reid, *John Selden: Measures of the Holy Commonwealth in Seventeenth-Century England* (Toronto: University of Toronto Press, 2003).
Barnett, R.D., ed., 'The Burial Register of the Spanish and Portuguese Jews, London 1657–1735', *Miscellanies of the Jewish Historical Society of England*, VI (1962), 1–72.
Bartels, Emily C., *Spectacles of Strangeness: Imperialism, Alienation, and Marlowe* (Philadelphia: University of Pennsylvania Press, 1993).
Berkvens-Stevelinck, C., Jonathan Israel and G.H.M. Posthumus Meyjes, eds, *The Emergence of Tolerance in the Dutch Republic* (Leiden: E.J. Brill, 1997).
Bershadsky, Edith, 'Controlling the Terms of the Debate: John Selden and the Tithes Controversy', in Gordon J. Schochet, Patricia E. Tatspaugh and Carol Brobeck, eds, *Law, Literature and the Settlement of Regimes* (Washington: Folger, 1990), 187–220.
Bershadsky, Edith, 'Politics, Erudition and Ecclesiology: John Selden's Historie of Tithes', unpublished Ph.D. dissertation, University of Michigan, 1994.
Birch, T., ed., *The State Papers of John Thurloe* (London: Printed for the Executor of the late Mr. Fletcher Gyles, Thomas Woodward, 1742).
Blau, Joseph, *The Christian Interpretation of the Cabala in the Renaissance* (New York: Columbia University Press, 1944).
Blunt, Elijah, *A History of the Establishment* (London: Printed for Saunders and Benning, 1830).
Blunt, John Henry, ed., *The Dictionary of Sects, Heresies, Ecclesiastical Parties, and Schools of Religious Thought* (London: Rivingtons, 1874).
Bodian, Miriam, *Hebrews of the Portuguese Nation: Conversos and Community in Early Modern Amsterdam* (Bloomington, IN: Indiana University Press, 1997).
Bornstein, Diane, 'The Style of the Countess of Pembroke's Translation of Philippe de Mornay's *Discours de la vie et de la mort*', in Margaret P. Hannay, ed., *Silent But for the Word: Tudor Women as Patrons, Translators, and Writers of Religious Works* (Athens, OH: The Kent State University Press, 1985), 126–49.
Borst, Arno, *The Ordering of Time: From the Ancient Computus to the Modern Computer* (Cambridge: Polity Press, 1993).
Boutcher, Warren, 'The Renaissance (c. 1500–1650)', in Peter France, ed., *The Oxford Guide to Literature in English Translation* (Oxford: Oxford University Press, 2000) 45–54.
Bowman, J., 'A Forgotten Controversy', *Evangelical Quarterly*, 20 (1948), 46–69.

Boyarin, Daniel, *Carnal Israel: Reading Sex in Talmudic Literature* (Berkeley: University of California Press, 1993).
Brailsford, H.N., *The Levellers and the English Revolution* (London: Cresset Press, 1961).
Brown, Cedric C., 'Great Senates and Godly Education: Politics and Cultural Renewal in some Pre- and Post-Revolutionary Texts of Milton', in David Armitage, Armand Himy and Quentin Skinner, eds, *Milton and Republicanism* (Cambridge: Cambridge University Press, 1995), 43–60.
Burnett, Stephen G., *From Christian Hebraism to Jewish Studies* (Leiden: E.J. Brill, 1996).
Burns, J.H., ed., *The Cambridge History of Political Thought 1450–1700* (Cambridge: Cambridge University Press, 1991).
Capp, Bernard, *The Fifth Monarchy Men: A study in seventeenth century English Millenarianism* (London: Faber and Faber, 1972).
Cesarani, David, 'Dual Heritage or Duel of Heritages': Englishness and Jewishness in the Heritage Industry', in Cesarani and Tony Kushner, eds, *The Jewish Heritage in British History: Englishness and Jewishness* (London: Frank Cass, 1992), 29–41.
Cesarani, David, *Reporting Anti-Semitism: The "Jewish Chronicle" 1879–1979*, The Parkes Lecture 1993 (Southampton: University of Southampton, 1993).
Cesarani, David, *The "Jewish Chronicle" and Anglo-Jewry, 1841–1941* (Cambridge: Cambridge University Press, 1994).
Cesarani, David, 'The Changing Character of Citizenship and Nationality in Britain', in Cesarani and Mary Fulbrook, eds, *Citizenship, Nationality and Migration in Europe* (London: Routledge, 1996), 57–73.
Chazan, Robert, *Medieval Stereotypes and Modern Antisemitism* (Berkeley, CA: University of California Press, 1997).
Cheyette, Bryan and Nadia Valman, eds, *The Image of the Jew in European Liberal Culture, 1789–1914* (London: Vallentine Mitchell, 2004).
Christianson, Paul, *Discourse on History, Law, and Governance in the Public Career of John Selden, 1610–1635* (Toronto: University of Toronto Press, 1996).
Claydon, Tony and Ian McBride, 'The Trials of the Chosen Peoples: Recent Interpretations of Protestantism and National Identity in Britain and Ireland', in Claydon and McBride, eds, *Protestantism and National Identity: Britain and Ireland, c. 1650–c. 1850* (Cambridge: Cambridge University Press, 1998), 3–33.
Coffey, John, *Persecution and Toleration in Protestant England, 1558–1689* (Harlow, Essex: Pearson, 2000).
Cohn-Sherbok, Dan, *The Crucified Jew: Twenty Centuries of Christian Anti-Semitism* (London: Fount, 1993).
Cole, A., 'The Quakers and the English Revolution', in T.H. Aston, ed., *Crisis in Europe, 1560–1660* (London: Routledge & Kegan Paul, 1965), 341–58.
Collinson, Patrick, *Godly People: Essays on English Protestantism and Puritanism* (London: The Hambledon Press, 1983).
Collinson, Patrick, *The Birthpangs of Protestant England: Religious and Cultural Change in the Sixteenth and Seventeenth Centuries* (Basingstoke: Macmillan, 1988).
Collinson, Patrick, *The Elizabethan Puritan Movement* (Oxford: Clarendon Press, 1990).
Collinson, Patrick, 'Biblical Rhetoric: The English Nation and National Sentiment in the Prophetic Mode', in Claire McEachern and Debora Shuger,

eds, *Religion and Culture in Renaissance England* (Cambridge: Cambridge University Press, 1997), 15–46.
Como, David R., 'The Kingdom of Christ, the Kingdom of England, and the Kingdom of Traske: John Traske and the Persistence of Radical Puritanism in Early Stuart England', in Muriel C. McClendon, Joseph P. Ward and Michael MacDonald, eds, *Protestant Identities: Religion, Society, and Self-Fashioning in Post-Reformation England* (Stanford, CA: Stanford University Press, 1999), 63–82.
Corns, Thomas N., ed., *The Literature of Controversy: Polemical Strategy from Milton to Junius* (London: Frank Cass, 1987).
Corns, Thomas N., *John Milton: The Prose Works* (New York: Twayne, 1998).
Coudert, Allison P., 'The Kabbala Denudata: Converting Jews or seducing Christians', in Richard H. Popkin, ed., *Jewish Christians and Christian Jews: From the Renaissance to the Enlightenment* (Dordrecht: Kluwer Academic Publishers, 1994), 11–35.
Coward, Barry, *The Stuart Age: A History of England 1603–1714* (London: Longman, 1994).
Cressy, David, *Bonfires and Bells: National Memory and the Protestant Calendar in Elizabethan and Stuart England* (London: Weidenfeld and Nicolson, 1989).
Crowley, Weldon S., 'Erastianism in the Westminster Assembly', *The Journal of Church and State*, 15 (1973), I, 49–65.
Cunningham, W.A., *Alien Immigrants in England* (London: Cass, 1969).
Cust, Richard and Ann Hughes, eds, *Conflict in Early Stuart England: Studies in Religion and Politics 1603–1642* (London: Longman, 1989).
Dan, Joseph, ed., *The Christian Kabbalah: Jewish Mystical Books and their Christian Interpreters* (Massachusetts: Harvard College Library, 1997).
Davies, Julian, *The Caroline Captivity of the Church: Charles I and the Remoulding of Anglicanism 1625–1641* (Oxford: Clarendon Press, 1992).
De Beauval, Basnage, *The History of the Jews, from Jesus Christ to The Present Time: Containing, Their Antiquities, their Religion, their Rites, the Dispersion of the Ten Tribes in the East, And the Persecutions this Nation has suffer'd in the West* (London: J. Beaver and B. Lintot et al., 1708).
De Beer, Esmond Samuel, ed., *The Diary of John Evelyn: Now Printed in Full from the Manuscripts belonging to Mr. John Evelyn* (Oxford: Clarendon Press, 1955).
Diamond, A.S., 'The Cemetery of the Resettlement', *TJHSE*, 19 (1960), 163–90.
Dimmock, Arthur, 'The Conspiracy of Dr. Lopez,' *English Historical Review*, 9 (1894), 440–72.
Dimmock, Matthew, *New Turkes: Dramatising Islam and the Ottomans in Early Modern England* (Aldershot: Ashgate, 2005).
Endelman, Todd, *Radical Assimilation in English Jewish History 1656–1945* (Bloomington, Indiana: Indiana University Press, 1990).
Endelman, Todd, *The Jews of Britain, 1656–2000* (Berkeley, CA: University of California Press, 2002).
Faulkner, Robert K., *Richard Hooker and the Politics of a Christian England* (Berkeley: University of California Press, 1981).
Feldman, David, 'Jews in London, 1880–1914', in Raphael Samuel, ed., *Patriotism: The Making and Unmaking of British National Identity* (London: Routledge, 1989), II, 207–29.
Feldman, David, *Englishmen and Jews: Social Relations and Political Culture 1840–1914* (New Haven and London: Yale University Press, 1994).

Ferguson, Arthur B., *Clio Unbound: Perception of the social and cultural past in Renaissance England* (Durham, North Carolina: Duke University Press, 1979).

Fielding, John, 'Arminianism in the Localities: Peterborough Diocese 1603–1642', in Kenneth Fincham, ed., *The Early Stuart Church, 1603–1642* (Basingstoke: Macmillan, 1993), 93–115.

Figgis, J. Neville, 'Erastus and Erastianism', *The Journal of Theological Studies*, 2 (1901), 66–101.

Filloy, Richard A., 'The Religious and Political Views of John Selden: A Study in Early Stuart Humanism', unpublished Ph.D. dissertation, University of California at Berkeley, 1977.

Fincham, Kenneth, 'Episcopal Government 1603–1640', in Fincham, ed., *The Early Stuart Church, 1603–1642* (Basingstoke: Macmillan, 1993) 71–92.

Fincham, Kenneth and Peter Lake, 'The Ecclesiastical Policies of James I and Charles I', in Fincham, ed., *The Early Stuart Church, 1603–1642* (Basingstoke: Macmillan, 1993) 23–51.

Firth, Katharine R., *The Apocalyptic Tradition in Reformation Britain 1530–1645* (Oxford: Oxford University Press, 1979).

Fletcher, Eric, *John Selden 1584–1654: Selden Society Lecture delivered in the Old Hall of Lincoln's Inn, July 9th 1969 by The Right Hon. Sir Eric Fletcher, MP, President of the Society* (London: Bernard Quaritch, 1969).

Fraser, Antonia, *Cromwell, Our Chief of Men* (London: Weidenfeld and Nicolson, 1973).

Freeman, Thomas S., '"Great Searching out of Bookes and Autors": John Foxe as Ecclesiastical Historian', unpublished Ph.D. dissertation, Rutgers University, 1995.

Friedman, Jerome, *The Most Ancient Testimony: Sixteenth-Century Christian-Hebraica in the Age of Renaissance Nostalgia* (Ohio: The Kent State University Press, 1983).

Fussner, F. Smith, *The Historical Revolution: English Historical Writing and Thought 1580–1640* (London: Routledge and Kegan Paul, 1962).

Gardiner, S.R., *The First Two Stuarts and the Puritan Revolution: 1603–1660* (London: Longmans, Green and Co., 1878).

Garnett, George, ed., *Vindiciæ contra Tyrannos; a Defence of Liberty against Tyrants. Or, Of the lawfull power of the prince over the people, and of the people over the prince. Being a treatise written in Latin and French by Junius Brutus, and translated out of both into English* (Cambridge: Cambridge University Press, 1994).

Gatti, Hilary, *The Renaissance Drama of Knowledge: Giordano Bruno in England* (London: Routledge, 1989).

Glassman, Bernard, *Anti-Semitic Stereotypes Without Jews: Images of the Jews in England 1290–1700* (Detroit: Wayne State University Press, 1975).

Godwin, William, *History of the Commonwealth of England, from its commencement, to the Restoration of Charles the Second* (London: Printed for Henry Colburn, 1828).

Golding, Louis Thorn, *An Elizabethan Puritan: Arthur Golding the Translator of Ovid's Metamorphoses and also of John Calvin's Sermons* (New York: Richard R. Smith, 1937).

Grafton, Anthony, *Joseph Scaliger: A Study in the History of Classical Scholarship* (Oxford: Clarendon Press, 1983).

Graham, Timothy and Andrew G. Watson, eds, *The Recovery of the Past in Early Elizabethan England: Documents by John Bale and John Joscelyn from the Circle of Matthew Parker* (Cambridge: Cambridge Bibliographical Society, 1998).
Grant, Robert M., *Eusebius as Church Historian* (Oxford: Clarendon Press, 1980).
Greene, C.H., 'Trask in the Star-Chamber 1619', *Transactions of the Baptist Historical Society*, 5 (1916–7), 8–11.
Greenhalgh to Thomas Crompton, 22 April 1662, reprinted in *TJHSE*, 10 (1924), 49–57.
Grell, Ole Peter and Roy Porter, eds, *Toleration in Enlightenment Europe* (Cambridge: Cambridge University Press, 2000).
Grell, Ole Peter, Jonathan I. Israel and Nicholas Tyacke, eds, *From Persecution to Toleration: The Glorious Revolution and Religion in England* (Oxford: Clarendon Press, 1991).
Grosser, Paul E. and Edwin G. Halperin, *The Causes and Effects of Anti-Semitism: The Dimensions of a Prejudice. An Analysis and Chronology of 1900 Years of Anti-Semitic Attitudes and Practices* (New York: Philosophical Library, 1978).
Guibbory, Achsah, *Ceremony and Community from Herbert to Milton: Literature, Religion and Cultural Conflict in Seventeenth-Century England* (Cambridge: Cambridge University Press, 1998).
Guibbory, Achsah, 'Conversation, Conversion, Messianic Redemption: Margaret Fell, Menasseh ben Israel, and the Jews', in Claude J. Summers and Ted-Larry Pebworth, eds, *Literary Circles and Cultural Communities in Renaissance England* (Columbia, MI: University of Missouri Press, 2001) 210–34.
Guy, John, 'The Henrician Age', in J.G.A. Pocock, ed., *The Varieties of British Political Thought, 1500–1800* (Cambridge: Cambridge University Press, 1993), 22–30.
Gwyer, John, 'The Case of Dr Lopez,' *TJHSE*, 16 (1952), 163–84.
Halasz, Alexandra, *The Marketplace of Print: Pamphlets and the Public Sphere in Early Modern England* (Cambridge: Cambridge University Press, 1997).
Haller, William, *Tracts on Liberty in the Puritan Revolution 1638–1647* (New York: Columbia University Press 1934).
Haller, William, *Foxe's Book of Martyrs and the Elect Nation* (London: Jonathan Cape, 1963).
Hannay, Margaret P., *Phillip's Pheonix: Mary Sidney, Countess of Pembroke* (Oxford: Oxford University Press, 1990).
Happe, Peter, *John Bale* (New York: G.K. Hall & Company, 1996).
Hastings, James, ed., *A Dictionary of Christ and the Gospels* (Edinburgh: T. & T. Clark, 1906).
Hastings, James, *A Dictionary of the Apostolic Church* (Edinburgh: T. & T. Clark, 1915).
Helgerson, Richard, *Forms of Nationhood: The Elizabethan Writing of England* (Chicago: University of Chicago Press, 1992).
Henriques, H.S.Q., *The Return of the Jews to England: Being a Chapter in the History of English Law* (London: Macmillan, 1905).
Herbermann, C.G., et al., eds, *The Catholic Encyclopaedia*, 15 vols (New York: Robert Appleton Company, 1910).
Hill, Christopher, *Economic Problems of the Church: From Archbishop Whitgift to the Long Parliament* (Oxford: Clarendon Press, 1956).
Hill, Christopher, *Society and Puritanism in Pre-Revolutionary England* (London: Secker and Warburg, 1964).

Hill, Christopher, *The World Turned Upside Down: Radical Ideas during the English Revolution* (London: Maurice Temple Smith, 1972).

Hill, Christopher, *The Century of Revolution 1603–1714* (Walton-on-Thames: Thomas Nelson, 1980).

Hill, Christopher, 'Till the Conversion of the Jews', in Richard H. Popkin, ed., *Millenarianism and Messianism in English Literature and Thought 1650–1800* (Leiden: E.J. Brill, 1988) 12–37.

Hill, Christopher, *The English Bible and the Seventeenth-Century Revolution* (London: Penguin, 1993).

Holmes, Colin, *Anti-Semitism in British Society 1876–1939* (London: Edward Arnold, 1979).

Hosmer, James, *The Jews: In Ancient, Medieval and Modern Times* (London: T. Fisher Unwin, 1886).

Hughes, Ann, *The Causes of the English Civil War* (Basingstoke: Macmillan, 1998).

Huie, James, *The History of the Jews, From the Taking of Jerusalem by Titus to the Present Time: Comprising, A Narrative of their Wanderings, Persecutions, Commercial Enterprises, and Literary Exertions; with an Account of the Various Efforts made for their Conversion* (Edinburgh: Oliver & Boyd, 1840).

Hume, Martin A.S., *Treason and Plot: Struggles for Catholic Supremacy in the Last Years of Elizabeth* (London: James Nisbet & Co., 1901).

Hume, Martin A.S., 'The So-called Conspiracy of Dr Ruy Lopez,' *TJHSE*, 6 (1908), 32–55.

Hutton, Ronald, *The Restoration: A Political and Religious History of England and Wales 1658–1667* (Oxford: Clarendon Press, 1985).

Inowlocki, Sabrina, *Eusebius and the Jewish Authors* (Leiden: E.J. Brill, 2006).

Israel, Jonathan, *European Jewry in the age of Mercantilism 1550–1750* (Oxford: Clarendon Press, 1985).

Israel, Jonathan, 'Menasseh ben Israel and the Dutch Sephardic Colonization Movement of the Mid-Seventeenth Century (1645–1657)', in Yosef Kaplan, Henry Mechoulan and Richard H. Popkin, eds, *Menasseh ben Israel and his World* (Leiden: E.J. Brill, 1989), 139–65.

Israel, Jonathan and David Katz, eds, *Sceptics, Millenarians and Jews* (Leiden: E.J. Brill, 1990).

Jasper, David, ed., *Translating Religious Texts: Translation, Transgression and Interpretation* (Basingstoke: Macmillan, 1993).

Johnson, Paul, *A History of the Jews* (London: Weidenfeld and Nicolson, 1987).

Jonathan R. Ziskind, 'Petrus Cunæus on Theocracy, Jubilee and the Latifundia', *The Jewish Quarterly Review*, 68 (1978), 4, 235–55.

Jones, Edwin, *The English Nation: The Great Myth* (Stroud, Gloucestershire: Sutton, 1998).

Jordan, W.K., *The Development of Religious Toleration in England, from the Beginning of the English Reformation to the death of Queen Elizabeth* (London: Allen and Unwin, 1932).

Jowitt, Claire, 'Radical Identities? Native Americans, Jews and the English Commonwealth', *The Seventeenth Century*, 10 (1995), 101–19.

Jowitt, Claire, '"Inward" and "Outward" Jews: Margaret Fell, Circumcision and Women's Preaching', *Reformation*, 4 (1999), 139–68.

Jowitt, Claire, '"The Consolation of Israel": The Representation of Jewishness in the Writings of Gerrard Winstanley and William Everard', *Prose Studies*, 22 (1999), 83–99.

Kamen, Henry, *The Rise of Toleration* (London: Weidenfeld & Nicolson, 1967).
Kaplan, Yosef, Henry Méchoulan and Richard H Popkin, eds, *Menasseh ben Israel and his World* (Leiden: E.J. Brill, 1989).
Katz, David, *Philo-Semitism and the Readmission of the Jews to England, 1603–1655* (Oxford: Clarendon Press, 1982).
Katz, David, 'English Redemption and Jewish Readmission in 1656', *Journal of Jewish Studies*, 34 (1983), 73–91.
Katz, David, *Sabbath and Sectarianism in Seventeenth-Century England* (Leiden: E.J. Brill, 1988).
Katz, David, 'The Marginalization of Early Modern Anglo-Jewish History', *Immigrants & Minorities*, X (1991), 60–77.
Katz, David, 'The Phenomenon of Philo-Semitism', in Diana Wood, ed., *Christianity and Judaism: Papers Read at the 1991 Summer Meeting and the 1992 Winter Meeting of the Ecclesiastical History Society* (Oxford: Published for the Ecclesiastical History Society by Blackwell, 1992), 327–62.
Katz, David, *The Jews in the History of England 1485–1850* (Oxford: Clarendon Press, 1994).
Katz, Jacob, *From Prejudice to Destruction: Anti-Semitism, 1700–1933* (Cambridge, MA: Harvard University Press, 1980).
Kelley, Donald R., 'The French School', in J.H. Burns, ed., *The Cambridge History of Political Thought 1450–1700* (Cambridge: Cambridge University Press, 1991), 78–80.
King, John N., *Milton and Religious Controversy: Satire and Polemic in Paradise Lost* (Cambridge: Cambridge University Press, 2000).
Kingdon, Robert M., *Church and Society in Reformation Europe* (London: Variorum Reprints, 1985).
Kingdon, Robert M., *Myths about the St. Bartholomew's Day Massacres 1572–1576* (Cambridge, MA: Harvard University Press, 1988).
Kishlansky, Mark, 'The Emergence of Adversary Politics in the Long Parliament', in Richard Cust and Ann Hughes, eds, *The English Civil War* (London: Hodder Headline, 1997) 62–83.
Klein, William, 'The Ancient Constitution Revisited', in Nicholas Phillipson and Quentin Skinner, eds, *Political Discourse in Early Modern Britain* (Cambridge: Cambridge University Press, 1993), 23–44.
Knappen, M.M., *Tudor Puritanism: A Chapter in the History of Idealism* (Chicago: University of Chicago Press, 1939).
Knoppers, Laura Lunger, *Constructing Cromwell: Ceremony, Portrait and Print 1645–1661* (Cambridge: Cambridge University Press, 2000).
Knott, John R., *Discourses of Martyrdom in English Literature, 1563–1694* (Cambridge: Cambridge University Press, 1993).
Kohler, Max J., 'Dr. Rodrigo Lopez, Queen Elizabeth's Jewish Physician, and his Relations to America,' *Publications of the American Jewish Historical Society*, 17 (1909), 9–25.
Kunze, Bonnelyn Young, *Margaret Fell and the Rise of Quakerism* (Basingstoke: Macmillan, 1994).
Kushner, Tony, 'Heritage and Ethnicity: An Introduction', in David Cesarani and Kushner, eds, *The Jewish Heritage in British History: Englishness and Jewishness* (London: Frank Cass, 1992), 1–28.
Kushner, Tony, 'The End of the "Anglo-Jewish Progress Show": Representations of the Jewish East End, 1887–1987', in Kushner, ed., *The Jewish Heritage in*

British History: Englishness and Jewishness (London: Frank Cass, 1992), 78–105.

Laing, David, ed., *The Letters and Journals of Robert Baillie*, 3 vols (Edinburgh: Alex Lawrie & Co., 1841).

Lake, Peter, 'Calvinism and the English Church, 1570–1635', *Past and Present*, 114 (1987), 32–76.

Lake, Peter, 'Presbyterianism, the Idea of a National Church and the Argument from Divine Right', in Lake and Maria Dowling, eds, *Protestantism and the National Church in Sixteenth-Century England* (London: Croom Helm, 1987), 193–225.

Lake, Peter, *Anglicans and Puritans? Presbyterianism and English Conformist Thought from Whitgift to Hooker* (London: Unwin Hyman, 1988).

Lake, Peter, 'The Laudians and the Argument from Authority', in Bonnelyn Young Kunze and Dwight D. Brautigam, eds, *Court, Country and Culture: Essays on Early Modern British History in Honor of Perez Zagorin* (New York: University of Rochester Press, 1992), 149–77.

Lake, Peter, 'The Laudian Style: Order, Uniformity and the Pursuit of the Beauty of Holiness in the 1630s', in Kenneth Fincham, ed., *The Early Stuart Church, 1603–1642* (Basingstoke: Macmillan, 1993), 161–87.

Lamont, William, *Marginal Prynne 1600–1669* (London: Routledge & Kegan Paul, 1963).

Lamont, William, 'The Puritan Revolution: a Historiographical Essay', in J.G.A. Pocock, ed., *The Varieties of British Political Thought, 1500–1800* (Cambridge: Cambridge University Press, 1993), 119–46.

Lander, Jesse, *Inventing Polemic: Religion, Print, and Literary Culture in Early Modern England* (Cambridge: Cambridge University Press, 2006).

Lang, Timothy, *The Victorians and the Stuart Heritage: Interpretations of a discordant past* (Cambridge: Cambridge University Press, 1995).

Langmuir, Gavin, *History, Religion and Antisemitism* (London: Tauris Press, 1990).

Langmuir, Gavin, *Toward a Definition of Antisemitism* (Berkeley, CA: University of California Press, 1990).

Laursen, John Christian and Cary J. Nederman, eds, *Beyond the Persecuting Society: Religious Toleration before the Enlightenment* (Philadelphia: University of Pennsylvania Press, 1998).

Lecler, Joseph, *Toleration and the Reformation* (London: Longman, 1960).

Lee, Sidney, 'Elizabethan England and the Jews', *Transactions of the New Shakespeare Society*, I (1887–1892), 143–66.

Lewalski, Barbara K., *Protestant Poetics and the Seventeenth-Century Religious Lyric* (New Jersey: Princeton University Press, 1979).

Liljegren, S.B., *James Harrington's Oceana* (Lund: C.W.K. Gleerups Forlag, 1924).

Lipman, Vivian D., ed., *Three Hundred Years: A Volume to Commemorate the Tercentenary of the Re-settlement of the Jews in Great Britain 1656–1956* (London, Vallentine, Mitchell & Co., 1956).

Lipman, Vivian D., *A History of the Jews in Britain since 1858* (Leicester: Leicester University Press, 1990).

Lloyd, Howell A., 'Mixed Constitution or Mixed Government', in J.H. Burns ed., *The Cambridge History of Political Thought 1450–1700* (Cambridge: Cambridge University Press, 1991), 273–9.

Lloyd, Jones Gareth, *The Discovery of Hebrew in Tudor England: A Third Language* (Manchester: Manchester University Press, 1983).

Loades, David, ed., *John Foxe and the English Reformation* (Aldershot: Scolar Press, 1997).
Mantel, Hugo, *Studies in the History of the Sanhedrin* (Cambridge, MA: Harvard University Press, 1961).
Manuel, Frank E., *The Broken Staff: Judaism through Christian Eyes* (Massachusetts: Harvard University Press, 1992).
Matar, Nabil, *Turks, Moors and Englishmen in the Age of Discovery* (New York: Columbia University Press, 1999).
McDowell, Nicholas, *The English Radical Imagination: Culture, Religion, and Revolution, 1630–1660* (Oxford: Clarendon Press, 2003).
McDowell, Nicholas, 'The Stigmatising of Puritans as Jews in Jacobean England: Ben Jonson, Francis Bacon and the Book of Sports Controversy', *Renaissance Studies*, 19 (2005), 348–63.
McGinn, Bernard, 'Cabalists and Christians: Reflections on Cabala in Medieval and Renaissance Thought', in Richard H. Popkin, ed., *Jewish Christians and Christian Jews: From the Renaissance to the Enlightenment* (Dordrecht: Kluwer Academic Publishers, 1994), 11–35.
McKisack, May, *Medieval History in the Tudor Age* (Oxford: Clarendon Press, 1971).
McRae, Andrew, *Literature, Satire and the Early Stuart State* (Cambridge: Cambridge University Press, 2004).
Mechoulan, Henry and Gerard Nahon, eds, *Menasseh ben Israel, The Hope of Israel: The English Translation by Moses Wall, 1652* (Oxford: Oxford University Press, 1987).
Milton, Anthony, 'The Church of England, Rome and the True Church: The Demise of a Jacobean Consensus', in Kenneth Fincham, ed., *The Early Stuart Church, 1603–1642* (Basingstoke: Macmillan, 1993), 187–211.
Milton, Anthony, *Catholic and Reformed: The Roman and Protestant Churches in English Protestant Thought 1600–1640* (Cambridge: Cambridge University Press, 1995).
Morrill, John, 'The Religious Context of the English Civil War', in Richard Cust and Ann Hughes, eds, *The English Civil War* (London: Hodder Headline, 1997), 159–81.
Morrill, John and John Walter, 'Order and Disorder in the English Revolution', in Richard Cust and Ann Hughes, eds, *The English Civil War* (London: Hodder Headline, 1997), 310–40.
Myers, Jack, *The Story of the Jewish People, Being a History of the Jewish People since Bible Times* (London: Kegan Paul, Trench, Trubner & Co., 1909).
Nederman, Cary J. and John Christian Laursen, eds, *Difference and Dissent: Theories of Toleration in Medieval and Early Modern Europe* (Lanham, Maryland: Rowman & Littlefield, 1996).
Nevitt, Marcus, 'Agency in Crisis: Women and the Pamphlet Culture of Revolutionary England, c. 1640–c. 1660', unpublished Ph.D. dissertation, University of Sheffield, 1999.
North, J.D., 'The Western Calendar: "intolerabilis, horribilis, et derisibilis", Four Centuries of Discontent', in G.V. Coyne, M.A. Hoskin and O. Pedersen, eds, *Gregorian reform of the calendar: proceedings of the Vatican conference to commemorate its 400th anniversary, 1582–1982* (Vatican Press, 1983), 75–117.
Olsen, V. Norskov, *John Foxe and the Elizabethan Church* (Berkeley: University of California Press, 1973).

Osborn, James M., *Young Philip Sidney 1572–1577* (New Haven: Yale University Press, 1972).
Osborne, John, *An Indictment Against Tythes: or, Tythes no Wages for Gospel-Ministers* (London: Livewel Chapman, 1659).
Osterman, Nathan, 'The Controversy over the Proposed Readmission of the Jews to England (1655)', *Jewish Social Studies*, 3 (1941), 301–28.
Parker, Kenneth L., 'Thomas Rogers and the English Sabbath: The Case For a Reappraisal', *Church History*, 53 (1984), 335–48.
Parker, Kenneth L., *The English Sabbath: A Study of Doctrine and Discipline from the Reformation to the Civil War* (Cambridge: Cambridge University Press, 1988).
Parmelee, Lisa Ferraro, *Good Newes from Fraunce: French Anti-League Propaganda in late Elizabethan England* (New York: University of Rochester Press, 1996).
Parry, Glynn, 'John Foxe, "Father of Lyes", and the Papists', in David Loades, ed., *John Foxe and the English Reformation* (Aldershot: Scolar Press, 1997), 295–306.
Patterson, Annabel, *Reading Holinshed's Chronicles* (Chicago: University of Chicago Press, 1994).
Paul, Robert S., 'Oliver Cromwell and the Jews', in Vivian Lipman, ed., *Three Hundred Years: A Volume to Commemorate the Tercentenary of the Re-settlement of the Jews in Great Britain 1656–1956* (London, Vallentine, Mitchell & Co., 1956), 9–14.
Paul, Robert S., *The Assembly of the Lord: Politics and Religion in the Westminster Assembly and 'The Grand Debate'* (Edinburgh: T. & T. Clark, 1985).
Pedersen, O., 'The Ecclesiastical Calendar and the Life of the Church', in G.V. Coyne, M.A. Hoskin and O. Pedersen, eds, *Gregorian Reform of the Calendar: Proceedings of the Vatican Conference to Commemorate its 400th Anniversary, 1582–1982* (The Vatican: Vatican Press, 1983), 17–75.
Pedersen, O., 'Eusebius and the Paschal Controversy', in Harold W. Attridge and Gohen Hata, eds, *Eusebius, Christianity and Judaism* (New York: E.J. Brill, 1992), 311–26.
Peltonen, Markku, ed., *Classical Humanism and Republicanism in English Political Thought 1570–1640* (Cambridge: Cambridge University Press, 1995).
Perry, Thomas, *Public Opinion, Propaganda, and Politics in Eighteenth-Century England: A Study of the Jew Bill of 1753* (Cambridge, MA: Harvard University Press, 1962).
Phillips, H.E.I., 'An Early Stuart Judaizing Sect', *TJHSE*, 15 (1946), 63–72.
Picciotto, James, *Sketches of Anglo-Jewish History* (London: Trubner & Co., 1875).
Pocock, J.G.A., *The Ancient Constitution and the Feudal Law: A Study of English Historical Thought in the Seventeenth Century* (Cambridge: Cambridge University Press, 1987).
Pocock, J.G.A., ed., *The Commonwealth of Oceana and A System of Politics* (Cambridge: Cambridge University Press, 1992).
Pollins, Harold, *An Economic History of the Jews in England* (London and Toronto, Associated University Presses, 1982).
Poole, Kristen, *Radical Religion from Shakespeare to Milton: Figures of Nonconformity in Early Modern England* (Cambridge: Cambridge University Press, 2000).
Poole, Robert, *Time's Alteration: Calendar reform in early modern England* (London: UCL Press, 1998).
Pooley, Roger, 'Anglicans, Puritans and the Plain Style', in Francis Barker, Jay Bernstein, John Coombes, Peter Hulme, Jennifer Stone and Jon Stratton, eds,

1642: Literature and Power in the Seventeenth Century: Proceedings of the Essex Conference on the Sociology of Literature ([Colchester]: University of Essex, 1981), 187–201.
Porter, H.C., 'Anglicans, Puritans and American Indians: Persecution or Toleration?', in Ole Peter Grell, Jonathan I. Israel and Nicholas Tyacke, eds, *From Persecution to Toleration: The Glorious Revolution and Religion in England* (Oxford: Clarendon Press, 1991), 189–99.
Prall, Stuart E., *Church and State in Tudor and Stuart England* (Arlington Heights, IL: Harlan Davidson, 1993).
Questier, Michael, *Conversion, Politics and Religion in England, 1580–1625* (Cambridge: Cambridge University Press, 1996).
Quilligan, Maureen, 'Sidney and his Queen', in Heather Dubrow and Richard Strier, eds, *The Historical Renaissance* (Chicago: Chicago University Press, 1988), 101–23.
Ragussis, Michael, *Figures of Conversion: "The Jewish Question" and English National Identity* (Durham: Duke University Press, 1995).
Raitiere, Martin N., *Faire Bitts: Sir Philip Sidney and Renaissance Political Theory* (Pittsburgh: Duquesne University Press, 1984).
Rashkow, Ilona N., *Upon the Dark Places: Anti-Semitism and Sexism in English Renaissance Biblical Translation* (Syracuse: Sheffield Academic Press, 1990).
Raymond, Joad, *Pamphlets and Pamphleteering in Early Modern Britain* (Cambridge: Cambridge University Press, 2003).
Reay, Barry, 'Quaker Opposition to Tithes 1652–1660', *Past and Present*, 49 (1980), 85–120.
Reay, Barry, *The Quakers and the English Revolution* (Middlesex: Temple Smith, 1985).
Rosenblatt, Jason P., *Torah and Law in Paradise Lost* (Princeton: Princeton University Press, 1994).
Rosenblatt, Jason P., 'John Selden's De Jure Naturali . . . Juxta Disciplinam Ebraeorum and Religious Toleration', in Allison P. Coudert and Jeffrey S. Shoulson, eds, *Hebraica Veritas?: Christian Hebraists and the Study of Judaism in Early Modern Europe* (Philadelphia: University of Pennsylvania Press, 2004), 102–24.
Rosenblatt, Jason P., *Renaissance England's Chief Rabbi: John Selden* (Oxford: Oxford University Press, 2006).
Roth, Cecil, 'Leon da Modena and England', *TJHSE*, 11 (1928), 206–25.
Roth, Cecil, 'New Light on the Resettlement', *TJHSE*, 11 (1928), 112–42.
Roth, Cecil, *Magna Bibliotheca Anglo-Judaica* (London: Published for the JHSE, 1937).
Roth, Cecil, *A History of the Jews in England* (Oxford: Clarendon Press, 1941).
Roth, Cecil, 'Leone da Modena and his English Correspondents', *TJHSE*, 17 (1953), 39–43.
Roth, Cecil, 'The Middle Period of Anglo-Jewish History (1290–1655) Reconsidered', *TJHSE*, XIX (1960), 1–12.
Roth, Cecil, 'The Resettlement of the Jews in England in 1656', in V.D. Lipman, ed., *Three Centuries of Anglo-Jewish History* (Cambridge: Published for the JHSE by W. Heffer and Sons, 1961), 1–26.
Roth, Cecil and Geoffrey Wigoder, eds, *Encyclopaedia Judaica*, 16 vols (Jerusalem: Keter Press, 1972).
Roth, Cecil, *Catalogue of an Exhibition of Anglo-Jewish Art and History: In Commemoration of the Tercentenary of the Resettlement of the Jews in the British*

Isles (Published by the East and West Library for the Tercentenary Council and printed by the Shenval Press, London, Hertford and Harlow).
Rowse, A.L., *Four Caroline Portraits: Thomas Hobbes, Henry Marten, Hugh Peters, John Selden* (London: Gerald Duckworth & Co., 1993).
Rubinstein, William D. and Hilary L. Rubinstein, *Philosemitism: Admiration and Support in the English-Speaking World for Jews, 1840–1939* (Basingstoke: Macmillan, 1999).
Russell, Conrad, *The Crisis of Parliaments: English History 1509–1660* (Oxford: Oxford University Press, 1971).
Salmon, J.H.M., *The French Religious Wars in English Political Thought* (Oxford: Clarendon Press, 1959).
Salmon, J.H.M., 'Catholic Resistance Theory, Ultramontanism, and the Royalist Response, 1580–1620', in J.H. Burns, ed., *The Cambridge History of Political Thought 1450–1700* (Cambridge: Cambridge University Press, 1991).
Sampson, Margaret, '"Property" in Seventeenth-Century English Political Thought', in Gordon J. Schochet, ed., *Religion, Resistance and Civil War, Proceedings of the Folger Institute Centre for the History of British Political Thoughts*, Vol 3 (Washington: Folger, 1990), 259–76.
Samuel, Edgar, 'The First Fifty Years', in V.D. Lipman, ed., *Three Centuries of Anglo-Jewish History* (Cambridge: Published for the *JHSE* by W. Heffer and Sons, 1961), 27–44.
Samuel, Edgar, 'The Readmission of the Jews to England in 1656, in the Context of English Economic Policy', *Jewish Historical Studies*, 31 (1988), 153–69.
Samuel, Raphael, 'The Discovery of Puritanism, 1820–1914: A Preliminary Sketch', in Jane Garnett and Colin Matthew, eds, *Revival and Religion since 1700* (London: The Hambledon Press, 1993), 201–48.
Samuel, Wilfred, *The First London Synagogue of the Resettlement (Founded in 1657, Enlarged in 1674)* (London: Published by Spottiswoode, Ballantyne and Co. ltd for the *JHSE*, 1924).
Shapiro, James, *Shakespeare and the Jews* (New York: Columbia University Press, 1996).
Sharpe, Kevin, *Politics and Ideas in Early Stuart England: Essays and Studies* (London: Pinter, 1989).
Sharpe, Kevin, *The Personal Rule of Charles I* (New Haven: Yale University Press, 1992).
Sharpe, Kevin and Steven N. Zwicker, eds, *The Politics of Discourse: The Literature and History of Seventeenth-Century England* (Berkeley: University of California Press, 1987).
Sheils, W.J., ed., *Persecution and Toleration: Papers Read at the Twenty-Second Summer Meeting and the Twenty-Third Winter Meeting of the Ecclesiastical History Society* (Oxford: The Ecclesiastical History Society, 1984).
Sherwin-White, A.N., *Roman Society and Roman Law in the New Testament: The Sarum Lectures 1960–1961* (Oxford: Clarendon Press, 1963).
Shoulson, Jeffrey S., *Milton and the Rabbis: Hebraism, Hellenism and Christianity* (New York: Columbia University Press, 2001).
Shuger, Debora K., *Sacred Rhetoric: The Christian Grand Style in the English Renaissance* (New Jersey: Princeton University Press, 1988).
Shuger, Debora K., *The Renaissance Bible: Scholarship, Sacrifice and Subjectivity* (Berkeley: University of California Press, 1994).

Shuger, Deborah K., '"Societie Supernatural": The Imagined Community of Hooker's Lawes', in Arthur Stephen McGrade, ed., *Richard Hooker and the Construction of Christian Community* (Temple, AZ: Arizona State University Press, 1997), 307–31.
Siegel, Paul N., 'Shylock and the Puritan Usurers', in Arthur D. Matthews and Clark M. Emery, eds, *Studies in Shakespeare* (Florida: University of Miami Press, 1953), 129–39.
Smith, Nigel, *Perfection Proclaimed: Language and literature in English radical religion 1640–1660* (Oxford: Clarendon Press, 1989).
Smith, Nigel, *Literature and Revolution in England 1640–1660* (New Haven: Yale University Press, 1994).
Sommerville, J.P., 'James I and the Divine Right of Kings: English Politics and Continental Theory', in Linda Levy Peck, ed., *The Mental World of the Jacobean Court* (Cambridge: Cambridge University Press, 1991), 55–71.
Springborg, Patricia, 'Hobbes on Religion', in Tom Sorell, ed., *The Cambridge Companion to Hobbes* (Cambridge: Cambridge University Press, 1996), 346–81.
Stacey, Robert, '1290–1260: A Watershed in Anglo-Jewish Relations?', *Historical Research*, 61 (1988), 35–50.
Stacey, Robert, 'The Conversion of the Jews to Christianity in Thirteenth-Century England', *Speculum*, 67 (1992), 263–83.
Stewart, Alan, 'The Birth of a National Biography: The Lives of Roderigo Lopez, Solomon Lazarus Levi and Sidney Lee', *EnterText* [e-journal] 3:1 (2003), 183–203.
Stow, Kenneth, *Alienated Minority: The Jews of Medieval Latin Europe* (Cambridge, MA: Harvard University Press, 1992).
Sullivan, Ceri, *Dismembered Rhetoric: English Recusant Writing, 1580–1603* (London: Associated University Press, 1995).
Sutcliffe, Adam, 'Enlightenment and Exclusion: Judaism and Toleration in Spinoza, Locke and Bayle', in Tony Kushner and Nadia Valman, eds, *Philosemitism, Antisemitism and 'the Jews': Perspectives from the Middle Ages to the Twentieth Century* (Aldershot: Ashgate, 2004), 177–93.
Sutherland, N.M., 'The English Refugees at Geneva, 1555–1559', in Richard C. Gamble, ed., *Calvinism in France, Netherlands, Scotland, and England* (London: Garland, 1992), 271–80.
Toomer, G.J., 'Selden's Historie of Tithes: Genesis, Publication, Aftermath', *Huntington Library Quarterly*, 65 (2002), 345–78.
Torrance Kirby, W.J., *Richard Hooker's Doctrine of the Royal Supremacy* (Leiden: E.J. Brill, 1990).
Tovey, D'Blossiers, *Anglia Judaica: Or the History and Antiquities of the Jews in England, Collected from all our Historians, both Printed and Manuscript, as also from the Records in the Tower, and other Publick Repositories* (Oxford, 1738).
Trevor-Roper, Hugh, *Archbishop Laud, 1573–1645* (Basingstoke: Macmillan, 1988).
Tubbs, J.W., *The Common Law Mind: Medieval and Early Modern Conceptions* (Baltimore: The Johns Hopkins University Press, 2000).
Tuck, Richard, *Natural Rights Theories: Their Origin and Development* (Cambridge: Cambridge University Press, 1979).
Tuck, Richard, *Hobbes* (Oxford: Oxford University Press, 1989).
Tuck, Richard, *Philosophy and Government 1572–1651* (Cambridge: Cambridge University Press, 1993).

Twomey, Vincent, *Apostolikos Thronos: The Primacy of Rome as Reflected in the Church History of Eusebius and the Historico-Apologetic Writings of Saint Athanasius the Great* (Munster: Aschendorff, 1982).

Tyacke, Nicholas, *Anti-Calvinists: The Rise of English Arminianism c. 1590–1640* (Oxford: Clarendon Press, 1987).

Tyacke, Nicholas, 'The "Rise of Puritanism" and the Legalizing of Dissent, 1571–1719', in Ole Peter Grell, Jonathan I. Israel and Nicholas Tyacke, eds, *From Persecution to Toleration: The Glorious Revolution and Religion in England* (Oxford: Clarendon Press, 1991), 17–51.

Tyacke, Nicholas, 'Puritanism, Arminianism and Counter-Revolution', in Richard Cust and Ann Hughes, eds, *The English Civil War* (London: Hodder Headline, 1997), 136–59.

Urban, Sylvanus, ed., *The Gentleman's Magazine*, 36 (1851), 451–9.

Van Dorsten, Jan A., 'Sidney and Franciscus Junius the Elder', *The Huntington Library Quarterly*, 42 (1978), 1–13.

Van Rooden, Peter, 'Conceptions of Judaism as a Religion in the Seventeenth-Century Dutch Republic', in Diana Wood, ed., *Christianity and Judaism: Papers Read at the 1991 Summer Meeting and the 1992 Winter Meeting of the Ecclesiastical History Society* (Oxford: Published for the Ecclesiastical History Society by Blackwell, 1992), 299–309.

Vitkus, Daniel J., *Turning Turk: English Theatre and the Multicultural Mediterranean* (New York: Palgrave, 2002).

Wallace, Dewey D., 'Puritan and Anglican: The Interpretation of Christ's Descent into Hell in Elizabethan Theology, *Archiv fur reformationsgeschichte*, 69 (1978), 248–88.

Walzer, Michael, *The Revolution of the Saints: A study in the Origins of Radical Politics* (London: Weidenfeld and Nicolson, 1966).

Watt, Tessa, *Cheap Print and Popular Piety 1550–1640* (Cambridge: Cambridge University Press, 1991).

Webster, Charles, ed., *Samuel Hartlib and the Advancement of Learning* (Cambridge: Cambridge University Press, 1970).

White, Peter, 'The Rise of Arminianism Reconsidered', *Past and Present*, 101 (1983), 24–54.

White, R.B., 'John Traske (1585–1636) and London Puritanism', *Transactions of the Congregational Historical Society*, 20 (1968), 223–33.

Whitrow, G.J., *Time in History: The Evolution of Our General Awareness of Time and Temporal Perspective* (Oxford: Oxford University Press, 1988).

Wolf, Lucien, *A Lecture Delivered at the Anglo-Jewish Historical Exhibition, Royal Albert Hall, 12th May 1887* (London: Wertheimer & Co., 1887).

Wolf, Lucien, *The Resettlement of the Jews in England* (London: The Jewish Chronicle, 1888).

Wolf, Lucien, 'American Elements in the Resettlement', *TJHSE*, 3 (1899), 85–93.

Wolf, Lucien, 'The Whitehall Conference: Celebration of the 250th Anniversary', *TJHSE*, 5 (1908), 276–98.

Wolf, Lucien, 'Henry Straus Quixano Henriques, K.C., 1866–1925', *TJHSE*, 2 (1928), 247–51.

Wolf, Lucien, 'Jews in Elizabethan England', *TJHSE*, (1928), 1–91.

Wolf, Lucien, 'Cromwell's Jewish Intelligencers', in Cecil Roth, ed., *Essays in Jewish History by Lucien Wolf* (London: JHSE, 1934), 91–114.

Wolf, Lucien, *Essays in Jewish History*, Cecil Roth, ed., (London: Published for the JHSE, 1934).
Wolf, Lucien, 'Jews in Tudor England', in Cecil Roth, ed., *Essays in Jewish History* (London: Published for the JHSE, 1934), 71–90.
Wooden, Warren W., *John Foxe* (Cambridge, MA: G.K. Hall & Company, 1983).
Woodhouse, A.S.P., ed., *Puritanism and Liberty* (London: Dent, 1938).
Woolf, D.R., *The Idea of History in Early Stuart England: Erudition, Ideology, and 'The Light of Truth' from the Accession of James I to the Civil War* (Toronto: University of Toronto Press, 1990).
Woolrych, Austin, *Commonwealth to Protectorate* (Oxford: Clarendon Press, 1982).
Wootton, David, ed., *Divine Right and Democracy: An Anthology of Political Writing in Stuart England* (Harmondsworth: Penguin, 1986).
Worden, Blair, 'Toleration and the Cromwellian Protectorate', in W.J. Sheils, ed., *Persecution and Toleration* (Oxford: Blackwell, 1984), 199–234.
Worden, Blair, *The Sound of Virtue: Philip Sidney's* Arcadia *and Elizabethan Politics* (New Haven: Yale University Press, 1996).
Worden, Blair, *Roundhead Reputations: The English Civil Wars and the Passions of Posterity* (London: Penguin, 2001).
Zagorin, Perez, *Ways of Lying: Dissimulation, Persecution, and Conformity in Early Modern Europe* (Cambridge, MA: Harvard University Press, 1990).
Zagorin, Perez, *How Religious Toleration came to the West* (Princeton: Princeton University Press, 2004).
Zeitlin, Solomon, 'The Political Synedrion and the Religious Sanhedrin', *The Jewish Quarterly Review*, 36 (1945), 109–40.
Ziggelaar, August, 'The Decree of 1582', in G.V. Coyne, M.A. Hoskin and O. Pedersen, eds, *The Gregorian Reform of the Calendar: Proceedings of the Vatican Conference to Commemorate its 400th Anniversary, 1582–1982* (The Vatican: Pontifica Academia Scientiarum, 1983), 201–30.
Zim, Rivkah, *English Metrical Psalms: Poetry as Praise and Prayer 1535–1601* (Cambridge: Cambridge University Press, 1987).
Ziskind, Jonathan R., 'Petrus Cunæus on Theocracy, Jubilee and the Latifundia', in Abraham I. Katsh, ed., *The Jewish Quarterly Review*, 68 (1978), 235–55.
Ziskind, Jonathan R., *John Selden on Jewish Marriage Law: The* Uxor Hebraica (London: E.J. Brill, 1991).

Index

Abrabanel, David (Manuel Martinez Dormido), 10
Abravanel, Isaac, 130
Achinstein, Sharon, 146n103
adiaphora, 35, 65, 68
Admonition, to the Parliament, An (anon), 38–41, 67, 154n56, 171n78
Aliens Act (1905), 8, 19, 20
altar controversy, 69–73
Ames, William, 66, 68, 71, 76, 82–3, 86–7
Amsterdam, 1, 2, 9, 10, 12, 55, 112, 128, 167n24, 188n60
Andrewes, Lancelot, 55–6
Anglicans
  use of term, 31–2, 149n10
  altar controversy, 69–74
  ceremonalism, 65–76, 90–1
  and religious constitution, 78–85
  prelates, 77–8
  Sabbatarianism, 89–91
  and Sanhedrin, 84–5
  and Tabernacle, 74–6
  and tithes controversy, 87–89
Anglo-Jewish Historical Exhibition, 19, 26
antisemitism, 134n17
  see also Judeophobia
Apologeticall Narration, An (Goodwin et al.), 102–3
Arminianism, 68–9, 103, 166n16, 167nn24, 26, 27, 179n24
'Arminius' (James Harmensen), 167n24
Arraignment of Mr. Persecution, The (Overton), 103–4

Baillie, Robert, 87, 98, 99–100, 107, 179n27, 180nn30, 31, 181n61
Balcanquhall, Walter, 77, 169n51
Bale, John, 59, 60, 61–2, 87, 163nn160, 162, 164n171

Balfour, Arthur, 134n2
Bancroft, Richard, 32, 48, 66, 84, 158n104
Barkesdale, Clement, 79, 171n74
Barlow, Thomas, 15
Bastwick, John, 66, 67, 166n12, 169n63
Beaumont, Thomas and Carleton, 13
Beauval, Jacques Basnage de, 133n6
ben Isaac, Solomon (Rashi), 46, 156n77
Berkshire, Earl of, 13
Bevis Marks Synagogue, 1, 12
Beza, Theodore 42, 43–4, 49, 54, 179n27
Bilson, Thomas, 38, 46–8, 84, 151n21, 156nn76, 80, 82, 83, 84
Blastus, 58, 63, 164n177
Bloudy Tenent, of Persecution, The (Roger Williams), 95–6, 100–2, 109, 111–12, 178n8, 180nn32, 34, 36, 37
Blunt, Elijah, 16–7
Bodin, Jean, 107
Book of Common Prayer, The, 48, 59, 96
Bourne, Immannuel, 88, 89, 173n112
Brabourne, Theophilus, 55
Bridge, William, 102
Bristol, 9
British Academy, 20
Broughton, Hugh, 27, 42, 53, 108, 130–2, 151n21, 152nn27, 28, 29, 30, 31, 32, 33, 34, 35, 36, 156nn76, 78, 79, 82, 87, 88, 89, 160n123
  attitude to Jews, 63, 130–1
  and Christ's descent to Hell, 46–9
  Hebrew scholarship, 36–9, 152nn33, 35
Bryce, James, 2, 140n73
Bunny, Edmund, 79–80
Burges, John, 66, 71, 168n36

Burnhardt, Jacob, 3
Burroughs, Jeremiah, 102
Burton, Henry, 66–7, 69, 76, 77, 91, 114, 166n12
Burton, Thomas, 142n82
Buxtorf, Johannes, 79, 185n30
Bynneman, Henry, 42

calendar reform, *see* Easter controversy
Calvin, Jean, 42–4, 85
Calvinism, 42–4, 69, 167n24
Canne, John, 87, 88–9, 173n112
Canon law, 51, 53, 121, 158nn103, 104, 186n34
Carleton, George, 158n104
Carlyle, Thomas, 21, 22
Cartenright, Johanna and Ebenezer, 10
Cartwright, Thomas, 35–6, 41–2, 43, 66, 69, 80–3, 84
Carvajal, Antonio Fernandez, 9
Caryll, Thomas, 115
Castellio, Sebastian, 94
ceremonialism, 34, 65–78, 88–91
Cesarani, David, 6, 139n63
Chaderton, Laurence, 34
Charles I, 32, 52, 67, 69, 97, 167n27
Charles II, 6, 12–13, 14, 15, 16, 17, 21, 23, 138nn33, 38, 141n77, 142n79
Chevallier, Anthony, 34, 36
Christianson, Paul, 157n99,
Christ, and controversy over descent into Hell, 46–9
circumcision, 56, 71, 82, 87, 161n146
Civil law, 51, 121
Coffey, John, 65, 178n8
Cohen, Lord, 92
Coke, Edward, 51, 114, 126, 158n104, 187n53
Coleman, Thomas, 54
Collier, Thomas, 117
Collinson, Patrick, 38, 39, 153n39
Common Law, 49, 51, 53–4, 79, 113, 119–26, 157nn95, 96, 158n103, 159n118, 186nn34, 35, 187nn53, 57
Conformists, *see* Anglicans

constitution, *see* English constitution
Conventicle Act (1664), 13
conversion
 of Jews to Christianity, 9–10, 12, 18, 36, 95, 104, 114–15, 117–18, 128, 147n108
 of Christians to Judaism, 56, 147n108
Coryat, Thomas, 95
Cotton, John, 98, 100–2
Council of Nice, 58
Council of Trent, 59
Covell, William, 173n102
Cromwell, Oliver
 attitude to Jews, 7, 11, 13, 21–3, 92–3, 137n33, 140nn75, 76, 176n5, 178n8
 posthumous reputation, 7, 13, 16, 20–7, 92–3, 140nn64, 67, 68, 76, 141n77, 144n96, 176n5
 Whitehall conference and aftermath, 1–3, 11–12, 13–15, 23–5, 137n33, 139n62, 142n82, 143n83, 144nn91, 94, 96, 145n97
Crouch, Nathaniel, 11, 114, 128
Crowley, Weldon S., 160n123
Cunæus, Petrus, 49, 79, 170n71, 171n74

Damascus Affair, 17
Davies, Julian, 167n27
Dee, John, 59
Dering, Edward, 35, 40
discalceation, 72, 168n38
'D.L.', 123–4, 128
Dormido, Manuel Martinez (David Abrabanel), 10, 13, 136n16
Drusius, John, 34
Dury, John, 9, 115, 117

Easter controversy, 58–63, 86–7
Eden, Anthony, 1
Edward I, 1, 8, 16, 20, 114–5, 119, 120, 125, 139n62, 145n97, 179n15
Edwards, Thomas, 94–5, 103, 178n11, 180n31, 181nn49, 53
Elizabeth I, 26, 38, 50, 59, 67, 69, 77
Endelman, Todd, 144n94

216 Index

English Association, 20
English constitution, 97–100, 104–12
Erastians, 52, 53–4, 78–9, 80, 83–7, 98–100, 160n123, 170n69, 179n26
  and Sanhedrin, 105, 107–12
  Westminster Assembly, 98
Erastus, Thomas, 78–9, 106, 170nn68, 69
Eusebius, 57, 58, 63, 164n174
Evelyn, John, 23, 113

Fairfax, Lord, 10
Falconer, John, 55–8, 62–3, 71
Fardinando, Anthony, 14
Fetherstone, Christopher, 40
Field, John, 38–40, 42, 44, 45, 81, 153nn39, 40, 41, 45
Fincham, Kenneth, 69, 167n27
Fletcher, Eric, 148n5
Foxe, John, 27, 59, 60, 61–2, 87, 127, 146n103, 162nn152, 154, 163nn160, 161, 163, 164nn164, 170, 171, 174
Fraser, Antonia, 140n67
Freeman, Thomas S., 164n174
Freud, Sigmund, 140n67
Fulke, William, 42, 46, 63
Fuller, Thomas, 55, 160n128

Gardiner, S.R., 22, 177n6
Geneva, 2, 42–3, 79, 154n60
Geneva Academy, 43
Gilby, Anthony, 40, 43–4, 45
Gillespie, George, 30, 98, 99–100, 105–9, 179n27, 180n37, 181n56, 182n72
  see also Late Dialogue Betwixt a Civilian and a Divine, A
Godwin, William, 17, 21–2, 137n24, 143nn85, 86
Golding, Arthur, 43, 44, 97, 154nn58, 61
Goodwin, John, 31, 32, 94, 110, 181n53
Goodwin, Thomas, 30, 98, 102
Greenhalgh, John, 12, 137n23
Gregory XIII, 59–60
Grell, Ole Peter, 178n8
Grindal, Edmund, 79

Grotius, Hugo, 49, 54, 79, 94, 107, 170n71, 171nn73, 74, 185n30, 186n35
Guibbory, Achsah, 165n7, 167n23
Gwyer, John, 135n6

Haller, William, 180n31
Hanmer, Meredith, 162n154
Harding, Thomas, 164n164
Harmensen, James ('Arminius'), 167n24
Harpsfield, Nicolas, 164n164
Harrington, James, 79, 170n70, 171n72
Hartlib, Samuel, 10
Hebraism, 4, 27, 34–9, 43–5, 46–9, 54, 56, 63, 91, 108, 130
  see also Broughton, Hugh; Puritans; Selden, John
Hebrew, Christian interest in, *see* Hebraism
Helgerson, Richard, 126, 147n5
Helwys, Thomas, 96, 179n19
Henriques, H.S.Q., 22, 23, 133n7, 141nn77, 79, 143n85, 145n99
Henry VIII, 9, 26, 34
Herbert, George, 64–5, 68, 165n1, 167n23
Heylyn, Peter, 66, 70–1, 73, 77, 90, 91, 166nn12, 13, 167n30, 169nn51, 59
Highland, Samuel, 185n33
Hill, Christopher, 68,
Historie of Tithes, The (Selden), 50–4, 82, 87, 130, 148n6, 157n96, 158n107, 159n121
Hobbes, Thomas, 157n92, 170n72
Hoffman, Michael, 145n97
Hogarth, William, 15
Holinshed, Raphael, 127, 163n159
Holmes, Colin, 139n54
Holweck, Frederick G., 162n151
Hooker, Richard, 27, 67, 83–5, 97, 105, 147n5, 166n22, 171n87, 172n93, 173n102
  see also Lawes of Ecclesiastical Polity, Of the
Hope of Israel, The (Menasseh), 9, 116, 117

Index 217

Hosmer, James, 18, 138*n*47
Hotman, Francois, 154*n*58, 157*n*95
Howell, James, 9, 172*n*92
Hughes, William, 112, 124, 126, 127–8
Huie, James, 17, 18, 138*n*47
Humphrey, Laurence, 34

Independents, 22, 95, 98–101, 108, 110–12, 178*n*11
  Westminster Assembly, 98–9, 108, 110–1
Isaiah, Paul, 9
Israel, Jonathan, 178*n*8

Jackson, Hamlet, 55, 161*n*134
Jacob, Henry, 47, 48, 156*nn*76, 81, 86
Jacobs, Joseph, 138*n*47
James II, 13, 23, 140*n*76
Jessey, Henry, 2, 114, 116, 118, 183*n*3
Jew Bill, *see* Jewish Naturalisation Act
Jewish Historical Society of England, 19, 20, 21, 24, 141*n*77
Jewish Naturalisation Act (1753), 15–16, 20, 138*n*44
Jews
  in Amsterdam, 1–2, 9, 10, 12, 112, 128
  in early modern London, 9, 10–12, 24–7, 144*nn*94, 95
  expulsion from England, 1, 8–9, 13, 16, 20, 26, 114–15, 119–20, 124–6, 135*n*5, 139*n*62, 145*n*97, 185*n*27, 187*n*47
  in Old Testament, 33, 39–42, 79, 83–5, 88, 106–7, 109–12, 131, 165*n*1
  readmission to England, 1–5, 7, 10–17, 23–7, 65, 68, 92–3, 113–20, 122–3, 126–9, 132, 134*n*2, 137*n*33, 138*n*38, 139*nn*62, 63, 141*nn*77, 79, 142*nn*80, 81, 82, 143*n*86, 144*n*96, 145*nn*97, 98, 178*n*8, 185*n*27
John (King of England), 126, 178*n*15
Jones, Edwin, 187*n*57
Jonson, Ben, 33, 36
Jordan, W.K., 92, 176*nn*1, 2
Josephus, Flavius, 73, 80

Judaism, meanings of, 27–9
  see also Judaizing
Judaizing, 28–9, 34, 41–2, 48, 54–8, 62–3, 65, 73–4, 78, 81, 107, 131, 146*nn*106, 107
Judeophobia, 8, 12, 20, 26, 28, 63, 134*n*17
Junius, Franciscus, 44–5

Katz, David S., 5, Katz, David, 5, 134*n*14, 136*nn*10, 16, 144*nn*95, 96, 145*nn*98, 100, 175*n*129
Knox, John, 43
Kushner, Tony, 6

Lake, Peter, 68, 69, 167*n*27
Lamont, William, 148*n*6
Languet, Hubert, 154*n*58
Late Dialogue Betwixt a Civilian and a Divine, A (Gillespie), 105–7, 108
Laud, William, 65, 67, 69, 71, 120, 167*n*30
Laudian reforms, 4, 66, 68–9, 73–4, 86, 90–1, 102, 160*n*124, 165*n*7, 166*n*17, 167*n*27, 169*n*51
Lawes of Ecclesiastical Polity, Of the (Hooker), 83–4, 147*n*5
Lee, Sidney, 19, 20, 135*n*7, 139*n*57
Levellers, 94, 98, 99, 103, 174*n*115
Lightfoot, John, 54, 95, 98, 100, 107, 109, 160*n*123
Lipman, Vivian D., 65
Lively, Edward, 34–5
Lopez, Roderigo, 9, 135*n*6, 144*n*95

Maimonedes, Moses, 159*n*117, 171*n*73
Maitland, F.W., 188*n*57
Manuel, Frank, 157*n*99
Martin, Gregory, 36, 46
Massachusetts, 95, 101, 102, 120–1
Mede, Joseph, 72–3, 90, 163*nn*38, 39, 40
Medina, Solomon de, 138*n*48
Menasseh ben Israel, 1–3, 7, 9–12, 23, 26–7, 115, 116–18, 120, 125, 127–8, 133*nn*1, 4, 137*n*26, 144*n*95, 171*n*74
  see also Hope of Israel, The

218 Index

mercantilism, 114, 118–19, 184*n*21
Mildmay, Sir Walter, 34, 36
millenarianism, 114–15, 118–19
Milton, John, 9, 27, 28, 87, 88, 148*n*5, 175*n*128, 178*n*9, 182*n*73
Modena, Leon, 95, 136*n*11, 178*n*12
Montagu, Richard, 30, 32, 50, 51, 52, 88, 159*n*117
Montefiore, Moses, 17
Montezinos, Antonio de (Aaron ha-Levi), 9, 115, 136*n*13
Mornay, Philippe de, 42, 43, 44
Morton, Thomas, 68, 71, 82, 84–5, 86–7, 97, 105, 172*nn*93, 94, 96
mos gallicum, 49, 157*n*95
Mosaic law, 11, 55, 63, 71, 182*n*73
Myers, Jack, 18, 138*n*47

nationhood, English, 126–8
Nettles, Stephen, 51, 52, 88, 158*nn*100, 107
New England, 98, 101–2, 120–1, 129
Norice, Edward, 57
Nye, Philip, 102

Overton, Richard, 94, 98, 103–4, 181*n*53
  see also *Arraignment of Mr. Persecution, The*

Pagitt, Ephraim, 56, 71–2, 160*nn*129, 130, 132, 133, 161*nn*134, 135, 136
Parker, Kenneth L., 175*n*129
Parker, Matthew, 60
Parliament, 8, 12, 14, 15–16, 17, 25, 50–2, 83, 87, 95, 97–8, 105–7, 114, 120–2, 124–9, 140*n*73, 142*n*82, 159*n*118, 172*n*93, 184*n*25, 187*n*57
Passover, observation of by Christians, 4, 34, 57–9, 62, 71–2, 132, 161*nn*143, 146
Paul, Robert S., 65
Pearson, Anthony, 174*n*115
Pembroke, Countess of, 44, 155*n*71
Pepys, Samuel, 12
Persons, Robert, 59, 60, 61–2, 163*n*154, 164*nn*164, 165, 171, 172, 173, 175, 177

Peter, Hugh (Hugh Peters), 118, 120–4, 126, 148*n*4, 181*n*53, 185*nn*28, 32, 186*n*38, 187*n*45
'Philo-Judaeus', 73, 117
philosemitism in England, 1, 4–6, 7–8, 17–20, 27–9, 33–4, 63, 93, 134*n*2, 139*n*53
  use of term, 134*n*17
Picciotto, James, 19, 139*n*56
Pocklington, John, 66, 70, 75, 77, 168*n*30
Pocock, J.G.A., 187*n*53
polemic, 30–3
Presbyterians, 30, 38, 67, 94–5, 165*n*8, 172*n*96, 173*n*101
  and religious constitution, 80–2, 85
  and tithes controversy, 87–9
  Westminster Assembly, 98–105, 108–12, 179*nn*26, 27
Prideux, John, 91
Prynne, William, 27, 28, 31, 32, 66, 67, 70, 102–3, 108, 119–20, 121–9, 165*n*2, 166*n*12, 168*n*30, 169*nn*61, 62, 63, 173*n*112, 177*n*6, 185*nn*28, 30
  on church discipline, 77–8, 169*n*61
  on constitutional debate, 109–11
  Judeophobia of, 28, 122, 124–6, 127–9
  and tithes controversy, 87–8, 175*n*128
  Westminster Assembly, 98–9
  see also *Short Demurrer, A*
psalms, 45, 155*n*71
Puritans
  use of term, 31–2, 149*n*10
  opposition to ceremonialism, 67–8, 76
  and religious constitution, 80–2
  and Christ's descent into Hell, 46–9
  and Continental thinkers, 42–5
  Easter controversy, 58–63, 86–7
  and Jewish customs, 54–63
  and Old Testament, 39–42, 65
  study of Hebrew, 34–9, 46–9
  and tithes controversy, 49–54, 87, 130–1

Quakers, 87, 88, 173*n*114, 174*n*115, 175*n*128
Quartodeciman heresy, 58, 61–3, 86–7, 162*n*148, 164*nn*171, 172, 174, 177
  see also Easter controversy

Rashi (Solomon ben Isaac), 46, 156*n*77
Raymond, Joad, 31
Read, Alexander, 74
readmission of Jews to England, *see* Jews
Reeve, Edmund, 70, 71, 75, 78, 90, 169*nn*51, 55
religious toleration in England, 4, 11, 13–15, 21–5, 27, 65, 85, 92–97, 98–104, 108–12, 113–19, 120, 122, 125–6, 127, 132, 140*nn*75, 76, 176*n*1, 2, 5, 177*nn*6, 7, 8, 178*nn*9, 11, 180*n*43, 182*n*73, 188*n*60
Reuchlin, Johannes, 49
Ridley, Thomas, 158*n*104
Robarts, Foulke, 73–4, 75, 90, 158*n*104
Robinson, Henry, 94, 103
Robles, Antonio Rodrigues, 10–11, 136*n*17, 145*n*98
Rogers, John, 105
Rogers, Thomas, 32, 150*n*14, 175*n*129
Romain, Jonathan, 145*n*97
Romaine, William, 16
Roman Catholics, 12, 31–2, 34–5, 37, 38–9, 40, 42, 46, 54, 56, 85, 86, 109, 131
  calendar reform, 59–63
  ceremonialism, 64, 109
Ross, Alexander, 113, 117
Roth, Cecil, 5, 24, 136*n* 17, 138*n*47, 140*n*76, 142*n*81, 143*n*85, 144*nn*91, 96
Rothschild, Baron de, 18, 140*n*73
'R.T.', 73–4, 76, 168*nn*41, 45
Russell, Lord John, 140*n*73
Rycaut, Paul, 13

Sabbatarianism, 4, 33, 34, 54–6, 86, 89–91, 117, 132, 150*n*14, 160*nn*125, 130, 175*nn*128, 129

Sabbath, *see* Sabbatarianism
Sacks, Jonathan, 145*n*97
St Policarp, 58
Salomons, David, 17, 140*n*73
Salvetti, Francesco, 142*n*82
Sampson, Thomas, 34
Samuel ben Israel, 10, 12
Samuel, Edgar, 92
Samuel, Lord, 1
Samuel, Raphael, 21
Samuel, Wilfred, 25, 142*n*82
Sanhedrin, 4, 38, 50, 65, 78–80, 84–5, 93, 99–100, 104–9, 111, 170*n*67, 171*nn*72, 73, 172*n*98, 182*n*65
  see also Anglicans; Erastrians; Selden, John
Sasportas, Jacob, 12
Scaliger, Joseph Justus, 49, 54, 79, 107, 157*n*94, 171*n*74, 185*n*30, 186*n*35
Sclater, William, 28, 29, 51, 88, 89, 148*n*6
Seccombe, Thomas, 178*n*8
Selden, John, 27, 30, 63, 79, 106–8, 148*nn*5, 6, 156*n*92, 157*nn*95, 96, 98, 99, 159*nn*107, 109, 110, 111, 116, 117, 121, 171*n*74, 182*n*68, 185*n*30, 186*n*35
  Hebrew scholarship, 49–50, 52, 107–8
  and Parliament, 51–?, 100
  and Sanhedrin, 79, 100, 107
  and tithes controversy, 49–54, 82, 87, 89, 130–1
  Westminster Assembly, 87–8
  see also Historie of Tithes, The
Sempill, Sir James, 51, 53, 88, 89, 90, 148*n*6
Serres, Jean de, 154*n*58
Shakespeare, William, 3, 6, 19
Shapiro, James, 6, 125, 185*n*27
Sharpe, Kevin, 68
Shelford, Robert, 70, 73, 74, 167*n*30, 168*nn*34, 42, 169*n*49
Short Demurrer, A (Prynne), 88, 119–20, 121–3, 124–8, 185*nn*28, 30
Sidney, Philip, 42, 44–5, 155*nn*65, 69, 70

Simon the Zealot, 62
Simpson, Sidrach, 102
Spelman, Henry, 158n104
Spencer, Edward, 116–18
St Paul, 77, 161n146
St Bartholomew's Day Massacre, 42, 154n57
Stacey, Robert, 8
Stow, John, 114, 127, 183n2
Stow, Kenneth, 8, 125, 187n47
Stubbs, John, 42–3, 45
Sutcliffe, Matthew, 59–61, 164n174
Swan, John, 169n48, 51

Tabernacle, 70, 71, 74–8, 110–11, 168n44, 169nn49, 51, 182n78
Talmud, 27, 34, 43, 46, 49, 56, 66, 79, 80
Temple (Jerusalem), 17, 40, 64, 72–6, 78, 88, 111, 182n78
Thirty-Nine Articles, 48, 80
Thomason, George, 148n8
Thorowgood, Thomas, 9
Thurloe, John, 118
Tillesley, Richard, 51, 52, 53, 88
tithes controversy, 49–54, 87, 130–1
toleration, *see* religious toleration in England
Tovey, D'Blossiers, 2–3, 15, 17, 114, 119, 133nn6, 7, 138nn33, 39, 46
Traske, John, 55–8, 62–3, 90, 160nn127, 130, 161n134, 161n146
Tremellius, Immanuel, 34, 44–5, 155n68
Tyacke, Nicholas, 69, 177n6, 178n8

Udall, John, 34–5

Vaughan, Rice, 120, 121–2, 124, 126, 185n28
Vautrollier, Thomas, 45, 154n58
Violet, Thomas, 13–15
Viret, Pierre, 42

Wall, Moses, 9
Walwyn, William, 94, 103, 149n9

Walzer, Michael, 177n7
Ward, Nathaniel, 120–2, 126, 185n28, 186n38, 187n45
Welwood, William, 49
Westminster Assembly, 52, 87, 97–9, 102–4, 144n94, 160n123, 179nn25, 26
see also Erastians; Independents; Presbyterians; Prynne, William; Selden, John
Whalley, Major-General, 140n75
Whitaker, William, 34
White, Francis, 90–1, 175n133
White, Peter, 167n27
White, R.B., 160n127
Whitehall Conference, 1–3, 7, 11–13, 16, 23, 113–15, 118–20, 124, 128, 134n1, 137n19, 142n82, 143n85, 145n96
see also Cromwell, Oliver
Whitgift, John, 27, 38, 41–2, 46, 47, 48, 69, 80–1, 83
Wilcox, Thomas, 38, 40, 42, 45
Wilfrid, Abbot of Ripon, 61
William the Conqueror, 8, 120, 124
Williams, John, 66, 70, 73, 167n30, 168n44
Williams, Roger, 94–7, 98, 100–3, 108–10, 111–12, 120, 129, 177n8, 178nn15, 16, 17, 180nn32, 34, 37, 38, 39, 42, 43
see also Bloody Tenent, of Persecution, The
Wilson, A.N., 145n97
de Wilton v. Montefiore, 141–2
Wolf, Lucien, 2–3, 5, 7–8, 19–20, 23, 24, 26, 133nn3, 8, 134nn1, 2, 136n16, 137n33, 138nn38, 47, 139nn56, 62, 141n77, 143nn83, 85, 144n94
Woodhouse, A.S.P., 92, 176n2
Wootton, David, 177n8
Worden, Blair, 140n68, 177n6

Zagorin, Perez, 177n7
Ziskind, Jonathan, 50